Information Technology
CAREERS
The Hottest Jobs For The New Millennium

Drew Bird

Mike Harwood

CORIOLIS

President and CEO
Keith Weiskamp

Publisher
Steve Sayre

Acquisitions Editor
Shari Jo Hehr

Development Editor
Deb Doorley

Product Marketing Manager
Brett Woolley

Project Editor
Hilary Long

Production Coordinator
Carla J. Schuder

Cover Designer
Jesse Dunn

Layout Designer
April Nielsen

Information Technology Careers: The Hottest Jobs For The New Millennium

Limits of Liability and Disclaimer of Warranty

The author and publisher of this book have used their best efforts in preparing the book and the programs contained in it. These efforts include the development, research, and testing of the theories and programs to determine their effectiveness. The author and publisher make no warranty of any kind, expressed or implied, with regard to these programs or the documentation contained in this book.

The author and publisher shall not be liable in the event of incidental or consequential damages in connection with, or arising out of, the furnishing, performance, or use of the programs, associated instructions, and/or claims of productivity gains.

Trademarks

Trademarked names appear throughout this book. Rather than list the names and entities that own the trademarks or insert a trademark symbol with each mention of the trademarked name, the publisher states that it is using the names for editorial purposes only and to the benefit of the trademark owner, with no intention of infringing upon that trademark.

The Coriolis Group, LLC
14455 N. Hayden Road, Suite 220
Scottsdale, Arizona 85260

(480)483-0192
FAX (480)483-0193
www.coriolis.com

Library of Congress Cataloging-in-Publication Data
Bird, Drew
    Information Technology Careers: The Hottest Jobs for the New Millennium/
by Drew Bird and Mike Harwood.
        p.   cm. -- (Exam cram)
    ISBN 1-57610-680-2
    1. Information technology--Vocational guidance.   2. Electronic data
processing personnel--Certification.   I. Harwood,
Mike. II. Title. III. Series.
    T58.5 .B49 2000
    004'.023--dc21   00-046616

Printed in the United States of America
10 9 8 7 6 5 4 3 2 1

The Coriolis Group, LLC • 14455 North Hayden Road, Suite 220 • Scottsdale, Arizona 85260

ExamCram.com Connects You to the Ultimate Study Center!

Our goal has always been to provide you with the best study tools on the planet to help you achieve your certification in record time. Time is so valuable these days that none of us can afford to waste a second of it, especially when it comes to exam preparation.

Over the past few years, we've created an extensive line of *Exam Cram* and *Exam Prep* study guides, practice exams, and interactive training. To help you study even better, we have now created an e-learning and certification destination called **ExamCram.com**. (You can access the site at **www.examcram.com**.) Now, with every study product you purchase from us, you'll be connected to a large community of people like yourself who are actively studying for their certifications, developing their careers, seeking advice, and sharing their insights and stories.

I believe that the future is all about collaborative learning. Our **ExamCram.com** destination is our approach to creating a highly interactive, easily accessible collaborative environment, where you can take practice exams and discuss your experiences with others, sign up for features like "Questions of the Day," plan your certifications using our interactive planners, create your own personal study pages, and keep up with all of the latest study tips and techniques.

I hope that whatever study products you purchase from us—*Exam Cram* or *Exam Prep* study guides, *Personal Trainers*, *Personal Test Centers*, or one of our interactive Web courses—will make your studying fun and productive. Our commitment is to build the kind of learning tools that will allow you to study the way you want to, whenever you want to.

Visit ExamCram.com now to enhance your study program.

Help us continue to provide the very best certification study materials possible. Write us or email us at **learn@examcram.com** and let us know how our study products have helped you study. Tell us about new features that you'd like us to add. Send us a story about how we've helped you. We're listening!

Good luck with your certification exam and your career. Thank you for allowing us to help you achieve your goals.

Keith Weiskamp

Keith Weiskamp
President and CEO

About the Authors

Drew Bird (MCNI, MCNE, MCT, MCSE, CNE) has been working in the IT industry for over 11 years. After starting out working with mainframes, he quickly moved into the PC networking arena where he has worked ever since. In 1995 Drew became a technical instructor teaching networking topics and has since moved in and out of technical training and consulting roles. Drew is a regular contributor to a number of Internet Web sites and computer magazines.

When not working, Drew enjoys anything that has nothing to do with technology, including sailing, mountain biking, snowboarding, and other outdoor pursuits. He lives in Kelowna, BC, Canada with his wife Zoe.

After experimenting with other professions, **Mike Harwood** entered the IT industry just about the time plug and play was introduced. Since then he has worked in a variety of settings, including everything from PC support to network design and implementation. Currently Mike manages a multisite network and trains on technology subjects. Along the way Mike has collected his MCSE, MCR, and A+ certifications.

When not working, Mike spends time with his four-year-old daughter Breanna and her two-year-old sister Paige, entertaining them with stories of magical lands where networks configure themselves and users are always friendly.

Acknowledgments

We would like to thank our friends and families for putting up with the long hours required to complete this project.

Of The Coriolis Group, we would like to thank Deb Doorley and Hilary Long for their ongoing support and for listening to the ramblings of two overworked writers.

Also, we'd like to thank all others who assisted with this project—Shari Jo Hehr for making this book possible, Carla Schuder for her production coordination, April Nielsen for her assistance with interior design, and Wendy Littley for assisting with the production efforts.

Thank you, also, Laurel Ann Spivey Dumas, Tcat Houser, and Matt Simmons for your contributions to the book, as well as Harold Ketchell for your research and contributions.

Special thanks is extended to Shawn McNutt for his incredibly careful and conscientious technical review, and Glen Chamberlain of Matrix Resources, who provided commentary from the perspective of an IT Recruiter.

Contents at a Glance

Table of Contents

About This Book

There was a time when Java was just coffee, Web designers were of the arachnid variety, and "C" represented mediocre academic performance. But times have changed, and these same words or slang now represent particular "hot" areas in the field of Information Technology (IT). Individuals with competency in any one of these skills now roam freely through the IT industry, often commanding huge salaries and benefits such as stock options and sometimes even personal trainers.

The fact is that the IT industry currently has an extreme shortage of skilled staff. If you are considering or have chosen to pursue a career in IT, then this book provides you with a valuable resource to help you make decisions about your choices. It is written from a commercial, rather than an academic perspective. The observations given are designed to help you choose and attain the right job.

As you consider a commitment to a career in IT, note that the shortage of skilled IT staff will not only continue for many years, but it is also predicted to heighten. According to a U.S. Department of Commerce study entitled "America's New Deficit – The Shortage of Information Technology Workers," more than 137,800 new IT workers per year will be needed to fill newly created jobs in the technology industry. As if that was not enough, the report also predicts that this trend will continue until at least the year 2006. Despite a steady stream of newcomers to the IT industry, demand continues to outstrip supply. As the continued level of integration between technology and our personal and business lives increases, the skills shortage may actually become the limiting factor in how quickly we can progress. Already, computers and technology pervade almost every aspect of our daily lives. Even when we may not realize that we are using technology, it is still there working for us. The point is that to make it work for us, we have to make it work. That takes skilled people, and there are simply not enough to go around.

By picking up this book, you have expressed an interest in joining the fastest growing and most dynamic industry in the world. It is an industry that provides opportunities that are not limited by geographical boundaries and that can make you a valuable commodity in your own hometown or in another country. The IT industry gives those who participate in it the potential for a career with good salaries, a high level of flexibility, unparalleled mobility, and perhaps most importantly—job security. For those seeking a new profession or entering the labor force, a career in IT can provide diversification and opportunities not readily found in other fields.

Unlike other professional career areas, many aspects of IT do not require a university education, though for certain positions and employers, it still remains a fundamental requirement. In almost every area, IT is an industry where the person and the experience are as important as the paper. For those without the necessary academic qualifications, alternative paths into the industry are available. IT certification, which is discussed in this book, provides a path into IT that can be achieved by anyone with the aptitude and attitude to do so.

With this high degree of flexibility however, comes a degree of complexity. A career in IT brings with it many issues. First, there are so many different areas, each with its own set of skills and requirements. Then, there are such a wide variety of areas to which you can apply those skills. To people outside the industry wanting to get in, the array of choices and chances can at times seem bewildering. That's where this book comes in.

Information Technology Careers: The Hottest Jobs for the New Millennium attempts to demystify the IT industry as a whole. Rather than just looking at the obvious career choices, we have sought to explain how the IT industry functions, what the highest demand skill areas are, and how you get into them. We look at the factors that you need to consider when choosing an IT career path, and then how you can turn those paper choices into a practical reality. We look at how you prepare for and then execute an IT job search, as well as how IT job searches differ from other job searches. After you get the job, we also look at how you can keep it while maintaining your marketability, should you exercise your right to move on.

One thing is for certain. If you have chosen to pursue a career in IT, you have made a wise choice. A career in IT can be challenging as well as rewarding, and offer almost endless opportunities as technologies and the industries that support them continue to change.

Incidentally, if you do think that Java is just coffee, you can be sure that by the end of this book, you will know that Java is a programming language, a Web designer possesses some of the most sought after skills, and, although "C" does still represent mediocre academic performance, it's actually another very popular programming language.

How to Make This Book Work for You

Information Technology Careers: The Hottest Jobs for the New Millennium is designed to provide you with a comprehensive and accurate resource that can help you make informed and educated decisions about a career in IT. It is for those who know nothing about IT, as well as for those already familiar with the industry, but perhaps in need of some assistance with how to move from one area of IT into another. Although some of the listings and Web sites provided as resource material may be limited to a national audience within the United States, whenever feasible, various international sites and listings have been added to accommodate an international audience. Important to note is that the basic information regarding the IT industry, the technical areas and job descriptions described, is universal. Therefore, whether coming from a national or international perspective, this guide can assist you with your career in IT.

The organizational structure of this book takes a practical approach in providing assistance to you. There are three main parts of the book, all of which are described below:

Part I —What's IT All About? provides some background information about the IT industry, then guides you into a general understanding of some of the most common factors that could affect your decision of whether you choose to work in IT. After you learn that IT is for you, it makes recommendations of how to decide what area of IT is right for you by providing some overview of specific IT areas.

Part II—Which Job Is Right for You? explores the possibilities of the job market in IT as it is today. Each chapter is dedicated to a particular career in IT and describes areas of specialty, as well as relevant job roles. Each job role description discusses such things as daily tasks, job demand, qualifications and requirements, as well as listings of various useful resources, such as training and certifications. Each chapter ends with at least one "day in the life" interview of an IT professional working in that relevant area of IT.

In *Part III—Making It Happen* pulls it all together and advises you on how to make your career decisions and plans work for you. This is where we help you prepare to find a job, talk about what company type is right for you, how to seek the job you want, then how to hold on to it, and how to move on from there.

Also included in this book is a useful resource called "IT Lingo," a glossary not in the traditional sense in that it does not necessarily include all and/or only those terms used in this book, but those that are considered to be most common and frequently used overall in the IT industry. In this section, you'll find jargon such as upload and download, and platform defined in laymen terms, as well as things like MCSE and SCSI. What's it all mean? If you don't know, you can look it up here.

Finally, the five appendixes included in this book supply you with some extremely useful information. Such things as listings of specialized placement services, major IT employers, Internet career resources, and recommendations for further reading are included. Consider these sections resources that can save you an enormous amount of research time, as well as provide you with helpful listings that can enhance your own findings.

To Our Audience

Although this book is targeted primarily at those entering the IT industry, it can also provide a great deal of useful information to those who have been working in IT for only a short time, or those seeking to rejoin the industry after a break. In view of this target audience, little or no knowledge of the IT industry is required, although a basic understanding of computers, the Internet, and general business computing terms is helpful. Also, as described earlier, the basic information regarding the IT industry, as well as the technical areas and job roles described in this book, are universal. Therefore, whether coming from a national or international perspective, this guide can assist you with your career in IT.

What's IT All About?

*I*nformation Technology Careers was designed to assist you through the process of choosing and starting a career in IT. With that in mind, Part I is an orientation exercise, providing you with background information to help you decide whether a career in IT is the right direction for you to take. Part I also gives an overview of some common career choices available to you in the IT industry.

We begin by looking at the IT industry as a whole, examining a little of its history, as well as how it all looks today. From there, we take a look into the future to see how things may shape up in coming years.

Armed with a bit of background info, we then start to look at how a career in IT may relate to you. What kinds of jobs are you best suited to do, and what type of company do you want to work for? The IT industry presents a myriad of opportunities. It's completely possible to create a career path that suits your needs, ambitions, and desires. By understanding the things that are important to you and seeing how they relate to an IT career, you can make choices that will serve you best and allow you to pursue your career goals.

By the end of this section, you should have the answer to one very important question. Is a career in IT right for you?

CHAPTER ONE

The Landscape of the IT Industry

Trying to describe the IT industry in a few pages is a bit like using an Etch A Sketch™ to draw a circle. You think you've got it licked, then someone comes along and says, "Hey, that's a nice box!" The IT industry has so many different parts, personalities, aspects, and facets that there will always be something significant you leave out.

Probably the most sensible thing to do is to start at the beginning.

The Past

Many events and occurrences have shaped the IT industry into the creature it is. Its history is filled with myriad names, brands, ideas, and concepts, all of which have played their part in making IT one of the most dynamic industries in the world. The history of computers is an interesting subject; indeed entire books have been written about it. Although understanding the history of computers may not help you secure a career in IT, they make for an interesting read and are a useful source of background information. Included in Appendix E are some suggestions for further reading.

To convey the entire history of computing in a few paragraphs is difficult indeed. So, rather than try to cover all of the bases, the following is a summary of the some of the more significant happenings that have influenced the evolution of the computer industry over the past 50 or so years.

The 1940s: In the Beginning

The roots of digital computing can be traced back to 1946 when the world's first digital computing device called ENIAC was put into service. This event, in digital terms at least, marked the beginning of the information age. In terms of size and complexity, ENIAC was a monster, occupying an entire room and needing a team of engineers and scientists to operate it. Despite its impressive size and appearance, it had less processing power than today's hand-held electronic organizers.

As well as being regarded as the world's first real digital computer, ENIAC is also famous for helping to define the term *bug*, due to the fact that a moth was found to have shorted out the system, causing it to stop. The term those early engineers coined to describe the fault is still used today to refer to a problem with a computer system or program.

Shortly after ENIAC was being brought to a standstill by flying insects, another significant event occurred: the invention of the transistor. The transistor was the first step toward the development of microprocessors. It was a very significant invention, as today's microprocessors have literally millions of individual transistor switches in them.

The formative years at the end of the 1940s served as the foundation to the computer and IT industry as we now know it. Those early technical pioneers sowed the seeds of discovery that would shape the world. As the saying goes, the rest is history.

The 1950s: The Territory of the Mainframe

Realizing the obvious potential of computers, the inventors of the ENIAC continued their work into the 1950s, designing and subsequently manufacturing a more powerful machine than ENIAC, called the UNIVAC. The UNIVAC is regarded as the first commercially available digital computer.

It was also during the 1950s that IBM, who had made a name for itself producing calculating machines, made its first foray into digital computing with a system called the Type 701 EDPM. The 701 was the first machine in a series that would propel IBM into the mainframe computer market and make the company one of the most significant and well known in the computer industry.

The 1960s: The Decade of Downsizing

The problem was that although they performed tasks useful to many businesses, mainframe computers were incredibly expensive to buy and subsequently run. What was needed was a computer that was smaller and more affordable than a mainframe. The answer was the minicomputer, originally manufactured by the Digital Equipment Corporation. These new minicomputers, though still only affordable by good-sized businesses, were considerably cheaper to buy than mainframes and had lower operating costs.

Before computers could get even smaller, the computer industry needed to develop a way to make the processing elements of the systems smaller and even more powerful. The solution to that problem arrived when Robert Noyce teamed up with fellow engineer Gordon Moore and started a company called Intel.

Intel did not actually start out as a microprocessor company; initially the company designed and manufactured memory chips. It wasn't until a Japanese calculator company asked Intel to produce a set of chips to put into a programmable calculator, that one of its engineers hit on the idea of an all purpose processor. By 1971, Intel was selling its first fully functioning microprocessor, the 4004, for the tidy sum of $200.

Though the development of the microprocessor was a major event, the '60s also saw many other important developments and achievements for the computer industry. Perhaps one of the most significant was the advent of computer networking. It was in the late 1960s that work began on the ARPAnet, the network that would eventually become today's Internet.

Also significant in the 1960s was the development of the Unix operating system, which has become the operating system of choice for use on the Internet. Unix, though obviously upgraded and updated, is still used by many large companies today. The current trend toward Linux, also has much to thank the Unix operating system for. Linux is actually based on a computing standard called POSIX, which was originally developed for Unix software.

The 1970s: The Industry Takes Shape

In a trend that is now just a little too familiar, Intel released a new chip called the 8008 less than a year after the 4004. The 8008 chip is worthy of mention because it led to the release of what is generally regarded as the world's first personal computer, or PC, called the Altair 8800. But the Altair was just the beginning.

During the 1970s a variety of other personal computers came on to the market as well. Although some were in kit form, and of more interest to enthusiasts than general home and business users, the personal computer market started to gain pace, aided in no small part by the popularity of the Apple computer, which also became popular with business users. Another boost for the PC was the introduction of applications such as Visicalc and WordStar that turned the PC into an easy-to-use and multifaceted business tool.

The 1970s also saw businesses completely embrace computing and information technology. Businesses of all sizes were buying mainframes or mini-computers and employing teams of operators to run the systems.

The 1970s were also the formative years for today's Internet. Initially created as a tool for the Department of Defense, the ARPAnet had been in use and growing for a number of years, and prompted research and development into technologies that served to further the general goals of networking. As the Internet is now, the ARPAnet of the 1970s was the network of all networks.

Still on the subject of networking, it was during the 1970s that Ethernet, the standard on which a large proportion of today's local area networks (LANs) are based, was created. The standard and the technology to support LANs would not be released for some time, however.

The 1980s: The Decade of the PC

The start of the 1980s saw an event that would change the computing landscape completely. IBM, who by now had confirmed its place as a major player in the computing world, launched its first personal computer that ran with a new operating system, called PC-DOS. Subsequent versions of this operating system were produced under the now familiar name of MS-DOS. PC-DOS was the product of a small software company called Microsoft that had been started by two college students some years earlier. As every new business owner does, these two students had aspirations for success, but neither could have expected that within 20 years their company would become one of the largest and most successful in the world.

In 1983, with the total number of computers in use in the U.S. passing the one million mark, *Time* magazine took the rather unusual step of naming the personal computer as the "1982 Man of the Year." That such an esteemed publication would give the prize to an object rather than a human being indicated the level of impact that the world was feeling from technology and from personal computers in particular.

As the decade drew on, PCs appeared in homes and offices all over the globe. Applications started getting increasingly powerful, peripherals such as printers became more affordable, and people started to look for new ways to use the power of the PC to the maximum. Computer games with advanced graphics and amazing sound effects began to drive PCs toward the arena of multimedia. The PC was becoming more than just a device for working and playing games, it was turning into an entertainment center. All that was needed was an efficient method to get the entertainment to the masses.

The 1990s: The Internet Explosion and the Bug of All Bugs

The 1990s saw the growth of the IT industry surpass everyone's expectations. Millions of people the world over realized the power of the Internet and logged on to use email, chat rooms, and the World Wide Web (WWW). The initial burst was driven by providers such as CompuServe and America Online (AOL), but it was quickly followed by smaller providers, all competing for a share of the increasing lucrative market. At first, access was expensive, then it became cheap, then it was almost free, and by the end of the decade you could get a free PC if you signed up for an Internet access agreement.

The increases in speed, functionality, and availability of PCs continued apace, with many businesses surrendering their mini- and mainframe computers in favor of powerful PC-based systems. Microsoft's operating systems continued to dominate the market. Possibly one of the oddest moments of television in the 1990s was the pictures of people sleeping outside computer superstores so that they could be the first to own a copy of Microsoft's new Windows 95 operating system. But it was not just the home and business PC market that Microsoft was starting to dominate. They were also making drastic inroads to the PC networking market, initially with LAN Manager, and subsequently with Windows NT.

The decade ended with a wake-up call for the IT industry. The fact that many of the world's computer systems and programs had been created with a built-in bug caused panic among the IT community. Governments, companies, and individuals across the globe braced themselves for the passing of that great date when, it was forecast, the airliners would drop out of the sky, hospital power plants would fail, and, more significantly, fast-food chains would run out of burgers. Some minor problems were reported, but the world celebrated the coming of a new millennium without any massive computer failures. No nuclear weapons fired themselves and no banks ran out of money. Most people began to wonder what all the fuss had been about.

Some people put the non-event of Y2K down to extensive preparation and diligence of the governments of the world. Others pointed an accusing finger at software manufacturers and consultancy companies and accused them of scare mongering. In reality, most companies and individuals alike were just happy that New Year's Eve passed without too much drama. With the removal of the last obstacle, the world, and the IT industry, were able to look forward to a new era of development, with nothing to hold them back.

The Present

Today, technology is everywhere. If the Y2K bug scare did nothing else, it served to remind us of just how reliant we have become on technology and the industry that supports it. Without computers, modern day life would look very different—indeed it would take a very creative mind to imagine life without it. The milk carton you used this morning was almost certainly designed on a computer, and this book was written on one. Look around you now and think for a moment about how technology affects you.

The Internet Age

Of all of the individual aspects currently influencing technology, the Internet must surely be the most significant. The Internet now pervades almost every aspect of the IT industry, as it does our daily lives. Any company that is not already on the Internet in some form or other is looking for a way to get on, because more and more an Internet presence can mean the difference between success and mediocrity.

Companies use the potential of the Internet in a variety of ways. Some use it as a way of communicating their message to customers. Considering the relatively low costs involved, companies can make the Internet a completely viable 24 hour a day, 7 days a week advertisement. Furthermore, the potential customer base the Inter-net gives access to is in the millions. Others companies use it as a medium for supplying information or advice on their products, reducing the need for telephone call centers and operators. The Internet provides limitless opportunities to creative and entrepreneurial businesses.

Perhaps the biggest driver of all for the Internet from a business point of view, however, is the development of e-commerce. The sale of goods and services over the Internet has come a long way. Not too long ago, you would go online, find a product that you wanted, and then phone the company directly and order it. Pioneers of e-commerce such as Amazon.com have developed and presented new ways to shop, making the whole process much more comprehensive, convenient, and considerably more consumer friendly. Further, recent Internet security advances have increased consumer confidence, all but alleviating previous concerns of credit card details being viewed by unwanted eyes.

Perhaps the massive increase in spending online is not by chance. Advertisers themselves use technology to watch people's Web habits and build consumer profiles based on actual buying patterns. This, perhaps invasive approach, allows companies to target their advertising campaigns and advertising dollars directly at those people most likely to purchase their products. Whether this is a good or a bad thing is a matter of personal preference. It is, however, how things work in the information age and acts as a demonstration of the kind of power and functionality that technology provides.

Of course the Internet is not restricted to business use. Many individuals have embraced the Internet using it for entertainment, information, and recreation. The lure for many modern surfers is that the Internet provides a relatively impersonal and seemingly anonymous communication medium. Nowadays virtual chat rooms connect human beings from all over the world.

In a way though, the Internet is merely a front end, a visual presentation if you like, of a wide range of aspects of the IT industry. It is a user-friendly medium that provides people with the tools to access information and systems that run applications and store information. The important thing to remember is that every Web page has to be designed, every site has to be run on a server of some description, every request passed over a network and every PC that runs a browser needs to be designed, built, configured and supported. In other words, from an IT professional's perspective, the Internet is simply a window through which people can view our, dare we say, art.

The Bigger Picture

The IT industry today is certainly not just the Internet. Even though they may well have some connection or relationship with the Internet, companies use computers and technology to perform day-to-day tasks. Any company with more than a few computers is likely to have its own technical support person, or at the very least a relationship with a local computer company so that in time of failure, help is readily at hand. The important thing to remember is that for many companies, it is not the computer that is the focus of their business, but rather the functionality that the computer provides. Companies have become dependent on this functionality and ultimately on the computers.

Businesses with more than a few PCs are very likely to have installed a computer network. Depending on requirements, some companies may use PC-based operating systems such as Microsoft Windows 98 or Windows NT Workstation to share files from system to system, while larger companies have server-based networks. Nowadays, most companies opt for server-based networks. These server systems run operating systems from manufacturers such as Microsoft, Novell, or a version of Unix or Linux.

Companies may use a standard suite of applications such as Microsoft Office. Server-based networks provide the option to store applications and files locally on the user's PC or on the server. The servers, along with offering the capacity for centralized file storage, may offer services such as email, databases, or specialized applications.

Today's office networks are powerful and diverse, connecting computers in offices, irrespective of location. The standardization of protocols has also meant that today's PC is a window to almost any other type of system, be it micro, mini, or mainframe computer, whether it be on the network locally, across the Internet, or over a private network.

Though they were responsible for bringing PCs to the mass market, IBM's share of this market has shrunk considerably since those early days. Now, you are more likely to see PCs from companies such as Compaq, Dell, Gateway, or other less well-known manufacturers on a user's desk. Modern mainframes, though smaller than their predecessors, still perform a key role in many companies, delivering processing power and storage capabilities not available in smaller computers.

On the Sidelines

As with the rapid advances of technology, the industry that supports it has grown in a similar fashion. Not only are more and more people becoming employed by the IT industry directly, but other industries, such as publishing, have evolved and expanded as part of the IT industry. Because IT is so information-based, magazines and publications fill the newsstand, and the Internet is filled with technically related Web sites and forums.

Education for IT has become big business. In particular, the technical training and certification industry has become massive, with almost every vendor offering some kind of certification and accreditation program. Much of this growth has come from the skills shortages that plague almost every sector of the industry. It is not just commercial education that has seen changes. Secondary school and college curriculums have all been modified to accommodate the new demand for technical skills requirements that will be placed on students.

For those that have completed their studies, the recruitment industry has developed with the IT industry. Recruitment agencies and Web sites that advertise technical jobs compete with each other to offer job opportunities. You may think that being a recruitment agent in an industry that has more jobs than candidates to fill them would be an easy task, but competition between agencies to get the vacancies from the employers is fierce, and equally as fierce to match the right candidates to the jobs. In the past few years, the trend toward Web-based recruitment has accelerated, and many employers and candidates are matched online.

The Way We Work

Technology today does not just affect what we work at, but also how we work. The advances in communications technology have made working from home, or telecommuting to give it its proper name, a practical reality. People are able to dial-in from their spare room and videoconference with people at the office who have struggled through an hour of traffic to do the same thing. In this way, technology not only gives us a new way to work, but may also help to alleviate other societal concerns such as traffic congestion, pollution, and urban crowding. If you don't have to travel to work each morning, then does it really matter how far away you live from the office?

Nowadays, people are as likely to work on projects and collaborate through email and instant messaging, rather than meetings and memos. The use of fax machines, though still popular, is on the decline as people find faster and easier ways to communicate. High-speed networking and Internet access have provided people with the ability to create vast networks that span countries and continents, providing access to information for all.

Cutting the Ties That Bind

Because we can now work practically from home, the next logical step is to be able to work and have access to the office from anywhere. Most recently, big steps toward a truly wireless world have been made with the development and introduction of wireless devices and the communications standards to support them.

The first portable hand-held devices were small versions of desktop computers, with mini versions of the same applications that you had in the office. Now they are fully functional hand-held Internet portals, using new communications technologies such as wireless access protocol (WAP), which will allow you to trade stocks, check email, or read the news from anywhere. When you examine these trends and the rapidity with which they develop, the science fiction idea of a videophone on your wrist doesn't seem too far away.

The New Threat

It's not all good news; new technologies bring with them new concerns. Recent increases in email viruses and Web site hacking have made the news all over the world. Unfortunately, viruses are now a daily risk of using the Internet. Although computers can almost always be vaccinated against a specific virus, developers play a constant game of catch up with the people who develop the viruses.

Our relative susceptibility, coupled with our increased reliance on technology, have caused politicians and governments to look at the risks, and attempt to find ways to discourage these attacks from affecting the populous. One of the biggest problems with the enforcement of laws and standards is not only is the Internet anonymous, it also crosses geographical boundaries. Good news for the hackers and virus authors, but bad news for law agencies and governments.

For someone pursuing a career in the IT industry, computer security is sure to become one of the fastest growing areas. To many people, it also appears to be an exciting aspect of the industry.

The Future

Predicting what will come in an industry that evolves on an almost daily basis is a thankless and almost futile task. Things change at such a rapid rate, and many of the technologies are so fluid, that a shift in direction can occur in weeks rather than months.

Of course the easiest thing to do is make sweeping statements such as PCs will get faster, the Internet will grow, and wireless devices will become commonplace. These facts are indisputable, but as someone pursuing a career in technology, you are interested in not just what the future trends will be, but also how they will affect the job market. Detailed below are just a few of the things that will affect the IT industry over the coming years. How they affect you and your career will depend on which field of IT you choose to enter, and how long it will be until you start work.

The Internet and E-commerce

If we think that today's Internet and e-commerce opportunities are technically advanced, we have not seen anything yet. Not only will the existing uses of the Internet get more and more advanced, but new ways will be found to exploit the opportunities it provides.

The delivery of these services will not just be dependant on new formats and programming, but also on the mediums that deliver them. For this to happen, certain changes will need to take place, not just technological, but legal as well. Protection of consumers needs to be examined, as well as considerations such as copyright protection and piracy prevention. The unmanaged nature of the Internet also makes it the ideal medium for scams and schemes—hard to control, and often even harder to identify the people behind them.

The Transport of the Future

With the Internet being used in more and more different ways, not only will the speed need to be improved, the functionality will need to be examined. One of the biggest concerns facing the Internet is the depletion of computer addresses. As each device that is connected to the Internet needs a unique address, known as the

IP address, the more devices that are connected the more addresses are required. The protocol that is used on the Internet today, TCP/IP, dates back over 20 years, and has been a faithful and reliable servant, but is now insufficient for current needs in terms of both technology and capacity. The current version, IPv4, has almost run out of addresses. To alleviate the problem, the Internet community has been working on the development of a new version of IPv6 that will offer more addresses, better security, and improved handling of multimedia applications.

The transition to IPv6 is likely to be a leisurely and smooth procedure, as hardware and software manufacturers are working hard to find a method of migration that will allow existing network devices and computers to "talk" to the new version. Even so, it is highly likely that anyone entering the IT industry at the beginning of the 21st century is going to hear a great deal about IPv6.

It's a Wireless World

As well as using conventional methods to connect to the Internet, wireless access will also become a common approach. Although we already have wireless data devices, the wireless computing industry is still in its relative infancy. With wireless transmission speeds developing at a rapid rate, coupled with the availability of wireless data services, this is one area of technology that is sure to become a big mover. Even now, hand-held computers or Personal Digital Assistants are becoming commonplace.

Doing Your Homework

The boundaries between companies' Internal network and the Internet will become blurred, and the skills to manage that boundary will become high in demand. The increase in speed for home Internet access through cable, DSL, and satellite will further drive telecommuting, creating a need for engineers and systems analysts who can diagnose and repair a problem with a PC remotely. These same engineers will need to have a deep understanding of network technologies and the Internet, as companies come to rely on email and videoconferencing not just as a luxury, but as a necessity.

The Ultimate Directory

With networks and the Internet growing ever larger, we will need to find new ways to manage the large volumes of users that are connected to them. The use of directory services systems and technologies such as XML will become commonplace, as we have the functionality to electronically contact and connect to anyone connected to the Internet.

1

When 1Ghz Is Just Not Enough

The personal computer will get progressively more powerful. Already processors are available that process data at 1Ghz. Strangely, for home PCs at least, the driving force behind PCs is games and multimedia. These are two areas that will have strong growth for IT careers in the coming years. As computers do more and more for us in the workplace, we will be looking for ways for them to do more for us in the home as well.

The Only Sure Thing

One thing is certain. Although we can predict generally the direction in which the IT industry is headed, there can be no surefire way to predict exactly what will happen in the coming years. It's just one of the reasons why a career in IT is so exciting!

Chapter Summary

The IT industry has come a long way since digital computing was first introduced in the mid 1940s. From mainframe to PC, from ARPAnet to the World Wide Web, each decade has brought with it technical advances that offer new challenges and opportunities for those working in IT.

Technology continues to advance, constantly changing how we work, where we work, and the skills we need to work. What the future holds for IT is impossible to predict, but it's guaranteed to be a wild ride.

CHAPTER TWO

So You Want to Work in IT?

When you were young, did you ever dream of being a firefighter, a train driver, or a police officer? Maybe you did, maybe you didn't, but it's unlikely that you dreamt of becoming a Web designer or network manager. Though there are exceptions, the decision to pursue a career in a field such as IT is a decision of the mind rather than the heart.

It's not that a job in IT cannot be rewarding, because it can. As with any other profession, IT can be rewarding *if* you are working in the right area. Although this example is a bit out of context, consider the choices a professional chef has to make. He trains to become a chef and then goes out to work. The only position he can find is as a short order chef in a diner. Sure, he's using some of the skills he learned during training (in most professions, only a small percentage of the skills learned during training are used daily in the workplace), but the environment in which he uses those skills may not have been what he had in mind. The same goes for a career in IT. You can train to become a programmer or network designer and work in a variety of situations, but finding the right situation for you will have an important bearing on how content you are.

Though the focus of this book is IT careers, the situation or career you choose is important no matter what field you are in. Consider this: The average person lives to the age of 75 and works from the ages of 22 to 60, and you spend an average of 8 hours a day, 5 days a week at work; therefore, in the span of 38 years, you will spend over 62,000 hours at work. That's too much time to spend in boredom or disappointment. As previously stated, part of the intent of this book is to assist you in anticipating some of the factors and variables that play significant roles when you're deciding whether or not to pursue a career in IT.

In this chapter, we'll look at some of the factors that govern not just why you might want to work in IT, such as job security and portability, but also things that you should consider that can influence your decision about which companies you may choose to work for and where. We will start by looking at the major factors that influence why people want to work in IT.

The Main Factors

Many factors will influence your reasons for wanting to work in IT. Some will be more important to you than others. We'll leave it to you to decide which ones are most important, but in the sections that follow, we'll outline some of the major ones. They aren't listed in any specific order of priority, because personal preference dictates the factors of most importance.

Money

Let's not beat around the bush. Few things motivate people more than money. Sure, there are jobs that people do through choice, many of which are not that financially rewarding, but unless you are fortunate enough to have some special kind of financial advantage, you are going to have to pay the rent and put food on the table. In this respect, IT is an attractive field indeed. Wages and salaries for IT professionals can be quite good. You are not, as a programmer or network engineer, likely to earn the same as a major league baseball player or a film star, but with a few years of experience and some hard work, you can earn salaries similar to those of other professional fields (such as the legal and medical professions) without having to invest several years of your life in school and internships. One of the advantages of IT is that much of the learning is done on the job—while you are being paid for it! However, if you think a career in IT is a "shortcut" to making money fairly quickly and easily, you are mistaken. You'll find that there are no shortcuts here—you will truly pay the price, but you'll reap the benefits of the investment you make in IT in a different manner than you would the benefits of an investment of another profession.

Salaries in IT do tend to be on the better side of average, but by how much? That is a difficult question to answer. Even when talking about first jobbers, it is hard to predict what pay scales are likely to be. A trainee PC support person will earn considerably more working for a software company in California's Silicon Valley than a person going for the same role in a small manufacturing business in Des Moines. In that respect, IT is no different from any other industry. The type of company and the location are all likely to have a large impact on what you will be paid. One thing that does make a difference, though, is the demand factor. Companies in small towns struggle just as much as the big boys do to attract the best IT staff. What the smaller companies may be able to offer, which perhaps the larger companies cannot, is a working environment that may appeal to certain people.

So why is the money so good? IT, like anything else in life, is subjected to the forces of supply and demand. As long as there are fewer people available to do IT jobs, the money will continue to be good. If a point in time arrives when the gap between the demand for IT skills and the individuals who possess them begins to close, then expect wages for IT staff to start dropping. In the foreseeable future at least, this outcome seems unlikely.

Your earning potential will depend on many factors, including how flexible you are prepared to be about your work, but the two major forces are simply your level of experience and your qualifications. Although there is no quick way to gain experience, you can do things to make the experiences you have count for more, such as following up what you do at work by studying outside of the workplace or keeping detailed notes of everything you are shown or that you do. As for qualifications, the thinking is reasonably simple. The more relevant qualifications and certifications you hold, the more you are likely to be paid, though increasingly, employers are only recognizing qualifications and certifications if you have experience to back them up.

Though money can be a major force in your decision to work in IT, it should not be a major driver in your overall career choice. Working in IT is very different from other job areas in that it demands a high level of continual personal development at a pace that can, at times, be overwhelming and difficult to keep up with. If you enter the IT field only for the money and you're not interested in the subject, you are likely to find this continual development an uphill (not to mention stressful) struggle. For this reason, and to encourage you through those sometimes difficult times, it is essential that the level of interest is there. There is no shortcut to this developmental cycle either. If you don't take the time to upgrade your skills, your earning potential will be short-lived indeed. So basically, the monetary rewards that working in IT can bring are great as long as you enjoy what you are doing. If you're not interested in technology, a career in IT is unlikely to be right for you. Besides, there are plenty of other ways to make a living.

How's your curve ball?

Job Security

It's somewhat hard to quantify the importance of job security in an individual's life, but it should, and does, have a distinct influence on career decisions.

In general, people's perception of job security is determined by a number of factors:

➤ *The size of the company*—In these days of billion dollar corporate buyouts, even the largest of companies cannot escape the fact that they will sometimes be closed down, either through assimilation or merger. In broader terms, however, large companies are generally "safer" than smaller ones in terms of job security because they are better able to weather fluctuations in the market or economy. Larger companies also tend to have a degree of diversity that offers even more protection.

➤ *The nature of the industry*—Some industries are more volatile than others. Particularly in times of recession, industries that serve luxury markets tend to get hit harder than those that deal with necessities such as foodstuff and

2

clothing. This is a factor that you should consider if you are aiming your career search toward a certain market sector. There are some sectors, such as government, that are affected much less by the economy and more by political policy. For this reason, though they may be thought of as "safe" jobs, they are still somewhat at risk from outside influences that may be difficult to anticipate.

➤ *The type of work*—Some careers fields are more secure than others for a variety of reasons, such as overall demand and the importance of their role within the company. Though there are few employees that are not needed, those that are deemed less important may be the first to go.

➤ *The history of the company*—As the old investment saying goes, "Past performance is no guarantee of future performance." That said, certain companies have developed reputations as good companies for which to work. Many have earned this reputation by being outstanding in a variety of areas, one of which may be their recognition of employees' job security needs.

Though these factors apply to most any career, as well as a career in IT, there are a few small twists in the tale. First, as we have discussed already, people with IT skills are highly sought after. To most companies and organizations, technology is not a luxury. When it comes time to tighten belts and the budgets, people from the IT department don't usually feature too highly on the list of optional employees. In addition, companies struggle to find suitably skilled staff, so if you are doing your job and doing it right, you are likely to remain a permanent fixture.

But that is not the biggest factor influencing IT job security. As an IT worker, you have the additional comfort of knowing that you work in an industry that provides a wide range of opportunities outside of the company in which you work. Effectively, a career in IT offers you great *job* security, but it offers even greater *career* security. With this in mind, you may find yourself taking comfort in the fact that, if your current job does not work out for any reason, you may find it reasonably easy to find further work.

Having said all of this, there is one fact that is inescapable. Employees who do not perform to expectations, and those who do not play by the rules, can and will be fired, recession or not. Working in IT is no protection for employees with low standards or those with a poor attitude. They will be fired as quickly as an employee in any other department who acts the same way. As the old saying goes, "No one is irreplaceable." What IT does offer is a mechanism by which individuals can make themselves valuable and hard-to-replace assets.

What's Your Interest?

Some jobs are boring; some are not. Some jobs in IT are boring; most are not. What is boring to one person may be a source of endless enjoyment to another. That diversity is what makes us human. The key to finding a specific IT career that keeps you satisfied for many years to come is deciding what area of technology is appropriate for you. These points will be discussed in greater detail in chapters to follow. What we are referring to here is just a general level of interest.

To the untrained, nontechnical eye, working in the IT industry may look a bit mundane—spending endless hours in front of a computer screen performing a variety of tasks, day in and day out. But those on the inside are well aware that the IT industry is anything but dull. In fact, if it were widely known how interesting it can be, there would be a stampede to the nearest training center. It is also worth mentioning that, although the common perception is that people spend countless hours staring at a screen, that is not the case for many areas of IT. In many IT roles, you are also likely to be spending time talking to other people, attending meetings, or crawling under desks.

There are other things that make IT an interesting and stimulating field. Most occupations in the computing industry require that IT professionals use, or at least have knowledge of, the latest and greatest products and programs. There is nothing dull about working in an industry that requires its workers to be on the cutting edge. Even if your chosen field means that endless hours are spent in front of a computer screen (and here's one of the big IT secrets), a lot of this time is spent playing around with cool and interesting stuff. In fact, "playing around" with cool stuff (testing new software, for example) can be a large part of the job, even if it is typically disguised as seeking a more efficient method to conduct business.

Whatever your chosen IT area, there will be times when you need to try a beta version of a program, or new features of an existing program, or maybe even new products like voice recognition software or some sort of multipurpose printer. The point is that technology progresses at an ever increasingly rapid pace, and it is, to say the least, very interesting to have access to the products and programs of the future. For many people working in IT, it is this ability to work with new products that provides the greatest satisfaction of all.

If testing and working with the most recent and innovative software and hardware does not perk your interest, do not despair; there are plenty of other interesting elements to the IT industry. Consider for a moment the on-the-job diversity that a career in IT can provide. Small to mid-sized companies that employ few IT professionals require the ones they do have to be able to perform a variety of different tasks. One day you might show up to work and need to troubleshoot a bad network connection. The next day you find yourself upgrading a PC with a larger hard drive and sound card. The next day you may be training users on a new database program. This kind of diversity provides ongoing interest, and in many cases the opportunity to try new and different things. And you never know; you may find that you enjoy a certain aspect of the job a great deal, in which case you can choose to focus on that.

Those whose interest fades when faced with the same task every day may find that they enjoy the diversity that some IT jobs provide. With some jobs, you may not know what needs to be done on any given day.

Still not convinced? Try this one. Essentially, in IT, nothing is ever assumed to be as good as it gets. All programs, from Web browser to operating system, and all hardware, from hard drives to network cards, are temporary. They are used in the interim until something else comes along, and when that something else comes along, it too is temporary. Hardware and software are replaced as soon as someone conceives and designs a better product. That someone could be you.

Portability

A career in information technology can act as a mechanism for traveling and seeing other parts of the country or even the world. Because every company worldwide has a technology infrastructure of some sort, every country can become part of your target market. Though some experience will almost certainly make things go a little smoother, there is no reason why those starting a career in IT should not be able to take advantage of out-of-town or even out-of-country opportunities.

The language of technology is international. The skills and experience you bring to a job in your hometown are valid practically anywhere else in the world, provided of course that you have the language skills to back up your technical knowledge. In fact, the addition of a foreign language to your skills set can be a valuable and worthwhile asset if you are seeking work with a large multinational corporation who may be supporting customers worldwide.

IT is unique in that many other fields require participants to have their qualifications evaluated or recognized by a certifying body in the country to which they want to go. In the IT field, this is not the case. A C++ programmer in the United States can be a C++ programmer in Australia with no such hurdles.

A further enhancement of this worldwide portability can be found with certifications, which are recognized globally. Whereas industry degrees or professional certifications often require that the holder be recertified or have his qualifications recognized by the foreign country, this problem doesn't exist in IT. Take, for example, the Microsoft Certified Systems Engineer (MCSE) certification, which is one of the most popular certification programs available. The MCSE is recognized in every country in which Microsoft has a presence, and even those that it doesn't. Effectively, the MCSE, as with other certification programs, has become a global standard by which technical capability can be measured. Because the testing strategy is the same the world over, employers know that a person who has gained his or her MCSE in the United States has demonstrated the same level of knowledge and understanding that a person from England has. This gives employers an advantage too because it provides them with a meaningful and relevant way to compare the skills of two people irrespective of nationality and background.

If you do have aspirations of world travel and jet-setting, just bear one thing in mind. Starting a new job, let alone a new career, can be a stressful and intimidating experience. Starting off in a place where family and friends are around to lend a bit of moral support can be a big bonus. Also consider that a supportive circle of friends, some of whom perhaps work in IT, can serve as a useful resource in times of need. Email can be a great tool, but there is nothing like sitting and talking about a day at work over a coffee or iced tea.

Which IT Job Environment Is Right for You?

Now that we have examined why you would want to work in IT, it's time to look at some of the factors that will influence your decisions about what kind of environment you would like to work in. We are not referring to specific job areas yet—that's covered in the next chapter. What we will be discussing here are things like your work hours, environment, and surroundings. You would be surprised about how much these factors can influence your overall happiness.

Where Do You Want to Work?

When you imagined yourself working in the IT industry, did you imagine yourself working in a skyscraper and wearing a three-piece suit to work every day? Is your picture of your job less formal, such as working in a small office wearing jeans and a T-shirt to work? Or is it even less formal, like no office and wearing a bathrobe and boxer shorts while you work?

The IT industry may be one of the few industries that allow its workers to choose any one of these environments. On the one extreme, IT professionals can find themselves working in environments that demand a high level of formality. Conversely, with the increase in the amount of contract work and the advances

2

in telecommuting, many IT professionals can work from the comfort of their homes. The workload, pressures, and demands of the job remain constant; only the scenery changes.

Basically, there is no standard work environment for the IT professional, which is a true strength of the industry. Each area of IT has its own unique occupational setting, giving those interested in a career in IT a chance to customize and choose a job that has a work environment best suited for them. Some programmers may enjoy, and are more productive, in an office setting; some may be better working in their home.

The possible working environments can be broken down into some common categories, namely office based, field based, project based, and home based. Though you may find a job that does not fit into one of these categories, most do. Listed here are the categories, along with some of the characteristics of each:

➤ *Office-based*—Having an office-based position generally means that you are working at the same location and with the same people on a permanent basis. That's good if the journey to work is an easy one and you enjoy spending time with these people. It's not so good if the journey is a nightmare and the office environment leaves a lot to be desired. A large proportion of IT jobs are office based, and although you may not like everyone, the fact that you are likely to have a common interest (technology) with your workmates will usually make it easier to get along. Most offices require employees to work regular business hours, but office-based jobs in IT aren't always a 9-to-5 affair. In many areas, especially support roles, you'll find shift systems that require staff to work very early in the morning, late at night, or even overnight in certain cases, so this is something to consider if you are person who has trouble getting up early or staying up late.

➤ *Field-based*—Though not all IT fields are conducive to field-based positions, many, such as support engineers, are. The basic premise of field-based work is that you travel from one location to the other, attending to jobs at each location. This means that field-based personnel usually work alone and do not have a fixed "home" base. The idea of hours on the road with no manager to look over you may seem attractive at first, but as with anything, it has a downside. Field-based positions do not suit everyone. It can tend to be a lonely existence, traveling (sometimes for a number of hours) between sites where you don't know anyone, with nothing but the radio and your thoughts for company. If you like traveling, though, and driving in particular, then it could be for you.

➤ *Project-based*—Some positions are regarded as project based, meaning that you work for a company who moves you from one client site to another. These positions differ from field-based positions in that you generally spend a longer period of time, such as weeks or even months, in a single location. For people who prefer being around others and in a familiar environment, project based positions can be ideal, offering a chance to work in a range of different situations and environments while at the same time maintaining consistency in employment. The only problem with finding project-based positions is that they are often not advertised as such, and you find out the details only when you get to the interview. If you are dealing with a recruitment agent (which we will talk about in Section 3), you can specify that you would ideally like a project-based position. Another solution is to target companies that commonly operate in this manner, such as facilities management or outsourcing companies.

➤ *Home-based*—To many, the idea of working from home seems like the ultimate in luxury. Drag yourself out of bed at 8:55 and be in the office by 9:00! It sounds ideal. Remember that there's a price to pay for every good thing that comes along; it's just a matter of knowing what's most important to you and what you're willing to sacrifice for it. If, for example, a flexible schedule is important to you, you may not mind the discipline that is required in order to get your job done.

Probably the most misunderstood of these categories is the home-based environment. There are a few factors that play integral roles in the success of a work-from-home situation:

➤ Creating a suitable environment

➤ Self discipline and dedication

➤ Time management

To create an environment that is conducive to work, many recommend that you have a dedicated room or space specifically designated as your work "office." Because you can be distracted by home-related environmental factors, you have to be able to focus on your work and be dedicated and self-disciplined enough to not only accomplish your task, but also continue to strive toward a higher level of quality. And because you might have the luxury of a more flexible schedule, you must manage your time efficiently and be willing to do what it takes to meet the requirements of your job, regardless of the time of day or day of the week. If you're considering this option, it is sometimes helpful to talk to others who work from

2

home; they can provide you with valuable insight learned through their own experiences.

The reality of this situation is that, unless you work well alone and have the motivation to keep at a (what may be boring) task while the sun is shining outside, then a home-based working environment may not be for you. You should also consider that, although technology is providing more and faster ways to work from home, there is still a very small percentage of people who work solely from home, and a number of professions simply do not lend themselves well to a home-based work setup.

Some Other Things to Think About

As the saying goes, "Even the little things can make a big difference." Having focused on some of the major factors regarding your career selection, we'll now look at some other things that you can consider. These "little things" may not seem that important at first, but as time goes on, you'll be surprised at the difference they can make between a job you like and a job you love.

Be Around the Things You Like!

Though not always the case, a career in IT can allow you to combine the work you do with other interests. Because practically every company has an IT function, it's possible for you to match up the companies you would like to work for with an interest you have. In this particular case, the importance of other factors, such as money and job security, may become less relevant. An IT professional who likes airplanes, for instance, might want to look for an IT job within the aviation industry or even at an airport.

Another way of looking at the comfort factor is this. If you have previously worked in another profession such as accounting and you enjoyed it, try mixing a career in IT with your accountancy skills. This will make you doubly valuable in certain environments. Not only will you have an understanding of IT systems, you will also understand the specifics of the implementation and how they are used.

Another angle that you should consider is whether you want to work for a technical company or whether you want to work as a techie in a nontechnical company. Does the idea of working for Microsoft or Cisco or even Yahoo! appeal to you? These companies have just as much if not more of a need for technically capable staff as nontechnical companies do. You may find that technical companies also have a more positive approach to training than nontechnical companies.

Company Size—Does It Matter?

Though it may seem like an odd thing to consider when you are starting a career in IT, the size of company you work for can make quite a difference in the early stages of your career, which is likely to consist of the most formative years. It is difficult to characterize companies by size, but different size companies have many features in common.

Small Companies

People who work in a small company need to be highly flexible, moving between tasks such as answering the phone or signing for a delivery while still doing their IT job. From a job security perspective, though, small companies offer less because they are more prone to fluctuations in the economy. That said, there are some significant upsides. Because you are working in a small unit, there is a better chance that you will understand how the company works overall, which will provide you with the ability to realize a tenable link between the work you do and the success of the company. This can provide a great deal of job satisfaction.

On a more personal level, working in a small company may make it easier to be recognized for your talents, but there may also be fewer places to go. In a small company it may also be that you are the only IT resource employed, which in itself can be a double-edged sword. On the one hand, you get to do all of the IT related tasks yourself, on the other, there is the fact that there is no-one around to help you if you come across a problem that you have trouble fixing. Working for a small company can often seem like a trial-by-fire.

Though it is not always the case, smaller companies tend to pay slightly less and have a less structured benefits system than larger companies, the impact of which should be fully considered when comparing offers. One of the best things about working for a smaller company is the sheer speed at which things move. Often in small companies, budgets are tight, which mean that staffing levels are generally at or below required levels, meaning that you are likely to be constantly pushed to produce more work. If this sounds appealing to you and you like the cut and thrust of working in a dynamic and constantly changing environment, a small company could be the right place for you.

Medium-Sized Companies

A medium-sized company offers the benefits of working for a small company (such as the ability to be recognized for your skills) along with the increased security that working for an established company brings. Because medium-sized businesses are likely to have been trading for some time, they may have already weathered harder times and learned how to survive, making them somewhat less susceptible to fluctuations in the economy. In addition, medium-sized companies are likely to have more funds available for training and also for adopting new technologies, both of which will help you to increase your skills and knowledge. Though there is still likely to be a touch of the dynamic to the environment, it will be a little more tempered because the larger the company is, the more time it takes to respond to changes in the market. In terms of benefits, medium-sized companies are more likely to offer a complete package, such as healthcare, pensions, and so on.

Though many medium-sized companies do have a defined IT department, the chance of these "departments" consisting of just a few people is high. For this reason, your ability to relate well to the other people is particularly important, as is your willingness to pitch in with any task at hand. Many people find the combination of security and flexibility found in medium-sized companies particularly suitable for a first job, but this can sometimes make competition for these types of positions particularly fierce.

Large Companies

This is the point where you are more likely to be working as part of a large IT department rather than in a small team. Most procedures—such as those regarding vacations, pay, and promotion—will be set and standardized. Though you will have the ability to shine within your department, you might find it hard to be noticed outside of that environment, a fact that some people can find a little frustrating. You will often find that your role is heavily defined within a larger company, which is good if you prefer to work within reasonably strict parameters. Larger companies also tend to have a highly organized management structure, another factor that appeals to some people and not to others. Large companies generally use high-quality equipment and software and realize the benefit of training individuals to maximize their investments in those products. They also usually have the money to make this happen. Though not always the case, the benefits available to those working in large companies are often better than in smaller companies. These benefits may include such things as medical and dental plans and even subsidized restaurants, gymnasium facilities, and the like. Large companies will also tend to be more tolerant to those new to the IT field because they have the ability to "absorb" any lack of knowledge the newcomers may have within the team environment.

Corporate

These are the kind of companies whose names are familiar to most everyone—a point that can work heavily in your favor if you are moving on. Large corporate companies usually provide you with many opportunities and, most likely, a professional and highly organized working environment. However, the nature of large corporate organizations can sometimes leave employees feeling uncertain as to how their specific efforts are helping "the big picture." Another aspect of this is that it can sometimes be hard to shine in a large corporate company, where employees rely heavily on their managers to recognize talent and develop it.

It does happen, though, and if you're willing to stay put and work your way up the corporate ladder, then a certain amount of wealth and recognition may await you, but be prepared for what can potentially be a long and arduous haul. As with anything that promises wealth and riches, you'll more than likely have your fair share of stress and pressure to endure from various sources. One side benefit of working for a corporation is that corporations often have offices in other parts of the country or the world, which can provide opportunities to travel or perhaps to relocate. Corporate companies tend to be at the leading edge when it comes to adopting new technologies, often even to the point of acting as test sites for manufacturers. The availability of funds will usually mean that technology projects are fully staffed and fully equipped, a major boon to those involved within these projects. Because corporate companies often go to great lengths to attract candidates of the highest quality, you can often find yourself working alongside some of the best individuals in your chosen field, a fact that can only enhance the career of someone new to IT.

As long as you are okay with the relative anonymity that working for a corporate company can bring, the benefits of working for such an organization are huge. This is a fact not lost on many people who are new to the IT field. When you combine this with the fact that many of these corporate companies are household names, you can begin to appreciate that competition for positions at these companies is often extremely fierce.

Punching the Clock—Your Working Hours

Stories of programmers working long hours to meet deadlines or network administrators working weekends to ensure proper network functioning are well documented. Ever wonder just how many hours an IT professional typically works in a week? The simple answer is that it all depends.

Those working in IT professions such as PC repair and help desk support can expect to work a standard 40-hour workweek with very little deviation. In theory,

2

IT professions such as Web designers and programmers work a 40-hour week. However, those entering these professions and expecting to be home by five for supper every day may be in for a bit of a surprise. The workweek in these professions starts out as 40 hours and increases depending on what needs to be done, and no one is going anywhere until it is done. Products, programs, and client-required services are extremely time sensitive, and deadlines are unforgiving; this is reflected in the actual amount of working hours.

Other areas of IT require that workers be at the job at unusual hours. Network administrators, for instance, who need access to the server for upgrades or repairs will find themselves working evenings and weekends to accomplish their needs. The work of network administrators needs to be done when the network is least used to minimize the inconvenience to the end user. It will not be uncommon to drive by the office at 6:00 on a Saturday and see a car belonging to an IT professional in the parking lot. Don't feel too badly for him, however, because come Monday morning he is likely to be sleeping in.

It's Not All a Bed of Roses

Working in IT is no different than anything else. There is always a downside. In the introduction, we promised to tell you about not just the good, but the bad as well. That said, this section is not meant to discourage you from working in IT—far from it. We are just trying to make you aware of the fact that it's not all a bed of roses.

Consider the Challenges

The list of reasons why people should explore a career in IT is long. Factors such as job security, high salaries, and benefit packages can perk the interest of even the most technically resistant person. There are, however, other factors that you should be aware of before you head on down to the nearest training center. Computer operators, network administrators and technicians, and indeed all of those working in IT face challenges and problems in the workplace that are unique to the IT industry. Those wishing to work in the field need to be aware of the unusual and potentially negative aspects that can appear in an IT work environment. We'll discuss some of these negative aspects in the sections that follow.

Consider Your Needs

Those needing recognition or validation for a job well done may not find it in the IT industry. Typically, a supervisor or a boss has a reasonably good understanding of what the employees are doing and knowledge of what their jobs entail and the daily challenges they face. Because of the technical nature of the occupations within the IT industry, many supervisors are unaware of the issues facing their computer staff. Nontechnical businesses, for instance, that employ a network administrator often have no idea what is done behind the mysterious door located somewhere near the basement. All they are concerned about is that when they press the print icon, something comes out of the printer, that when they need to log on, they can, and that they can access their database with ease. If, for instance, Monday morning comes and users are unable to send out important emails, expect frantic and sometimes hysterical calls. If, however, come Monday morning all systems are working and the email is sent with no difficulty, do not expect a call congratulating you on your efforts. Even if you spent your entire weekend reconfiguring your Dynamic Host Configuration Protocol (DHCP) scopes, subnetting your network, and troubleshooting miscellaneous logon anomalies just so Monday's emails would be sent.

It is not that people are insensitive or unappreciative of the work that an IT professional does, it is simply that the computer skills are specialized and the technical details and behind-the-scenes work is not readily understood or recognized by the end user or supervisor. All that can be seen is the end result, and as cold as it may sound, the end result is not a luxury but rather an expectation of your employment. Unfortunately, because a lot of computer work is done behind closed doors, it is difficult for others to gauge your work performance and determine how good, or how poor, you are at doing your job. This often leaves resourceful and energetic IT professionals feeling unappreciated and not-so-good ones feeling just fine.

Consider the Stress Factors

Where's the fire? IT professionals have been somewhat accurately referred to as "technical firemen." A computer-related job can at times be bizarrely serene and calm, especially when things are running smoothly and programs are functioning as they should. An experienced IT professional would suggest that you savor these moments because, if there is one constant in the IT world, it's this—if something can go wrong, eventually it will. Just when you've settled in for a Friday afternoon of water cooler conversation and some mind-numbing computer task, the phone rings and a program release date has been moved forward, a client demands an immediate redesign on a Web page by Monday, and furthermore, no one is able to log on to the network. You are required and expected to fix the problems in an efficient and expedient manner. It is up to you to calmly and confidently put out the fire.

It's times like these that are perhaps the hardest part of an IT job and the reason more than a few people have quit or avoided either particular areas of IT or the whole IT profession. The stress involved in these situations can be intense, and the impatience and urgency of those relying on your ability to correct the problem only serve to fuel the fire.

The amount of stress and the number of potentially stressful situations are greater in some IT professions than others, but none have the ability to escape it altogether. Essentially, IT professionals have unique technical skills, be they programmers, Web developers, or network administrators. Companies depend on your knowledge and ability to utilize these skills to ensure that their applications and their business function reliably. Those hired in IT are hired on the assumption that when the chips, or perhaps the computers, are down, they are able to get everything operational.

All experienced IT professionals are more than willing to entertain you with stories of system crashes, corrupt databases, and working unbelievable hours to meet a seemingly impossible deadline. Certification, education, and training cannot adequately prepare you for the feeling of having a boss, client, or entire company waiting on you. This is a situation that IT professionals are likely to face and a situation that determines your aptitude and suitability for a career in IT. To a great degree, the satisfaction that you get from the job in IT depends upon how well you're able to "weather the storms," as well as your continued level of interest. Needless to say, possessing an even temper and being able to "absorb" comments without taking them personally and letting them interfere with getting the job done can be two personal attributes that will benefit you more in your IT profession than possibly ever before.

Consider the Pace

It is a long and often arduous process to get the qualifications, training, and certifications you need to secure an IT career. After months or years of training, you are finally ready to face the world and take your place in the IT workforce. Then you discover that you are not out of the training woods yet, nor are you going to be in the future. By the time you've finished your education, the technology and the training programs that support it have been updated or amended to support a new product range or even a new product. If you want to play the game, you have to keep paying, both financially and intellectually. An even more frustrating factor is that you can often discover that much of the skills you learn during training are not applied in the workplace. It is not worth getting disheartened by this. It is the nature of the beast.

The point is that the IT world is a dynamic one, changing and progressing at a pace that makes much of what we know today become obsolete in six months. That's just the nature of technology—it constantly and rapidly progresses and, therefore, sets the pace for the demands of most IT professionals whose daily tasks involve trying to accommodate for such rapid change and growth. There is always a new and improved way of doing things, and you are required to make it work. Training and the IT industry go hand in hand, and if there is a second constant in the computer world, it's that you will never be finished with your training. There will always be technical workshops, seminars, exams, and certifications. To ignore the need to upgrade your skills is to ignore your IT career. You'll simply be left behind if you don't continue to march with the band and at the band's pace. Ultimately, insufficient training reduces your effectiveness on the job and makes you a lot less marketable in the IT realm.

Consider Yourself!

Hello! Anybody! Depending on the exact area of IT you choose and the environment in which you are employed, you can find yourself working alone a large part of the time. Small to mid-sized companies may not need or have the money for more than one technician. This can create an isolated and lonely working environment. There can be few things more demoralizing than sleeping on the floor under your desk waiting for a data restore to complete while the rest of the company's employees are at home enjoying an evening with their families. We mention this as just another item for you to factor into your equation when trying to calculate whether IT is right for you.

Chapter Summary

Don't take our word for it. Deciding on a career in IT and then on a specific area can be a big decision. This book is a valuable resource to assist you along the way and provide you with some useful and honest insight, but there are other avenues and methods you can use to assist you in making a solid career decision.

Ask around; someone you know or someone a friend knows probably works in IT. Give that person a call and ask some questions, get the inside scoop into the industry. Nothing can give you better insight into the job you are seeking than to talk to people already in the profession. Ask to hear both the good aspects and the possible negative aspects of the job. It is best not to view the profession through rose-colored glasses. If at all possible, it can be very beneficial to visit the workplace of an IT profession you are interested in. Seeing a network administrator or programmer at work can give you a clearer picture of what the job entails. Also, ask about the company: What size is it? What is the environment like? What type of company is it? The environment and working conditions are an important consideration when choosing a particular area of IT.

Log on to the Internet and search out information pertaining to the area of IT in which you are interested in becoming employed. Check out employment sites to determine the demand for your target job and the locations in which the job is in most demand. Relocation may be necessary. Refer to the job tasks listed by employers to get a better idea of what your typical day would look like. Would you be in front of a computer all day? Would you be dealing with end users? Would you be working in an office or working off-site?

Explore the training curriculum for your chosen career. The material presented in the training program can provide a clear indication of what the job requirements will be and what you need to know. If you find the training materials extremely uninteresting and you find yourself having to force yourself to read it, that may be an indication of trouble brewing. As mentioned, IT careers require ongoing training and upgrading of skills, and there really needs to be some interest in the chosen field right from the onset.

3

Choosing the Area of IT That's Right for You

Can you remember the best job you ever had? What about the worst? Did you enjoy working directly with others, or did you prefer to work alone? As discussed in the preceding chapter, an awareness of what you want and need from a job and a work environment is essential when choosing a career in IT. IT jobs offer many types of working conditions—some require working long hours alone, some require working exclusively with clients, and others require ongoing collaboration with co-workers. The number and diversity of IT work environments allow those entering the industry the opportunity to choose an area that best suits their personality.

The previous chapter provided a general look at the IT industry including such things as work environment and the type and size of company that you choose to work for. Armed with this information, you may now want to match your personality to a specific area of IT that interests you. By matching your personality, we simply mean to learn and take into consideration such things as stress factors, personal attributes, and soft skills that may be specifically relevant and necessary for particular job types in IT.

The intention of this chapter is two fold:

➤ To provide a general introduction to five primary technical areas in IT.

➤ To discuss the various stress factors, personal attributes, and soft skills that are advantageous to particular jobs in such areas of IT.

This chapter addresses five primary areas of IT—Computer Programming, PC and Computer Support, Networking, Internet Technologies and Web Design, and Database Design and Administration. Each area discusses the stress factors, along with the general personal attributes needed for each job area. The "personality checkpoints," included as notes in these sections, will be of particular interest to you as well.

The technical areas introduced in this chapter, though by no means inclusive of all areas, represent the current hotspots of the IT industry—the general areas in which several job types reside. The next five chapters focus on the actual jobs in these particular areas and describes these positions in greater detail, along with their requirements. Please keep in mind that the duties of some of these jobs overlap, as do the working conditions.

When selecting the area you think is right for you, consider how well you deal with stress, the variety of work you want to do, and other factors such as whether you crave interaction with others, and whether your skill sets are suited for that position. Of course, the only way to really know whether a job is right for you is to do it, but at least by looking at what kind of things you can expect from a certain job based on the experiences and observations of others, you can narrow the possible field in terms of what job you believe suits you best.

Why These Five Areas?

We have chosen the five preceding technical areas for good reason. They represent not only a wide range of possible job choices, but also paths into an IT career that can be obtained by those who only have a little technical knowledge. We say little technical knowledge because there is one thing you need to consider. If you have made it this far in life without expressing an interest in IT that has prompted you to buy a PC, get on the Internet, and start thinking about how things work, then a career in IT will be challenging indeed.

The five areas we have chosen to cover are all accessible to people who have no college degree or other formal training. These areas can be pursued through self-study, certification, and perseverance. If you are fortunate enough to have a university or college degree, all the better, as it will almost certainly work in your favor.

More than anything else though, we chose these career areas because they are now, and are expected to remain, the areas of strongest job demand within the IT industry. Demand equals jobs, and that is where you want to be.

As we start to talk more specifically about job roles, it is worth talking briefly about one of the confusing aspects of the IT industry, that of terminology. Many job and skill areas have a variety of descriptions or job roles that are all related to the same skills set, though the positions themselves have certain unique demands and characteristics. At this early stage of the proceedings, the subtle differences between some of these roles are not so important. As your career progresses, however, the difference between, for example, a software designer and a software tester becomes all the more significant.

A Closer Look at the Five Areas of IT

In this section, we look at our chosen areas in a little more detail. For each, we discuss such things as the likely work environment, and look at factors such as stress. Also included are personality checkpoints that can help you to decide whether a specific area is matched to your personality.

Computer Programming

Programs make the technical world go round. We use computer programs every day. They are the widely used word processors, operating systems, games, and Web pages that make our computers functional and productive.

Naturally, someone has to write these programs, and it is the job of the computer programmer. Programmers are generally a determined bunch of people, dedicated to keeping us up-to-date in the ever-changing world of IT. It is up to the programmers to design, test, and fix all programs we use, which is no small task given the speed at which the masses demand more functionality from their computer systems.

As a profession, becoming a programmer is a solid choice. The demand for programmers is predicted to rise, a trend that is likely to continue as long as the industry-wide shortage of programmers persists. This shortage of skilled and experienced personnel has put many companies and businesses in the unenviable position of having to aggressively recruit programmers, which in turn has led to ever more creative and lucrative benefit packages, luxury work conditions, and higher salaries.

Computer programmers can be found working in a variety of different environments, though typically they find themselves in an office setting. Companies of all sizes need and use computer programmers, from the largest corporation to the smallest Internet startup. Regardless of the setting, if you like spending large parts of time directly at the computer, then this is the job for you.

That said, the old stereotype of the lone programmer hunched over the keyboard in the corner of the basement is somewhat far from the truth. Although it is true that some programming jobs require extensive hours directly working with the computer, programmers often work in environments where direct programming hours are tempered with project meetings and discussions. Essentially, programming cannot be done in a bubble. There is a good chance that a number of people may be working on the same program, and the need for good communication and cooperation is essential for the successful completion of the project.

Personality Checkpoint: Programmers must be self-motivated and ready to work long hours to meet deadlines. When writing code, programmers are often required to work independently of others. Conversely, when a program is in the development stage, there is often a great deal of collaboration on the project. Programmers who do not function well in a cooperative environment will need to develop the skills to do so.

Stress Factors

Okay, so working independently is no problem, and you function well with team collaboration. You need to consider other factors before entering a career in programming. If you want to work in a stress-free environment, you are not going to find it in programming. As we already know, bananas have a longer shelf life than computer programs, and software is constantly in a state of change. It is up to the programmers of the world to keep these programs coming and coming fast. The release dates and deadlines for software applications, software upgrades, and patches are often unforgiving. To miss one deadline is to potentially give the edge to the competition and disappoint clients.

Programmers are hired on the assumption that they are able to write, design, and debug programs in their chosen language in a timely fashion. This expectation means that the responsibility is squarely on the shoulders of the programmers to deliver quality and on time. Although it means potentially working long hours, good programmers meet their deadlines, and those who don't will not be programmers for very long.

Personality Checkpoint: When deadlines are approaching, programmers may find themselves working in a stressful environment as the push is on to meet the deadline. Programmers must be able to maintain composure and remain productive in a stressful environment.

Character Sketch

Much of a programmer's time is spent writing programming code. To do the job well, programmers need the ability to think logically, while at the same time, creatively. They must take a thorough and methodical approach when writing and debugging programs. Programming can often be a painstaking process, and to rush through the job can mean having to retrace steps to fix problems. With tight deadlines, no one has time for that. Procrastination is a programmer's nightmare. With the speed at which things can happen, tasks simply can't be put off until tomorrow.

Personality Checkpoint: Whether programmers are debugging an existing program or writing new ones, they need to pay close attention to detail. For programmers, patience is definitely a virtue.

PC and Computer Support

We've all been there—hard drive failure, modem doesn't work, screen doesn't come on, or your Shift key is stuck. At times a piece of hardware in a PC will need repair, maintenance, or upgrading. Other times a new application will need to be installed, configured, or taught. PC support will always be in demand.

All companies, agencies, and even home users that use computers will at some point need to crack open the case on a PC, whether to install a new component, replace an old one, or to troubleshoot a hardware error. Nowadays, a growing number of people are taking matters into their own hands and attempting their own upgrades and fixes. Upgrading your own PC is comparable to changing the oil in your car instead of taking it to a garage. Changing the oil is easy, and many people choose to do it themselves. If the transmission goes, however, you probably take it to a mechanic. Many people are highly successful at doing their own PC upgrades and minor repairs, but the major work and troubleshooting is always left to those who have the training.

It is not just individuals. Companies of all sizes need PC support in one form or another, and as the number of PCs keeps growing, the demand for people who are suitably qualified to work on them is likely to follow suit.

Personality Checkpoint: Those doing PC support need to keep apprised of current hardware, as they will most certainly be working and configuring it. They need to have a wide range of knowledge that includes not only extensive hardware knowledge but software knowledge as well. The rate of change within the PC environment does not make this an easy task. Keeping up with an ever increasing pace is something that you should be able to do well.

If there were ever an easy way to get into IT, then PC support would be it. Fundamentally a PC support role combines technical skills such as knowledge of PCs and common application programs with a high degree of communication skills and a passion for hard work. Easy to get into it may be, limited in potential it is not. PC support starts from the ground up and just keeps on going. Many highly capable technical individuals work and prefer to remain in a PC support role for the reason that it lends a degree of human interaction and an amazing range of variety to the work.

Unless a company is of a reasonable size, most do not retain PC technicians on staff solely for PC repair and maintenance. Many companies, when faced with a computer hardware problem, will call an outside PC support technician. A quick trip through the Yellow Pages reveals numerous computer sales and service companies that offer these facilities.

It is within these companies that many PC technicians can be found. These computer outlets typically require a certified PC support person to deal with customers' questions and problems with their systems. Many of these technicians are also required to go into the field to work as needed. They may be required to go to a customer's home or business for after sales service, or they may be contracted out to companies for onsite repair and maintenance.

In PC support, personality is everything. Whether you are talking to users, to company clients, customers, or doing telephone support, PC technicians spend a lot of time discussing computer problems with users. The proliferation of computer service organizations means that customers and clients have a degree of choice when selecting who maintains and upgrades their systems. They will choose to get their PC support from the company with technicians that are competent as well as personable.

3

Personality Checkpoint: PC repair, maintenance, and upgrading require a large amount of interaction with computer users. Support personnel must be able to relay technical information in an understandable, and often diplomatic, way. Keep in mind, people generally only call PC support when something is wrong. Typically, the callers may not be at their best, but the PC support person will need to be.

Stress Factors

PC support is not without its stresses, but by comparison to other areas of IT such as programming, is not too bad. The main source of stress from the job of PC support comes directly from the customers or clients. When a computer is purchased, it is assumed that it will work seamlessly, and this does not always happen. When hardware doesn't work as it should, frustrations can be high, and the PC technician often bears the brunt of the frustration. Further stress can be added as the repairs are often done onsite, under the watchful eyes of clients and customers.

Personality Checkpoint: PC repair is often done in front of the user. Hardware problems can be difficult to troubleshoot at the best of times, and the pressure of having clients on hand when repairs are done can make the situation even more tense.

Character Sketch

PC support technicians need to have access to, and extensive knowledge of, current hardware. New hardware designs including everything from graphic cards to motherboards are introduced almost daily. It is essential that support technicians keep up-to-date with the new technology.

In addition to their hardware knowledge, PC support technicians must have a general knowledge of the common software used. They will need to be able to set up, configure, and in some cases, train clients in its use. Some software packages, whether games or applications, may have difficulties running with particular hardware configurations, and the PC support person's understanding of the relationship between the two entities will be a key factor in the resolution of the problem.

The cause of many PC problems is not always obvious, and the support technician needs to be an expert troubleshooter. The Internet and other PC professionals remain a valuable resource for technicians, and a thorough knowledge of where key information can be found is essential.

Personality Checkpoint: When presented with a particularly difficult hardware or software problem, PC support technicians may have to swallow some pride and ask a fellow technician for some pointers. Furthermore, there will be times when you may have to tell the customer or client that you are unable to locate a problem. Even PC support technicians are not invincible.

Network Administration

Computer networks initially started out as a means of sharing peripheral devices, such as printers, between computers to avoid having to purchase redundant equipment. The idea of networking from there has, to say the least, become quite popular. There can be no doubt that nowadays companies, whether large or small, are reliant upon their computer networks. Local area networks (LANs) and wide area networks (WANs) are the name of the game for businesses, providing the connectivity and communication backbone for companies.

Essentially, a computer network is comprised of several computers connected together for the purposes of sharing files between them, sharing devices between them, and maintaining security. Sounds simple doesn't it? Well the theory isn't, and the practice is often even harder.

The complexity of computer networks has advanced significantly to the point that a layman entering a network server room may mistake his surroundings for the cockpit of a space shuttle. Network administrators of today must contend with many technical factors associated with maintaining a network, and also the person-alities of the people who are reliant upon the network. In addition, they must have the ability to support products from various manufacturers, all of which need to be made to work with each other.

Network administrators can be employed in any size of business that uses a computer network. All types of businesses use these networks—from banks, to schools, to large corporations. Smaller companies, however, may rely on a local networking company rather than having their own full-time staff. In many larger companies, there may be network professionals whose time is dedicated solely to the functioning of the network. In small to mid-sized companies, network administrators often manage not only the network but may also find themselves doing PC repair, upgrading, and training.

3

Personality Checkpoint: Network administrators often work in environments that require minimal contact with end users and involve extensive time monitoring and improving the network. Other network administrators will find themselves spending large amounts of time with end users and less time monitoring the network. In either case, network administrators must have good communication skills and the ability to relay technical information in an easy, non-threatening manner.

Stress Factors

Unfortunately, network administration is not without its stresses. Most companies rely on networks for everything from printing to Internet access. If a network goes down, often times so does the business. To some businesses, such network disruption is an inconvenience, but to other companies, a non-functioning network can be a devastating financial blow. In either case, network administrators will be getting a call, and will be expected to be a swift and effective resource in what can be a troubling time.

It is not just about fixing problems, however. Long hours on weekends and evenings are sometimes required to upgrade networks or to maintain them in an effort to keep them up and running. Much of the time, upgrades and maintenance need to be performed outside of normal office hours. If you become a network administrator or network engineer, don't be surprised to be working after everyone else has gone home.

Personality Checkpoint: When network problems occur, administrators must be ready to address the problem in a timely fashion despite the complexity of the problem. When the network is down, you must be prepared to be in the spotlight, and a very bright spotlight it is.

Character Sketch

Network administrators have to be self-motivating because networks require continuous routine maintenance. If they are left unattended for extended periods, it can have serious repercussions for the stability of the network. Administrators must keep one eye on network monitors, keep another eye on users' activities, and a third eye on error logs, or other activities. The best network administrator has the ability to foresee problems before they occur and develop a plan so that the problem never surfaces. They are also resourceful. The diversity of the networking arena may often mean that when faced with a problem they do not know the answer, but they do know where to look for the answers.

Personality Checkpoint: Networks need a lot of care and attention. To avoid or delay the day-to-day maintenance and procedures is to eventually lessen the reliability and functionality of a network. Good administrators pay close attention to detail, establishing and monitoring performance baselines to keep ahead of potential network problems.

Internet and Web Design

Web design and Internet related jobs are a relative newcomer to the field of IT, though these occupations didn't take long to establish themselves as career front-runners in the industry. The skills required for Internet related jobs are varied, ranging from desktop publishing, to technical networking, security, and even sales. Within this area of IT there is a little something for everyone, and no shortage of companies looking for skilled professionals.

It seems like nowadays everyone has a Web page whether for information purposes, e-commerce purposes or just to promote their business. Whatever the reason for the Web page, someone has to design it, develop it, link it to the Internet and host it on a server.

So if Internet skills are in such demand, why doesn't everyone become a Web designer? Web page design is one of those few areas of IT in which a required skill cannot be learned. The skill we refer to is that of artistic ability. Modern Web page creation software can make the creation of Web sites relatively easy, and the programs themselves are designed to be easy to use. Even so, a page created by someone with little artistic ability will look distinctly amateur in comparison to one created by a person who has true artistic flair.

Web design often transcends mere page design to encompass other areas of IT, such as the platform support on which the Web server that serves the pages are run. In addition, an in-depth knowledge of other Internet related technologies is needed, such as file formats, encryption, and networking. The wide range of skills that are required in the Internet industry provides a good indication of the range of job related tasks needed on a day-to-day basis. Essentially, those with more skills can expect greater variation on the job. For those wanting job variation and a desire to be working on different aspects of the IT industry, Web design and the Internet is a good place to look.

Personality Checkpoint: Perhaps one of the most important qualities for Web designers is creativity. For a Web page, layout and design is everything. A page can have all the information, but without the organization and the proper presentation, it will not be useful.

Stress Factors

The stress for a Web designer is not that of other areas of IT, but it can still be present. Often Web designers and developers work directly with non-technical, clients—a situation that can present a whole range of challenges. It is important to remember that when a business or company decides to publish a Web page it is representative of their business, and therefore an important marketing tool. Some businesses rely entirely on Internet marketing. Businesses take marketing very seriously and are prepared to pay a lot of money for a well-designed page. They will expect a professionally designed page, and it is up to you to ensure they get it. The job of a Web designer can be relatively stress free when customer and clients are happy with your end product. Rest assured however, that they won't always be happy.

Personality Checkpoint: Not every page a Web designer turns out will be a winner. A client may look at the design and layout of a page you have spent hours working on and decide on something completely different. There is always the possibility you will have to go back to the drawing board. Remember, the client has the last say on the Web page. Although you can provide input, at the end of the day, the customer is always right.

Character Sketch

Web designers have to be able to take the business information given by a client and translate that information into a creative and well-designed Web page. They must be able to visualize the end product and effectively communicate their vision or suggestions to the client.

Web designers need to have a spirit of adventure and be willing to try new methods and new technologies to incorporate into the Web pages they design. To meet the demands of clients, they need to be fully aware of the products and tools available to them. As we know, technology moves at a rapid pace, and Web design is no different. Those who do not learn the latest tools will be left behind.

Personality Checkpoint: The complexity of Web pages has advanced considerably. Putting together a page means more than just adding some HTML text. Web pages can promote products and information using everything from sound to 3D graphics. To be competitive, Web designers need to be in touch with the latest and greatest tools that are used for Web page development, in combination with their visual and creative skills. This person, therefore, needs to continuously keep up with new technologies, along with the day-to-day responsibilities of the job.

Web designers will find themselves working within a strict time limit. While it would be nice if Web designers were given unlimited time to perfect a Web page, this is not the case. Businesses and companies are generally impatient and want to get their ideas or products to the Internet market as soon as possible. Web designers must be able to work within these strict timelines while still producing a quality product.

Personality Checkpoint: Web designers need to be able to take criticism in their stride. Often, a page will be created that the client does not like. The Web designer must have the objectivity to be able to take the criticism and rework the page.

Database Design and Administration

Consider the phrase "Information is Power." If it is true, then there can be no more a powerful tool than a database. Databases are literally everywhere. They store almost every conceivable type of information, from your Social Security number, to your credit history, to your purchasing habits, to your movie rental preferences. Each item of information is stored and sorted, ready for retrieval at the touch of a keystroke. Keeping these behemoth vaults of data in a ready-to-run and error free format is a job in itself, though the same person who now manages the database may well be the same one who designed and coded it in the first place. Such is the diversity of the database developers and administrators role.

Personality Checkpoint: For those looking for more responsibility in their lives, look no further. Database administration can provide you with just that. Companies, whether large or small, are dependent on the information held in their databases to the point that without it, companies cannot function. Database administrators are responsible for this information, and an awesome responsibility it is.

In many instances, the information stored in databases is intended for "future" reference; the client does not really know how best to use the information. The role of a database administrator is that of a facilitator. The data is in there, and it has to be retrieved and used for a productive purpose. As well as designing the structure of the database, the administrator is responsible for its maintenance as well.

Personality Checkpoint: Database administrators need to maintain communication with other IT professionals to ensure proper functioning of the database. Therefore, good communication skills are essential. This communication may be between the system administrators of the systems that the databases run on, and other developers whose systems interface with the database.

Database design is very similar to programming in that developmental languages are used to develop the database. Unlike programming languages that are used in a multitude of situations, however, database development languages are reasonably focused in their purpose. Most modern database languages are based around the Structured Query Language (SQL), which means that some of the knowledge gained working with a particular database system can be transposed to others.

Many of the most modern technologies, including e-commerce, rely and are dependent on high powered and high performing database systems. These systems need to be designed, created, and optimized to provide users and companies with the ability of performing literally tens of thousands of transactions per second. This high level of integration with the Internet and Web sites means that the line between database designers and Web site designers has become unclear.

Where it gets different is in the actual administration of the database. In this role, the database administrator, often referred to as the DBA, performs routine tasks such as the creation and execution of reports, the maintenance of user accounts (which are sometimes separate from those that the users use to log on to the main systems), and the management of backups.

Personality Checkpoint: If there is no development to be done, and the system is running smoothly, then the database administrator's life can seem a little dull, with only standard maintenance tasks and preventative checks to fill the day. Having the ability to make good use of down time, therefore, is advantageous.

Another thing that can add a level of interest to the database administrator's role is that of needing to understand a reasonable amount about the operating system on which the database runs, mainly for the purposes of optimization and management.

Stress Factors

Because companies now rely so heavily on their database systems, when an error occurs, the pressure is truly on. Consider an e-commerce outfit that cannot process any orders because its database is down, or a sales force that cannot make any sales calls because the customer database is unavailable. In normal times, the database administrator's life is reasonably calm, with what could even be described as a monotonous range of daily administration tasks. However, excitement, if you can call it that, is only moments away.

Personality Checkpoint: When the database goes down, the database administrator becomes both the hero and the villain. Companies and individuals stand to lose valuable revenue if the database is unavailable. For this reason, quick thinking and careful actions are required.

Character Sketch

Database programmers need a wide range of skills to cover the many facets of their work. When developing systems, they need the patience and diligence of a programmer combined with the creativity of a Web page designer. In the day-to-day operation of the system, they need the procedural ability and method of a network administrator, and when the chips are down they need the troubleshooting capabilities of a network engineer, combined with an ability to work under lots of pressure.

Personality Checkpoint: A database designer has to wear many hats. Although the majority of tasks are related to one common product or system, there can be a great degree of diversity in the tasks that need to be performed.

Chapter Summary

This chapter explored five occupations of the IT industry. This general information on each occupation can help assist you in matching your personality to occupations within IT. From this general overview you are now ready to further explore the jobs you feel you are suited for.

This chapter provided a starting point from which you can match your personality to a profession in IT. From here, a more detailed and in-depth exploration is required. Part II of this book describes these occupations in greater detail and is a good resource for additional information. Do not stop there however. Log on to the Internet and check out some sites dealing with your chosen interest. If at all possible, locate someone who is doing the job you are interested in. When choosing a career, the more information you have the better.

Which Job Is Right for You?

Welcome to Part II. You made it this far, which may mean that you've chosen to pursue a career in IT and that you have some idea as to which areas of IT are of most interest to you.

In Part I, we dealt with whether a career in IT is the right direction for you to take and took a look at what your general choices are in terms of job possibilities. Now it is time to look at some of the specific jobs that are available in your chosen skill area(s).

The career areas addressed in Chapters 4 through 8 represent the areas for which demand is currently the strongest in the IT industry. Although some job roles discussed may be a bit more in demand than others, all of those discussed here are considered the most "in demand" in the industry. In an industry that is having its growth stunted by the lack of skilled people, there are few areas that are not currently suffering from a skills shortage.

Chapters 4 through 8 are broken down into the following career areas:

➤ Computer programming—Literally dozens of computer programming languages exist, but which ones are in demand and what are they used for?

➤ Computer networking—Should you be an MCSE, CCIE, or MCNE? This section hooks you up with the information you need for a career in computer networking.

➤ PC and computer support—A PC sits on every desk and uses ever more complex applications that require user support. But it doesn't stop there. In addition, there is a need for people who can maintain and upgrade hardware.

➤ Internet technologies and Web Design—Ever fancied being a Webmaster or a B2B guru? We look at what you need to get you going in the fastest growing sector of them all.

➤ Database design and administration—Behind every great e-commerce Web site there is a great database. You could be in charge of gigabytes of valuable data!

The varied nature of IT means that in some cases there is a degree of overlap between these general classifications. For example, it is quite likely that a computer programmer will work on an Internet-related project, though the actual programming and the specifics of working as a programmer would remain largely the same.

Each chapter describes each subject area, then describes particular relevant job roles. Each job role or specialty area includes such things as a description of daily tasks, discussion regarding job demand, qualifications and requirements, as well as various resources such as training, course and certification options, study options, jargon typically used in that field, and other useful resources. Also included at the end of each chapter is a "day in the life" interview with professionals in the field.

The information provided in this section provides a comprehensive look at specific occupations within the IT industry. It provides you with the information necessary to make an informed decision of which IT career is right for you.

CHAPTER FOUR

Careers in Programming

A computer without a program is like a joke without a punch line. Computer programs provide instructions that tell the computer what to do and how to do it. In the absence of programs and instruction, the computer becomes quite useless and like a joke without a punch line, there's nothing funny about that.

Essentially, a program is a set of instructions or directions understood by the computer allowing it to perform predetermined functions. These instructions are given to the computer with the use of specific programming languages. A computer language is basically a form of communication understood by both programmers and machines.

A variety of these computer languages have been developed for creating software programs, although some have proved more useful than others. Languages, such as BASIC, FORTRAN, COBOL, C, and Pascal, are known as high-level programming languages, meaning that they use language more readily understood by humans. By contrast, low-level languages, such as assembly or machine language, are difficult to use because they are closer to the language that the computer uses. Machine language in fact, uses binary numbers. Because of the obvious difficulties in using low-level languages, most programs are written in a high-level language. These high-level languages must eventually be translated into computer, or machine, language, which is done through the use of compilers, assemblers, or interpreters.

This chapter provides a detailed description of four high-level languages, C++, Java, Perl, and Visual Basic (VB). An overview of each language is provided as well as its marketability in the IT industry, the strengths of the language, training requirements, and additional resources for further reference. At the end of the chapter, two factual on-the-job interviews with programmers are presented in order to give you a feel for what "a day in the life" of a programmer is like.

Deciding to become a programmer is just the first step; isolating and choosing a language or languages to learn is a required second step. Like most technologies, computer languages are developed through a transitional process. New programming languages are created and old ones enhanced by examining the shortcomings of previous languages and making necessary improvements. Larger and more complex computer programs demand the continued development and evolution of programming languages that are able to take full advantage of current technology. Without continually modifying and developing these languages, programs would be unable to meet the current and future needs of users. For this reason, the future for programmers in the workforce is secure. The IT industry is reliant upon skilled programmers who are able to create, modify, and expand programming languages as well as programs they create.

Computer programmers hold the communicative keys to computer systems. They form the section of the IT industry that writes, tests, and maintains the programs end users need. From word processors and spreadsheets to operating systems and drivers, it's the programmers and the programs they create that keep computers functioning. In some cases, the development of a simple program may take a skilled programmer just a few hours to complete. However, other programs, such as operating systems that require complex detailed instructions, can take more than a year of work for a group of programmers. Even though programmers often work behind the scenes, far removed from the view of the end user, their influence on the daily usage of computers is keenly felt.

4

Daily Tasks

Programmers usually find themselves working in highly creative and technical environments. Often programmers must work independently, but at the same time possess a strong sense of teamwork and maintain a collaborative spirit. It is essential that programmers be reliable, dependable, self-motivated, and have the ability to cope with the stress of inflexible deadlines. Programmers are frequently called upon to perform a variety of jobs and sustain many responsibilities. Programming duties may include, but are not restricted to, the following:

➤ Develop, test, and debug client/server applications. As a programmer, you will often find yourself writing, testing, and fixing programs that may be written by you or by another member of your team. These tasks are likely to constitute a large portion of your time.

➤ Convert designs and specifications into computer code. This means working with a specification or design that someone else has produced. Your task is to turn these concepts into a programmed reality. If the design is very detailed, you may not have any room for creative flourishes, but if you receive just a basic outline, the rest is up to you.

➤ Analyze existing program code to discover causes of errors and revise code as necessary. The process of running down errors in a program, known as debugging, is a fundamental programming skill. A thorough knowledge of your chosen programming language is essential.

➤ Deliver high quality and useable code in a timely fashion. Programmers are often faced with inflexible time lines in order to meet market demands. Late nights may become an occasional but unavoidable part of your work.

➤ Develop code in order to implement well-structured and reusable design that follows technology standards. You may produce the initial program, but there is no guarantee that you will work on the same code the next time around. By writing programs that adhere to stringent guidelines, your code will be easily understood by other developers. Keep in mind that the next person to analyze and dissect someone else's program may be you!

➤ Analyze, install, and test upgrades of externally developed application programs. You may not like what you see, but you'll have to work with what you have. In some cases it is quicker, easier, and cheaper to have someone else write a needed program for you, in which case, you should reasonably expect it to work the first time. But then again, this isn't always the case.

➤ Monitor performance of programs after implementation to keep up-to-date with users' needs and possible software bugs. Your work does not end when the program is passed to the user. Even if there are no errors in the program, users have a way of changing their minds about aspects of the program. Alternatively, they may like it so much that they'll think of even more useful things that it can do and request updates and modifications.

➤ Write or review documentation that describes installation and operating procedures, which may be tedious, but is absolutely essential. The documentation of a product can make a huge difference in its overall usability. And, in fact, the information contained in the documentation can help other developers maintain the product.

➤ Design and code screen layouts, graphical user interfaces, printed outputs, and interfaces with other systems. Sometimes the appearance of a program can be like an electronic signature that a programmer leaves behind. Creating a usable and effective user interface can heavily influence a users opinion of the usability of a program.

➤ Compile programs and correct errors detected in the compiling process. Looking for your own mistakes is perhaps not the most encouraging of pastimes, but it is essential nevertheless. Fortunately, modern programming languages have the capability to track down and draw your attention to errors in the code. Keep in mind that historically this was a completely manual process.

➤ Interact with users at times to keep in touch with the everyday problems and bugs that may be found by the user. Often programmers have to attend meetings with users outside of their own group or company. For these events, a certain degree of communication skills coupled with a smart and businesslike appearance makes a big difference.

➤ Provide technical assistance by responding to inquiries regarding programming errors, problems, or questions. Sometimes programmers need to assist with simple tasks, such as helping a user install the program, and other times they may need to troubleshoot a major problem with an application. Whatever the situation, a friendly, approachable personality either on the phone or in person is a major asset.

Overall, the programmer is typically responsible for software design, coding, compiling, debugging, and program testing and revision. Programmers generally work in an office setting and may have to work evenings or weekends to meet deadlines or debug programs. With advancing technology, however, the option for programmers to use telecommuting as a means to work outside of the office has become a reality. It is now possible for programmers to write and troubleshoot programs and perform their daily tasks during off hours away from the office environment.

Job Outlook

As with most areas of the IT industry, the job outlook for programmers is exceptionally positive. In fact, the U.S. Department of Labor predicts that employment for programmers is expected to grow faster than the average for all occupations. Further, they believe this trend will continue through the year 2008.

The need for programmers will remain constant because businesses, software developers, schools, and other companies continually require new applications and modifications to existing ones to meet their ever increasing needs. An online search of companies seeking qualified programmers reveals this huge demand. To some extent, programmers are in the driver's seat with regards to their employment. Companies that do not pay their programmers market value may find themselves looking for another programmer.

In spite of all of the good news for prospective programmers, there are some factors that may serve to dampen employment growth. These factors include companies using programming businesses outside of the country at a lower cost, and with the increased level of knowledge of some users, they are able to design and write more of their own programs.

Nevertheless, the job forecast for programmers is solid. Considering the current labor market, money, time, and effort spent on obtaining certifications and skills in the programming field would be well spent. Keep in mind that despite the job availability and often high salaries, programming is definitely not for everyone. Even with the necessary programming knowledge and aptitude, programming requires a personality that can handle spending considerable amounts of time in front of a computer screen often with little interaction with others.

Qualifications and Requirements

It is not difficult to search the Internet and find an employer looking to hire skilled programmers. In these advertised jobs, there seems to be little variation on the tasks and responsibilities employers require from their programmers. There is, however, a confusing level of variation of job qualifications and educational requirements.

Interestingly, some employers demand an overwhelming, and seemingly impossible, amount of education and experience from potential candidates. These employers require extensive knowledge in numerous operating systems, languages, and a bachelor's degree or higher. Other employers are far less concerned with formal education and focus their requirements on the number of years of experience a programmer has. Some companies are in such need for a programmer they actively try to recruit programmers away from other companies.

The discrepancy in qualifications an employer will accept from candidates can leave those interested in pursuing programming as a career confused as to what level of knowledge and training is required to get a job. It is no secret that the IT industry as a whole is experiencing a shortage of skilled professionals and programming is no exception. It is because of this shortage that employers will hire a programmer with no formal education, based solely on experience and a proven ability to program.

Those with two to three years experience may find that as programs become more complex, employers will increase their job requirements. Inevitably, a candidate in an interview with a bachelor's degree and experience is much more likely to get the job than someone with experience and no degree. Furthermore, a bachelor's degree can provide significantly more mobility with regards to changing careers within IT or advancement in the same job.

Those companies requiring bachelor's degrees from candidates specify that degrees, if held, should ideally be in Computer Science, Mathematics, or Information Systems. Computer science degrees are preferred because graduates are trained in a number of specific computer areas, programming being one of many.

Degrees and diplomas are not the only form of training in the IT world—far from it. IT certifications are widely sought by students and widely recognized by employers. Certifications have several key advantages over degree or diploma programs:

➤ Certification programs are shorter, meaning that training is quicker and students are typically ready to enter the workforce sooner.

➤ Certification courseware and training material is focussed and directed, whereas degree programs often require elective courses that are not always related to the specific area of IT.

➤ Shorter, more focussed certification programs are better able to accommodate retraining for rapidly changing technology.

4

Certification and training options are covered in greater detail in Part III of this book.

Why These Computer Languages?

The computer languages discussed in the following sections were chosen not only for their popularity in today's programming environments, but also to show the diversity of computer languages. Currently, many programs can be adequately written in several different languages, meaning that the language used for a specific job is often chosen based on personal preference, familiarity, or as a requirement of the employer. Keep in mind, however, that there are definitely computer languages that are more in demand and more marketable than others. It is easier to find an employer advertising a position for a C++ programmer rather than a Perl programmer, which is not to say that Perl is not in demand. Overall, there are numerous languages used to write programs. Knowledge of a lesser used language coupled with the experience of programming in a high demand language may be a determining factor in obtaining a job.

Programming with C++

C++ is a high-level programming language whose raw code is translated into machine language with the use of compilers. Though it is a high-level language, it is not for the faint of heart. Programming in C++ can be complicated, and beginners first looking at C++ code may be intimidated by its hieroglyphic look. The basic syntax and structure used in C++ comes from its predecessor, a language simply called "C," although C++ has many additional features and advantages. One of the key features added to C++ is its object-oriented capabilities.

Object-oriented programming (OOP) developed rapidly in the 1980s and 1990s. Numerous languages began to emerge that took advantage of the technology.

Essentially, when using OOP, small pieces of code are written into *objects*. Programs written using an object-oriented language consist of a number of these objects. These objects are independent modules combined together to form the whole program.

By creating a program with separate independent objects, programmers are able to take objects and reuse them elsewhere within the current program or in other programs. It's a lot like recycling. Object-oriented languages make all parts of an existing program extendible and reusable. Objects can be used separately or be grouped together differently to create new programs.

Object-oriented languages have gained considerable popularity among programmers, and in many environments, have replaced older, more traditional structured programming techniques. C++ in particular has become one of the most popular languages for the development of large-scale applications used in both Macintosh and Windows environments. Some examples of these large-scale application programs are word processing programs, database programs, image editing programs, and communication programs.

Why Choose C++?

For a computer language to gain popularity, it must be able to meet the demands and expectations of programmers. And these expectations are high. C++ has a proven track record and has gained a loyal following among programmers. It is a versatile language and can be used to create a wide range of applications. C++ has conceivably become the computer language in most demand today. So why choose C++?

Object-Oriented Programming

C++ and its object-oriented capabilities allow the programmer to design applications that are based less on a sequence of code and more towards communication between separate objects. OOP allows the reusability of code in a more logical and productive way. The recycling of code can limit the repetitive rewriting of code prevalent in other languages.

Portability

It is possible to compile the same C++ code for almost any type of computer and operating system with a minimal amount of changes. For this reason, C++ is one of the most used and widely deployed programming languages.

Programs written in C++ can be made up of several source code files that are compiled separately and then linked together. Because these source code files are compiled separately, it is not necessary to recompile the complete application when making a single change—only the required section needs to be recompiled. This provides a very efficient way to modify and maintain C++ programs.

Marketability

C++ has become a key language used for the development of efficient, portable software, ranging from operating systems to databases and numerous business applications. The potential of this powerful language has created the need for C++ programming professionals whose skills can be applied to a broad variety of applications. Skilled C++ programmer's are a hot commodity in the IT industry and are constantly in high demand. Current trends and expected growth indicate that this demand shows no sign of weakening.

Training Options and Resources

Like many other areas of the IT industry, training options and opportunities for those interested in becoming programmers are varied and diverse. This diversity allows you to choose the training method that best suits your learning style and the one that provides you with the necessary training to be competitive in the labor market.

It is important to keep in mind that regardless of which training method you choose, employers will have their own preference with regards to training. Today, employers look more favorably upon someone who has completed training in a college or university. Degrees and diplomas obtained from respected post secondary institutions are a definite asset and provide quality instruction. This instruction, however, does not come cheap. Certifications are also widely sought, but these certifications are more valuable when obtained from a recognized source.

Courses and Certifications

There are a number of options available for specific C++ training. Microsoft offers the Microsoft Certified Solution Developer (MCSD), which includes detailed training using Microsoft's Visual C++. Details of the MCSD program can be found on the Internet at Microsoft's Training and Certification site at **www.microsoft.com/trainingandservices**.

In addition, the other commercial C++ vendor, Borland Software, also provides training and certification programs. They too offer a certification program. Although it may not be as well known outside of the industry, Borland's training courses and certification are well recognized by employers. More information on

Borland's training courses and certification programs can be found on its Web site at **www.borland.com/services/training/certification**.

Online Training

There are many online schools that teach everything from C++ basics to advanced C++ concepts. Before choosing any of these training agencies, it is a good idea to read over their course descriptions to ensure that the course covers the material you desire and in a delivery method that will work for you. Furthermore, reading course outlines will enable you to confirm whether you have the right equipment and prerequisites for the course. The following list contains three online training schools that will give you some idea of the material offered and how it is offered:

➤ eKnowledge Concepts (**www.pcon.com**) offers Web-based Microsoft official curriculum training. Delivery of courseware includes instructor led segments and video captures to assist students through the various sections. Students enrolled in the course also have access to instructor email, online chats, and practice exams.

➤ Infotec (**www.infotec.com**) offers courses and certifications including Microsoft's Visual C++. It is a good site to check out to get an understanding of what Web-based training is all about.

➤ Element K (**www.elementk.com/**) offers several online C++ courses that start with introductory level courses and continue with more advanced topics. Courses begin by introducing C++ concepts and language basics. You can then continue on to more advanced topics using more complex features.

Self-Study Options

One of the great aspects of learning a computer programming language is that you do not need a great deal of equipment to learn the basics. With a language like C++, all you need is a copy of the software, a personal computer, and a certain amount of patience.

To obtain a copy of the C++ compiler, you will need to spend some money. When learning a new product or technology, it pays to stay in the mainstream. In C++ terms, that means using a product from Borland or Microsoft.

Microsoft has three different offerings in its Visual C++ product family. The Standard Edition, which costs around $100, is suitable for those starting out in C++ development and perhaps offers the most practical way to get a solid foundation in the language. The next version, called Professional Edition, costs quite a bit more at around $500, but comes with advanced features and capabilities. Finally, the Enterprise Edition, which retails around the $1300 mark, offers even more features.

You can find more detailed information concerning Microsoft C++ products at **http://msdn.microsoft.com/visualc**.

Borland has offerings at similar price points and uses the same terminology, Standard, Professional, and Enterprise, to define the different levels of capability. Approximate prices for the Borland C++ product are $100, $800, and $2500, respectively. To find out more information about Borland products, visit Borland's Web site at **www.borland.com/bcppbuilder**.

Additional Resources

For those seeking more information on C++, there are limitless resources both online and in local bookstores. Whether you need information on job postings, associations, or assistance from other programmers, the information is readily available. The following section provides information on C++ resources, but the list is by no means comprehensive or exhaustive. It does however provide all the information necessary to begin your quest towards a possible career as a C++ programmer.

C++ Jargon Buster

When searching for more information about C++, you may come across phrases or words that you may not be familiar with. To help you better understand the information you find, the following list contains some definitions and explanations that you may find useful:

> *Source Code*—Source code refers to the code or instructions written by a programmer. Source code is not in executable format and is not ready to run on the computer. It must first be translated by interpreters or compilers.

> *Compiler*—A program that translates high-level computing languages into object code or machine code. Numerous compilers are available for all computer languages.

> *Object Code*—The end product after the compiler has finished. This code is executable and ready to be used by the computer.

> *Class Library*—A reusable collection of software code, or routines. There are numerous references and resources online to access these libraries. The libraries often contain heavily used graphical user interface (GUI) functions.

Additionally, OOP has its own distinct terminology. Although they do sound somewhat unusual, a few common acronyms used are object-oriented technology (OOT), object-oriented programming language (OOPL), object-oriented design or databases (OOD), and object-oriented graphics (OOG). There are more OO terms, but this list provides you with enough lingo to recognize that when you overhear someone complaining about his OOG or his OOT, he is most likely an object-oriented programmer.

Books

There is no shortage of books on the subject of C++ programming. The difficult part is finding the one that best suits your needs. When learning C++, it is important to get a good introductory book that is informative and easy to read.

Beginner Book Titles

➤ Lawlor, Steven C. *The Art of Programming: Computer Science with C++.* PWS Publishing, 1997. ISBN 053495135X.

➤ Eckel, Bruce. *Thinking in C++, Vol. 1 (2nd Edition).* Prentice Hall, 2000. ISBN 0139798099.

➤ Riley, Richard. *C++ (Teach Yourself Books).* Teach Yourself, 2000. ISBN 0658006967.

Advanced Books

➤ Ladd, Scott Robert. *Advanced C++ Techniques.* O'Reilly & Associates, 2000. ISBN 1565927338.

➤ Meyers, Scott. *Effective C++: 50 Specific Ways to Improve Your Programs and Designs.* Addison-Wesley, 1997. ISBN 0201924889.

➤ Langer, Angelika, and Klaus Kreft. *Standard C++ IO Streams and Locales: Advanced Programmer's Guide and Reference.* Addison-Wesley, 2000. ISBN 0201183951.

Reference Books

➤ Josuttis, Nicolai M. *The C++ Standard Library: A Tutorial and Reference.* Addison-Wesley, 1999. ISBN 0201379260.

➤ Schildt, Herbert. *C++: The Complete Reference.* 3d ed. Osborne/ McGraw-Hill, 1998. ISBN 0078824761.

➤ Volkman, Victor. *C/C++ Treasure Chest: A Developer's Resource Kit of C/C++ Tools and Source Code with CDROM.* CMP Books, 1998. ISBN 0879305142.

Online Information and Resources

Perhaps the first place programmers go when needing information is the Internet. It is important to bookmark a list of resources available, which can be accessed when needed. The following sections contain a few links to get you started.

Newsgroups

Newsgroups are Internet based message boards that allow users to post messages or reply to messages that other people post. Newsgroups are descriptively named to give an idea of what the newsgroup is about. For instance, comp.os.netware, is the NetWare discussion group under the computer operating system section. There are thousands of newsgroups on almost every possible subject. Newsgroups can be a valuable resource for anyone involved in the IT industry. Almost every part of the IT industry has related newsgroups.

Newsgroups can be accessed via a newsreader such as those included with Microsoft Outlook or Netscape Communicator, or via a Web interface. Accessing newsgroups through a Web interface on a site such as **www.dejanews.com** usenet is the easiest way to get started. For more information on newsgroups, refer to Appendix C.

Internet newsgroups are a favorite haunt of programmers, and C++ programmers are no exception. The following is a list of some informative newsgroups:

➤ **comp.lang.c++**

➤ **comp.std.c++**

➤ **comp.sys.lang.c++**

➤ **it.comp.lang.c++**

➤ **alt.comp.lang.learn.c-c++**

Magazines and Journals

There are also a number of magazines and journals on the subject of C++ programming. Most offer a Web site that provides a detailed look at what the publication provides, so that you can assess whether or not the information is relevant to your needs. These Web sites also provide the capability to subscribe online:

➤ *The C++ Report* (**www.creport.com**)—By Subscription, $79 for 10 issues. The C++ Report provides an extensive list of how-to articles, hands on programming techniques, and reusable source code.

➤ *C/C++ Users Journal* (**www.cuj.com**)—By Subscription, $29.95 annually. This journal covers everything you need to know about the world of C++. A great resource for both beginners and advanced programmers.

➤ *C++ Builder Developer's Journal* (**www.reisdorph.com**)—By Subscription, $79 annually. This journal helps you learn the tips and techniques to becoming a better and more efficient C++ programmer.

Web Pages

The vast array of C++ related Internet Web sites will keep those looking for information busy for a considerable amount of time. The following list contains just a few links to get you started:

➤ *Ask the C++ Pro* (**www.inquiry.com/techtips/cpp_pro**)—Browse this site for a C++ search engine and links to numerous other programming resources.

➤ *Eg3* (**www.eg3.com/softd/cplus.htm**)—A great source for links and other resources. A good place to start your C++ journey.

➤ *C++ Bookmark* (**www.vb-bookmark.com/vbCpp.html**)— Another good starting point that contains even more resources, more links, tips and tricks, compilers, and the inside scoop.

➤ *DevCentral Learning Center* (**http://devcentral.iftech.com/learning/ tutorials**)—A site that offers tutorials on C++ as well as general information on OOP.

Professional Associations

Networking with other programmers can be invaluable. Invariably, programmers will come up against a problem that is very difficult to solve. Having a connection to other programmers who have had the same or similar problem can be a valuable resource, which can save lots of programming time and frustration. The following list contains a few professional associations that may be of interest to you:

➤ *Association of C and C++ Users* (**www.accu.org**)—The ACCU is a worldwide association that is open to both advanced and beginner programmers. It offers book reviews, training seminars, and numerous other services to assist you on your C++ journey. There is a fee for membership.

➤ *The International Programmers Guild Society* (**www.ipgnet.com**)—The IPG is a good resource for those wanting to connect with other programmers. It is not specific to C++, but rather is a site for programmers in general. It does, however, provide links to many C++ related Web sites. The site also includes a newsletter and a job search index. It appears to be a good site to bookmark and provides good links to further programming resources. As with the ACCU, there is a fee for membership.

Summary

C++ is a modern programming language that has gained considerable favor with programmers. Used in countries all over the world, C++ provides a wide range of excellent career opportunities to those with a desire to succeed in the IT industry. Though qualifications are still important, the most successful C++ programmers are likely to be those that can demonstrate their skills and abilities in a variety of situations and environments. C++ is not the only programming language in use today, however, those using it know that it is a very versatile and powerful development tool.

Along Comes Java

What do you get when you take several disgruntled programmers, give them a cool code name like "Green," and ask them to develop a revolutionary new programming language? The answer of course is several half drunk cups of coffee and an untold number of empty Nacho chip bags. Well, that and the development of one of the most versatile programming languages ever written.

In 1990, Sun Microsystems commissioned a handful of its employees the monumental task of anticipating the next big craze in the computer industry. Initially, this team of technological prophets concluded that the next big trend would be the integration of digitally controlled consumer devices and computers. The team then set out to design a platform that could be used in every component including the remote control, the toaster, gaming machines, the VCR, and of course, the computer. Originally, the Green team intended on using C++ for its project, but it soon became apparent that C++ would not meet its needs. Instead, the team developed a new high-level, object-oriented language named Oak. Oak was designed as closely as possible to C++, keeping much of its syntax and structure. Some of the features considered to be unnecessary or overly complicated were intentionally excluded. Keeping the design close to the heavily used C++ meant that the transition to Oak would be easy for programmers.

In 1994, Sun decided to reconstruct Oak and gear the direction of the language towards the Internet. This move was a fundamental decision for the future of the language and significantly changed the face of the Internet. The newly modified language, apart from being able to create stand-alone applications, was able to create applets that could be transmitted over the Internet. These applets, and their possible uses, generated a great deal of excitement in the Internet world.

Basically, applets are programs designed to run inside a Web browser. Applets allow the animation of Web pages. This new feature sparked considerable excitement for the Internet surfing public. This excitement, however, was tempered as animation overuse and on some pages created a lot of frustration for those connecting to the Internet with slow dial-up connections. Of course, because the speed of Internet access has increased considerably, it has alleviated the previous frustrations of low speed connections. Now Java flourishes all over the Internet bringing users an abundant variety of Web page animations as well as providing everything from interactive programs to games.

Eventually, this new language needed a new name, and soon the name Oak was discarded and replaced with Java. In an industry previously dominated with humorless names, such as C++, Delphi, and Visual Basic, the name Java opened a floodgate of potential coffee puns. There was no shortage of writers and companies eager to take advantage of the new opportunity, seemingly unwilling or unable to stop until all coffee related references had been utterly and completely exhausted. This book will endeavor to avoid the apparently unstoppable Java pun machine.

What Makes Java So Hot?

Java is widely regarded as the tool used to spice up Web pages, adding sound, pictures, or video to an otherwise mundane Web page. To gain widespread acceptance, however, Java had to offer considerably more than the capability to animate Web pages. Because Java has this animation capability and does it well, it has almost become typecast in this role. It is true that Java has a strong association with the Internet, but Java is not limited to the creation of quality Web counters. Java has become a viable development tool able to seduce programmer's loyalties away from the status quo.

Portability

In just a few short years, the popularity of Java has skyrocketed, propelling the language into the often skeptical, mainstream programming world. This popularity was partially inspired by its slogan—"write once, run anywhere"—truly a bold statement from the creators of the Java language. Essentially, the implication behind the statement is that code written for Java is portable, meaning that it can be written once and used on several different operating systems. With most other languages, written code, or programs, are translated into machine code with the use of compilers. The code translated by the compiler is understood only by the operating system it is translated for. Consequently, the program needs to be recompiled for other operating systems. Java avoids this redundant programming with the use of the Java Virtual Machine (JVM). The introduction of this virtual machine and the write once promise significantly reduces the work programmers need to do and perhaps also, inadvertently, reduces the increasing number of Carpal Tunnel Syndrome claims.

Distributed Computing

Portability and the "write once" promise may perk the interest of some programmers, but those employing these programmers may be less concerned with convenience and more concerned with Java's capability to perform as a useful business and company tool. Managers can rest easy as the benefits of Java extend well into the business world. Java was intended to have a significant impact in the area of distributed, or client/server, computing. Distributed computing is a type of computing where the objects comprising an application can be located on different computers on a network. The purpose for segregating components may be for security reasons or for centralized administration.

Java was designed to provide a simpler method of delivering client/server, or distributed, applications that run over the internal local area network (LAN). It quickly became a viable alternative to the heavily used C++ for such application development. Java simplifies the deployment of applications over a network and can save a company money in the process. Java's portability allows applications to be shared over the network without needing to modify any computer platform, saving time and money that would have been needed to write programs for multiple platforms.

Marketability

The combining factors of Java being a new language, the overall shortage of skilled programmers, and the high demand for Java skills in the workforce creates a situation in which entry into the labor force as a Java programmer is relatively easy for those interested. Formal education, though often preferred, is not mandatory for Java because the need is simply too high for employers to be overly picky. It's a seller's market when it comes to Java skills.

Java Pro, a Java magazine, and a company called Wilson Research recently conducted a salary survey for Java careers. Recognizing the demand for Java programmers, the results were not surprising. Worldwide, the United States pays the highest salary for Java programmers at an average of $86,000 followed by Canada, which pays an average of $53,000. Within the United States, the regions around California pay the highest salary in the country on average. As the need for Java programmers is destined to continue to rise, so too will these salaries.

The downside to these high salaries is that they are not always earned by punching the clock between 9 and 5. The same survey discovered that on average Java programmers in the United States work 48 hours per week. That of course is just the average, some programmers work considerably longer days than that.

The shortage of skilled Java programmers has led to another interesting factor in the labor market, that being the aggressive recruitment of potential employees. Companies in need of a programmer may contact employees from other agencies to lure them away. Whether right or wrong, this type of practice is quite common. The loss of key IT professionals can be devastating to a company, which creates the need for employers to attempt to ensure a high level of job satisfaction for their employees. Considerably more attention has been given to staff retention. For now at least, Java programmers can expect to be well taken care of. Keep in mind, however, that there was a time when the IT industry was screaming for Pl/1 programmers. Now Pl/1 programmers are sought only by weekend archeologists. At this point in time, Java programming is a hot commodity, maybe even the hottest, but as Robert Frost once said, "Nothing gold can stay."

Training Options and Resources

There are numerous training opportunities and methods for those interested in learning more about the Java language. Whether for general interest or certification, there is something for everyone.

Courses and Certifications

Perhaps the first place to look when seeking Java training is to go right to the source—Sun Microsystems. Sun offers many courses, which range from beginner level to very advanced. Sun delivers a wide range of recognized certification programs that provide a solid background for Java programming. Sun offers three key certification programs:

➤ Sun Certified Programmer for the Java Platform

➤ Sun Certified Developer for the Java Platform

➤ Sun Certified Enterprise Architect for Java 2 Platform

To find more about available courses from Sun browse its Web page at **http:// java.sun.com/aboutJava/training**.

Java training is also provided by many postsecondary institutions as part of degree or diploma programs, or as separate more focussed certification programs. Obtaining postsecondary degrees, diplomas, and certifications are widely recognized and sought after by employers. They are, however, considerably more expensive and time intensive than obtaining certification through self-study. The choice is yours.

Online Training

The Sun Web Learning Center (**http://suned.sun.com**) is an interactive online training resource. Sun's online courses are available by subscription and allow access to Sun's IT courseware anytime, anywhere. That is, of course, if you have an Internet connection.

Experquest (**www.experquest.com**) offers technical computer courses online including some Java courses. It may be worth your time to read their course descriptions to ensure that the course covers the material you desire. Furthermore, it is important to ensure that you have the right equipment and prerequisites for the course.

Infotec (**www.infotec.com**) offers courses and certifications including Java. It is a good site to check out to get an understanding of what Web-based training is all about.

Self-Study Options

As with C++, one of the great aspects of learning a computer programming language is that you do not need a great deal of equipment to learn the basics. With a PC, a copy of the Java program, and a little spare time, you can begin to learn the language.

Those interested in self-study to obtain Java certification have a wide range of resources at their disposal to assist them. Numerous books on certification and self-study guides are available, including:

➤ Tittel, Ed. *IT Certification Success Exam Cram*. 3d ed. The Coriolis Group, 2000. ISBN 1576107922—This book is a good "first stop." It provides a detailed description of Sun's Java Certification program, among others, and provides many valuable resources, such as how to locate training and certification information, obtaining descriptions and objectives for the relevant exams, and identifying training and self-study options.

➤ Brogden, Bill. *Java 2 Exam Cram.* The Coriolis Group, 1999. ISBN 1576102912—This book assists you as you actually prepare and study for the exam. It focuses on those areas that are critical to passing the exam and provides tips and other helpful notes that aid in exam preparation.

➤ Roberts, Simon, Philip Heller, and Michael Ernest. *The Complete Java 2 Certification Study Guide.* Sybex, 1999. ISBN 0782127002—This book also assists you in preparing for the exam. The book itself was written by Sun Java course instructors, giving it an added bonus. The book starts out explaining the core syntax of Java, and then progresses into the more graphical and sophisticated aspects of development. As an additional feature, each chapter includes a practice test complete with an answer guide.

➤ Jaworski, Jamie. *Java 2 Certification Training Guide.* New Riders Publishing, 1999. ISBN 1562059505—This book focuses on the specifics of what you'll need to successfully pass the certification tests. It also includes practice exams, which follow Sun's format and style. A CD is included, which includes a sample of the actual computer based tests.

Where to Go for Good Java—Additional Resources

Those seeking to find more information on Java can type "Java" in any search engine and access an enormous amount of Java resources. Some of the information found is quite detailed, descriptive, and easy to follow, whereas other information seems to be written in incomprehensible code understood only by a select few. Java was designed as an easy to learn language, so if a resource is confusing find another one; there is no shortage of useful resources on the Internet. The following sections provide a quick look at some of the resources available.

Java Jargon Buster

When exploring Java resources, you may come across phrases or words that you may not be familiar with. To help you better understand the information you find, the following list contains some basic definitions and explanations that you may find useful:

➤ *Applet*—A small program designed to be executed within a larger one. Java applets run within Web browsers. Applets are designed for and work well with small Internet applications accessible from a browser. Java applets perform interactive animations and many other simple tasks without having to send a user's request back to the server.

➤ *Bean*—Small reusable software components that can be joined to create an application. These JavaBeans can be developed only in Java, however, they can run on any platform.

➤ *HotJava Browser*—A browser developed by Sun Microsystems that is written in the Java programming language.

➤ *Java Virtual Machine*—The program that actually executes the Java programs. This virtual machine is what allows the same Java code to run on different computers and platforms. The virtual machine is basically a software program that converts the Java language into machine language and executes it.

➤ *JavaScript*—A Java based scripting language developed by Netscape. Even though it shares many of the features of the Java language, it was developed independently. JavaScript is supported by both Netscape browsers and Internet Explorer.

To find more of the common Java terms and definitions that you may come across, check out the following Web sites.

➤ Sun Microsystems (**http://java.sun.com/docs/glossary.html**)

➤ TechWeb (**www.techweb.com/encyclopedia**)

Books

Many books are available for those already using Java and those interested in learning Java programming. Such books can become an important reference and resource for all levels of programming knowledge. Below is just a few books to get you started.

Beginner Book Titles

➤ Pawlan, Monica. *Essentials of the Java Programming Language: A Hands-On Guide.* Addison-Wesley, 2000. ISBN 0201707209.

➤ Holzner, Steven. *Java Black Book.* The Coriolis Group, 2000. ISBN 1576105318.

➤ Chapman, Stephen J. *Introduction to Java.* Prentice-Hall, 1999. ISBN 0139194169.

Advanced Books

➤ Berg, Daniel J., and Steven Fritzinger. *Advanced Techniques for Java Developers, Revised Edition.* John Wiley & Sons, 1999. ISBN 0471327182.

➤ Wigglesworth, Joe, and Paula Lumby. *Java Programming Advanced Topics.* Course Technology, 1999. ISBN 0760010986.

➤ Hunt, John, Alexander McManus, and Alex McManus. *Key Java : Advanced Tips and Techniques (Practitioner Series [Springer-Verlag]).* Springer-Verlag, 1998. ISBN 3540762590.

Reference Books

➤ Haggar, Peter. *Practical Java Programming Language Guide: The Addison-Wesley Professional Computing Series.* Addison-Wesley, 2000. ISBN 0201616467.

➤ Winston, Patrick Henry, and Sundar Narasimhan. *On to Java.* Addison-Wesley, 1998. ISBN 0201385988.

➤ Flanagan, David. *Java in a Nutshell : A Desktop Quick Reference (Java Series).* O'Reilly & Associates, 1999. ISBN 1565924878.

Online Information and Resources

The Internet provides a seemingly endless number of Java links and resources. Everything from programmer support, newsletters, columns and workshops can be found. The following sections contain just a few of the online resources available for those wanting more information on Java.

Newsgroups

Start with these Java newsgroups if only because you have to start somewhere:

➤ **comp.lang.java.advocacy**

➤ **comp.lang.java**

➤ **comp.lang.java.programmer**

➤ **comp.lang.java.help**

➤ **comp.lang.java.security**

Magazines and Journals

A wealth of resources available on Java programming is provided in the following list. Some sites also provide links to other Internet sites of interest.

➤ *Javaworld Magazine* (**www.javaworld.com**)—Contains loads of articles, tips, hints, and tricks as well as information relevant to Java developers of all levels.

➤ *Java Boutique* (**http://javaboutique.internet.com/other.html**)—Contains a searchable library of Java applets, a free email newsletter, and a wide range of useful information.

➤ *Java Developers Journal* (**www.sys-con.com/java/index2.html**)—Contains the latest Java news, upcoming Java events, interviews, and articles. This type of resource is valuable before and after you become a Java programmer.

Web Pages

➤ *JavaRanch* (**www.javaranch.com**)—This site provides interesting and entertaining information and is an excellent place to start for those interested in familiarizing themselves with Java.

➤ *The Java Tutorial* (**http://java.sun.com/docs/books/tutorial/ index.html**)—This site is part of the Sun Web site and provides detailed tutorials that will help you learn the Java language and write your first Java program.

➤ *Programmers Source* (**www.progsource.com**)—This site is a good resource page offering Java documentation and other literature, tutorials and training, as well as some Java employment resources.

➤ *TeamJava* (**http://teamjava.com**)—This site offers some employment information and links to other programming and Java related sites.

➤ *DevCentral Learning Center* (**http://devcentral.iftech.com/learning/ tutorials**)—This site offers tutorials on Java and JavaScript programming.

Professional Associations

Professional associations provide a means of communicating with other programmers. The IPG (**www.ipgnet.com**) is a good resource for those wanting to connect with other programmers. It is not specific to Java, but rather is a site for programmers in general. It may, however, provide links to Java related Web sites. The site also includes a newsletter and a job search index. It appears to be a good site to bookmark and provides good links to further programming resources. There is a fee for membership.

Summary

The early 1990s saw the introduction of Java, a new OOP language. Within a short amount of time Java has become a popular choice for programmers for both application and Web development. Due to the versatility of the language, employment demand for skilled Java programmers has increased and is predicted to continue to rise. Because of Java's increasing marketability, those interested in pursuing programming as a career choice should explore and consider Java as their primary programming language.

Perl

Practical Extraction and Report Language (Perl) is a high-level programming language, and according to its supporters, the best scripting language to use for the Web. Perl is used to write Common Gateway Interface (CGI) programs. CGI programs are designed to allow Web servers to interact with users.

Perl was introduced in the late 1980s and is based on a Unix platform. Perl was designed and developed to be an easy and fun to use language. It does use some of the more generic features of C, making the transition between the two languages easier. Perl supporters maintain that the language is as powerful as other well-known languages, such as C and C++, but with greater simplicity.

As noted in the previous sections, object-oriented technology has become high on the average programmers wish list. Beginning with Perl 5, this language takes a leap into the OO world. OOP is included in Perl as an additional tool that can be used by the supporters of OOP or omitted by programmers who do not wish to use it.

A survey of some online job postings reveals that although the market is saturated with demands for the more mainstream languages, like Java and C++, Perl does have a niche market. There are several employers looking specifically for Perl devel-opers. Remuneration for these jobs is on par with its C++ and Java counterparts.

For those interested in focusing their programming careers towards Web development, knowledge of Perl would be an excellent start. Those individuals with a few years of experience with Perl, a working knowledge of Web development, and experience with Unix would find themselves in demand for certain positions. Also, other advertised programming jobs may list experience with Perl as a requirement or at least a recommendation for employment.

Why Choose Perl?

Although Perl cannot claim to have the industry-wide popularity that languages like C++ and Java enjoy, it does have a loyal following of programmers. The following sections list some clear reasons why those interested in learning programming may want to try Perl.

Perl Is Easy to Learn

According to those who use Perl, it is an easy language to learn. Perl supporters contend that with this language difficult programming tasks are made easy. The language can handle some of the more tedious aspects of programming automatically, such as memory allocation and garbage collection. This isn't to suggest that you will be a skillful Perl programmer in a matter of hours. However, it does mean that those interested at trying their hand at programming may want to give Perl a shot.

Perl Is Compiled on the Fly

Compiling, if you recall from the beginning of this chapter, is the process of translating a high-level language into machine code. On the fly compiling suggests that as soon as a program is written it can be executed. Additionally, because programs don't need to be compiled on specific computers, they can run anywhere and within all operating systems that have a Perl interpreter installed.

Perl Has Strong Web Development Capability

Perl has become popular in the development of Web server programs for such tasks that may include automatic updating of user accounts and newsgroup postings, synchronizing databases, and generating reports.

Perl Can Be Fun to Use

Perhaps the most ambitious statement made by those who use Perl is that it is fun. Programming or the ability to produce programs can be highly creative, and those that use this language feel that Perl puts a little creativity back into programming. The enthusiasm with which devoted Perl programmers describe the language should make anyone want to give it a try.

Perl Is Free

What better reason to try a programming language than being able to obtain it free of charge. The latest version of Perl can be downloaded from **www.perl.com**.

Marketability

Perl may not be in the forefront of the programming world, but it does have its niche. Many employers, especially in the area of Web development and Internet related jobs, are seeking programmers skilled in Perl programming. Some of these employers specifically request Perl skills, whereas others, even though advertising for another language, suggest Perl knowledge as a secondary requirement. Although Perl is not as widely sought, employers looking for Perl programmers offer competitive wages and benefits. Those interested in the marketability of Perl may want to search online IT jobs sites to get information on the jobs that are currently available for Perl programmers and the duties and tasks they are required to perform.

Training Options and Resources

As might be expected, the options for formal training are not as widespread as C++ or Java. This is not to say there isn't any. Many skilled Perl programmers have learned their skills through hands-on usage. Those new to Perl would probably find it easier to at least have some basic instruction on the language before attempting to use it professionally.

Many postsecondary institutions offer Perl instruction either as separate training or as part of a degree or diploma program. An investigation of offerings at local colleges and universities is a good place to look for more formal training. For those interested in self-study, Perl instructional books for both beginning as well as advanced programmers are available at most bookstores.

Courses and Certifications

The Internet is home to numerous companies offering Perl training. Some of these companies offer strictly home study courses, whereas others offer classroom and even onsite training for companies. Regardless of the training method, these training centers suggest a minimum requirement of computer literacy, knowledge of Unix, Linux, or Windows. The following is a list of a few resources online offering Perl training. The list does not include all online training options, but rather lists just a few places for you to start your Perl journey:

➤ A Web page suitably entitled "Brainbench" at **www.tekmetrics.com** offers general training in many areas, Perl being one. Those looking for a general introduction to Perl may find it at this site. All Brainbench certification examinations are delivered via the Web and use adaptive computer testing. All Brainbench certifications are not endorsed by major vendors, such as Microsoft or Novell. Brainbench advertises itself as an independent certification authority.

➤ Perl.com, one of the largest Perl Web sites, offers onsite training. Course costs, outlines, and other relevant information can be located at **www.perl.com**.

➤ Perl training is also offered on Stonehenge at **www.stonehenge.com**. According to its outline, the course presumes no prior knowledge of Perl and promises to provide comprehensive instruction on the basics of the language as well as lay the groundwork for more advanced Perl instruction. Course rates and instructor information is also available.

➤ The Institute for Advanced Technology Training offers Perl courses as well. Information can be found at **www.itte.org**. Courses include advanced Perl programming, CGI scripting with Perl, and accelerated Perl programming.

Online Training

There are many options for those wanting to learn Perl through online training. Element K (**www.elementk.com**) is a sample of the types of schools and training centers that offer online training. Element K offers online Perl courses that give you an introduction to Perl and enough information for you to begin to create your own Perl programs. These courses focus on programming skills related to CGI programming.

Remember to always examine the course content, courseware, and delivery conditions before enrolling in any course. It is important that the course provide the information necessary to prepare you for the job you are pursuing. Keep in mind that not all courses will do this.

Self-Study Options

Obviously, the best place to start learning through self-study is to acquire the actual program. Perl is offered free of charge and can be obtained from the Perl Web page at **www.perl.com**. From this Web site, you can get the source code for both the Unix and Windows platforms.

Once you have the program, there are several good books to assist you in learning Perl. Refer to the "Beginner Book Titles" section provided later in this chapter for a list of Perl resources for beginning programmers.

Additional Resources

There are numerous resources available for those wanting to know more about Perl both online and in bookstores. The following sections describe some of the available resources.

Perl Jargon Buster

Before heading off into the world of Perl resources, it is a good idea to learn a few of the more common terms you may come across.

➤ *CGI Script*—CGI scripts are small programs used to allow Web sites to interact with databases and other applications.

➤ *Object-Oriented Programming*—Objects are smaller, independent programming modules that form the building blocks of a larger application. The later versions of Perl offer object-oriented programming capabilities.

➤ *Interpretive Language*—Perl is referred to as an interpretive language. For computer languages, there are two ways to translate and prepare high-level code to be executed as programs: the first is with the use of compilers and the second is with interpreters.

For more information on Perl definitions, terminology, and programming basics, the Perl home page at **www.perl.com** is a good place to visit.

Books

Reference and introductory level books can augment the online Perl resources. The following is a list of a few available books.

Beginner Book Titles

➤ Cozens, Simon, Peter Wainwright. *Beginning Perl.* Wrox Press Inc, 2000. ISBN: 1861003145.

➤ Walsh, Nancy, and Linda Mui (editor). *Learning Perl/Tk: Graphical User Interface with Perl (O'Reilly Nutshell).* O'Reilly & Associates, 1999. ISBN 1565923146.

➤ Sebesta, Robert W. *A Little Book on Perl.* Prentice-Hall, 1999. ISBN 0139279555.

Advanced Books

➤ Hall, Joseph N. *Effective Perl Programming: Writing Better Programs with Perl.* Addison-Wesley, 1998. ISBN 0201419750.

➤ Roselius, Rob. *Advanced Perl Programming.* DDC Publishing, Inc., 2000. ISBN: 1562439774.

➤ Wall, Larry, Tom Christiansen, and Jon Orwant. *Programming Perl (3rd Edition).* O'Reilly & Associates, 2000. ISBN 0596000278.

Reference Books

➤ Holzner, Steven. *Perl Black Book.* The Coriolis Group, 1999. ISBN 1576104656.

➤ Holzner, Steven. *Perl Core Language Little Black Book.* The Coriolis Group, 1999. ISBN 1576104265.

➤ Johnson, Andrew L. *Elements of Programming with Perl.* Manning Publications,1999. ISBN 1884777805.

Online Information and Resources

Although Perl does not have the widespread use of some of the more mainstream programming languages, it is not lacking in its available resources. The Internet provides all the information and links required to access the Perl resources you need.

Newsgroups

Here are some Perl newsgroups to check out:

➤ **comp.lang.perl**

➤ **comp.lang.perl.misc**

➤ **comp.lang.perl.modules**

➤ **comp.lang.perl.tk**

➤ **comp.infosystems.www.authoring.cgi**

Magazines and Journals

➤ *Perl Month* (**www.perlmonth.com**)—A Web-based monthly magazine featuring links, columns, and other information about the world of Perl.

➤ *The Perl Journal* (**www.itknowledge.com/tpj**)—A magazine devoted to Perl offering columns and articles from experienced Perl programmers. This site is informative as well as entertaining.

➤ *Take Ten Minutes to Learn Perl* (**www.geocities.com/SiliconValley/7331/ten_perl.html**)—Beginners will find the instructions on this page easy to follow; a good place to start.

➤ *Nik Silver's Perl Tutorial* (**http://agora.leeds.ac.uk/Perl**)—This site provides good tutorials and is geared more toward Perl and Unix.

Web Pages

➤ *Perl.com* (**www.perl.com**)—The Perl home page. Your first stop for information, news, and updates for Perl. The site is a good reference site and provides information on everything from training to additional online resources.

➤ *O'Reilly* (**www.perl.oreilly.com**)—This site offers everything from book resources to articles on Perl. A great site for general information and links to other Perl resource pages.

➤ *The Perl Archive* (**www.perlarchive.com/**)—This page has several useful articles as well as some Perl tips and tricks. It is definitely worth a look.

➤ *Perl Crawler* (**http://perlsearch.hypermart.net**)—A search engine that is just for sites related to Perl and CGI programming. This tool can help focus your search and save you time when seeking Perl resources.

➤ *Webring* (**http://nav.webring.org/cgi-bin/navcgi?ring=perl;list**)—A comprehensive list of available Perl Web resources for those that take the time to type this lengthy URL. You can also access this Web site from its home page at **http://nav.webring.org**; just follow the links.

Professional Associations

Professional Associations provide a means of communicating with other programmers. The IPG (**www.ipgnet.com**) is a good resource for those wanting to connect with other programmers. It is not specific to Perl, but rather is a site for programmers in general. It may, however, provide links to Perl related Web sites. The site also includes a newsletter and a job search index. It appears to be a good site to bookmark and provides good links to further programming resources. There is a fee for membership.

Summary

Perl is a powerful programming language that, once learned, lets you quickly and easily develop Web applications. Perl is a general purpose programming language originally designed for Unix platforms but has expanded to virtually every other platform. Most programmers using Perl comment on its ease of use and its versatility. For these reasons, Perl enjoys a loyal following within the world of programmers.

Visual Basic

Visual Basic was introduced to the programming world in the early 1990s with the introduction of Visual Basic 1.0. Visual Basic represented the first visual development tool from Microsoft and was intended to compete with the popular languages of the day, like C, C++ and Fortran. Visual Basic 1.0 struggled to gain acceptance with programmers, but the release of versions 2.0 and 3.0 saw the popularity of the language increase significantly.

Visual Basic has its programming roots in a language known as Basic, but has now far exceeded the simplicity of its predecessor. Within a few short years, Visual Basic has earned itself the status of a professional programming language and is used by many programmers for the development of quality programs. Visual Basic has become part of a collection of programming tools from Microsoft called Visual Studio. The latest offering from Visual Studio is version 6.0 and has Basic Learning, Professional, and Enterprise editions. The difference in the editions are as follows:

➤ *Visual Basic Learning Edition*—As you might expect, the Learning Edition includes everything you need to get up and running. This edition provides you with the tools you need to create programs, but omits the advanced features included in the other editions.

➤ *Visual Basic Professional Edition*—Included in the Professional package are a comprehensive set of tools including, Visual FoxPro, Visual C++, Visual InterDev, and Visual J++. Further, it includes all of the features from the Learning Edition and also includes ActiveX controls, Integrated Data Tools and Data Environment, and the Dynamic HTML Page Designer.

➤ *Visual Basic Enterprise Edition*—The Visual Basic Enterprise Edition contains all of the features included in the Professional Edition and includes some additional features, such as: BackOffice tools, Internet Information Server (IIS), Systems Network Architecture (SNA) Server, Visual SourceSafe, and Microsoft Transaction Server (MTS).

The Learning Edition may be the most common edition purchased by people who want to try Visual Basic. It does omit many features you will want as you get better at programming with Visual Basic. Professional is probably the most commonly used edition. Able to find a balance between the two editions, it includes most features needed by beginning as well as intermediate Visual Basic programmers. The Enterprise edition includes all features contained in the other two editions, but adds the capability to perform heavy duty database programming and client/server programming. An additional factor in choosing a particular edition may be its cost. The full package product for the Enterprise edition is just under $1,300, Professional comes in around $550, and the Basic Learning package is just over $100.

Regardless of the edition used, Visual Basic provides a friendly programming environment that has become quite popular with programmers of all levels. Although easy to learn, it also provides the advanced tools, functions, and routines necessary to create programs capable of competing in the programming market. Overall, Visual Basic has become an excellent choice for both beginning and expert programmers.

Why Visual Basic?

Visual Basic offers a very friendly and familiar graphical interface, making the learning of the language a little bit easier. It has become popular for those interested in trying programming because of its graphical interface. Microsoft has accommodated the beginning programmer by supplying a learner's edition of Visual Basic. For the novice user, this edition provides an inexpensive means to try the product. Although Visual Basic is a good product for the beginner, it provides all the tools necessary to create high-end, professional applications and programs. There is no doubt that Visual Basic is a versatile and marketable language. The following is a list of further benefits of Visual Basic:

➤ Visual Basic allows the rapid development of high quality data forms, all with the ease of drag and drop.

➤ Visual Basic creates applications for the increasing number of mobile users. After some familiarity with the product, it is possible to write client/server applications that work with databases and are accessible to users whether they access the database from a LAN or from the Web.

➤ With the newly integrated Visual Database Tools, it is possible to perform common database activities without exiting Visual Basic.

➤ The Package and Deployment Wizard easily deploys Internet applications.

➤ Visual Basic allows you to secure your source code by using Microsoft Visual SourceSafe.

Familiarity and Ease of Use

Those who have used Microsoft Windows will find the interface of Visual Basic familiar and comfortable, and by using Windows they may have mastered many of the skills needed to use Visual Basic. To write programs with Visual Basic, it is not necessary to write numerous lines of code. Instead, programmers use prebuilt objects to make a program. Because of its familiarity and the relative ease in which programs are created, novice programmers are able to build a Visual Basic application in a short amount of time. Although it is easy to create programs within Visual Basic, it also has the ability and tools to be used to create highly complex programs.

Marketability

Since its inception in the early 1990s, Visual Basic has placed itself in the forefront of the programming world. It has gained popularity with both beginning programmers as well as advanced programmers. Visual Basic is a powerful language used for the development of programs from client/server applications to Web based solutions.

By surveying many online IT job sites, they reveal that a number of employers are seeking programmers skilled in Visual Basic. Many programming jobs, although not asking specifically for Visual Basic programming skills, look favorably on those candidates with Visual Basic skills. The salaries and benefit packages offered to Visual Basic developers is comparable to those of developers versed in higher profile languages.

Visual Basic has something for everyone and is constantly improving to keep pace with the demands of the IT industry.

Training Options and Resources

Microsoft offers a widely recognized certification program, the MCSD. Those who pursue and obtain the MCSD are given the skills necessary to design and develop leading edge business solutions with Microsoft development tools, technologies, and platforms. The types of applications MCSDs are trained to program include desktop, multiuser, Web-based, and transaction-based applications. Successful MCSD candidates possess the qualifications to complete at such job tasks as analyzing business requirements to maintaining and designing business solutions. Information on the MCSD can be found on the Microsoft Web site at **www.microsoft.com/trainingandservices**.

Online Training

Many online training centers offer Visual Basic training. The difficult part may be finding the one that best suits your educational, not to mention financial, needs. Take the time to investigate the course or certification program to ensure it provides you with what you need from the training. The following list contains samples of what is available for online study:

➤ Netdesk Corporation (**www.netdesk.com**) advertises Visual Basic 6.0 training from Microsoft Certified Trainers. Students have 24 hour access to Netdesk resources and ongoing support and feedback from the trainers.

➤ IMGUniversity Online (**www.imgwebu.com**) offers online training for Microsoft's MCSD certification program. The courses are a combination of self-study and instructor led classes. The courses allow students to set the pace of their own learning.

➤ ARIS OnLine (**http://online.aris.com**) advertises Web-based IT training with the assistance of a certified instructor. Interaction with instructors is offered through real-time chat sessions, email, newsgroups, and live instructor lecture Webcasts.

➤ Magellan University (**http://magellan.edu**) is an institution that offers its classes entirely online. Students are required to complete assignments by specific due dates, but have the flexibility to design their own study time to accomplish these tasks. Class size is restricted to less than 20 students, and communication between students is encouraged.

Self Study Options

Those interested in learning Visual Basic will find that it is part of the MCSD certification. At least two courses within the program focus specifically on Visual Basic; Exam 70-176: Designing and Implementing Desktop Applications with Microsoft Visual Basic 6.0 and Exam 70-175: Designing and Implementing Distributed Applications with Microsoft Visual Basic 6.0. Those interested in pursuing MCSD certification, through self study may find the following books useful in passing the Visual Basic component.

➤ Syngress Media Staff (editor). *MCSD Visual Basic 6 Desktop Applications Study Guide: Exam 70-176.* Osborne/McGraw-Hill, 1999. ISBN 0072119306.

➤ Syngress Media Staff (editor). *MCSD Visual Basic 6 Distributed Applications Study Guide: Exam 70-175.* Osborne/McGraw-Hill, 1999. ISBN 0072119322.

➤ MacDonald, Michael D. *MCSD Visual Basic 6 Desktop Exam Cram.* The Coriolis Group, 1999. ISBN 1576103765.

➤ Hawhee, Howard, Thomas Moore, Felipe Martins, Richard Hundhausen, and Corby Jordan. *MCSD Visual Basic 6 Exams: Exams 70-175 and 70-176 Training Guide.* New Riders Publishing, 1999. ISBN 0735700028.

The MCSD certification can be obtained through home study, classroom instruction, or a combination of these methods. Classroom training can often give beginners a better understanding of the material as well as access to the programs and equipment they will see on the job. However, the cost of classroom training can be prohibitive, making the option of a mixture of class time and self-study an attractive one.

Additional Resources

The resources available for all levels of Visual Basic programmers seem almost unlimited. The information available on the Internet and in bookstores for Visual Basic is extensive, offering something for everyone from the novice to the experienced Visual Basic programmer.

Visual Basic Jargon Buster

As with other programming languages, Visual Basic introduces its own terminology. Knowing a few of the common VB terms may help you understand jargon you may come across in the available resources.

➤ *Class*—Within an object-oriented technology class is a user defined data type that defines a collection of objects that share the same characteristics. For instance, you might make a class called "shapes," which is comprised of objects that are just that—boxes, circles, and triangles.

➤ *Encapsulation*—Allows the programmer to group subroutines and variables in a single class.

➤ *Client/Server*—A computing model in which the client or workstation requests information from another computer known as a server. The client requests the information and the server provides it.

➤ *Compiler*—Translates code into an executable file.

➤ *Source Code*—VB statements that are instructions for your program to follow.

Books

Save some room on your bookshelf for a few Visual Basic titles, because a programmer's library wouldn't be complete without them.

Beginner Book Titles

➤ Smiley, John. *Learn to Program with Visual Basic 6.* Active Path, 1998. ISBN 1902745000.

➤ Halvorson, Michael. *Microsoft Visual Basic 6.0 Professional (Step by Step).* Microsoft Press, 1998. ISBN 1572318090.

➤ Halvorson, Michael. *Learn Microsoft Visual Basic 6.0 Now (Learn Now).* Microsoft Press, 1999. ISBN 073560729X.

Advanced Books

➤ Freeze, Wayne S. *Expert Guide to Visual Basic 6.* Sybex, 1998. ISBN 078212349X.

➤ Petroutsos, Evangelos. *Mastering Database Programming with Visual Basic 6.* Sybex, 1999. ISBN 0782125980.

Reference Books

➤ Holzner, Steven. *Visual Basic 6 Core Language Little Black Book.* The Coriolis Group, 1998. ISBN 1576103900.

➤ Aitken, Peter G. *Visual Basic 6 Programming Blue Book.* The Coriolis Group, 1998. ISBN 1576102815.

➤ Shelly, Gary B., Thomas J. Cashman, John F. Repede, and Michael L. Mick. *Microsoft Visual Basic 6: Complete Concepts and Techniques (Shelly Cashman Series).* South-Western, 1998. ISBN 078954654X.

Online Information and Resources

Those seeking to find additional information on Visual Basic will have little difficulty finding what they need on the Internet. The following is a list of resources to get you started.

Newsgroups

Just like the other languages, there is a slew of newsgroups for the Visual Basic curious. Here are just a few:

➤ **comp.lang.basic.misc**

➤ **comp.lang.basic.visual**

➤ **comp.lang.basic.visual.misc**

➤ **comp.lang.basic.visual.database**

➤ **comp.lang.basic.visual.3rdparty**

Magazines and Journals

➤ *Visual Basic Programmers Journal* (**www.vbpj.com**)—This is a well-organized and informative site offering links, articles, and a newsletter. A valuable site to bookmark.

➤ *Visual Basic Developer Online* (**www.pinpub.com/VBD/home.htm**)—This site looks at what is new in Visual Basic and provides articles, programming tips, and other relevant information. This is a subscription service that offers a free trail subscription to see if it is what you are looking for.

➤ *vbwm.com* (**www.vbwm.com**)—Another helpful resource page. If nothing else, log on and get its electronic newsletter.

➤ *Visual Basic Online Magazine* (**www.vbonline.com/vb-mag**)—A comprehensive site for Visual Basic developers.

Web Pages

➤ *Visual Basic Explorer* (**www.vbexplorer.com**)—This site is a very interesting site that offers everything you can imagine from the world of Visual Basic.

➤ *Searchvb.com* (**www.searchvb.com**)—This site offers a Visual Basic search engine with access to 2000 VB sites. On this site you will find information that covers all areas of the language. Those interested in Visual Basic will find no end to the information, tips, hints, and resources offered on this page. For those hungry for a little Visual Basic, this page is a feast.

➤ *Visual Basic Compendium* (**www.cyber-matrix.com/vb.htm**)—This site offers beginning tutorials to get you up and programming. Book reviews, training information, newsgroups, tips, and tricks can all be found on this site.

➤ *DevCentral Learning Center* (**http://devcentral.iftech.com/learning/ tutorials**)—This site offers tutorials on Visual Basic and VBScript.

Professional Associations

Professional Associations are a means of communicating with other programmers. The IPG (**www.ipgnet.com**) is a good resource for those wanting to connect with other programmers. It is not specific to Visual Basic, but rather is a site for programmers in general. It may, however, provide links to Visual Basic related Web sites. The site also includes a newsletter and a job search index. It appears to be a good site to bookmark and provides good links to further programming resources. There is a fee for membership.

Summary

Originally, Visual Basic struggled to gain acceptance with programmers. With improved version releases, Visual Basic has now gained approval from many programmers and is considered to be a powerful and useful tool for the development of quality software solutions.

Three separate editions of Visual Basic are available: Basic Learning, Professional, and Enterprise editions. These edition choices allow you to save money by not paying for features you may not need. The versatility of Visual Basic allows it to be used by both beginners and experienced programmers. Its familiar interface and drag and drop features make it a good choice for those interested in trying their hands at programming.

Programmers skilled in Visual Basic are in demand in the IT industry, and the product itself is constantly improving to keep pace with the advancements in the IT industry. Visual Basic is a solid programming language and will be a favorite of programmers for some time to come.

A Programmer's View

The following sections contain two on-the-job interviews that may be helpful in providing you with an understanding of what "a day in the life" of a programmer might be like. Interviews with those already on the job is often the best way to get the real scoop.

Interview One

Joe Sapiano, a C++ programmer based in Seattle, provides some insights into the life of a programmer.

Why do you choose to program with C++?

[Joe]: I use C++ for many reasons: its object-oriented capabilities, the ability to reuse code, and code encapsulation. Basically, I use it for its flexibility and reusability features.

What are your qualifications, training, and years of experience?

[Joe]: I have not been using C++ for all that long. Most of my experience is with C. The languages are quite similar. C++ has an object-oriented component that takes some time to learn.

As for formal training, I hold a master's degree in geophysics. This isn't to suggest you need a master's degree to get a job as a C++ programmer. The master's degree required several skills that are transferable to a career in programming. During the degree program, I was involved in some coding using both C and Pascal. Furthermore, my degree required strong mathematical skills. I chose programming work because, essentially, it was available and as it turns out, I find it quite enjoyable to do.

What is required in maintaining and upgrading your skills? Do you pay for your upgrading or does your employer?

[Joe]: Those working directly in software development know that keeping up-to-date and constant upgrading go with the job, and it is a very important part of the job. On my own, I spend time reading to keep current. There is also a strong focus on training where I currently work. My employer currently pays for upgrading, and courses and workshops are readily available.

Basically, the goal of the company is to stay ahead of the competition. To do this, if there is a better, faster, or more secure way of doing things, we need to know. Even programmers that have fifteen years experience still have things to learn. There is always a better way of doing things.

What are your likes and dislikes with the profession or with the language? What are the job stressors?

[Joe]: To be honest, I have to admit it is a lucrative profession and that is definitely nice. Also, it is an exciting field to be working in. We are always on the cutting edge. If there are new products, new methods, or new designs, we are going to be among the first to know. There is always something new to learn.

I do not always like the hours that are required to stay ahead. The problem with working on the cutting edge is that you have to spend the time to stay there. The constant need to retrain can be draining.

Don't expect to get a job programming and work from 9 to 5. Sometimes when it is necessary to meet a deadline, you may work 60 hours per week or more until the project is complete or until you just get too tired. There are considerable time pressures when trying to get a product out; everybody's working hard, and people can sometimes get a little stressed. That is when the job becomes less enjoyable.

Another aspect of the job that I don't like is sitting for long periods of time. The job can be pretty inactive; you definitely need to stay away from the snack foods.

What are your current job responsibilities and daily tasks?

[Joe]: Previously, I was working on some end user applications. Now there seems to be more demand to program in the Web development area. That's mainly how I spend my time now.

There are essentially two main parts of my job: The first is on design and the second is on writing the actual code. Programming is not as isolated as you may think. When it comes to the design of the project we are working on, there is a lot of teamwork. Numerous discussions and meetings are needed to make sure we are all on the same page. However, when it comes to writing the code for our designs, we are pretty much alone at our computers. The coding can take a long time depending on the complexity of the project we are working on.

What kind of environment do you typically work in?

[Joe]: I have always had an office with a door that closes, although the offices are typically shared with another person. Within the office, there is a lot of collaboration on projects. It would be impossible to come to work, sit at the computer, and work independently. Although some independent work is required, there is a strong teamwork requirement to the job.

The only thing I miss in my office is a window, but that is something to work towards.

What are your job prospects?

[Joe]: There are a lot of assumptions that because the IT industry is short of skilled programmers that it is easy for anyone to enter the profession. Although this may be true in some instances, it is not necessarily the case. I have found that people with two years or less experience may have trouble getting a job as a programmer. The reason for this is that the products we are working on need to be turned out quickly, faster than the competition. To get the products out fast enough, employers need programmers who can step in and do the job. It is difficult to train new people and meet project deadlines with the tight timelines we have.

It is possible for those with two years or less experience to get into programming, but they usually have to demonstrate an ability to catch up and be willing to spend considerable time doing self-study. Furthermore, it is essential that these new programmers show that they have a strong work ethic. Unfortunately, this may mean working longer hours.

Having said that, the market is wide open for those programmers with four years or more experience. Programmers with years of experience and a proven ability to do the job and meet deadlines are a valuable resource for the company.

Interview Two

To get a actual idea of what the life of a Java programmer is like, it is best to ask one. Wade Wurm is a Java programmer based in California. This is what he had to say about working in one of the most active IT career fields.

4

Why do you choose to program with Java?

[Wade]: Basically for its ease of use, access to the full development tool set, its memory management and hiding of pointers features, and the use of object-oriented methodology. Java was written for the Web and offers a full range of support tools, such as debuggers and integrated development environments. Furthermore, there is a wide range of uses for the language; it offers a rich set of components including JSP, EJB, applet, servlet, and so on; and the abstraction of data.

Essentially, it combines all of the latest innovations into one language.

What are your qualifications, training, and years of experience?

[Wade]: I currently hold a degree in computer science and degree in management. I have been an application developer for more than seven years in database processing and am currently a technical consultant for a major credit bureau in the United States. I am currently working on the integration of legacy systems into the Web environment and will be changing to a project leader for a major consulting service provider.

What is required in maintaining and upgrading your skills? Do you pay for your upgrading or does your employer?

[Wade]: Training is typically based on individual needs. Employees should take advantage of employer skill development programs based on how the training fits with their personal goals.

A technical writer who wishes to become a manager might focus more on nonreimbursable external leadership courses rather than on reimbursable writing courses. When it comes to training, the first question should be   Does the benefit outweigh the cost? Don't waste your time taking courses you won't use in the next six months. Chances are you will forget everything and waste your time as well as your employer's money.

What are your likes and dislikes with the profession or with the language? What are the job stressors?

[Wade]: I would say that there are key forces that are associated with the profession. It then comes down to whether you have the personality to adapt to working within those forces. For example:

➤ *Product to market/branding*—In the e-commerce world, half the battle is being first. This means long hours, tight deadlines, and unsympathetic stakeholders.

➤ *Competition*—A typical technical professional is geared to be the best. This means you're often working in an environment of egos. Team skills are a definite requirement.

➤ *Change*—What you know today will be obsolete in one year.

➤ *Niching skill sets*—Value is found in expertise; techs need to niche their most durable skills.

As for the language, Java is like Legos for the Internet. You're able to build most anything, but don't expect to be able to create the blocks yourself. Still, I prefer to use Java over C++. C++ is one of the most technically efficient languages available today, but it's not for the lighthearted.

The stressors of the job can be summed up in three words: better, faster, cheaper.

What are your current job responsibilities and daily tasks?

[Wade]: Architecture, scoping, development, and integration using the best tool for the problem presented. A typical day includes product support, maintenance support, documentation, standards development, infrastructure enhancement, product development, and implementation.

What kind of environment do you typically work in?

[Wade]: Distributed processing on various platforms including PC, mainframe, Unix, and Tandem.

What are your job prospects?

[Wade]: Experienced techs can typically expect to see a flood of opportunities available to them across the country in all areas of business. In today's market, techs are in a very strong negotiating position and have the opportunity to find jobs that closely match their overall goals.

5

Careers in Computer Networking

Of all the IT career fields currently available, few can offer the diversity that computer networking provides. First, the networking industry is huge, encompassing hundreds of companies and a massive range of technologies. Second, the sheer demand for skilled individuals means that opportunities with companies of all sorts and sizes abound. The reason for this high level of demand is simple. Practically every company has a network and almost all have the need for a skilled individual to manage their network. Even if they cannot justify having a full-time administrator of their own, they are likely to have an arrangement with a computer company that does. For the past few years, computer networking has been, is now, and is forecasted to remain one of the primary growth areas of the IT industry.

Getting Connected

When computer networking is discussed, it refers primarily to the process of connecting two or more computers together. The true meaning of a network is answered by a question. Why would you want to join two computers together in the first place?

In the early days of networking, the two main uses of a computer network were the sharing of data and the shared use of expensive peripherals, such as printers. Today, these two tasks still form the basis of most networks, but networks are now used in many other ways as well. The explosive popularity of email has meant that a user is as likely to use the network for sending and receiving mail as he or she is to connect to a shared printer. The popularity in database applications has also sparked the growth of facilities and capabilities in the networking area.

Without a doubt, the defining point in the history of networking was the creation of the Internet. Although it is difficult to convey in just a few lines, the Internet is basically a massive collection of connected networks. In fact, the term Internet (with a capital I) is derived from the term internetwork (with a lowercase i), meaning a group of connected networks. Although it is obvious that the scale of the Internet makes for differences in the technology used, the basis for the Internet is the same as that of many of the networks used in businesses around the world.

Essentially, networking is a concept or principle that requires two kinds of products: hardware and software. These products are the components that make up the network. Effectively, there is a computer networking hardware industry (cables, devices for attaching PC's to a network, etc.) and there is a networking software industry (software for sharing files, email, etc.). Although there are exceptions, there are relatively few instances where companies have large scale participation in both areas.

There is a great need for individuals to work on the hardware aspect of networking (sometimes called the infrastructure). However, there is more of a demand for those that are skilled with the software that powers the networks. In addition, although there are certain companies who will take people fresh out of school and through training turn them into a networking gurus, many infrastructure companies require people who possess an understanding of the functionality a network provides. This understanding normally comes from working with network operating systems, such as Windows NT and Windows 2000 from Microsoft, NetWare from Novell, and Unix and Linux.

It is not so much the understanding of the operating system software that the infrastructure companies are interested in, it is more the depth of understanding of what a network can provide. In almost every case, the purpose of a network is to connect two PCs. Having a thorough understanding of the functions and capabilities of those PCs and their operating systems not only helps individuals to realize the point of the network in the first place, it also serves to provide an understanding of the "big" picture.

In essence, starting a career in computer networking may best be served by starting at the beginning, which in networking terms means connecting two computers to provide services. As your career progresses, you may begin to look more at the necessary steps to connect two networks, which is where products, such as those from Cisco and Nortel, and technologies, such as ISDN and ATM, come into play.

Unlike other areas of technology, networking is about brand names: Microsoft, Novell, Cisco, Nortel, 3Com, and Compaq, to name but a few. The companies involved in the networking industry drive the technology forward, most of the time playing catch up with the demands of the companies and organizations that use their products.

One of the most attractive features that a career in networking offers is sheer diversity. There are so many different aspects to the networking field. As a network administrator, you need to have an understanding of the network operating systems that are in use, the products that provide backup capabilities, and (at least to some extent) the products that run on the servers you are supporting. You need to have an understanding of network infrastructure issues, cabling, machine locating, and so on. In addition to these skills, there are a number of other areas you need to have experience in, such as printing and email. And, almost every network administrator needs to have at least some general knowledge of computer hardware. From a personal perspective, network administrators must also possess excellent troubleshooting and communication skills. Because there are so many areas and avenues to explore in the networking field, a person could spend an entire career in this field and still find something new and different.

This chapter focuses on three major technologies in networking—Microsoft Windows NT, Novell NetWare, and Unix and Linux. Let's start by taking a look at the difference between PC support and networking.

The Difference between PC Support and Networking

In this book, we have split PC support and Networking into two separate sections. The reason for this is that even though both share common areas of technology, they are quite different. Networking is about managing and supporting the fabric that connects PCs and includes the services that such a fabric provides. It is about user management, provision of Internet access, corporate email, and so on. PC support, on the other hand, deals with the applications and issues that turn a computer into a productivity tool and the hardware that makes it possible.

The gray area between PC support and networking is revealed when the two are combined. In many companies, the PC support person and the network administrator are one and the same person. This is particularly true of smaller companies. The reason they have been separated in this book is simply to illustrate that they are very different technology areas, and individuals who choose to do so can pursue positions that are almost completely networking in nature or strictly PC support.

The Name Game

The networking field has a bewildering range of job titles, many of which refer to very similar, and in some cases identical, roles. A quick scan through an Internet job site will turn up occurrences of network administrator, network engineer, network analyst, network systems analyst, and so on. A great number of these jobs are similar in nature and encompass many of the same roles and responsibilities. Because job titles are defined by an individual or company in many areas of IT, these titles can become confusing. There are no set standards regarding which job title corresponds to which role. So, to make matters easier, from this point on in the book, the title of network administrator will be used to represent these roles. Even though this label may be a little inaccurate in some cases, those that gain employment in the networking field have a better than average chance of holding this title for their first job.

Daily Tasks

As stated in the introduction, networking is a truly diverse field. Network administrators will find themselves in a variety of situations during a working day, which is part of the attraction of the role. Much of their time will be spent working with systems rather than with users, although in many environments there is still a reasonably high level of interaction. The following list contains some of their most common tasks:

➤ *Performing general system maintenance*—Even the most basic computer network is a complicated device. The primary task of a network administrator is to ensure the overall health of the network. For this to be the case, continuous attention to all systems is necessary, although many companies use a management system to make the monitoring easier. Even so, the data supplied by the monitoring systems must be interpreted, and if necessary, acted upon. All of which can serve to ensure that the network administrator is kept busy.

➤ *Dealing with system failures*—Three words a network administrator never likes to hear are "the system's down." Unfortunately, even the most diligently maintained network is likely to experience occasional problems. In many cases, the problems will be minor and isolated, but every so often a major problem will come along that will test not only your troubleshooting skills, but also your patience and ability to deal with stress. These are the times when network administrators really earn their money. Every minute that the system is unavailable can potentially cost a company money. When the systems are down, the meter is running, and everyone has their eyes on the person who can make everything work again.

➤ *Applying software updates and fixes*—The complexity of software packages coupled with the need for them to work with such a diverse range of products results in the necessity for manufacturers to release updates to their software. The installation of these updates is essential to ensure the consistent smooth running of systems. In addition, certain software programs, particularly programs such as virus checkers, require frequent updating. Though most updates are easily applied, network administrators must always consider what effect the updates may have on other software products, and if suitable equipment is available, test the products before implementation.

➤ *Attending to network related PC support issues*—In many cases, PC support staff will fix problems on a specific workstation. Other times, the network administration staff will be called in, especially if the problem is related to a networking issue. This is where communication skills and diplomacy come into play. The

5

network administrator will need to take the time to understand and fix a problem for sometimes impatient and irate users. Just smile and say thank you. More often than not, the users won't.

➤ *Attending meetings*—Those working in computer networking must understand that they are basically working in a service industry. For the service to be kept in line with the customer's wishes, a certain degree of communication is necessary. Communications will often take the form of meetings, where the current state of the network is discussed along with the analysis of any recent issues. In addition, because networks are in a constant state of advancement, new projects and products must be discussed.

➤ *Evaluating new solutions*—Just because an administrator has the network up and running smoothly does not mean that his or her job is done. The versatility of computer networks means that there will always be some other enhancement to add to the network. This extra functionality often involves products that will change the layout of the network and could potentially affect the other components. For this reason, any solution that is considered must be tested fully, and the results of those tests documented. Many larger companies provide a dummy test network for these purposes, although not all do. Because implementation of new solutions can require the network to be taken "offline," a great deal of this kind of work takes place in the evenings or on weekends, so users are not disrupted. Network administrators must be flexible in this respect.

➤ *Documenting systems*—One of the most overlooked and avoided of all network administration tasks is that of documentation. Documentation serves to provide a reference point for the configuration of the network and is an invaluable resource when troubleshooting problems or investigating network related issues. It also is very useful when planning upgrades to the system or when deciding to introduce new products. Unfortunately, the ever changing nature of the network means that the process of updating the system documentation can be endless. The good news is that no one is awarding prizes for creativity either. An easy to read, concise, and above all accurate run down on the specifics of the system is more than sufficient.

➤ *Performing backups*—Sometimes referred to as a disaster recovery measure, backing up system data is probably one of the most important tasks performed each day. Most modern backup systems are highly automated, and the maintenance and checking of the system is very important. In addition, network administrators will periodically restore data from a backup to test that the system is working as it should, and that the data being restored can be used in the event of a failure.

➤ *Maintaining hardware*—Much of a network administrator's work is software related, but because the software runs on hardware, a good knowledge of computer hardware is also required. Tasks that a network administrator may perform will range from upgrading or replacing individual components to replacing an entire PC. The PCs used as network file servers often bear little physical resemblance to the PCs that appear at home or on users' desks, but they are still basically the same albeit more powerful and with more disk space and RAM.

➤ *Maintaining cabling and network devices*—Cabling is the medium that makes computer networking happen. Even though a cabling contractor may install the main cabling system, there will always be computers that need to be relocated, new systems added, and faults with existing equipment diagnosed and corrected. In addition, many modern networks use hardware devices to connect systems together. Although novice network administrators may be excused from knowing all about these devices, those with even a few months experience will almost certainly have to deal with them, though on a relatively infrequent basis.

Job Outlook

The outlook for careers in the networking arena is very positive. The phenomenal growth of computer networking has fueled demand to a point where there are simply not enough people to fill the vacancies available. The certification programs introduced by many of the computer networking software and hardware companies have addressed the shortfall, at least in part. The relative ease with which people can train for these certifications has meant that large numbers have taken the tests and have then started careers in the networking field. Even so, the amount of people joining the marketplace remains insufficient, and as software manufacturers begin to tighten their certification programs (which some people have criticized for being too easy), the gulf between the people required and the people available will probably remain huge. Some feel it may even begin to widen.

Although you can be fairly sure of the fact that the demand for certified, qualified, and experienced personnel will continue, it is not clear in what areas that growth is likely to be strongest. Toward the end of the last decade, Linux was being touted as the answer to practically everything (even the common cold). Now, at the beginning of the twenty-first century, the future seems a little less clear. Microsoft remains the dominant player in the field, but Novell's recent product releases have caused its products to regain some ground. Even though the ground swell that is

Linux appears to have abated somewhat, it continues to garner a growing support among the Internet fraternity and is becoming a more frequent sight in corporate server rooms.

From a career perspective, this movement can only work in your favor. The more products that are available effectively means that you would be working in a subsector of the networking industry. This brings up the question of whether it is best to acquire knowledge in more than one area, thereby ensuring yourself against any one area becoming more popular than another. It is the issue of specialization versus generalization.

Specialization vs. Generalization

Although it can be said of almost any technical field, networking is one area where there is truly an issue of specialization versus generalization. Because there are so many different facets of the industry, a person could focus almost entirely on one specific product or technology and make a career of it. In fact, many people do. From the perspective of someone just starting a career in IT, there are certain issues that need to be considered in this respect.

For a specialization to be successful, you need to know more (usually a good deal more) about a certain product that a generalist. You must also ensure that the area of expertise you have chosen is in demand and will remain so for an appropriate period of time, which can be tricky to determine. Although the networking industry is not that fickle a creature, products do rise and fall in popularity. If a specialist has made a poor choice, he or she may reach a position where it may be difficult to stay in a particular field. The solution, if you are interested in specialization, is to become specialized in a technology rather than a product. Technologies tend to evolve, whereas products are often replaced. Although it can be argued that in either case, the knowledge gained from the previous specialization can be transferred to another, there is always the challenge of conveying that fact accurately to a potential employer. It is somewhat easier to do so regarding a technology rather than a product because in a technology, a very great portion of previously learned knowledge remains useful, if only as background information.

Can you be both a specialist and a generalist? Well, the answer is probably yes. The old phrase "jack of all trades, master of none," has been turned on its head by many enthusiastic network administrators, who train and educate themselves to the point where they are "jack of all trades, master of more than one." In reality, the breadth of technologies and products that are presented to network administrators results in the fact that they often develop specializations in certain areas, often without actually realizing it.

Qualifications and Requirements

Some argue that networking cannot be learned from a book or in a classroom and must be learned through real-world, on-the-job experience. The problem is, as with almost every other field, getting the experience before you can get a job invokes the old chicken and egg situation. This section deals with the qualifications and requirements that will hopefully open some doors and get you that invaluable experience.

From an academic perspective, any college or university degree in a computer related field is likely to be a valuable tool. For many graduates, the path to a given company will be via a graduate intake program, where the company recruits graduates, and then grooms them for certain positions. Without a graduate intake program, many graduates will find it necessary to display some specific knowledge in their chosen area of technology.

So how do employers choose the people for the positions they have? Increasingly, it is by the use of vendor certification programs, of which there are many. Currently, the most popular certification program is the Microsoft Certified Systems Engineer (MCSE) program, closely followed by Novell's Certified Novell Engineer (CNE) offering. Aside from these, there are also other programs that are gaining increasing popularity including those from Cisco and CompTIA. The relative popularity of these programs against each other is no mystery—they closely reflect demand (and reward) in the marketplace.

From a personal perspective, those in the networking field must possess a wide range of skills, not limited to: an ability to deal with stress, excellent communication skills, and a the ability to remember (and at the appropriate moment retrieve) a wide range of facts on an even wider range of products.

Why These Areas?

So why does this chapter focus on the these areas? As with other technology areas discussed in this book, attention is focused on just a handful of products and systems. The reason for this is simple. The focus of this book is to help you find a job, and the topics discussed represent the fields or areas that are in the highest demand. They also represent fields that are accessible to individuals starting a career in IT.

Networking diehards may look at this section and ask why certain paths or fields are not included. Some paths into the networking industry are easier than others, and some areas are easier to learn than others. The technology areas presented are those that can be learned (in theory at least) by individuals with access to a reasonable amount of computer hardware, the Internet, and a local bookstore. Surely, there are some who want to become network security specialists or networking gurus. The problem is that unless you have the means to obtain literally tens of thousands of dollars worth of equipment to study with, you will find the going very hard. Besides, it might be beneficial to consider that old phrase about learning to walk before you run.

Pick a Card, Any Card

To make things a little more complicated (as if they weren't already), you should be aware of the fact that a great number of companies use more than one network operating system within their organization. By doing this, they often capitalize on the strengths of each operating system and expect their network administrators to have an understanding of each. The depth of understanding required will vary depending on the environment and the organization. You should not feel obliged to learn more than one area to start with, although it may well help in your job search. After you have learned and mastered one area of networking, you may find yourself in a situation where you need to learn another.

Competition is fierce between the manufacturers, particularly Microsoft and Novell. Both companies release products that can help the migration from one platform to another. Manufacturers of Unix and Linux operating systems tend to distance themselves from such arguments, safe in the knowledge that their products and the roles that they fulfill are not only key to many organizations, but also that their products and the ideals on which they are founded have a strong and very dedicated following.

From your personal perspective, remain objective. Keep in mind that computers do a job. They perform a task. The best network operating system for a certain task is the one that does it best— plain and simple. The best network administrators are those that remember this and do not get involved in debates over the general merits of one operating system over another. If you can remain objective on this issue, you will be able to make decisions based upon business needs rather than personal preference—a skill that eludes many of even the most seasoned network administrators.

Microsoft Windows NT

Windows NT is one of the most popular network operating systems in the world. Originally derived from a product called LAN Manager, Windows NT has become the platform of choice for businesses in every sector and of every size. The

NT stands for new technology, although in the latest release, the NT has been replaced by some, er, newer technology and has been renamed Windows 2000, keeping it in line with Microsoft's habit of naming its products after the year in which they are released. There are distinct differences between Windows NT and Windows 2000, but they are also closely related. Anyone considering pursuing a career in networking in the near future would do well to learn both operating systems because more and more companies are likely to replace their Windows NT systems with Windows 2000. Much of the information in this section applies to both products, so they will be referred to as Windows NT/2000.

Each release of Windows NT comes in different versions, designed for different purposes. For Windows NT 4, there is a Workstation product designed for use by individuals on a PC workstation, and a Server product designed for use as a centralized file/application/print server. For Windows 2000, the Workstation product is now called Professional, and there are three variations of the Server product, namely Server, Advanced Server, and Datacenter Server, which are designed to be used in different environments.

Why Use Windows NT?

One of the main reasons Windows NT has been so widely adopted is its capability to perform many functions very well. The basic product, which is very affordable by software standards, comes with most of the tools that a modern organization needs to operate. Although the functionality of these tools may not be as complete as other commercially available products, many companies simply stick with them rather than spend money on other products.

Common Interface

The user interface (sometimes referred to as the "front end") for both Windows NT and Windows 2000 are very similar to other Microsoft operating systems, such as Windows 95, 98, and Millennium Edition, which many people are already using on their home computers. This commonality has a number of benefits. First, it means that the interface, and subsequently the administration of Windows NT/2000 systems, is relatively straightforward. Second, it means that any applications that are designed to run on the server look the same, which in turn make them easier to learn.

Business Features

Although the visual presentation of Windows NT/2000 is similar to that of other Microsoft operating systems, that is where the similarity ends. The Windows NT/2000 products are designed for use primarily in a business environment and must accommodate different needs than the operating systems used on home computers. These extra business features include a much greater degree of security, better support for applications, and an increased level of reliability. Windows NT/2000 also supports systems that require a significant amount of processing power and those that require huge amounts of RAM.

Ease of Administration

One of the reasons that Windows NT has proved so popular with companies of all sizes is the ease with which it can be administered. Not only are the administration tools easy to find and use, but also those with little or no knowledge of the utility can often rely on a comprehensive help system or in many cases a wizard, which takes them through basic tasks, such as creating a new user, group, or printer. Another factor is that Windows NT/2000 are designed to be run "out of the box" with little or no alterations to the default configuration. That is not to say that it cannot be tuned, because it most surely can be. Many companies, in particular small businesses, like the idea of having an easy to install, easy to administer, good-at-pretty-much-everything operating system.

Third-Party Product Support

The list of products that are written to run on a Windows NT system is practically endless. Products include accounting, personnel, databases, graphics, booking systems, network management, inventory, Internet Web servers, and so on. Many companies, not using Windows NT/2000 originally, have now found themselves using one or more of these servers, so that they can use an application or system that was written to run on a Windows NT/2000 system.

The Differences between Windows NT and Windows 2000

The biggest difference between Windows 2000 and its predecessor is the way in which they deal with information about objects (users, groups, etc.) on the network. Windows NT operated on what is known as a domain model, where users and computers were grouped into logical units called domains. These domains had one or more Windows NT servers, which acted as central repositories for information on users and groups within the domain. Within each domain, one Windows NT server was nominated as the "master or primary." To reduce the load on this server, increase performance, and provide a degree of fault tolerance, other servers could be nominated as "backups" to the master and receive a copy of all the user and group information that the master held. This domain model system was well understood and widely implemented. Even so, some people criticized the domain model for its lack of scalability, in other words, for its inability to handle very large numbers of user accounts in a practical and easily administrable manner.

The new version of Windows NT, Windows 2000, still has the capability to operate using this domain model, but also comes with a new method of management called Active Directory. In an Active Directory environment, the database does not have a master and backups. All servers participating in the directory can hold information on objects on the system. In addition, these objects can be divided into separate units, allowing them to be managed and administered on a local basis. This function is in direct contrast to the Windows NT 4 model, where all objects were held in a single area. Not only does Active Directory provide the capability to compartmentalize areas of the network, it also has the capability to relate to other areas of the network and create an object called a *tree*. Multiple trees can then be grouped to form a *forest*. This extra level of organization effectively addresses any potential issues that Windows NT 4 had in regard to scalability, and makes Windows 2000 a truly scalable network operating system.

As time goes on, you are likely to see more and more implementations of Windows 2000. The proliferation of Windows NT 4 in the market means that anyone entering the Windows networking sector, or indeed any area of networking, should try to obtain at least some knowledge of the Windows NT 4 product.

Job Demand

Demand for individuals with Windows NT/2000 skills is currently exceptionally high. Vacancies can be found at almost every level, in almost every town or city, and with almost every type of company.

Many employers looking for Windows NT/2000 skills specify Microsoft certifications as a base requirement rather than an option. In addition, many are looking for experience in a computing environment to match those skills, although there are plenty of employers willing to take on those with the right approach and attitude, even if they have no formal experience. Another common occurrence is that of employers looking for people who are not just skilled in Windows NT/2000, but also in other Microsoft products as well. Quite often, businesses that use Windows NT/2000 elect to take advantage of the integration of other Microsoft products, such as Exchange (email), SQL Server (database system), or Systems Management Server SMS (network management). If you want to make it easier to get a Windows NT network administration position, you would do well to learn one of these other products along the way.

It should also be noted that the demand for skilled Windows NT/2000 candidates makes for a happy hunting ground for those who do not have the appropriate skills or experience. In such cases, those that lack the required skills hope to cash in on employers who are finding it difficult to hire suitable staff. Although few of these applicants make it past the résumé stage, you should go to the extra effort to ensure that your résumé communicates your correct level of skills and experience, so that you are not mistaken for one of these other job seekers.

Training Options and Resources

The popularity of Windows NT/2000 has had a dramatic effect on many satellite industries, and training is no exception. There is an abundance of traditional training methods, such as classroom-based instruction. There is also a wealth of other resources, such as computer- and Web-based training modules.

Courses and Certifications

The MCSE program is recognized throughout the world as a measurement of an individual's knowledge of Windows NT/2000 and their associated products and technologies. To become an MCSE, candidates must pass a series of Microsoft Certified Professional (MCP) exams. However, the method of preparation for each exam is at the discretion of the individual. Once the required exams are successfully completed, Microsoft grants the designation of MCSE, allowing the holder to use the credentials and accompanying logo on résumés and business cards. For more information on the MCSE program, visit the Microsoft training Web site at **www.microsoft.com/trainingandservices**.

Microsoft itself provides a range of training options, including full instructor-led courses, that are delivered through a worldwide network of training centers.

Many other companies also offer training that will help you learn Windows NT and prepare for the certification exams. For a list of training companies in your area, check the Yellow Pages under Computers – Training. Training companies that are approved by Microsoft carry either the Microsoft Certified Technical Education Center (CTEC) designation or the Microsoft Authorized Academic Training Partner (AATP) designation. CTEC programs are designed for individuals who are already working in the IT industry and so are normally short in duration and presume a certain level of prior knowledge. AATP institutions are often community colleges or private colleges that run courses aimed at those new to the industry or those with little experience.

Online Training

Online, or Web-based, training continues to grow in popularity and, predictably, there are a variety of Windows NT and Windows 2000 courses available to those who prefer this method of learning.

A list of companies that provide Internet-based training on Microsoft products can be found on the Microsoft Training and Certification Web site at **www.microsoft.com/trainingandservices**.

Another online resource for Windows NT training is **www.freeskills.com**. As the name implies, the training is free and can be downloaded and studied at your own convenience. Although targeted at general training rather than toward specific exam objectives, it is professionally written and very useful.

Self-Study Options

The sheer volume of information and material available can make self-studying for a Microsoft certification an attractive choice. As well as traditional books, there are CDs, videos, flash cards, CBTs, and a plethora of other training aids that can help you understand Windows NT networking. Be forewarned though. There is only so much that can be learned from a book. The only real way to gain the knowledge you need is to use the product. The fact that Windows NT runs on any reasonably specified Pentium PC means that this goal is well within reach.

Although it cannot simulate a complete networking environment, building a small network at home can be of unfathomable benefit to those studying for their MCP or MCSE certification. The ability to try out scenarios, use a utility, or install the product over and again is experience that cannot be bought. To set up a suitable "lab," you will need two PCs of sufficient power to run the version of Windows that you want to load.

Even though the actual Windows NT or 2000 software costs hundreds of dollars, evaluation copies can be obtained with relative ease, and many Microsoft Self-Study kits come with 120 day evaluation copies of the software. This fact, coupled with the knowledge that you are "getting the straight goods" make the Microsoft kits well worth considering. It's also worth noting that some of the kits are designed to teach you overall network administration tasks and principles and do not necessarily focus on exam specific objectives.

Additional Resources

Finding out more information about Windows NT/2000 is an easy task. There are countless resources available on the Internet, through newsgroups, and in your local bookstore. The following sections contain resources that you may find useful as you start to look at Windows NT/2000 in more depth.

Windows NT Jargon Buster

When researching information about Windows NT, you may come across phrases or words that you may not be familiar with. To help you better understand the information you find, the following list contains some terms, definitions, and explanations that you may find useful.

➤ *Registry*—A database that forms part of the operating system on Windows NT computers and contains information about the hardware and software configuration of the system.

➤ *Domain*—Windows NT computers are grouped together into units known as domains. Each domain has a central computer that contains the user and computer accounts for that domain.

➤ *Active Directory*—A system implemented by Microsoft in the Windows 2000 product that allows information about users, computers, and other objects to be stored in a database, which can be distributed among the systems of the network.

➤ *Primary Domain Controller (PDC)*—A computer that acts as the central point of reference for a domain.

➤ *Backup Domain Controller (BDC)*—A computer that holds a copy of the user information stored on the PDC.

Books

The popularity of Windows NT has led to a huge range of books written about the operating system. As well as books that deal with the subject in general, there are a great many that deal with specific topics, such as security or internetworking. The following sections contain a small collection of the available titles.

Beginner Book Titles

➤ Davis, Peter T., Barry D. Lewis. *Teach Yourself Microsoft Windows NT Server 4 in 21 Days.* Sams, 1999. ISBN 0672315556.

➤ Tittel, Ed, Mary Madden, and Earl Follis. *Windows NT Networking For Dummies.* IDG Books Worldwide, 1996. ISBN 0764500155.

➤ Donald, Lisa, Patrick Ciccarelli (contributor), and Dan Newland (contributor). *MCSE 2000 JumpStart: Computer and Network Basics*. Sybex, 2000. ISBN 0782127495.

Advanced Books

➤ Wise, Eric R. *Performance Tuning Microsoft Networks*. Intelligentsia Publishing, 1999. ISBN 0966833414.

➤ Minasi, Mark, Christa Anderson, Brian M. Smith, and Doug Toombs. *Mastering Windows 2000 Server (Mastering)*. Sybex, 2000. ISBN 0782127746.

➤ Edmead, Mark T., and Paul Hinsberg. *Windows NT Performance Monitoring, Benchmarking, and Tuning (New Rider's Professional Series)*. New Riders Publishing, 1998. ISBN 1562059424.

➤ Nielsen, Morten Strunge. *Windows 2000 Server Architecture and Planning, Second Edition*. The Coriolis Group, 2000. ISBN 1576106071.

Reference Books

➤ Pearce, Eric, Robert J. Denn (editor), and Beverly Murray Scherf. *Windows NT in a Nutshell: A Desktop Quick Reference for System Administrators (Nutshell Handbooks)*. O'Reilly & Associates, 1997. ISBN 1565922514.

➤ Hunt, Craig, Robert Bruce Thompson, and Robert Denn (editor). *Windows NT TCP/IP Network Administration*. O'Reilly & Associates, 1998. ISBN 1565923774.

➤ Williams, Robert, Mark Walla, and G. Robert Williams. *The Ultimate Windows 2000 System Administrator's Guide*. Addison-Wesley, 2000. ISBN 0201615800.

➤ Wallace, Nathan. *Windows 2000 Registry Little Black Book The Definitive Resource on the NT Registry*. The Coriolis Group, 2000. ISBN 157610348X.

Online Information and Resources

The Internet provides a wide range of information on Windows NT/2000. There are a number of newsgroups from which you can gain valuable information as well as a variety of magazines. The following sections contain a few resources to get you started.

Newsgroups

Newsgroups are Internet based message boards that allow users to post messages or reply to messages that other people post. Newsgroups are descriptively named to give an idea of what the newsgroup is about. For instance, comp.os.netware, is the NetWare discussion group under the computer operating system section. There are thousands of newsgroups on almost every possible subject. Newsgroups can be a valuable resource for anyone involved in the IT industry. Almost every part of the IT industry has related newsgroups.

Newsgroups can be accessed via a newsreader such as those included with Microsoft Outlook or Netscape Communicator, or via a Web interface. Accessing newsgroups through a Web interface on a site such as **www.dejanews.com** usenet is the easiest way to get started. For more information on newsgroups, refer to Appendix C.

Here are some of the Microsoft Windows NT related newsgroups:

➤ **comp.os.ms-windows.nt.misc**

➤ **comp.os.ms-windows.nt.setup**

➤ **comp.os.ms-windows.nt.admin.misc**

➤ **comp.os.ms-windows.nt.admin.networking**

➤ **comp.os.ms-windows.nt.setup.hardware**

➤ **comp.os.ms-windows.nt.setup.misc**

Magazines and Journals

As you might expect, there are a great number of magazines and journals devoted to Windows NT. The trick is finding the one that best suits your needs and interests. Good magazines should be able to offer links, troubleshooting information, upcoming products and patches, and informative articles. There are many that fulfill this requirement:

➤ *Windows 2000 Magazine* (**www.winntmag.com**)—This magazine offers information on various aspects of Windows 2000, including networking. The articles included are comprehensive and can help administrators of all levels improve or troubleshoot their networks. The site is not free; subscription for this magazine is 14 issues (1 year)—US $49.95.

➤ *Ent Online* (**www.entmag.com**)—This site offers current headlines announcing industry highlights and provides up-to-date information on new products and features. The site offers a free subscription and a chance to subscribe to its twice a week newsletter, *Newsline*.

➤ *Element K Journals* (**www.elementkjournals.com/ewn**)—This magazine features articles, tips, and the very latest in the world of Windows NT. The articles are specific "how to" articles, giving detailed instructions, which makes them a very valuable resource. Access to these journals are not free; currently they are listed at $89 for 12 issues. Pay-per-view access for viewing articles is also offered.

➤ *Winmag.com* (**www.winmag.com/windows/win2knt.htm**)—This magazine offers articles, tips and tricks, reviews, and more. Log on and subscribe to its free newsletter.

Web Pages

Good network administrators will have a list of resources they can turn to when they need an answer. Having a list of Web sites to turn to can often make the difference between a good day and a bad day.

➤ *Newsnow* (**www.newsnow.co.uk/-NewsFeed.Tech.htm**)—The scroll bar on this page lets you access the latest news on a variety of products and platforms. Explore this site to find the latest news on Windows NT, service packs, and other relevant information. This is an excellent site to bookmark and an excellent site to use to keep in touch with changes in the industry.

➤ *Microsoft Technet* (**www.microsoft.com/technet**)—Got a problem? Go right to the source, Microsoft Technet. This site offers columns, reviews, and the latest news and products. Technet provides online support and access to a knowledge base that can help you solve a variety of networking problems.

➤ *Netadmintools.com* (**www.ntadmintools.com**)—Examine this site for some of the tricks of the trade brought to you by experienced programmers. It also offers utilities that could save you some valuable administrative time.

➤ *NT toolbox.com* (**www.nttoolbox.com**)—A great site for general Windows NT information and updates. It offers security information, downloads, and discussions. It's definitely worth a look and a bookmark.

Professional Associations

Professional Associations can frequently be helpful as a resource as well as a means to "meet" and associate yourself with other professionals with common interests in the field.

The Association of Windows NT System Professionals (NT*Pro), with over 33,000 members, provides a wealth of information and resources to those with an interest in Windows NT, Windows 2000, or related products. It offers a comprehensive Web site at **www.ntpro.org** that contains, among other things, a list of Windows NT usergroups in almost every area of the country. Membership in the association is open to any Windows NT computer professional and is free of charge.

Summary

Windows NT has become one of the most significant developments in PC networking to date. It's relative ease of use, coupled with its capability to fulfill a wide range of roles, has made it the first choice of companies all over the world. For those electing to pursue Windows NT skills, it is a solid career choice, and one in which the demand for skilled individuals shows little sign of diminishing.

Novell NetWare

Many companies are responsible for bringing PC networking to the masses, but none more so perhaps than Utah-based Novell, Inc. Its flagship network operating system, Novell NetWare, has been one of the best selling network operating systems of all time and continues to win over new users with its blend of speed, resilience, flexibility, and manageability.

Novell NetWare has for many years been regarded as the ultimate file and print server platform. Its speed, reliability, versatility, and support indicates that it is being used in a variety of situations, especially those where large amounts of network objects, such as users and groups, need to be managed.

Novell has traditionally been very strong in the government arena as well as other areas of public service. This is due in part to the fact that these were the first organizations to implement large scale networks many years ago at a time when the range of network operating systems capable of providing such services was limited.

Novell's continuing success can be attributed to a number of reasons. Many companies like the professional approach that Novell takes to its products, coupled with the fact that an extensive dealer and support network provides help and assistance when needed.

Why Use Novell NetWare?

There are a variety of reasons businesses use Novell's networking products. Many have been using these products for years and have upgraded as new versions have become available. Others have recently adopted these products, wanting to take advantage of their superb management capabilities and their reputation for reliability. A few reasons that a company or organization may choose to use Novell NetWare are discussed in the following sections.

Manageability

The key to understanding and managing a Novell network is to understand the "glue" that binds Novell networks together. The "glue" is Novell Directory Services (NDS). In line with Novell's vision of being an Internet services company, NDS was renamed NDS eDirectory for NetWare 5.1. NDS eDirectory is a database that holds information about practically every object on the network including users, printers, file servers, and many more. The NDS eDirectory database can be held, in whole or in part, on other servers around the network, allowing strategies for the improvement of speed and resilience to be implemented. It was version 4 of the NetWare operating system that first introduced this functionality. NDS eDirectory, though optimized to run on a NetWare system, can also run on other systems including Linux and Windows NT/2000.

NDS eDirectory's capability to hold and quickly retrieve information on vast numbers of objects has made it a popular choice in large corporate environments, where such a system can be fully utilized. Although NDS eDirectory is a reasonably complex system under the surface, Novell supplies administrators with all of the tools necessary to manage, troubleshoot, and control the NDS structure.

Cross Platform Support

An important part of Novell's strategy is that of providing cross platform support for networks. To this end, Novell has developed NDS into a product that can be deployed on other systems. Although Novell NetWare is deployed and used in a variety of situations, Novell acknowledges the fact that organizations will often choose to run more than one operating system. With a number of disparate systems, the management of users and objects becomes all the more complex and involved. NDS eDirectory effectively allows network administrators to bring the management of all their systems under one product.

Scalability

NDS eDirectory's capability to cope with literally millions of objects combined with being able to distribute the workload while fostering reliability and fault tolerance through replication, makes it the ideal choice for companies with large corporate networks that span countries or even continents. Equally, these features lend a degree of assurance to smaller users, who can rest safe in the knowledge that they are operating well within its limits on a network with just a few servers.

Performance

Although there are numerous tests pitting one operating system against the other, whatever the outcome, Novell NetWare is still regarded by many as the ultimate file and print server platform. When you combine these strengths with the flexibility and manageability of NDS eDirectory, you establish a strong case for businesses to use Novell NetWare.

Job Demand

Novell's maturity in the field suggests that the shortage for suitably qualified personnel in this area is perhaps not as acute as in other areas of networking. That said, there continues to be an abundance of (unfilled) positions available in the job market for those with Novell skills. As with any other field, hands-on experience is the most important asset you can have, a fact you should consider when starting your career search.

It is almost impossible to define what industry areas or company sizes are most suited to those seeking a NetWare related role because the product is used so widely and in such a diverse range of organizations.

Training Options and Resources

Novell has always been a pioneer in technical training. Its list of firsts includes being the first to introduce computer-based testing for certification programs and being the first to use simulations of real utilities in those exams. Novell has one of the most comprehensive technical training structures in the industry, but there are hundreds of other opportunities for people who want to learn about Novell products in practically every form imaginable.

Courses and Certifications

As mentioned previously, Novell offers a certification program that allows individuals to demonstrate their proficiency in Novell products. In fact, Novell was one of the first IT companies to create a certification program, when in 1989, they created the CNE program. There is now more than one certification track available for those wanting to train in Novell products. The base certification that Novell issues is that of Certified Novell Administrator (CNA). The next level of certification is the CNE, which can be pursued along a number of different paths. Those with enough interest and enthusiasm can take their studies even further and attain their Master Certified Novell Engineer (MCNE) certification. Full details on the requirements of all these programs can be found on the Novell Education Web site at **education.novell.com**.

In addition to Novell's own training programs, there are a great number of other training options, although most are still designed to prepare you for taking Novell's certification exams. For a list of training companies in your area, check the Yellow Pages under Computers - Training. As with Microsoft, Novell designates its training partners through the use of an accreditation scheme. Novell Authorized Education Centers (NAECs) provide courses that last between 2 and 5 days that are aimed at people who have prior experience in the computer field or those with some prior knowledge of Novell products. Novell Authorized Education Partners (NAEP) are academic institutions that have partnered with Novell to teach Novell curriculum.

Online Training

Novell, like other manufacturers, provides its own Web-based training programs that can help you prepare for the certification exams. These authorized online courses are offered through Novell's partner program. For more information on Novell's online course offerings, visit **www.novell.com/education/notp**.

In addition to Novell's training services, many other companies offer online training courses in Novell products.

Self-Study Options

Learning about Novell NetWare on a self-study basis is a viable alternative to other training methods. There is a wide range of books available that can help you study and some excellent training resources that can be obtained from sources on the Internet. For home study, you will need to set up a small network, so that you can learn about aspects of the product by trying out procedures and performing troubleshooting scenarios. To create a small network, you will need at least two PCs, one that can be configured as a server, and another that can be configured as a workstation. Additional PCs can be a benefit in certain scenarios, but in most cases, two PCs will be adequate.

The product itself requires a moderate level of hardware to run, and the installation process, if done correctly, forms a valuable part of your learning process. NetWare software can be obtained from Novell. Rather than buy a full copy, which costs hundreds of dollars, Novell makes demonstration and evaluation versions of the software available at low costs. Further information, including hardware requirements, can be found at **www.novell.com/products/netware/ evaluation.html**.

5

Although NetWare does come with utilities that allow management tasks to be performed from the server, most are normally performed from a workstation, which means that you will need an additional PC for these tasks. An additional PC is also necessary to fully understand how a NetWare network operates from a client perspective.

As with any self-study scenario, gaining hands-on experience with the product makes all the difference when it comes to taking exams or performing in the workplace. The creation of a small network using a PC as a workstation and a Novell file server will go a long way toward helping you understand how a NetWare network functions.

Additional Resources

Finding more information about Novell NetWare is an easy task. There are countless resources available on the Internet, through newsgroups, and in your local bookstore. The following sections provide some resources that you may find useful as you start to look at Novell NetWare in more depth.

Novell NetWare Jargon Buster

As you discover more information about Novell NetWare, you may encounter unfamiliar phrases or terms. The following list contains a few of the most common terms used when discussing NetWare along with a brief explanation of each:

➤ *NDS*—A database that holds information about objects such as users, groups, printers and servers, that are on the network. The NDS database can be divided into smaller parts (known as partitioning) and distributed among different servers on the network (a process called replication).

➤ *Bindery*—Before NDS, Novell NetWare operated on a one server, one database principle. The database, although it was comprised of three files, was collectively referred to as the Bindery. The Bindery contained information on the users, groups and printers, and print queues on the server.

➤ *ZENworks*—Although ZENworks (ZEN stands for Zero Effort Networking) is actually a satellite product of the main Novell operating system, it is worth mentioning because many companies using Novell NetWare choose to use ZENworks in light of the fact that it is tightly integrated with NDS. ZENWorks provides a range of tools that are designed to reduce administrative overhead of workstations and other network devices on a NetWare network.

➤ *NetWare Administrator*—A workstation-based utility that allows the administrator to perform much of the administration of the network.

➤ *NetWare Management Portal (NMP)*—New to NetWare 5.1, the NMP is a browser-based utility that lets you perform a wide range of network administration tasks.

Books

There are many books available on Novell NetWare and its associated products and technologies. The following sections contain some suggested titles that you may find useful.

Beginner Book Titles

➤ Lindberg, Kelley J. P., and Kevin Shafer. *Novell's NetWare 5 Basics.* IDG Books Worldwide, 1999. ISBN 0764545639.

➤ Currid, Cheryl C., and Mark A. Eggleston. *Novell's Introduction to Networking.* IDG Books Worldwide, 2000. ISBN 0764547003.

Advanced Books

➤ Kuo, Peter, and Jim Henderson. *Novell's Guide to Troubleshooting NDS.* IDG Books Worldwide, 1999. ISBN 0764545795.

➤ Kearns, David, Brian Iverson. *The Complete Guide to Novell Directory Services.* Sybex, 1998. ISBN 0782118232.

➤ Gaskin, James. *Mastering NetWare 5.1.* Sybex, 2000. ISBN 078212772X.

Reference Books

➤ Shafer, Kevin. *Novell's Encyclopedia of Networking.* IDG Books Worldwide, 1997. ISBN 0764545116.

➤ Sant'Angelo, Rick. *Novell's Guide to Troubleshooting NetWare 5.* IDG Books Worldwide, 1999. ISBN 0764545582.

➤ Lindberg, Kelley J. P. *Novell's NetWare 5 Administrator's Handbook.* IDG Books Worldwide, 1980. ISBN 0764545469.

Online Information and Resources

As with other areas of technology, the Internet provides an almost bewildering array of information on Novell NetWare. Many of the resources mentioned in the following sections are Internet-based and free, providing a great way to gather more information without committing yourself.

Newsgroups

The following are Novell newsgroups you might find interesting:

➤ **comp.os.netware**

➤ **comp.os.netware.security**

➤ **comp.os.netware.misc**

➤ **novell.administratorforwinnt**

➤ **novell.directoryservices**

In addition to these groups, Novell maintains a complete set of related newsgroups at **forums.novell.com**. The site allows the groups to be accessed via a Web browser or traditional news reader.

Magazines and Journals

There are a number of Novell related magazines and journals available, both electronically and in print. The following list contains a few that you may want to investigate:

➤ *NetWare Connection* (**www.nwconnection.com**)—A magazine aimed at Novell network administrators. A great resource for NetWare administrators.

➤ *Novell Appnotes* (**http://developer.novell.com/research**)—Novell's monthly technical journal for network design, implementation, and monitoring.

➤ *Inside NetWare* (**www.elementkjournals.com/inw**)—A comprehensive magazine covering the latest and greatest from Novell. It also includes useful articles and columns. The cost of the magazine is $90 for 12 issues.

Web Pages

➤ *Novell Corporate home page* (**www.novell.com**)—This site is the main source for everything new in the world of Novell. Browse this site to find the latest products, reviews, business and corporate information, news, and press releases.

➤ *Novell Support Page* (**http://support.novell.com**)—This site offers drivers, downloads, a knowledgebase, and product specific support. When troubleshooting a network, it is a good place to start.

➤ *Netwarefiles.com* (**www.netwarefiles.com**)—This site is a great place to go if you are looking for NetWare utilities that can make your network run smoother and your life a little bit easier. The site also offers a newsletter full of articles and a few tips and tricks for network administrators.

➤ *NDS Cool Solutions home page* (**www.novell.com/coolsolutions/nds**)—This site provides an informal medium for the communication of technical information regarding Novell's NDS system. As well as useful articles on new and existing products, it features a Q&A section, a "from the trenches" column.

Professional Associations

For those interested in finding out more about Novell and linking up with like minded individuals, look no further than NetWare Users International (NUI). NUI acts as a focal point for Novell user groups all over the country, and indeed the world. Membership is free and open to anyone by simply completing the online registration form. As well as special offers on training products, members can also get discounts on Novell partners products and even car rentals! All members receive a free technical resource CD when they join. For more information, visit the NUI home page at **www.novell.com/community/nui**.

Summary

Novell and its networking products have played an important part in the networking industry up to the present time and will surely be a major factor in the future. Novell is continually evolving as a company, and this proactive approach increases its presence of networking products in businesses and institutions all over the world. Even if you choose another technology area as your primary focus, sooner or later you are likely to come across a Novell product.

Unix and Linux

In computing terms, Unix is old. Effectively it is the granddaddy of all network operating systems. Developed initially by AT&T labs in the early 1970s, Unix was designed as a network operating system for computer scientists by computer scientists. Rather than having a graphical interface, command-line utilities with short, often meaningless names were, and still are, used to manage the system. It was fast, clean, and purposeful. Pretty was not a requirement.

As the product developed, it became a popular choice in universities, colleges, and governmental departments, where the need for a high-performance operating system that ran on a modest level of hardware was greatest. Because of its use in these environments, it became the basis for today's Internet, which is another reason for its continuing level of popularity.

It took some years for the Unix operating system to permeate fully from the educational and governmental institutions into the corporate server room, but it did happen. Businesses that had traditionally run mainframe computers liked the fact that there were versions of Unix that ran on minicomputers and microcomputers, yet still offered high levels of performance and reliability. This fact was the main reason businesses then, as they do today, used Unix as a platform to run very large and often very mission critical applications.

There are many different versions of Unix available, but most of the changes between versions have been subtle. These minor changes have enabled individuals skilled in one version of Unix to learn another version with relative ease. Much of this portability is due to the fact that Unix employs the use of programming languages, particularly C, to create functionality on the system. Anyone becoming involved with Unix from a systems administration perspective will almost certainly have to have a good understanding of the C language and programming principles in general to get on.

In 1994, the entire landscape of the computer industry was changed by a man named Linus Torvalds when he introduced a network operating system kernel called Linux. Nowadays, the low (or no) cost nature of Linux, and the fact that it runs on almost any modern PC, has attracted interest from users everywhere. Another reason that it is gaining such a foothold in the industry is that many hardware and software manufacturers have recognized Linux as a viable operating system and have started to create products that are compatible.

The fact that Unix and Linux are now competing against products such as Windows NT/2000 and Novell NetWare means that they have had to adapt in terms of packaging, marketing, and appearance. Even so, both platforms have managed to remain reasonably true to their roots, remembering that when all is said and done, they have a lot going for them.

More than with any other network operating system, those who choose to learn and become involved with Unix or Linux are joining a community of like minded people, many of whom have a generally unique and "open" view of technology. This sense of community appeals to many people and serves as a valuable tool, especially to those who are new to the IT industry.

Why Use Unix?

Companies usually choose a Unix system for one reason—because they need to. Either they choose it for its unparalleled reliability or because they need a system with the very highest levels of performance. Either way, they get exactly these features when they install almost any one of the currently available versions of Unix on their systems. However, utilizing Unix is not a simple undertaking. Unix is not an operating system for the fainthearted.

Unlike operating systems like NetWare and Windows NT/2000, Unix systems require a degree of customization, tuning, and configuration to maximize their capabilities. Also, the command-line nature of the operating system does little to soothe the nerves of a small business owner who is looking for a quick way to get up and running. These facts make Unix unattractive to small and medium-sized businesses that have limited technical support available. So, to a large extent, Unix is predominately used in the domains of big business, government, education and those in Internet related businesses.

Very powerful applications, often costing tens or even hundreds of thousands of dollars, are written to run on Unix's well understood and robust architecture. Many of these applications are not household names, and you won't find them on the shelf at your local computer store. They are highly specialized applications designed for specific purposes, such as Computer Aided Design (CAD), controlling industrial machinery, and advanced graphics. As stated earlier, businesses use Unix for one reason—because they need to.

However, applications for a Unix system don't have to be expensive. There are literally thousands of applications available, many of which are free, that can be run on a Unix system. They include games, productivity packages, such as word processors and spreadsheets, products for scientific uses, and utilities galore. All of them written to the same basic rules that make Unix computing what it is—make the best use of the hardware and make the best use of the operating system.

Why Use Linux?

Though not as prevalent in a corporate environment as Windows NT, Novell NetWare, or even Unix, Linux is beginning to gain a strong foothold in corporate computing. The fact that Linux runs on hardware that other operating systems cannot lays strongly in its favor, although the increasingly rapid drop in computer hardware costs has begun to negate this advantage somewhat. Linux is a low cost, fully featured, secure, resilient network operating system that provides many, if not all, of the functions a modern business requires. It is particularly suited for operation as a Web server and in Internet security applications, areas that have contributed greatly to the product's overall growth.

For those new to the networking industry, Linux represents a particularly interesting opportunity as more and more businesses want to use it, but often have no Linux related skills already in-house. Although employers may not hire employees directly for their Linux knowledge, it makes an interesting addition to an individual's skill set, especially if the organization has a use for other networking skills that the individual possesses.

For a low cost product, there is nothing cheap about the range of features that Linux provides. However, support by third-party manufacturers may not be as good as that for other operating systems, such as Windows NT. Manufacturers are catching on to the fact that Linux is here to stay, and if they want to stay in the game, they had better start producing compatible products.

Is Linux Really Free?

The answer to this often asked question is yes, Linux is free. Part of the driving force behind the Linux movement is that of open source software, which means everyone has access to the source code, the actual ingredients that make up the basic operating system. The problem is that if you don't know how to mix the ingredients in the right way, the recipe will fail. So, to make things easier, a number of companies have created Linux operating systems of their own variety. These products, which are known as distributions, are sold by the companies to the general public, but the software itself is still technically free. Effectively, by buying a distribution of Linux, you are choosing to pay a company for collecting all of the necessary components, packaging them, and in some cases providing support for the product.

So, if it's free, or at the very worst low cost, why isn't everyone using it? The answer to that question is not an easy one. Without being too controversial, there are a number of reasons Linux is not steamrollering Novell and Microsoft out of the network operating system marketplace (though some people would have you believe that it is). First, there is a simple matter of support. Linux skills are in short supply, as are those for Unix. Businesses only feel comfortable implementing a new operating system if they are able to find capable support staff. Second, there is the issue of association. Microsoft particularly, and to a lesser extent Novell, are both massive software companies with billion dollar turnovers and armies of shareholders. Their products come with slick marketing and packaging, and give those that install them a warm fuzzy feeling that if things go awry, there is backup available. It would be incorrect to say that there isn't any support staff available for Linux, and it would be wrong to say that the companies distributing Linux are not very professional and very supportive of their customers, but it all boils down to the perception of the consumer.

One last factor is this. There is an old saying in the IT industry, "No one ever got fired for buying IBM." This refers to the fact that in the early days of computing, IBM equipment was seen as a safe choice, even though there were other products available. The same, perhaps, can be said of Linux. Decision makers need to have a very compelling reason for not using one of the established network operating systems currently available and, surprisingly, the fact that Linux is low cost may actually work against it in this respect. After all, businesses have gotten used to paying for software. When they are offered something at a very low cost, they immediately start looking for the catch.

What's the Difference between Unix and Linux?

Having various versions of Unix available made it difficult in the past for software manufacturers to write programs that would work on all versions. To combat this problem, a standard called POSIX was created, allowing the companies that write Unix as well as the companies that write the software to have a common standard. Linux is a fully POSIX compliant operating system, which is said to be "Unix-like," although it does not actually use any of the programming code from other versions of Unix. Unlike Unix, which is a commercially available product, Linux is written, improved, and developed under the umbrella of the Free Software Foundations GNU project. The Free Software Foundations GNU project even enjoys charitable organization status.

Job Demand

Demand for individuals with Unix skills has been strong ever since it was introduced as a commercial computing platform. This demand continues, although it has now been joined by an equally unmet demand for Linux skills. This trend looks set to continue, if not increase, as use of Unix and Linux as a platform for Internet, and a multitude of other applications continues to grow. In fact, the limit to the commercial growth of Linux and Unix systems is seen by some as a symptom of the lack of availability of staff.

Another factor that may influence job demand in the Unix and Linux area is that of organization. As the high profile of some companies, such as Novell and Microsoft, draw people toward their products and into a career supporting them, the Unix and Linux market profile is somewhat less organized. Indirectly, this lack of exposure may mean that many people entering the networking industry don't even consider learning Linux or Unix at first. The lack of experience using these products probably won't affect most people in either the short or long term, but who's to say that they could have not had an equally or even more rewarding career as a Unix or Linux systems administrator.

Training Options and Resources

The fact that Unix has been around for such a long time, coupled with the eagerness of many companies to jump on the Linux bandwagon, means that anyone trying to track down some suitable training resources should not have too many problems.

There are a wide range of resources available that accommodate all levels of learning. In this field more than others, you should be wary of what you are getting for your money and what is expected of you. For example, if you are considering an instructor-led course, make sure the course is appropriate for your level of knowledge. Halfway through the first morning of a $1,500 course is no time to realize that you need to know how to program in C!

Courses and Certifications

The somewhat informal nature of the Unix and Linux industry means that although there are a number of certification programs available, there is no single outstanding certification. In a way, this is in keeping with the overall ethic behind Unix and Linux, but it does no favors for someone starting out in the industry who wants to choose and pursue the correct certification path. For more information on some certification programs for Linux products visit **www.examcram.com**.

Every organization that offers a certification program either runs courses themselves or has a network of training providers that does. In addition, you will find that nearly all of them produce supporting materials to accompany their certification programs. It is also worth checking your local colleges or universities for programs; you may find that they run part-time courses that are either Unix-based or involve Unix as a component.

The choice of whether or not to formalize your training into a certification is yours alone. However, those starting out in a career in IT usually find that any "supporting evidence" of their skills are very useful when looking for a job. Just be aware that certification tests are expensive. Only take them when you are ready and feel confident that you will pass.

Online Training

As you would expect, there are a variety of Unix and Linux courses available on the Internet. Both Unix and Linux can seem a little daunting to those new to these operating systems, so the ability to obtain the help of an experienced instructor at a fraction of the cost of classroom-based study makes online courses an attractive alternative.

There are more online training providers than can be practically listed in this section. To find a representative selection, use any Internet Web search engine. Available programs range from simple self-paced, Web-based courses to fully interactive virtual classroom scenarios.

More information on selecting an online learning course is provided in Part III of this book.

Self-Study Options

For Unix and Linux, perhaps more than any other network operating system, hands-on experience is vital to the learning process. Although you may choose to supplement your studies with a range of other materials available, it is the time spent at the keyboard that yields the greatest return in your learning experience. Setting up a Linux or Unix system at home is a relatively simple task, however, you are likely to find it hard work if you attempt it with no other help at all.

Linux especially can be obtained free or purchased for very little and installed on hardware that would be considered obsolete for other operating systems, such as Windows NT and Novell NetWare. The easiest way to set yourself up is to buy a copy of a Linux distribution, sit down with a cup of coffee, and follow the instructions provided. Even though the documentation that comes with the distributions is normally good, you may want to get some additional information as well. If you want to combine two steps into one, buying one of the many training kits that come complete with a distribution is good option. It eliminates the problem of buying a book for one version, and then purchasing the software for a different version (sounds improbable, but it can easily happen).

If you prefer to learn Unix rather than Linux, a good way to begin is by using one of the free Unix distributions that are available. One of the most prevalent is FreeBSD, a Unix operating system designed to run on PCs. More information on FreeBSD can be found on the FreeBSD Web site at **www.freebsd.org**. Along with information on the product, there are resources on the site that can help you with your self-study program.

As mentioned previously, once you feel that your knowledge has reached a suitable level, you can take the step of formalizing it through a number of certification programs available.

Additional Resources

Fortunately, the abundance of information on Unix and Linux makes the task of finding valuable resources particularly easy. The following sections contain some resources that can help you get started.

Unix and Linux Jargon Buster

As you find more information on Unix and Linux, you may come across terms that you are unfamiliar with. To make the information you read easier to understand, the following list provides some brief descriptions of a handful of terms that you may see during your search:

➤ *X-Window System*—A graphical-based application that is used to interface with a Unix system.

➤ *Kernel*—The operating system component of a Unix or Linux system. The kernel provides the interface between the applications and the computer hardware.

➤ *Daemon*—A program that runs in the background processing on a Unix system.

➤ *Vi*—A program used on Unix systems to edit files. Vi is not the only editing program available, but it is widely used.

➤ *Shell*—Part of a Unix operating system that accepts user commands and passes them to resources and applications. There are various different types of shells that can be used.

➤ *Root*—In terminology, root refers to the most powerful user account on the system. The root user can perform all actions on the system. Root is also used to refer to the top of a directory structure.

Books

A wide range of books are available on Unix and Linux, however, care should be taken to ensure that the book you buy is of the correct level for you to gain maximum benefit from it. Many books represent general information on the operating systems, and equally available are those that explore very specific issues, such as security or programming. For more input on a suitable book for your needs, posting a polite message on one of the Unix or Linux related newsgroups normally brings forth a number of suggestions.

Beginner Book Titles

➤ Peek, Jerry D., Grace Todino, and John Strang. *Learning the Unix Operating System (Nutshell Handbook)*. O'Reilly & Associates, 1997. ISBN 1565923901.

➤ Levine, John R., and Margaret Levine Young. *Unix For Dummies*. IDG Books Worldwide, 1998. ISBN 0764504193.

➤ Dawson, Terry, Olaf Kirch, and Andy Oram (editor). *Linux Network Administrator's Guide, 2d ed*. O'Reilly & Associates, 2000. ISBN 1565924002.

➤ Smith, Roderick W. *Linux: Networking for Your Office*. Sams, 1999. ISBN 0672317923.

Advanced Books

➤ Leblanc, Dee-Ann. *Linux System Administration Black Book*. Coriolis Publishing, 2000. ISBN 1576104192.

➤ Poniatowski, Martin. *Unix Users Handbook*. Prentice Hall Computer Books, 2000. ISBN 0130270199.

➤ Mann, Scott, Ellen L. Mitchell. *Linux System Security: The Administrator's Guide to Open Source Security Tools*. Prentice Hall, 1999. ISBN 0130158070.

➤ Asbury, Stephen. *Enterprise Linux at Work*. John Wiley & Sons, 2000. ISBN 0471363499.

5

Reference Books

➤ Rosen, Kenneth H., and Doug Host. *Unix: The Complete Reference (Unix Tools)*. Osborne/McGraw-Hill, 1999. ISBN 007211892X.

➤ Purcell, John (Editor). *Linux the Complete Reference*. Walnut Creek, 1999. ISBN 1571761659.

➤ Dent, Jack, Tony Gaddis. *Guide to Unix using Linux*. Course Technology, 1999. ISBN 076001096X.

➤ Volderking, Patrick, Kevin Reichard. *Linux System Commands*. IDG Books Worldwide, 2000. ISBN 0764546694.

Online Information and Resources

Not surprisingly, Unix and Linux's relationship with the Internet makes for a rich hunting ground for more information on these products. Listed in the following sections are just a few of the resources available. For even more information, simply type "Linux" or "Unix" into an Internet search engine.

Newsgroups

Here are some of the Unix and Linux related newsgroups:

➤ **comp.os.unix**

➤ **comp.unix.admin**

➤ **comp.unix.question**

➤ **comp.os.linux**

➤ **comp.os.linux.admin**

➤ **comp.os.linux.questions**

Magazines and Journals

➤ *Sys Admin* (**www.samag.com**)—A journal for Unix system administrators. The journal includes articles, newsletters, utilities, links to other resources, a buyers guide, and more. The subscription price is $39 for 12 issues, but well worth it for those who need to have the latest news and information regarding Unix administration.

➤ *The Linux Journal* (**www2.linuxjournal.com**)—A comprehensive monthly magazine written for anyone interested in the Linux operating systems and its associated applications. The magazine includes product reviews, book reviews, a Take Command section that discusses specific commands, and a Linux Apprentice section aimed at those new to the operating system. Subscription cost is $22 for one year and can be completed online. Alternatively, you should be able to track down a copy in your local bookstore or newsstand.

Web Pages

There are so many high quality Linux and Unix related Web sites on the Internet that to select just a few seems unfair to the others. However, you have to start somewhere, so contained in the following list are some links to a handful of sites. Think of these sites as starting points on your quest for more information.

➤ *Unix Guru Universe* (**www.ugu.com**)—This site is essentially a page for Unix administrators. The information and links provided on this site will be an asset to both the seasoned administrator and to the beginner. This site is a great place to start your Unix exploration.

➤ *Unix World* (**www.networkcomputing.com/unixworld**)—This home page provides information on Unix and Linux systems. The site has an array of useful resources including articles, tutorials, book reviews, and a research center. It, like many other sites mentioned in this list, also offers a free email newsletter service.

➤ *RootPrompt* (**http://rootprompt.org**)—This site includes in depth discussions and detailed tutorials on various aspects of Unix and Linux systems. It also includes links to the Unix and Linux webring, which contains more information on the two products than one person could ever want to read. Not only a good place to read about Unix and Linux issues, but a great place to start your Internet journey for related information.

➤ *Linux online homepage* (**www.linux.org**)—Those looking for more information on Linux would do well to make this site their first stop. As well as lots of information on Linux including what it is and how it works, there are links to more information and details of Linux user groups. This site is a must visit for anyone wanting to learn more about the Linux phenomenon.

➤ *Linux Today* (**http://linuxtoday.com**)—Visit this site for up-to-date news on what's happening in the Linux world. This site contains information on the latest developments affecting the Linux platform.

Professional Associations

USENIX is the Advanced Computing Systems Association (**www.usenix.org**). Although not specifically for Unix related systems, it is a magnet for Unix related topics. USENIX is also the home of the Systems Administrators Guild (SAGE), an organization specifically targeted at computer systems administrators. A membership fee is required to join both organizations, the details of which are provided on the Web site.

In addition to USENIX, there are many more localized user groups across the world.

Summary

Although the popularity of Unix has never been in question, the recent interest in Linux and the continuing rapid growth of the Internet has created a strong demand for related skills. The open nature of the platform as well as the software, coupled with the strong following that accompanies them, ensures that Unix and Linux will be major growth areas in the IT industry of the future.

A Network Administrator's View

What is it like to spend your life administering a network? No one can provide you with a better idea of what is involved than those who are currently spending their days troubleshooting connectivity issues and dealing with system problems. The following sections consist of two interviews with network administrators from two very different environments. From their answers, you will see that although network administration as a job is much the same wherever you go, the actual work environment can influence daily tasks.

Interview One

Marlon Gordon works for a financial institution in London, England. This interview was completed during one his (rare) quiet moments. The objective was to find out how he felt about his job and also to see what advice he could offer for those starting out in a career in networking.

What is your job title, and how long have you been doing this job?

[Marlon]: My actual title is Senior Network Analyst. I have been in this job now for just over a year.

What are your main duties?

[Marlon]: I generally look after the network, but also spend a lot of my time evaluating and implementing new solutions. More often than not, the products offer new features, but we are increasingly looking for ways to speed up the network and reduce administrative overhead.

What systems are you currently working with?

[Marlon]: We have a number of Novell 4.11 file servers, which we use for file and print services as well as email, intranet servers, and Internet access. We are also currently evaluating NetWare 5.1 as an upgrade. I also work with Tandem systems, which interface with our PC systems and Windows NT server.

What qualifications or certifications do you hold?

[Marlon]: I have college diplomas in electronics and computer maintenance as well as a college degree in Information Technology. I have started working towards my CNE certification, but between work and home I am having trouble finding time to study. Even so, I have managed to pass a few exams along the way, and I am determined to finish it one way or another.

How long have you been working in IT, and how did you get started?

[Marlon]: Ten years. My first job was repairing PCs, and it just started from there.

What hours do you normally work? If you work evenings and weekends, do you get paid for it?

[Marlon]: Things are very busy right now, so I am working somewhere in the region of 72 hours a week. I do get paid if I work on the weekend, and I also get a day off if I work on both a Saturday or a Sunday.

What do you find most interesting about your job?

[Marlon]: I really enjoy evaluating and implementing new products, and then seeing how those new products have an effect on the business. It can be very rewarding in that respect.

What is the least interesting aspect of your job?

[Marlon]: I am probably one of the happiest IT guys in the world because anything to do with my job I find interesting.

Do you consider your job to be stressful?

[Marlon]: There are no words to explain how stressful my job can be.

Do you work with other people or alone?

[Marlon]: I tend to do a lot of work on my own, although because of the amount of changes there have been recently, it's made it necessary for me to request some assistance. I have just taken on a trainee and have been busy training him.

If you could change one thing about your job, what would it be?

[Marlon]: The hours that I work don't leave a lot of time for anything else. If I could change one thing, it would be to have to work less hours.

Can you see yourself staying in this area of the IT industry, or would you like to try something different?

[Marlon]: I really enjoy the technology I work with and the environment I work in. If I were to change anything, I would probably like to remain doing what I am doing, but involve a bit of travel.

What do you consider to be the most challenging part of your job?

[Marlon]: Without a doubt, it is the implementation projects. More often than not they have to be implemented on short timelines and have to work 100 percent from day one. It can make for some exciting times.

What advice would you give to someone starting out in IT?

[Marlon]: My advice is to try to find a company that will take you on as a junior and train you to be certified in one of the platform technologies (Microsoft MCSE or Novell CNE). You will find that most companies offer certified training nowadays as part of the overall package. Most of all, good luck!

Interview Two—A Different Perspective

After speaking to Marlon, an opportunity arose to chat with Dave Strome, who works in the networking division of a software company in Canada. He was asked the same questions as Marlon, so that their different views could be compared.

What is your job title, and how long have you been doing this job?

[Dave]: My job title is Technical Analyst, or you can use my new title, Exchange Administrator. I've been doing this job for three years.

What are your main duties?

[Dave]: I manage three Windows NT corporate domains and one Windows NT resource domain. Those domains consist of approximately 30 servers and 180 client computers. I maintain all server functions including security, system stability, and uptime. I also coordinate all corporate projects for IS and act as primary upper-tier technical resource for all email, domain, OS, Internet, and security issues.

What systems are you currently working with?

[Dave]: Our systems currently consist of SQL 6.5 and 7.0, Windows NT Server 4.0, Windows 2000 Server and Advanced Server, Exchange 5.5, Linux, Internet Information Server, Proxy Server, Terminal Server, Windows NT Workstation 4.0, Windows 2000 Professional, and Windows 95/98.

What qualifications or certifications do you hold?

[Dave]: I am currently a Microsoft Certified Professional, although I only have one more exam to take before becoming an MCSE.

How long have you been working in IT?

[Dave]: I have been in the IT industry for about six years.

What hours do you normally work? If you work evenings and weekends, do you get paid for it?

[Dave]: I work a standard day: 9 to 5. Periodically, I work evenings or weekends to perform server maintenance. In my position, I have been routinely given days off for work done in "overtime." I have not been paid extra for my time.

What do you find most interesting about your job?

[Dave]: The ability to dive into new technologies constantly. I sometimes think of it as a multimillion dollar toy store. Although shaping the new technologies into a useful service for the corporation is even more interesting.

What is the least interesting aspect of your job?

[Dave]: Backups.

Do you consider your job to be stressful?

[Dave]: On average, the job is moderately stressful. Some days are completely routine, where there's no stress at all and everything's running fine. However, if any service that is required by users for any amount of time goes down, it costs the company money, and it can be extremely stressful if the service is unable to start back up immediately. Sometimes it makes you start wondering when the pink slip will arrive.

Do you work with other people or alone?

[Dave]: I work with an excellent IS team of six people including myself.

If you could change one thing about your job, what would it be?

[Dave]: If anything, I'd like to see the lack of respect for the IT industry become less widespread. People never really notice people in IT until something goes wrong. Unfortunately, we've become the psychiatrists of computing, listening to people's problems and how those problems interrupt their work. That is why we are here, to fix the problems. But the other 99 percent of the time, we're actually making life easier. My hope is that the general public will see that someday.

Can you see yourself staying in this area of the IT industry, or would you like to try something different?

[Dave]: I will definitely be in the IT industry for at least the next 10 to 15 years. There is no other industry that I know of that changes so quickly and provides so much interest. Although we're all in the same IT industry, the industry itself keeps changing every few years to accommodate new requirements and technologies. This fact in itself ensures that I'll never be bored, even if I'm in the same industry 30 years from now (although I'd like to be retired before then.)

What do you consider to be the most challenging part of your job?

[Dave]: Running headlong into the unknown. Every day I run into something that I either don't know or don't understand. Because of my position, I am constantly researching new technologies and methods. Keeping ahead of the requirements of the corporation requires me to constantly research and implement new technologies to ensure that the corporation is running as efficiently as possible.

What advice would you give to someone who is starting out in IT?

[Dave]: Expect to start lower on the ladder than you think you are capable of. Before you can progress, you need to prove that you're good at what you do. No matter how good you are at technical aspects and fundamentals, it takes years of experience to solidify troubleshooting skills. Most importantly, don't take a know-it-all attitude. That's the fastest way to lose respect in this industry. Admit you don't know, and someone will show you. They will also respect you for admitting it.

6

Careers in PC and Computer Support

Murphy's Law states that if anything can go wrong it usually will. Though it is unlikely that this statement was inspired by Murphy's personal computer troubles, it certainly captures the sentiment of computer users worldwide. At times, it seems that computers have a will of their own. One moment you are happily typing and printing, the next your PC is flashing warning messages, shutting down, and refusing to reboot.

Computer systems in general are becoming ever more complex. The generic "PC" that won the Time Magazine award back in 1982 bears only a physical resemblance to those now sitting on millions of desks and in homes all over the world. Few industries have experienced the combination of growth and progression that the IT industry has over the last 30 years, and a great deal of the driving force behind that trend has been the PC.

For many years, consumers pushed hardware manufacturers for faster and more powerful hardware. Now, at the beginning of the twenty-first century, with the advent of 1GHz personal computers, people are finally able to buy a system that is literally as fast as they need. For the time being at least. The one truth of PCs and technology in general is that there will always be someone or something that demands faster and more powerful hardware.

But a PC is so much more than hardware. Although the term personal computer is a definition of a hardware device, from the perspective of a PC support person, a PC is the hardware as well as the software broken down into their individual components. These components include the operating system, the application software, the input and output peripherals, such as printers and scanners, and just about any other component that can be put in, connected to, wired to, or set up with a personal computer. In fact, for many PC support people, their role transcends working with the actual PC and starts to touch on subjects such as ergonomics, health, and safety at work.

As if all of these areas were not enough, PC support technicians also have to work with products that are released at a furious rate by manufacturers so impatient to get their product to market that there are invariably errors or bugs in the products. As a PC technician, you not only have to keep up with the relentless release of new products, but you also have to learn what is wrong with them.

The role of a PC support person is multifaceted. Whether it is a conflict with computer software or a hardware malfunction, eventually, you are most certainly going to encounter a problem with your computer. Sleep easy; there is help at hand.

The Difference between PC Support and Networking

In this book, PC support and networking have been split into two distinct areas. The reasons for this are based upon the fact that they are two separate areas of IT, even though there may be areas in which the two are so closely related that the definitions become blurred. For the purposes of this book, PC support is defined as the task of supporting and maintaining PC hardware, workstation operating systems, and application software. Networking is defined as maintaining file servers, network operating system software, and network infrastructure components. There may be times when a PC support person is called upon to perform basic network administration tasks, just as there may be times when a network administrator is called to attend to an application software problem on a PC. Even so, the requirements for each area of IT are different, as is the knowledge needed to effectively operate in each case.

6

What Is a PC Technician?

Fundamentally, the term computer technician is another way of saying computer "repairman," a label not appreciated by some, but one that accurately describes the job. PC technicians are the tinkerers of the IT industry, working as much with their hands as their head. As mentioned previously in this book, repair and maintenance is the avenue many IT professionals use to enter the industry, and many other IT disciplines require rudimentary troubleshooting skills. But make no mistake; good technicians who make a career of it are born not made.

Good PC support personnel are a blend of two elements: technical excellence and communicative ability. In fact, in many environments, the PC support person's ability to communicate with a client is almost, and in some cases, more important than their technical ability. Of all the career fields in IT, PC support probably requires the highest level of communication. Those who are already working as PC support technicians will tell you it is more than the ability to accurately absorb and relate information to and from a customer or client. It is more of a case of sociability.

Imagine this scenario, your car is not running properly, so you take it to a garage. When you go to the service reception, the guy behind the counter asks what's wrong with the car. Your response, depending on how much you know about cars, will range between the completely informative to "there's an odd knock." As far as you are concerned, your job is done. But this is where the good mechanic takes over by asking probing questions, such as "When does the knock happen?", "How fast do you have to go to get it to make that noise?" and so on. The point is that he is doing you as much of a favor as he is himself. The more he can find out from you, the more likely he is going to find the problem. Apart from making him look good, these questions also save you money because the less time he spends on the problem the less you get charged. These are the qualities that make the difference between a good mechanic and a great mechanic.

A comparison between the mechanic and the PC support person works because of a certain commonality. PC support people, like mechanics, work with complex objects owned, used, and not understood by millions of people. Owners of cars and computers rely on specialists to fix the problems that owners cannot.

A PC support person's role differs from the mechanic's role in that generally, mechanics have the luxury of working on a vehicle without the customer sitting next to them. You have to wonder how long many mechanics would last if faced with that situation. PC support staff often have the rather unenviable task of working on equipment while the customer is looking on. This means that having excellent communication skills are even more important because you have to hold a conversation with someone while you are trying to perform a complex task. The upside is that, like a mechanic, you get to suck the air through your teeth and announce in a mock sympathetic tone how expensive the repair is likely to be.

PC support technicians interact with people to a much greater extent than their counterparts in networking, programming, and other areas of IT. This is because PC support people are the ones who maintain the "windows" to the systems operated and built by these other people in IT. Effectively, PC support people are the faces that are associated with computing in general.

The other curious characteristic associated with PC support people is that they are expected to know not just how to fix PCs, but also how to fix any other piece of technical equipment, be it a phone system, a fax machine, a video player, or a photocopier. Although it is quite reasonable to back away from these machines, most PC support people find that they are happy to undertake minor configuration and repairs as they develop a bent for fixing such devices.

What Makes a Good PC Technician?

Although many people have the ability to troubleshoot a PC, making a career out of PC support is a completely different endeavor. It requires a combination of certain personality traits:

➤ *Technical curiosity*—Support technicians always need to be one step ahead of new technologies. They need to be aware of what is coming and how to integrate the old with the new. This applies to both hardware and software.

➤ *Creative thinking*—Computer related problems and issues are diverse. Although much of the repairs and upgrades technicians do are routine, there are times when approaching a problem requires a creative solution.

➤ *Communication skills*—PC support often requires direct contact with clients, customers, and users. PC technicians must be able to articulate the problem or issue with the computer to the client. Effective communication also includes listening as well as talking, which is a fact that seems to escape many PC support people.

➤ *Ability to learn from experience*—Time is of the essence when repairing systems. Many of the problems PC support technicians encounter are repetitive. Keeping a record of past repairs can reduce the time needed to research solutions.

➤ *Resourcefulness*—Not all the problems faced by technicians are obvious. When faced with a particularly difficult problem, technicians must be resourceful in finding the answer. This may include Internet research or calling on another technician's expertise.

➤ *Lack of fear with new technologies*—The breadth of technologies that PC support technicians must deal with means that they will often be working with a product or system that they are unfamiliar with. In these situations, a combination of a cautious approach and a willingness to investigate the problem are necessary. In many situations, withdrawing from a problem is not an option.

➤ *Ability to work under pressure*—Many people rely on their computer systems and when the computers go down, so does their business. Technicians are required to work in situations where there is always pressure to fix systems in the shortest possible time. Almost every computer repair call that a technician undertakes will be accompanied by the question, "I can't work without my computer, how long is this going to take?"

➤ *Integrity*—Unfortunately, there is the potential for technicians to take advantage of unknowing customers. The onus is on the technician to find the most economic and expedient fix to the customer's problem. This involves the obvious traits, such as being honest about what is wrong, but also other attributes, like making sure that all avenues have been explored before performing costly repairs.

Can all of these characteristics be found in one person? Sure they can. The people who possess all of these skills and who know how to use them in the correct proportion are the superstars of the PC support world.

Daily Tasks

Due to the diversity and range of responsibilities and jobs a PC support technician is called upon to perform, it is difficult to nail down the exact daily tasks. The following list contains some of the common daily duties of a PC support person. Even though you are employed as a technician, do not be surprised to find yourself performing tasks other than those listed here:

➤ *Provide computer support services*—PC support technicians will find themselves providing technical support for clients or customers whether in person or over the phone. Supporting users comprises a large part of a PC support technician's job.

➤ *Software maintenance and upgrading*—Frequently, as soon as a new software package is released, it is immediately followed with a service pack or an upgrade package. These upgrades provide solutions to problems discovered in the program. Technicians have to be aware of these software patches and be able to use them to fix software related problems.

➤ *Keep a log of troubleshooting and fixes used*—Computer related problems are largely repetitive. Technicians who have worked in the IT industry for a number of years will have a detailed history of problems and their solutions.

➤ *Diagnose and troubleshoot software and hardware related issues*—The bottom line is, this is what a technician is trained and hired to do. Whether it is an illegal operation error, invalid boot disk, or faulty CD-ROM drive, a technician's job is to diagnose the problem, and then fix it. In many cases, the problem can be fixed while the PC is on the client's desk, but occasionally the computer needs to be removed and a replacement unit left in its place. This often necessitates the transferring of data from one PC to another.

➤ *Maintain inventory of software and hardware*—Technicians employed by companies are often required to keep track of the computers and software being used. This is an easy but sometimes mundane task that requires accuracy and diligence. License conformance is a weighty issue with companies and software manufacturers alike.

➤ *Set up of new equipment and software packages*—Companies spend a great deal of money purchasing new hardware and software. It is the PC support person's role to ensure that the new software and hardware is set up and configured correctly. In many cases, this may include the training of users in the use of the new systems or software.

➤ *Preventative maintenance schedules*—The best computer repair is the one that never has to be done. Preventative maintenance, such as defragmenting hard drives and cleaning systems, can prevent the need for future repairs. In many cases, PC support staff are required to create a schedule for such maintenance as well as carry it out.

➤ *Provide informal training*—Helping users may seem like just curing another problem, but in many cases, it becomes more than just help and develops into informal training. This requires that PC support technicians take their existing qualities of technical ability and communication skills and add patience to the mix. Helping someone with something they don't understand can be very rewarding, and many PC support people enjoy this facet of their role more than any other.

➤ *Evaluate new solutions and products*—New hardware and software products are released with amazing frequency. In many cases, before a company will adopt a new product or technology, an evaluation must be performed. This task often falls to PC support technicians because they have a detailed understanding of the systems currently in use and can accurately gauge how the new product will interact and work with existing solutions. They are also in an excellent position to evaluate the potential benefits a new product can bring to the company.

➤ *Update and deal with virus infections*—Nowadays, most companies have software that detects computer virus infections and prevents them from spreading. The task of dealing with virus outbreaks often falls to the PC support staff. As well as dealing with viruses once they have been detected, PC support staff are often assigned the task of installing and updating the antivirus software along with educating users in good antivirus practices.

➤ *Deal with printer issues*—The title of PC support technician does not mean that you will just be dealing with PCs. Printers are an integral part of today's PC systems, and many people assume that the PC support person and the printer support person are one and the same. For basic issues, such as configuration and the changing of toner or ink cartridges, this assumption is fine. However, if the printer is actually mechanically broken, then a PC support person is unlikely to be asked to fix it, but is expected to communicate the problem to a printer repair technician.

Where Can I Work as a PC Technician?

Practically every home, office, store, gas station, farm, government department, garage, hotel, police station, and just about every other place you can think of has PCs. In fact, it is becoming hard to think of places where people work that do not have computers. This diversity allows PC technicians to pick and choose the type of environment they work in.

The fact that your surroundings can have a great effect in how content you are in a job was discussed earlier in this book. Also discussed were the various job types, office-based, project-based, and field-based, and the fact that if possible, you should work in an area that appeals to your preferences and passions. Of all the areas of IT discussed in this book, PC support is probably the most flexible in this respect. If your passion is cars, you could look for a PC support job at a big car dealership. If your passion is films, you could look for a job with a film production company or boating—a boat company. You get the idea. PC support people are more likely than those in any other field to choose whether to work in an office-based role or a field-based role. Even if you are in one place all the time, it doesn't have to be an office. How about working in a retail environment, or on a cruise ship, or on an oil rig? In PC support, the opportunities are almost endless.

Job Outlook

Many people predicted that with plug-and-play technology and advances such as jumperless configurations and easier software installations, the demand for PC support technicians would decline. That, it would appear, was not an accurate prediction.

In essence, the PC industry is self-perpetuating when it comes to the requirement for support. When "wizards" that helped with software tasks were introduced a number of years ago, some people also predicted the demand for people with PC software support skills would decline. Although it is now easier to do more with today's PC hardware and software, today's PC hardware and software does more—much more in fact. Currently, PC support technicians are unlikely to have to help somebody with styling text in a word processor (though it still does happen) and are more likely to be reconfiguring an import filter for a spreadsheet or reconfiguring a scanner driver for higher resolution. The level of demand for support remains, only the requirements have changed.

The job outlook for PC support personnel is excellent. The Internet will continue to grow phenomenally over the next 10 years and connecting to the Internet will probably be done via PCs. Some people will elect to use a non-PC device to connect, but the reason that PCs have become so popular remains—they are truly versatile machines that provide a range of capabilities. And besides, won't these new "Internet devices" need repairs? And what about the new software on these Internet devices, won't it need support?

Another factor that will influence demand for PC support personnel are the software and hardware manufacturers who introduce new products. There will always be a need for people to install, upgrade, and support them.

Specialization vs. Generalization

Those who work in PC support have to be both specialists and generalists, though many do choose to be generalists with an area of specialization. Sounds a little confusing, but consider this: If you decide to become a PC hardware specialist, you will be expected to fully understand how a PC works at a very detailed level. To achieve this understanding, you must be familiar with PC operating systems because they often require configuration related to the hardware. Also, as a PC hardware technician, your job is effectively completed once the operating system is able to access the hardware.

PC software technicians are people who deal with and support software applications that are commonly used, such as word processors, Web browsers, spreadsheets, and so on. These applications run on the PCs, and the PCs run the operating systems. For PC software technicians to adequately perform their duties, they must at least have some knowledge of PC operating systems. Perhaps not as in-depth as the knowledge that a PC hardware technician has, but a good knowledge nonetheless.

A good PC support person knows a reasonable amount about all three areas: application software, operating systems, and hardware. Though they may elect to focus on one specific area more than another, having a general distribution of skills is most beneficial. When a PC support person with skills in all three areas attends a PC with a problem, he or she is much more likely to be able to help. When customers or clients report a problem with a PC, they often do not understand the problem enough to isolate the problem to a single area. This is when a multiskilled PC support person is of most benefit.

Effectively, those entering the PC support industry can choose to focus on hardware or software, or they can elect to learn about all of the three areas: hardware, operating systems, and applications. Once a certain level of knowledge is reached in each area, a specialization can be selected. One advantage of becoming familiar with all areas is that the individual will have had a chance to preview different areas of the industry and choose the area in which he or she is most interested.

Searching the Advertisements: What's in a Name?

Advertised jobs for PC support sometimes go by different names, which can be confusing for those first starting out. Although many of the tasks of the different titles overlap, there are some subtle differences in both the duties as well as the working environment. The following sections describe a list of the common job titles you will come across when researching PC support positions.

Help Desk Support

The term "Help Desk" generally refers to a role where a person or group of people are designated as a first line of resource for a company or product. Help Desk support involves assisting end users with a variety of concerns and problems and can be either software or hardware related. Much of the troubleshooting done by a help desk support professional is conducted over the phone or via email. Help Desk staff are often called upon to escalate user issues to other support personnel, a process that effectively turns the help desk person into a bridge between the nontechnical user and the highly technical support person.

Depending on where a support technician is employed, he or she may be required to have specialized knowledge of a specific hardware component or a specific software package. This is particularly true for those employed by major hardware or software vendors who must support customers or clients on the company's product range. In addition to this specialized knowledge, Help Desk support requires a working knowledge of commonly used applications, utilities, operating systems, and hardware configurations.

Help Desk support technicians working in smaller companies may combine the tasks of Help Desk support with the role of a technician. They may find themselves fixing, maintaining, and installing programs in addition to their Help Desk responsibilities.

PC Maintenance Technician

PC maintenance technician is the title given to those who typically are more involved in the maintenance, troubleshooting, and repairing end of the PC support world. These technicians have less of a need for specialized knowledge, but rather require a general knowledge of many areas of both hardware and software.

PC technicians are the jack-of-all-trades; they have to be prepared to address every problem that is presented to them, irrespective of whether or not they have seen the problem before. PC maintenance technicians need to be knowledgeable about peripheral devices, specifically, how they are configured and how they integrate with hardware and software.

PC Network Technician

Some companies require their PC technicians to have networking knowledge. The role of network technician often involves basic network administration duties in addition to the tasks of a PC technician. These professionals may assist the network administrator in basic tasks, such as setting up accounts or networking new systems, or they may act as liaisons for an outside networking company. In either case, PC network technicians need to have a reasonable understanding of network operating systems, procedures, and protocols. The role of PC network technician is, for many people, the first step on the path to becoming a network administrator or engineer.

Desktop Technicians

Desktop technicians are essentially the same as Help Desk support technicians. The subtle distinction may be that desktop technicians are generally less specialized in a specific area, but rather have an overall knowledge and so can respond to a variety of computer related issues. In addition, Help Desk support people may literally sit at their desks and troubleshoot using the phone or email, whereas desktop technicians may find themselves moving around an office building or even between sites, attending to problems wherever they occur.

Qualifications and Requirements

Although there are degree programs that include PC support training as part of the curriculum, most technicians choose to enter the field through certifications. Certification programs are available through self-study as well as vocational schools and colleges. The classroom-based programs offering PC support certifications have become popular due to the focused study material and the short period of time required to gain certification. Furthermore, vocational schools provide students with access to the hardware and software they will be using in the workplace. Because self-study does not always allow this option, it can cause training to become more theoretical than practical.

Regardless of the study method, employers often look for PC support candidates to have a recognized certification or diploma, and although not always possible, prefer candidates with experience. Employers require their technical staff to be familiar with a variety of technical aspects including, building and repairing computer systems, installing and configuring software, assisting users, and strong communication and documentation skills. In addition, a strong knowledge of computer peripherals is required as well as familiarity with commonly used operating systems and office software applications.

Having an understanding of what an employer requires from its PC support staff will help you decide which method of training to choose. It may be worthwhile browsing Internet job sites, such as those listed in Appendix D, to see exactly which skills employers are seeking from their PC support staff.

What Will I Be Expected to Know?

Regardless of the training method you choose, you will need specific knowledge to be able to do the job. The following list contains some general requirements that a training program, irrespective of the medium by which it is delivered, should prepare you for:

➤ *Hardware knowledge*—The job of PC support requires extensive hardware knowledge. Understanding basic hardware concepts, such as bus architecture, different random access memory (RAM) types (SIMMs, DIMMs, SDRAM, DRAM), central processing units (CPUs), motherboards, and hard drives is required.

➤ *Software knowledge*—A basic understanding of the most commonly used applications is required of a technician. Such applications include word processors, spreadsheets, graphics programs, virus detection software, Internet Web browsers, and even games. Many computer problems that appear at first glance to be hardware related are in fact software related.

➤ *Configuration knowledge*—Although advances such as Plug-and-Play and Universal Serial Bus (USB) have removed many of the configuration issues that previously plagued PC technologies, they do still appear. PC support technicians need a fundamental knowledge of hardware configuration, which includes such details as interrupt request (IRQ) settings, Direct Memory Access (DMA), and input/output addresses.

➤ *Device drivers*—By the time your training program is finished, you will most certainly have been introduced to the world of drivers, the translators between the device and the program Support technicians need to know how, when, and where to install device drivers. They also need to know where to get them.

➤ *Networking concepts*—Networks have become the name of the game, and many of the computers a technician will upgrade or repair will be part of a network. Oftentimes, to troubleshoot networked systems, technicians are required to have a general, though not necessarily detailed, knowledge of networks including cabling, network operating systems, network interface cards, and network architecture.

➤ *Internet skills*—Forget the dog, the Internet is a technician's best friend. Even the most difficult of computer problems can be solved with a little online help. The Internet provides more than just a resource for troubleshooting problems. The Internet gives the PC support technician access to vendor Web sites, information on latest products, access to latest software drivers, tips, hints, tricks, and a veritable gold mine of other useful information. The job of technicians is very much integrated with the Internet, not just from the perspective of supporting users who use it, but from the perspective of completing their own job.

➤ *Troubleshooting techniques and shortcuts*—Any training for PC support must provide a solid background of troubleshooting techniques. Many computer problems are repetitive, meaning that process and recollection of previous problems and their solutions becomes a major factor.

➤ *Knowledge of peripherals*—Printers, scanners, digital cameras, and other devices are used in the home and in the office. The integration of these devices is not always seamless, and the PC support person is the one expected to make all the various add-ons work together. The variety of peripherals that can be added to a PC system is mind boggling, and although a PC support person is unlikely to be expected to know how to configure every one, he or she should at least have some idea of how to get started.

➤ *DOS*— A technician should also be familiar with DOS, or more accurately, MS-DOS—the operating system that doesn't seem to go away. Even with today's Windows systems, much of the troubleshooting has to be done from the good old command prompt. Familiarity and the ability to use some of the basic DOS commands will be required from time to time for support technicians.

➤ *Preventative maintenance*—The job of the technician is not always reactive, good technicians are proactive. Scheduled maintenance of computer systems can prevent many problems before they arise. Training should teach the basics of a proactive maintenance strategy, detailing what should be done and when.

The Great Divide

As discussed earlier, PC support can be split into two areas, hardware and software. Both are required to make a computer function, therefore, the PC support technician needs to be versatile in both areas. Gaining competency in both hardware and software can seem a little overwhelming, especially considering the pace at which technology moves. However, these skills are very valuable for technicians to acquire.

PC Hardware Support

A career in hardware support deals primarily with the physical components of a computer system. Generally speaking, if you can touch it, it's hardware. Components such as monitors, keyboards, RAM, and video cards are all considered to be hardware. Those interested in pursuing a career in hardware support can expect to be working with these components on a daily basis. The job of hardware support involves installing, maintaining, troubleshooting, upgrading, and repairing this equipment.

To do the job of hardware support effectively, technicians need to be aware of past, current, and future hardware components. These hardware components will oftentimes be integrated into the same system, and the technician needs to make them work. In many cases, this can be a somewhat daunting task, especially when a certain interface board or component needs to work with a software application that has recently been upgraded.

As discussed previously, those choosing a career in hardware support need to learn a reasonable amount about computer operating systems, and in many cases, a certain amount about application software packages. Even so, the software element only constitutes part of the PC support persons role, and brings with it an advantage. PC hardware is largely generic. No one company controls the technologies available, meaning that the skills of a PC hardware technician are largely vendor independent. This is a benefit in one respect because it means that the PC hardware support person can work in almost any environment. On the other hand, it is a disadvantage in that it can sometimes be harder to quantify his or her skills.

To get an idea of the job of hardware support, it is necessary to review the technologies technicians will be working with.

Hardware Support Issues

All computer systems are comprised of some common hardware components. Hardware support technicians can expect to become very familiar with the following components, which will become part of your daily routine:

➤ *BIOS* (Basic Input Output System)—The BIOS provides the instructions needed to boot the computer, processing the steps the computer needs at start up. Technicians can expect to be working with and troubleshooting BIOS settings. BIOS settings are stored on a special chip called a CMOS (complementary metal oxide semiconductor). Most PCs come with a built in utility that allows technicians to access the BIOS settings of the PC. The boot sequence, hard drive settings, and other crucial setup information is set in the BIOS. PC support technicians will become very familiar with the BIOS settings.

➤ *Microprocessors*—Microprocessors are the heart of the computer system. Technicians will not be involved in repairing microprocessors and very rarely need to replace malfunctioning ones. Technicians will however find themselves upgrading systems with faster or even additional processors. As clients and customers install new peripherals and applications, the processor may not meet the new demands. Technicians will need to find bottlenecks in processor speed and make recommendations as required. Technicians will also need to keep up with advances in microprocessor technology. Newer microprocessors vary not only in speed, but also in the cache memory available on the chip.

➤ *Peripherals*—Peripherals are the components that are added on to a computer system. There are numerous peripheral devices ranging from printers and Zip™ drives to scanners and joysticks. Peripheral devices provide the PC technician with many challenges. Printers, for instance, can be purchased from various vendors and come in a variety of models: inkjet, laser, bubble jet, or dot matrix. Hardware support requires knowledge of current and future peripheral devices, as technicians will be involved with the installation and configuration of them.

➤ *Video Cards*—In most cases, a video card, or display adapter, is an expansion board that determines the resolution, number of colors, and refresh rate of the picture displayed by the computer. Video cards are not a component technicians repair, rather, when a video problem is a result of the card, it is simply replaced. Video cards are also frequently replaced to meet the demands of software applications that require higher resolution and enhanced color capabilities. In

6

addition to replacing a video card, technicians must be aware of the capabilities of the card to ensure it meets the demands of the customer or client. In the majority of cases replacement of the video card also requires new software drivers to be configured and installed.

➤ *Network Cards*—Network cards, as you might have guessed, are expansion boards that allow the computer to connect to a network. Network cards are available for different network mediums and in different speeds. As a hardware device, network cards are not difficult to physically install and rarely require upgrading or replacing. The challenge for network cards comes in their configuration after being installed. Networks have become very common, and hardware technicians need to be able to configure and manage a network card from within an operating system.

➤ *Memory*—RAM is a popular area of upgrade for computer owners, and hardware support technicians will replace and upgrade RAM often. In fact, of all the upgrades performed on computers, the addition or replacement of RAM may be the most common. In addition to upgrading RAM, technicians may find that it is the cause of malfunctioning systems. Hardware support technicians need to know the signs and symptoms of bad RAM. For the most part, this is learned on the job. There are different types of RAM that technicians will be required to work with including the older RAM, known as 30 or 72 pin SIMM RAM, as well as the more current technologies.

➤ *Hard Disk Drives*—As far as upgrades go, hard drives may run a close second to RAM. Hard drives have increased significantly in storage size in trying to keep pace with applications that are requiring more and more storage space. In addition to upgrading hard drives, hardware support involves the configuration of hard drives, and in some cases controller cards, which may include changing BIOS settings and partitioning the drive. In some cases, it may also require adding drives to create fault-tolerant configurations.

➤ *Operating Systems*—Hardware support technicians cannot do the job with only hardware knowledge; they need to know how to configure this hardware in relation to operating systems. Therefore, hardware support requires extensive knowledge of operating systems as well.

From Theory to Practice

The first step is to obtain an understanding of the hardware that will be used on the job. The second step is to find out exactly how the hardware is used and configured. When working on a computer system, technicians can expect to be performing one or all of the following tasks:

➤ *Installation and setup*—Installation and setup encompasses a massive range of tasks. In certain environments, PC support technicians will find themselves building entire PCs from a collection of parts. In others, it will be more a matter of checking over a fully installed and configured system prior to installation. In either case, the PC support technician is likely to use a gamut of different skills and abilities.

➤ *Upgrading*—Technology moves at an unrelenting pace. One day 16MB of RAM and a 2GB hard drive is plenty, the next day that same system is inadequate. Computer upgrades are very common. The components most likely to be upgraded include, RAM, hard drives, and video cards.

➤ *Repairs*—Everything breaks, and computers are no different. Repairing computers has in fact become less about repairing and more about replacing. Components such as video cards, modems, keyboards, and even monitors are rarely repaired. The trick for the PC technician is to isolate the malfunctioning hardware and get the computer up and running in the fastest time possible. In many cases, the technicians time is more expensive than the part or parts being replaced.

➤ *Troubleshooting*—Diagnosing computer related problems comprises a large part of the job of hardware support. To assist in troubleshooting, technicians need to understand the basics of hardware components and how they are meant to function.

➤ *Maintenance*—The goal of computer maintenance is to ensure a minimum amount of downtime due to a hardware failure. This requires that systems be monitored and cared for as required.

➤ *Software related tasks*—As discussed previously, PC hardware technicians need an understanding of today's computer operating systems. Most of a hardware technicians work involves dealing with how the hardware interacts with the operating system rather than any application setup or configuration. This may involve the loading of new device drivers or service packs.

Training Options for Hardware

As with the other areas of IT mentioned in this book, those interested in training for a career in PC hardware support have many options available to them. Training options include everything from self-study to classroom-based instruction.

Courses and Certification

Unlike other areas of IT, PC hardware support has relatively few recognized certification programs that accompany it. This is due in part to the fact that the computer hardware industry is much more distributed than its software counterpart. Although there are companies such as Compaq and Dell that lead the field in PC sales, there are still literally thousands of other companies that either manufacture or assemble PCs. This distribution has meant that the training and certification industry has been slower to seize upon hardware training opportunities.

Although there are a number of certification programs available from computer hardware manufacturers, they all tend to be very specific. Those who have been working in the IT industry for a number of years may find these certifications useful, but for someone new to the industry, they are probably a little too focused.

As far as vendor independent certification programs go, one certification program that stands out is the CompTIA A+ certification, which provides a solid grounding in PC hardware and operating system fundamentals as well as teaches topics such as safety and good working practices. For more information on the A+ Certification, visit the CompTIA certification Web site at **www.comptia.org/ certification**.

As the next step along the path to becoming a PC hardware specialist, CompTIA will soon be offering a new certification called Server+ . This certification focuses more directly on issues that face hardware specialists who work with network server computers. Again, further information is available at the CompTIA Web site.

In addition to hardware knowledge, PC hardware technicians need a solid grounding in PC operating systems, such as Microsoft Windows 98, Windows Me, Windows NT Workstation, and Windows 2000 Professional. Microsoft currently offers Microsoft Certified Professional (MCP) certifications in all of these disciplines, each requiring one exam to be taken to achieve certified status. For more information, visit the Microsoft Training and Education Web site at **www.microsoft.com/trainingandservices**.

Online Training

The physical nature of PC hardware does not lend itself well to online or Web-based training, and there are fewer companies offering online courses than for other areas of IT. Two reputable companies that do offer Web based CompTIA A+ preparation courses are **www.smartforce.com** and **www.knowledgenet.com**. Before signing up, ensure that you are comfortable with the teaching method.

The software aspect of PC hardware support is easier to provide for, with many online institutions offering courses in Microsoft operating systems. Microsoft also offers online training on its operating systems through its network of education partners. Information can be found at **www.microsoft.com/ trainingandservices**.

Self-Study Options

If there was ever a good way to learn about computer hardware, the process of building and dismantling a PC would have to rank as number one. That said, your own PC may not be the best place to start experimenting with BIOS configuration changes and device driver updates.

Warning: Before you consider self-study in PC hardware, remember that PCs are electrical devices and as such can be potentially fatal. Never open the case of a PC, monitor, printer, or any other device without first making yourself aware of the risks involved and the precautions you must take.

6

If you want to get some hands-on practice without risking costly accidents, consider purchasing a used computer that can become a test-bed for your experiments. A system that is neither cutting edge, nor rusting away, is perfect. In many cases, such a unit is quite representative of what you may end up dealing with in the field. If funds are tight, consider approaching local computer stores and asking them for old PC equipment, or even place a want ad in your local newspaper. Although this strategy may cause you to end up with a reasonable amount of junk, you may just find enough components to build a system. In fact, the older and weirder the components you get, the more likely they are to represent a challenge in configuration and setup. By experimenting with these types of components and troubleshooting the conflicts, you will learn a great deal more than if the system was complete at the outset.

Any system you use or put together should be capable of running one or more of the operating systems mentioned earlier. The system doesn't need to be extremely fast, and as a matter of fact, if the system is a little slow, then you will have the opportunity and associated experience of tweaking the operating system to its best performance.

A book or study guide is an almost essential companion to a self-study program, and most people find that it pays to learn some theory before actually diving into the box and trying things out. Preparing yourself in this way inspires confidence and can also help to prevent costly mistakes. Information on some suitable books is provided in the "Books" section.

Additional Hardware Resources

The following sections provide a collection of resources that can help you find out more about PC hardware and its associated technologies. Much of the information is supplied as a starting point.

PC Hardware Support Jargon Buster

As with the other areas of IT, PC support has its share of acronyms and professional jargon. The following list contains terms that you are most certainly going to encounter as you learn more about a career in PC hardware support:

➤ *Device Driver*—A device driver is a specific program that allows components, such as video cards and printers, to communicate with the operating system. These components are very particular about the device driver that is used, and incorrect drivers can cause all sorts of errors. Device drivers are one of the first places to look if hardware does not seem to be working.

➤ *Jumper*—A jumper is basically a small plastic covered metal clip that acts as an on/off switch. Jumpers are seen on expansion cards and motherboards and control a number of different settings. As technology advances, jumperless boards are being used more often. Even so, technicians are still required to know how to configure settings using jumpers.

➤ *CPU*—A CPU, also called the processor, is where the computing ability of the system comes from. The CPU processes instructions from hardware and software components of the PC.

➤ *Bus*—A bus, as it pertains to computers at least, is simply a path of wires through which data is transmitted. The bus allows internal computer components and expansion boards to access the CPU and RAM and vice versa. Common types of buses include peripheral component interconnect (PCI) and industry standard architecture (ISA).

➤ *RAM*—RAM provides the computer's temporary storage. This temporary storage area is used by applications for fast storage and retrieval of data. This method is much quicker than accessing the hard drive. RAM is referred to as volatile memory, meaning that when the computer is shut down, the information held in RAM is erased.

➤ *Read only memory (ROM)*—ROM is computer memory that has information written on it by the manufacturer. The information stored in ROM cannot be changed easily and is known as nonvolatile, meaning that the information is not lost when the computer is powered down.

➤ *Peripheral device*—Peripherals simply refer to any external device connected to a computer. Examples of such devices include keyboards, mice, scanners, printers and digital cameras.

Books

It is not difficult to find books on all levels of hardware information and configurations. It is important however, to find a book that is easy to read and fully explains the concepts and technologies. A few pictures can really help describe exactly what is being referred to, especially in consideration to PC hardware.

Beginner Book Titles

➤ Maran, Ruth. *Teach Yourself Computers and the Internet Visually, 2nd Edition.* IDG Books Worldwide, 1998. ISBN 0764560417.

➤ Chambers, Mark L. *Building a PC for Dummies.* IDG Books Worldwide, 1998. ISBN 0764503480.

➤ White, Ron, Stephen Adams (illustrator), and Timothy Edward Downs (Illustrator). *How Computers Work: Millennium Edition (How Computers Work, 5th Ed).* Macmillan Computer Publishing, 1999. ISBN 0789721120.

➤ Roman, Steven. *Understanding Personal Computer Hardware: Everything You Need to Know to Be an Informed PC User, PC Buyer, PC Upgrader.* Springer Verlag, 1998. ISBN 038798531X.

Advanced Books

➤ Englander, Irv. *The Architecture of Computer Hardware and System Software: An Information Technology Approach, 2nd Edition.* John Wiley & Sons, 2000. ISBN 0471362093.

➤ Blaauw, Gerrit A., and Frederick P. Brooks Jr. (Contributor). *Computer Architecture: Concepts and Evolution.* Addison-Wesley, 1997. ISBN 0201105578.

➤ Antonakos, James L., and Kenneth C. Mansfield. *Microcomputer Hardware, Software, and Troubleshooting for Engineering and Technology.* Prentice-Hall, 2000. ISBN 0130114669.

Reference Books

➤ Andrews, Jean. *A+ Exam Prep.* The Coriolis Group, 1998. ISBN 1576102416.

➤ Bigelow, Stephen J. *Troubleshooting, Maintaining & Repairing PCs, Millennium Edition.* McGraw-Hill, 1999. ISBN 0072122234.

➤ Glover, Thomas J., and Millie M. Young. *PC Reference 10TH Edition.* Sequoia Publishing, 2000. ISBN 1885071272.

➤ Shnier, Mitchell. *Computer Dictionary: Data Communications, PC Hardware, and Internet Terminology.* Macmillan Publishing Company, 1998. ISBN 0789716704.

➤ Croucher, Phil. *The Bios Companion, 3rd CD-ROM Edition.* Advice Press, 1999. ISBN 1889671207.

Online Information and Resources

The Internet is the fastest way to access information on any conceivable hardware component or configuration. PC support technicians can use the Internet to make their jobs considerably easier.

Newsgroups

Newsgroups are Internet-based message boards that allow users to post messages or reply to messages that other people post. Newsgroups are descriptively named by topic area. For instance, **comp.hardware**, is the hardware discussion group under the computer system section. There are thousands of newsgroups on almost every possible subject.

Newsgroups can be a valuable resource for anyone involved in the IT industry. Almost every part of the IT industry has related newsgroups. Newsgroups can be accessed via a newsreader, such as those included with Microsoft Outlook or Netscape Communicator, or via a Web interface. Accessing newsgroups through a Web interface on a site such as **www.dejanews.com/usenet** is the easiest way to get started. For more information on newsgroups, refer to Appendix C.

Hardware specific newsgroups are a good place to visit to read about what is going on in the hardware world. Newsgroups are also a great place to ask others for information on hardware questions you may have. Remember, newsgroup members are not necessarily professionals, but the information in these online discussions can provide very good information on a variety of hardware related issues:

➤ **alt.comp.hardware.pc-homebuilt**

➤ **comp.periphs**

➤ **alt.comp.hardware**

➤ **comp.sys.mac.hardware**

➤ **comp.hardware**

Magazines and Journals

Magazines provide PC support technicians with another means in which they can keep apprised of the new technologies heading their way. Magazines are a great place to go for product reviews, tips and tricks, and even some entertainment.

➤ *PC Magazine* (**www.zdnet.com/pcmag**)—PC Magazine offers everything from industry news and product reviews to software downloads. A one-year subscription to the magazine (22 issues) costs just under $27.

➤ *Byte Magazine* (**www.byte.com**)—Similar to PC Magazine, Byte offers hardware reviews and much more. Byte provides access to a variety of articles and columns including various software platforms, troubleshooting techniques, and hardware comparisons.

➤ *Wired Magazine* (**www.wired.com/wired/current.html**)—Wired Magazine is another magazine to investigate to stay ahead of the IT industry. Wired is currently offering a subscription of 12 issues for only $12.

➤ *Maximum PC* (**www.maximumpc.com/index.html**)—Maximum PC includes articles on upcoming hardware and software products. Maximum is currently offering a subscription price of $12 for 12 issues.

Web Pages

There are many Web sites offering PC hardware news, support, and general information. It is a good idea for technicians to have a few of these Web pages bookmarked.

➤ *Hothardware* (**www.hothardware.com**)—Is a good site to visit to find out about the latest hardware. The hardware on this page is cutting edge and are the very devices you can expect to be working with on the job.

➤ *Toms Hardware* (**www.tomshardware.com**) An excellent site that offers a wealth of technical information, news and reviews on all kinds of PC hardware. Toms Hardware should be a regular visit for those working in PC hardware support.

➤ *Cnet.com* (**www.cnet.com**)—Provides articles on the latest gear ranging from printers to Zip drives. The site offers technology news, hardware reviews, and the prices you can expect to pay for this new technology. The columns and articles on this page keep you in touch with the happenings in the IT industry.

➤ *Compinfo* (**www.compinfo-center.com**)—Offers up-to-date news on all aspects of the computer industry including hardware. The site also offers links to technical manuals to help you solve those maddening hardware problems. Compinfo is a good site to gain access to the latest news, drivers, and product information.

➤ *Driverguide.com* (**www.driverguide.com**)—Provides links and information on driver software for practically every PC and peripheral device imaginable. Membership is free. Simply sign up online and a username and password are sent to the email address you supply. Driverguide.com also provides the capability for you to upload a driver you have found in your travels to help others.

Professional Associations

The Association for Computing Machinery (ACM) has been around since 1947, which is a *long* time in the IT industry. There are two classifications of membership: student and professional. There are 36 special interest groups that cover specific areas of expertise. Chapters exist all over the country and indeed the world. The ACM also produces a range of magazines and journals, which are available for a further charge. More information including membership dues can be found on the ACM Web site at **www.acm.org**.

Summary

PC hardware support offers a career path in which little stays static for very long. Those who are successful in the field will possess many qualities, not the least of which will be the ability to systematically troubleshoot problems on a vast range of sometimes unfamiliar hardware.

PC Software Support

Software includes the operating systems, applications, utilities, and tools used on computer systems. As the software that is used becomes ever more complex, the skills required to support it become so as well. PC software support staff need to have a solid understanding of PC operating systems as well as a good grounding in at least a selection of the most popular application packages. As mentioned earlier in this chapter, a PC support person's role normally involves a great deal of human interaction, and in fact, software support tends to require a higher level than hardware support. Quite a range of skills are required to be a successful PC software support person.

Software can basically be broken down into two categories: application software and operating system software. Technicians need a knowledge of both to successfully complete their tasks.

PC Operating Systems

From the perspective of operating system software, the field is relatively narrow. Microsoft dominates the PC operating system market with products such as Windows 95, Windows 98, the new Windows Me, Windows NT Workstation 4, and Windows 2000 Professional. Detailed knowledge of at least a couple of these operating systems is needed by anyone considering a career in PC software support. Admittedly, there are other workstation operating systems, such as Macintosh Operating System (Mac OS) and Linux, but realistically, those looking to create a highly portable skill set would do best to focus on the Microsoft products.

With that said, you might think that narrows the field down a great deal, but it only helps a little. The problem is that although the most current Microsoft workstation operating system releases are Windows Me and Windows 2000 Professional, not everyone is using these products. In fact, you might just be surprised at how many times you will see Windows 98 or Windows 95 installed in homes and businesses. In addition, the increasing installed user base of Windows NT 4 means that, in a business environment at least, you are likely to be working with this software on a frequent basis. Furthermore, there are still those that run older Microsoft operating systems, such as Windows 3.1 and Windows for Workgroups. Although you are not going to find too many people running just MS DOS, PC support technicians still need to be versed in DOS commands, as all of these other operating systems still include some DOS functionality. Much of this knowledge is particularly useful when you are troubleshooting these systems.

PC Application Software

Microsoft is also a dominant force in the application software market, although it does not have quite the near monopoly that it exercises over the operating system market. The most common applications in use are word processors, spreadsheet applications, Web browsers, graphics packages, and so on. In some of these areas, Microsoft software, particularly the Office suite of software, is particularly popular. In the Web browser market, Microsoft's Internet Explorer product holds the lion share, but others, such as Netscape's Navigator and Communicator products, are still used by many people.

6

Outside of these mainstream applications however, things become less clear. As well as software that fits into accepted categories, such as graphics, desktop publishing (DTP), databases, email, scheduling, project management, and so on, there are a million other programs, utilities, and add-ons that do everything from telling time in 30 different countries to translating different languages to running traffic lights. The only problem is, as a software support specialist, you will be expected to know or at least have a general idea of how they work. Why? Because nowadays, a great deal of applications have something in common—a Windows interface.

It's a Windowed World

The number of PCs that run a Microsoft Windows operating system is literally staggering. If you are a company that develops software for PCs, you are going to need a very good reason to develop your software and not include a version for Microsoft Windows. There are those that do, but they are the exception rather than the rule. This does work in your favor, however. Applications that run on the Windows operating system have a common interface, which means that they are easy to install, configure, use, tweak, update, and remove. In many cases, menu systems and keystrokes are the same in different applications. Press F1, and you get a help screen. Go to Help | About, and you can see the product's serial number. This is not always true, but it happens enough that a seasoned PC support person will be able to figure out the software pretty quickly when faced with a common interface. This commonality, combined with the willingness to investigate problems is what allows the PC support person to track down and correct errors.

Turning Theory into Practice

The software support person's role revolves around tasks such as installing, updating, and removing application software on PCs. Many PC support people choose to take their knowledge further, learning how to customize and support specific applications in depth. This learning may include, for example, macro creation or even basic programming. In general, PC support people are normally required to know enough so that they can solve a wide variety of software related issues. They also need to have the ability to find help from other sources. In some cases, this involves calling the manufacturer's software Help Desk to discuss the problem. The following list contains some tasks that PC software support personnel will find themselves performing:

➤ *Installation of software packages and operating systems*—One of the main tasks a PC software support person will find themselves doing is installing new versions of operating systems or applications. Nowadays, many large corporate companies use automated network software installations, which means that each workstation does not have to be visited. Even so, the installations do not always go as planned, and PC support staff are often involved in preparing these rollouts.

➤ *Upgrade and update software*—Software packages are updated on a frequent basis. When they are, PC software support technicians are often responsible for installing the new packages and easing the transition for the users. This may involve training, and in many cases, researching the product to answer the users' questions.

➤ *Troubleshoot application and system errors*—The complexity of applications and operating systems can result in frequent errors. In some cases, these errors are not the fault of the software, but of the person using it. In these cases, PC software support technicians must be diplomatic in correcting the "problem."

➤ *Advise users on software use*—Although many users have a reasonable knowledge of the applications they use, to get the best of some of the more advanced features, some help may be needed. It is the responsibility of the PC software support technician to help users with the more advanced functions as well as help with tasks such as the importing and exporting of data.

➤ *Overseeing general PC usage*—Currently, most companies have policies regarding the use of computer systems within their organization. Because PC software support technicians often spend time around their company's systems, they become the eyes and ears of management in regard to employees' adherence to these policies. Although most PC support staffs' role in this context is that of reporting back to management, it is a side of the job that many professionals do not like.

This list is by no means comprehensive, and PC software support personnel will find themselves doing a multitude of other tasks as well.

Training Options for Software

To prepare for a career in PC software support, you will almost certainly need to undergo some degree of training. The following sections contain some training options that you should investigate.

Courses and Certifications

There are a number of certification programs that potential PC support people can consider when training for a career.

There is the CompTIA A+ certification programs for hardware. If you having a little bout of déjà vu, don't worry. We did mention the A+ certification back in the certification programs for hardware, but it really does deserve a place here as well. Not only does it teach the nuts and bolts of computer hardware that every person supporting PC's should know, it does have an operating system component as well. The A+ certification is widely recognized as a baseline certification for those pursuing a career in PC support. For more information and is a valid credential for anyone entering the industry. Visit the CompTIA A+ certification website **www.CompTIA.org/certification**.

The MCP program is a sound choice for those training to become PC support technicians. Currently, you can become MCP certified in Windows 98, Windows Me, Windows NT 4 Workstation, and Windows 2000 Professional. Many of these operating systems form part of the requirement for the Microsoft Certified Systems Engineer (MCSE) certification, should you choose to take your skills to the next level. Each MCP certification requires that you take one exam, which on passing, allows you to call yourself an MCP. More information on the MCP program can be found at Microsoft's Training and Certification home page at **www.microsoft.com/trainingandservices**.

For application software, Microsoft provides the Microsoft Office User Specialist (MOUS) certification, which is provided in two versions: Core and Expert. The Core version is designed for general tasks that end users will need. The Expert level is for those who are going to be intensive users of the products. The Expert level serves as a way of measuring the proficiency of an individual from a support perspective, but companies generally expect a more in-depth knowledge of the product than the MOUS program provides. The MOUS program is not promoted as strongly as the MCP certification, but is realistically one of the few certification programs available for Microsoft applications. For more information on the MOUS program, visit the MOUS Web site at **www.mous.net**.

The Help Desk Institute (HDI) offers a series of certifications for support professionals. While not as well recognized by employers as some of the other certifications mentioned here, the Institute has a highly professional image and a growing member base. Certifications include an Analyst, Support Engineer and Manager level. There are also separate Instructor and Auditor certifications. Find out more at the HDI Web site (**www.helpdeskinst.com**).

These certification programs represent a small selection of the most popular programs. A great number of software manufacturers now offer certification programs of their own. If you have a specific application or operating system in mind, look for a link to training and certification on the software manufacturer's home page.

Online Training

As with practically every other field of IT, PC software support has not escaped the attention of online training providers. One advantage of using a Web-based training company is that many offer certificates upon course completion, which can serve to reinforce your knowledge to a potential employer. If this is an important factor for you, make sure this is offered before signing up.

As with any other training method, Web-based training quite reasonably tends to focus on the most popular operating systems and applications. With the most popular being the Microsoft products, it's worth mentioning Microsoft's online training program, which is delivered through its network of training partners. Visit Microsoft's training and certification Web site at **www.Microsoft.com/ trainingandservices**.

A number of companies offer online training for the CompTIA A+ certification. Members of CompTIA that provide training services can be found at the CompTIA Web site at **www.CompTIA.org/certification**. It's worth noting that the companies listed on the site are only affiliated with CompTIA and not endorsed by them. Research training providers thoroughly before parting with any of your money.

For the best value in training courses, check out some of the free courseware from Freeskills. The courseware is downloadable, so it fits the self-study model better than the Web-based training, but it is training, and it is on the Web at **www.freeskills.com**. Courses include a wide range of PC applications from a variety of manufacturers as well as training courses for a number of popular operating systems.

For more online training providers, type "web based training" along with the operating system or application you are looking for training on into any Internet Web search engine.

Self-Study Options

For those choosing a career in PC support, self-study is a very feasible option. It's another reason why many people choosing to get into IT go into PC support.

There are a number of ways to get up to speed on software support issues. One of the most effective is to actually sit down at a PC with the product installed and study. Application software can be expensive, but some companies do provide evaluation versions of products, which allow you to understand and learn the features of a product for a free trial period.

If you have a home PC, then learning about the operating system is a relatively easy task, although it should be noted that the PC you use for your normal day-to-day computing is not the best tool for learning how the operating system works. Changes you make to the PC could make it unusable for your other tasks (or just unusable period). So proceed with caution.

A good approach, funds permitting, is to buy another PC to use as a test system. It does not have to be the fastest whiz bang system available, in fact, it is probably best if it's not. Buy a system that is sufficiently powerful to do what you need it to, but sufficiently old so you won't have to pay top dollar for it. Also, bear in mind that if you start to "play" with the hardware, there is a chance that you may break something. The less you paid for the PC in the first place the better. Check local papers for advertisements selling PCs to get an idea what they are going for. If you can pick up a bargain to use as your test machine, all the better. People often shy away from buying a used PC, but there is no reason to. You cannot destroy a PC like you can a car or a motorbike. If the PC is running when you look at it, and you test some of its components, such as the floppy drive, it should be okay to purchase.

Once you have a PC, use it as a test bed. Load and unload software. Try out different configurations. If it helps, use a self-study guide book to go through exercises, but remember that you must learn the product to a higher degree than those that simply use it, so buy a book that covers features and functions in depth. At the very least, your aim should be to cultivate your knowledge to the level of a power user, which is a term given to individuals who know more about a certain product than a regular user.

You may even choose to translate your knowledge learned through self-study into a certification if there is a certification program available for your chosen subject.

Additional Resources

There is a wide range of resources available to those looking for further information on PC software support and PCs in general. In the following sections, a number of links to books, newsgroups, magazines, and professional associations have been provided to get you started.

PC Software Support Jargon Buster

As you begin to find out more information on PC support, you may encounter terms and acronyms that you are unfamiliar with. The following list contains just a few definitions to help you along.

➤ *Operating system*—The operating system is without question the most important program installed on the computer system. It is the job of the operating system to control everything that happens on the computer. Examples of workstation operating systems include Windows 98, MS-DOS, MAC OS, and Linux.

➤ *Application*—Applications are the programs that turn PCs into a productivity tool. Common applications include word processors, spreadsheets, Web browsers, and database programs.

➤ *Macro*—A macro is a sequence of commands combined so that they can be executed by one other command. Macros are often used to reduce the need to perform repetitive (or boring) tasks within an application. Macros can be created by using a recorder which records key strokes and mouse clicks, or by using languages similar to programming languages

➤ *Software bug*—A software bug is an error in an application that causes it to malfunction. With the complexity of today's programs, bugs are quite common.

➤ *Patch*   A patch is a small program written to fix a bug within an application. Often, it isn't until after a program is released that issues are discovered. Software patches are written to address these issues.

➤ *Service Pack*   Service packs are a group of patches released to update a software package. Service packs generally represent a major update to software and address many concerns. In many cases, downloading and installing service packs is the first step in fixing many computer problems.

Books

There are books available on every subject and at every level of PC hardware, software, peripherals, and operating systems. The following list provides you with a few suggestions that you may want to consider.

Beginner Book Titles

➤ Bobel, Robert. *Active Introduction to Microsoft Windows 98.* Active Curriculum, 2000. ISBN 1586120549.

➤ Versdahl, Dave, and Leif Fedje. *Introduction to Personal Computers with Windows 98 and Office 2000.* ActiveEducation, 2000. ISBN 1582641234.

➤ Matthews, Martin S. *Windows 2000: A Beginner's Guide.* Osborne/McGraw-Hill, 2000. ISBN 0072123249.

➤ Rathbone, Andy, and Sharon Crawford. *Windows 2000 Professional For Dummies.* IDG Books Worldwide, 2000. ISBN 0764506412.

Advanced Books

➤ Stewart, James Michael (Editor), Lee Scales (Editor), and Ed Tittel. *Windows 2000 Foundations.* The Coriolis Group, 2000. ISBN 1576106799.

➤ Mueller, John Paul, and Irfan Chaudhry. *Microsoft Windows 2000 Performance Tuning Technical Reference.* Microsoft Press, 2000. ISBN 0735606331.

➤ Shelly, Gary B., Thomas J. Cashman, and Misty E. Vermaat. *Microsoft Office 2000: Post Advanced Concepts and Techniques: Word 2000, Excel 2000, Access 2000, Powerpoint 2000 (Shelly Cashman Series).* Course Technology, 1999. ISBN 078955691X.

Reference Books

➤ Czegel, Barbara. *Help Desk Practitioner's Handbook.* John Wiley & Sons, 1999. ISBN 0471319929.

➤ Minasi, Mark (Editor). *Mark Minasi's Windows 2000 Resource Kit.* Sybex, 2000. ISBN 0782126146.

➤ Ivens, Kathy, and Kenton Gardinier. *Windows 2000: The Complete Reference.* Osborne/McGraw-Hill, 2000. ISBN 0072119209.

➤ McFedries, Paul. *Paul Mcfedries' Windows 98 Unleashed, Professional Reference Edition.* Sams, 1998. ISBN 0672312247.

➤ Livingston, Brian, and Davis Straub. *Microsoft Windows Me Secrets.* IDG Books Worldwide, 2000. ISBN 0764534939.

Online Information and Resources

The Internet is an enormously valuable resource when searching for more information about careers in IT. PC software support is no exception. The following sections contain some Internet-based resources that you can use to find out more information on topics of interest.

Newsgroups

There is a wide range of Internet newsgroups related to PC software support. The following list contains a selection of some of the more relevant groups:

➤ **alt.windows98**

➤ **24hoursupport.helpdesk**

➤ **microsoft.public.win2000.general**

➤ **comp.software-eng**

➤ **comp.windows.misc**

➤ **comp.virus**☐

Magazines and Journals

Many of the magazines mentioned in the hardware section provide coverage of both hardware and software issues, so be sure to check out the Web sites listed in the previous "Magazines and Journals" section. There are other publications, however, that do focus specifically on software issues.

Element K journals (**www.elementkjournals.com**) produce a range of informative how-to journals covering a range of subjects and applications relevant to those working in PC support. The journals are nonadvertisement publications, so there is a subscription fee of $79 for the first year. A free issue is available on request to new subscribers. Journal subscribers also get free access to online training resources related to their journal. Find out more by visiting the Element K Web site.

Web Pages

The Internet is littered with sites offering help, advice, and tips to people using various software packages. The following list contains a few sites that you might find useful:

➤ *Winmag* (**www.winmag.com**)—Is an informative site that contains information, articles, and reviews on subjects related to the Windows computing platform. The Resource Center feature for operating systems and application software is particularly useful. Winmag.com is part of the Techweb network.

➤ *Microsoft* (**www.microsoft.com/office/using/tipstricks**)—Provides information on the Office suite of programs in a section of its Web site. From this site, you can access resources, software updates, and product information. You can also find out about Microsoft training and associated events.

➤ *Softseek* (**www.softseek.com/Utilities/Tips_Tricks_and_Help**)—Is an Internet Web site that provides access to shareware, freeware, and evaluation software. Part of this site is also dedicated to hints, tips, tricks, and information about software and hardware issues.

➤ *Cnet* (**www.cnet.com**)—Visit Cnet's Web site for access to tons of reviews of operating systems and application software. Also, check out the download link, which will take you to one of the most useful and complete collections of downloadable software anywhere on the Internet.

Professional Associations

Many IT professionals choose to join professional associations for the opportunity to network with other like-minded individuals. For software support personnel, there are a number of associations, but the Helpdesk Professionals Association (HDPA) is one that is particularly focused on the needs of those working in PC software support.

The HDPA is an organization that *"Champions for the advancement of the technical support profession."* Membership in this nonprofit organization costs $65 annually. For more information and to find out if there is a chapter near you, check out its Web site at **www.hdpa.org**.

Summary

PC software support is a challenging field that presents those participating with a varied and interesting range of tasks. The requirements for PC software support staff to understand PC hardware to some degree makes the position even more challenging. If you are looking for variety, flexibility, and interesting experiences, PC software support is for you.

Which Way Is Up to You

PC support is a truly diverse field. Those employed as PC support technicians need to possess more than just technical skill if they are to succeed. A thirst for knowledge is equally as important as communication and troubleshooting skills. Although there is room for those who choose to be a hardware or a software specialist, neither will escape the need to know a great deal about the other. PC support is a truly rewarding field.

A Support Technician's Perspective

To get a true idea of what it is like to be a PC support technician, the best people to ask are those that are doing the job on a daily basis. In the following interviews, two PC support technicians were asked a series of questions about their jobs. Their answers provide a valuable insight for anyone considering pursuing a career in this area.

Interview One

In the first interview, Derek Deschamps discusses his work as a PC network/ technician for a computer reseller in Canada. His job related tasks involve aspects of networking as well as PC support and maintenance.

6

What is your job title, and how long have you been doing this job?

[Derek]: My job encompasses two distinct areas of IT: the first is PC support and the second is networking. My title would therefore be a PC network and support technician.

What are your main duties?

[Derek]: I am involved with most of our company's warranty repairs and system builds. Warranty repairs involve diagnosing and replacing malfunctioning components. Furthermore, I am responsible for set up and maintenance of all our clients networks, which are usually in a Windows 9x/NT environment.

What systems are you currently working with?

[Derek]: My clients' systems range from Windows 9x/NT workstations, Exchange servers, and Proxy servers to Linux gateways.

What qualifications or certifications do you hold?

[Derek]: I have a diploma in electronic engineering, a year of computer science, a Microsoft Certified Systems Engineer certification, and I am a certified system builder. I am currently pursuing my Linux certification.

How long have you been working in IT, and how did you get started?

[Derek]: I have been working in IT off and on for about four years.

What hours do you normally work? If you work evenings and weekends, do you get paid for it?

[Derek]: I work 40 hours a week, but there is an expectation that if more hours are required to complete work, I may need to work more. This is generally not the case. I do get paid for the overtime hours I put in.

What do you find most interesting about your job?

[Derek]: The most interesting thing is getting to play with the new technology that comes out and working on expensive high-end servers.

What is the least interesting aspect of your job?

[Derek]: Phone support is very frustrating. It is very difficult to tell people how to update their drivers and address other computer related problems over the phone. Many of the customers calling for support have little or no knowledge of computer systems, which makes the task that much more difficult.

Do you consider your job to be stressful?

[Derek]: Certain aspects of the job are quite stressful. The time-sensitive nature of some of the repairs and network troubleshooting can be difficult. Also, dealing with customers or clients who are annoyed about their computer problems can add another stressful element.

Do you work with other people or alone?

[Derek]: On smaller jobs, such as straight PC repair, I tend to work alone. On larger jobs or when time is of the essence, I am assisted by other colleagues.

If you could change one thing about your job, what would it be?

[Derek]: To be honest, less contact with customers. I like the black box effect, comes in broken, goes out fixed. Having customers watch over your shoulder can be quite irritating. In fact, I have considered getting more into programming because of this factor.

Can you see yourself staying in this area of the IT industry, or would you like to try something different?

[Derek]: IT moves so fast that you don't have time to become bored with it. I may try and expand on my programming skills, but I am quite happy doing what I do now.

What do you consider to be the most challenging part of your job?

[Derek]: The most challenging part of my job is being called in to troubleshoot a machine and fixing it under the watchful eye of clients or customers, especially when the customers have already attempted to fix it themselves.

What advice would you give to someone starting out in IT?

[Derek]: Work experience is everything. If you are starting out with no experience, you can't expect a high paying job right out of the gate. If you have to, volunteer to get this experience, or take a low paying job to start out. I know people who have taken their MCSE and have been unemployed for a year after. However, if they had volunteered their services, they would have gained valuable experience.

Interview Two

In the second interview, Maurice MacGarvey, a seasoned IT professional, discusses his work with a variety of technologies and products.

What is your job title, and how long have you been doing this job?

[Maurice]: I have been in the IT industry for 12 years, working in many different areas including technician, management, and sales.

What are your main duties?

[Maurice]: I analyze needs, recommend the best options, and oversee the technical implementations.

What systems are you currently working with?

[Maurice]: To work as a technician, I am required to know Novell, Windows NT, and Windows 9x systems, but I specialize in Windows 9x/NT platforms.

What qualifications or certifications do you hold?

[Maurice]: I have a customer relations and personal development certificate, which has proved invaluable, and a project business certificate. When I entered the industry as a technician, if you knew that RAM was not just a male sheep, you were a technician.

How long have you been working in IT, and how did you get started?

[Maurice]: I have been working in IT for 12 years. I got started repairing and assembling 286s and XT computers.

What hours do you normally work? If you work evenings and weekends, do you get paid for it?

[Maurice]: I work 40 hours a week. I don't typically work overtime hours.

What do you find most interesting about your job?

[Maurice]: Being able to see and implement new technology and watch the development of leading edge products shape and mold our future. When I was a kid, I played Pong—two lines and a little ball bouncing across the screen. My five-year-old son turns on his Athlon 800 and plays games that requires technology that was not even available in the space program when I was a child.

What is the least interesting aspect of your job?

[Maurice]: Changing technology. Although it excites me, it also is the most frustrating part of the job. Every time a new product comes out, there are new bugs and quirks and new headaches for me.

Do you consider your job to be stressful?

[Maurice]: Yes, enough said.

Do you work with other people or alone?

[Maurice]: Some aspects require me to work with other people, both IT professionals and clients and customers. There are times though when I can expect to be fixing and troubleshooting computers with no one else around.

If you could change one thing about your job, what would it be?

[Maurice]: It is difficult dealing with customers that do not appreciate the value of doing things right the first time, but instead cut corners to save costs. I would like some time built into the job that allows for reading, researching, and keeping up with technologies.

Can you see yourself staying in this area of the IT industry, or would you like to try something different?

[Maurice]: I am happy to stay in this part of the industry. The speed at which technology changes means there is never a dull moment. Well, okay, maybe a few, but not many.

What do you consider to be the most challenging part of your job?

[Maurice]: By far the most challenging aspect is keeping up with technology.

What advice would you give to someone starting out in IT?

[Maurice]: Get work experience and use certificates for what they are meant for, not as a degree, but as a validation of knowledge.

7

Careers in Internet Technologies and Web Design

Of all the career paths available to you in the IT arena, Internet Technology is probably the broadest in scope. In order to understand how the Internet came to be what it is today, a bit of history is helpful.

The Internet was originally a government project that was started in the 1960s. The idea was to create a means of data communication between various computer systems that were separated by great geographical distances. The popularity of the Internet exploded in the early 1990s when Tim Berners-Lee of the Massachusetts Institute of Technology (MIT) created a language that allowed documents on the Internet to be linked to each other by means of *hyperlinks*. This language, the HyperText Markup Language (HTML), allowed authors of documents on the Internet to embed hyperlinks in these documents, which readers could follow for related information. The linking of these documents, now known as Web pages, soon created entire networks of Web pages that were linked both internally to other documents as well as externally to other Web sites. This cross-linking of Web sites came to be known as the World Wide Web (WWW).

The next significant advancement was the addition of graphics capabilities to Web pages. This advancement allowed HTML authors to broaden the scope of individuals to whom they were delivering content. Since its inception, the World Wide Web has seen amazing growth in the number of users as well as technological advancements. In comparing its history to what it has grown to be today, you can more fully understand and appreciate the magnitude of growth that has taken shape on the Internet, which directly coincides with the number of IT jobs it has created and continues to create.

The focus of this chapter is on three specific job roles in Internet Technology, which are in high demand in today's job market: Web developer, site designer, and Webmaster. In previous chapters, one major job role was discussed, which was then further divided into separate areas of expertise. For example, in Chapter 5 the job role of a network administrator was segmented into working with various network operating systems. However, in the field of Internet Technology, job roles are segmented by their various scopes of work and not necessarily by different competing technologies.

This chapter describes these roles and sites their differences as well as their commonalities. Let's begin by describing these roles on a very basic level. Web developers write the actual code that makes Web pages work. Site designers, on the other hand, formulate how the site is structured. This includes the organizational flow, navigational design, and usability features. Finally, Webmasters perform many of the administrative duties of maintaining the site including upgrading the Web server hardware, adding newly created Web pages, and troubleshooting hardware related challenges. Quite often, usually in smaller "dot com" companies, these three job roles are combined into one. Although such a multifaceted position can offer you varied experiences, the division of focus and attention that you might encounter on a daily basis may be difficult to manage and may host other challenges at times. Usually, however, these three job roles come with their own individual set of responsibilities.

Each of these three job roles is discussed separately in this chapter. Information addressed includes daily tasks, qualifications and requirements, job market, and training for each job role. Prior to moving on to the specifics of each role, the job outlook for the general area of IT is discussed. As each role is described and relevant terms are used, you might want to refer to the "Jargon Buster" sections included in each job role section of this chapter.

7

Job Outlook

For the most part, the job outlook for Internet professionals is phenomenal. This is due in part to the fact that so many companies are taking their businesses to the Internet. In order to accomplish this venture, a group of savvy developers is needed to create a site that serves the company's needs and is accessible to most Internet users.

Most companies that are based in Internet Technology are seeking individuals who are well rounded in all areas of IT. This is not to say that you need to be an expert at internetworking with Linux in order to be a Web developer, but you do need a general understanding of the underlying technology.

A quick search of a job board on the Web will give you a good understanding of the "wish lists" that many employers have. Understand that the phrase "wish list" is key. Many of these employers are willing to hire someone who doesn't have all of the qualifications listed. However, at a minimum, you should be familiar with the various qualifications listed, so that you can interface with other team members in the company during the development process.

In order to stay in demand in today's job market, Internet professionals must keep their skills current by learning about the various new technologies that develop on what seems to be a daily basis. The challenge lies in the fact that many of these technologies do not become commonly used on the Internet. Therefore, Internet professionals have to rely on resources, such as industry newsletters and news-groups, to get a feel for what technologies are taking off and will ultimately become industry standards.

The future growth in this area of IT is expected to be so high that it is difficult to even estimate its rate of growth. With the boom of the Internet economy, you can expect that in the next ten years most companies, both retail and service oriented, will rely heavily on the Internet to market their products and services. Given this fact, it will take thousands of talented developers, designers, and Webmasters to accomplish this amount of growth.

Specialization vs. Generalization

When it comes to the topic of specialization versus generalization and deciding on the best path to take, the answer lies in the size and type of organization for which you work. If the company's primary revenue stream is from online sales trans-actions, you will find that quite often there is an extensive team of developers, content writers, graphic artists, and programmers collaborating on creating the various parts and pieces that make up a large e-commerce Web site.

In such situations, a Web developer could specialize in one or more of the areas that comprise Web development. For example, you may be required to code Active Server Pages (ASP) for the purposes of integrating a database into the Web site. You could then find yourself interfacing with database architects to create your code, and then handing the code off to another Web developer to write the HTML code around the ASP code for presentation to the end user over the Internet.

However, in order to truly master an area such as creating ASPs, you must also be somewhat proficient at HTML coding, database technologies, and perhaps possess knowledge of some programming language, such as Visual Basic. Because these technologies are so interrelated, it is necessary to familiarize yourself with the various areas that relate to your specialty in order to truly master that field.

If you work for a smaller organization or one that uses a Web site as a sales tool to bring customers to a retail location, you will quickly find yourself handling many of these tasks or working with a group of developers with similar skill sets. The reason for this is that the Web site may not necessarily be generating a high volume of income for the company and therefore is not given a substantial budget to enable the hiring of staff who specialize in one area or another. The upside is that the site itself will not be required to perform very sophisticated tasks that require experienced specialists.

Web Developer

As stated earlier, the field of Web development consists of many various technologies and skill sets that are dependent on the specific needs of the company or client. These skills can include HTML authoring, programming Web applications, creating artwork optimized for the Internet, performing usability testing, and so on.

In general, most Web developers are responsible for coding content for Web sites into HTML. Oftentimes this involves creating custom scripts in JavaScript or ASP to enhance the functionality of the Web site.

Sometimes, programmers that create applications for Web sites are included under the title of Web Developer. In job listings, they are also referred to as Web Programmers. In addition, developers that integrate database solutions into a Web site can be included under this title as well.

Furthermore, artists who create the style and artwork for the Web site are also considered Web developers. Most of the time, however, these individuals are also skilled in HTML coding and have learned how to optimize graphics and artwork for the Web as part of their daily tasks. Rarely is there a separate department devoted entirely to creating artwork for a Web site.

Quite often two or more of these roles and responsibilities are given to one individual, depending on the size of the company. In many situations, a Web developer will interface primarily with programmers, database architects, and network architects. In larger development environments, Web developers also interface with graphic designers and content authors.

Daily Tasks

Most of a Web developer's day is spent in front of a computer generating the code for Web pages on the site. A more challenging aspect of being a Web developer is interfacing with all of the other individuals that create the content and design of the Web site. Generally, you will find yourself taking content from a copy editor, artwork from the art director, and combining it into the design that has been specified by the site designer. The challenge arises when each department has a specific idea of how their elements should be implemented into the final design. It is easy to find yourself being an ambassador of sorts for all of the departments.

7

However, this is what many Web developers feel is the most fulfilling part of their job. The following list contains some of the more common day-to-day tasks of a Web developer:

➤ *Develop end user interfaces*—This task involves interfacing with a site designer who has designed how the Web site will look and function. It is the responsibility of the developer to write the code that makes the design happen. An additional challenge is keeping the code compatible to both Netscape Navigator and Microsoft Internet Explorer browsers.

➤ *Author supporting client or server-side code*—In addition to writing HTML code, many Web developers find themselves writing scripting code that enhances user interactivity. The two most popular languages in use are JavaScript (client-side) and ASP (server-side).

➤ *Integrate supporting applications*—On many e-commerce sites, the programs that perform inventory checking, credit card transactions, and order processing are written in compiled languages, such as Java or C++. It is the duty of the Web developer to integrate these applications into the HTML code used on the Web site.

➤ *Integrate supporting databases*—Many sophisticated Web sites use databases for collecting and storing customer information, inventory, and user authentication. As with applications, it is up to the Web developer to integrate the database into the Web site. This usually involves writing scripts to parse the data and formatting it into HTML.

➤ *Write or update content*—The most common task of a Web developer is to write content in HTML, the standard programming language of the WWW. Some of the more common tools used for authoring web content are Microsoft FrontPage, Adobe PageMill, or Macromedia Dreamweaver. Furthermore, that content needs to be kept fresh and up-to-date. Therefore, updating current pages with new content becomes routine for a Web developer.

➤ *Produce or optimize graphics/artwork*—Although many Web developers think they are skilled artists, many lack the ability to design powerful and attractive looking Web sites. In the case of large commerce-based Web sites, there is usually a team of graphic designers that produce the artwork that is used on the site. However, many graphic artists produce work that is far too large to use on a Web site. Web developers, therefore, find themselves optimizing this artwork for better performance on the Web site.

Qualifications and Requirements for Web Developers

To be truly qualified in the area of Web development, you not only need to be proficient in HTML, JavaScript, and ASP, but you also need some extensive skills in graphic design and page layout. These skills are not limited to just image manipulation with a program like Photoshop, but also include the ability to combine images and content in such a way that it is useful and engaging to the site's visitors. The best Web developers have backgrounds in communication media, graphic arts, and computer science. A solid knowledge of networking technology is very useful to understand the underlying components that make the Internet work.

With the increased demand for Web developers, many continuing education schools and universities are offering courses in Web development. You should look for a training program that not only teaches you about HTML and Internet technologies, but also teaches you more intermediate and advanced level topics, such as JavaScript, ASP, and database integration. Additionally, some basic programming skills would be beneficial as well, such as JAVA, C++, or Visual Basic. Many of these programs offer graduate recruitment and internship offerings. Thereafter, the particular company that hires you will most likely provide you with any additional training in areas that are valuable to its business model.

For those who do not have the benefit of a job placement program, it is recommended that you create a personal Web site that showcases your abilities. Many Internet Service Providers (ISPs), like AOL and Earthlink, give their members personal Web site space as part of their service agreement. This Web site space provides you with the capability to create an "online portfolio" of sorts that will give a potential employer a good idea of what your skills as a developer are.

Job Demand

The demand for Web developers of all skill levels is at an all time high and is increasing rapidly. As more companies move to the Internet for their main source of revenue, the need for skilled developers will increase exponentially.

A recent query of a popular IT job Web site for the United States turned up over 39,000 job openings when given the keywords "Web developer." Many of the listings required individuals with basic Web development skills (HTML, JavaScript, ASP) and 1-2 years of experience, and offered salaries that ranged from $25 - $110 per hour on a contract or permanent basis. It is truly an employee's market.

The demand for individuals with more specific areas of expertise is lower, however, the pay is significantly higher. As your skills increase and you gain more experience with Web development, opportunities for better jobs will find you.

As new technologies develop and evolve, they will assist the role of a Web developer by providing more and better tools. An example is the existence of a Digital Subscriber Line (DSL). Because of the low implementation costs and monthly fees for DSL service, many Internet users are switching to DSL to access the Internet. This means that in the near future, Web developers will be able to create larger Web pages with more graphics and interactivity without worrying about slow response times to the user.

Training Options and Resources

Unfortunately, there are not nearly as many certification programs available to a potential Web developer as there are for network administration. Individuals seeking to break into the Web development field will find a handful of nonvendor specific certifications available from CompTIA and Prosoft, which test for entry-level knowledge, but do not go into specific areas of development, such as ASP or Flash.

This is not to say that these certifications are not valuable, however. They will provide you with the ability to prove to a potential employer that you know the basic skills required of a Web developer. This will greatly aid you in getting your foot in the door and working in a development environment. It is then up to you to train yourself to specialize in a particular skill that interests you.

Courses and Certifications

More and more certifications for Web development are beginning to appear on a regular basis. The following list contains a handful of the more widely recognized and accepted certifications available today:

➤ *CompTIA i-Net+ Internet Technician Certification*—This vendor neutral certification involves a single test on a broad range of Internet topics including HTML authoring, security, networking hardware, and databases. The exam is designed to test a candidate with 18-24 months of field experience. For more information, visit the official I-Net+ Web site at **http://comptia.org/ certification/inetplus/index.htm**.

➤ *Prosoft Certified Internet Webmaster (CIW) Foundations Certification*—This test is nearly identical in scope to the i-Net+ test from CompTIA. It is so similar in fact, that Prosoft is currently offering to give the Foundations certification to any candidate that has passed the i-Net+ test. For more information, visit the official CIW Foundations site at **www.ciwcertified.com/exams/ 1d0410.asp**.

➤ *Microsoft FrontPage 98 Certification*—FrontPage 98 is Microsoft's premiere HTML authoring tool that comes bundled with its Office suite. Passing the certification test earns you status as a Microsoft Certified Professional (MCP). For more information on the FrontPage 98 exam, visit **www.microsoft.com/ trainingandservices/exams/examasearch.asp?PageID=70-055**.

➤ *Microsoft Visual InterDev Certification*—Visual InterDev is a high-powered HTML and ASP authoring tool included in the Visual Studio suite from Microsoft. It is intended for use in a development environment where there are a number of individuals collaborating on a project. As with the FrontPage 98 certification, by passing this exam, you will become an MCP. For more information on this exam, visit **www.microsoft.com/trainingandservices/exams/ examasearch.asp?PageID=70-152**.

Online Training

Many online training schools offer well-developed courses on Web development. Individuals who have difficulty making a time commitment because of other life obligations may find that the 24-hour availability of these online classes makes the accomplishment of training much more feasible.

➤ *SmartPlanet* (**www.smartplanet.com**)—Students need only Web access and a credit card to sign up, pay for, and complete courses on this site. Within the Internet topics, students can choose from several options within tracks entitled Databases, Web Design & Graphics, Programming, Webmaster, and Networks & Servers. Within the Web Design & Graphics track, classes are offered in Photoshop, Paint Shop Pro, Illustrator, CSS, and basic design techniques. Wanna-be programmers can take courses in Perl and CGI, all things Java, and Visual Basic. SmartPlanet is a good choice for developers who want to dive quickly into a new technology or become familiar with an authoring tool without going deeper than the fundamentals of usage.

➤ *Techies.com* (**http://www.techies.com/Develop.html**)—Purchasing a $129.95 subscription to Techies.com gives you access to more than 200 online courses, which include instruction on Photoshop, Paint Shop Pro, Common Gateway Interface (CGI)/Perl, and Dynamic HTML (DHTML). The subscription is good for one year, and classes are entirely Web-based, meaning you can start a class at any time and complete it at your own pace. If you're a job seeker, one significant perk included with a Techies.com registration is the automatic inclusion of your vital stats and skill set in the nationwide job bank and résumé pool. Job descriptions matching your abilities and interest are emailed to the address of your choice, and employers can scan your résumé online.

Self-Study Options

A significant advantage to pursuing a career in Web development is the vast amount of online resources, both free and paid, that are available to you. Simply typing the words "HTML Tutorial" in your favorite search engine reveals hundreds of online tutorials on the topic. When used as a supplement to additional training and resources, these free online tutorials greatly benefit your learning of any related Web development topic.

➤ *C-Net Web Builder* (**http://home.cnet.com/webbuilding/0-3880.html?tag=st.cn.1.dir.3880**)—This site is full of tutorials and techniques not only for HTML, but also for graphics, programming, and e-commerce. Many of the articles and tutorials have been submitted by some of the most respected Web developers in the industry and are completely free of charge.

➤ *Westminster College* (**www.shire.net/learnwebdesign/index.html**)—This online tutorial on HTML authoring and Web design is completely free and can be used as a resource tool in concurrence with other training options.

Additional Information

The following sections include some additional resources that you may find useful in determining what it takes to be a Web developer. The "Jargon Buster" helps you translate some of the more frequently used terms, or jargon, specific to this field. There are also a number of additional online resources listed, which include newsgroups, discussion lists, and Web sites that you can visit to make your search for information easier.

Web Development Jargon Buster

As with any IT related field, there is a whole new set of buzzwords and acronyms that exist, which can confuse those new to the field. To help you better understand the information you find, the following list contains some useful definitions:

➤ *Intranet*—A Web-based network interface designed in HTML or other technologies for private, internal company use. Many intranets are designed to provide information, project scheduling, and company news to employees via an HTML compatible browser.

➤ *Extranet*—A Web-based network interface between two or more separate companies or vendors for the purposes of data exchange and project coordination. Unlike Internet sites, extranets are usually private connections between participating companies and involve higher levels of security. Like intranets, the information is accessible via an HTML compatible browser and can often be accessed via the WWW.

➤ *Applet*—Developed in the Java programming language, applets are small programs that are delivered to the visitor via a browser to provide additional functionality or visual presentation that is not easily available in standard HTML code.

➤ *ASP*—A Microsoft technology, ASP is becoming a staple of modern Web development. ASPs are authored in VBScript or JavaScript and allow sophisticated data interpretation and delivery to be computed by the Web server. Results are then sent to the visitor's browser in pure HTML.

➤ *JavaScript*—Developed by Netscape, JavaScript is not a subset of Sun Microsystems's Java programming language. It is however, the single most popular client-side scripting language in use today. Compatible with many current Web browsers, JavaScript allows HTML authors to create interesting and useful user interaction that is processed on the visitor's computer.

➤ *HTML*—HTML is the basic language used to author Web pages for use on the Internet, intranets, and extranets. HTML allows for data formatting, images, sounds, and animations to be delivered to a user with a Web browser.

➤ *DHTML*—DHTML is not so much a particular programming language as it is a method of using HTML, JavaScript, and Cascading Style Sheets (CSS) to create very interactive and attractive Web sites.

➤ *XML*—The eXtensible Markup Language is a powerful markup language that is gaining popularity among Web developers, especially those designing extranets, for the purposes of data exchange. XML allows authors to create their own markup languages by defining their own markup tags as well as the use of those tags. Unfortunately, XML is only supported by Internet Explorer 4.0 and higher and a number of more obscure Web browsers. Currently, no version of Netscape Navigator supports XML, therefore, its implementations on the WWW have been limited and cumbersome.

➤ *XHTML*—A recent addition to the World Wide Web Consortium's (W3C) recommendations, the eXtensible HyperText Markup Language was created to further standardize HTML authoring by using XML Document Type

7

Definitions (DTDs). DTDs are used in XML to define how tags are to be used and structured as well as what data types they can contain.

➤ *W3C*—The W3C is a quasi-standards organization that makes recommendations on various Web related technologies. Located at **www.w3c.org**, Web developers can get the latest information on which new technologies will be emerging as standards in the coming months.

Books

As with many IT fields, there are scores of books related to various Web development technologies available to you. The following sections contain a small list of books that are considered to leaders in the field.

Beginner Book Titles

➤ Houser, Tim Catura-Houser, Laurel Ann Spivey Dumas, and Matt Simmons. *i-Net+ Exam Prep.* The Coriolis Group, 2000. ISBN 1576105989.

➤ Oliver, Dick. *Teach Yourself HTML in 24 Hours.* Sams, 1999. ISBN 0672317249.

➤ Tyler, Denise. *Teach Yourself FrontPage 2000 in 21 Days.* Sams, 2000. ISBN 0672314991.

Intermediate Books

➤ Pitts-Moultis, Natanya, C.C. Sanders, Ramesh Chandak, and Jeff Wandling. *HTML Black Book.* The Coriolis Group, 2000. ISBN 1576101886.

➤ Buser, David, and Jon Duckett et al. *Beginning Active Server Pages 3.0.* Wrox Press, 2000. ISBN 1861003382.

➤ Milburn, Ken, and John Croteau. *Flash 4 Web Animation f/x and Design.* The Coriolis Group, 1999. ISBN 1576105555.

➤ North, Simon. *Teach Yourself XML in 21 Days.* Sams, 1999. ISBN 1575213966.

Advanced Books

➤ Williams, Al, Kim Barber, and Paul Newkirk. *Active Server Pages Solutions.* The Coriolis Group, 2000. ISBN 157610608X.

➤ Homer, Alex, and David Sussman et al. *Professional Active Server Pages 3.0.* Wrox Press, 1999. ISBN 1861002610.

Reference Books

➤ Goodman, Danny. *Dynamic HTML: The Definitive Reference.* O'Reilly & Associates, 1998. ISBN 1565924940.

➤ Goodman, Danny, and Brendan Eich. *JavaScript Bible.* IDG Books Worldwide, 1998. ISBN 0764531883.

➤ Harold, Elliotte Rusty. *XML Bible.* IDG Books Worldwide, 1999. ISBN 0764532367.

Online Information and Resources

The Internet provides a great number of informative resources for learning and reference on Web development. The following list contains just a smidgen of what is available.

Newsgroups

Many newsgroups are available on the Usenet network that will provide you with a good idea of what being a Web developer is like. You will also find some good information about what technologies are taking off and which ones are on the horizon.

➤ **microsoft.public.frontpage**

➤ **microsoft.public.inetserver.asp.general**

➤ **netscape.public.dev.html**

➤ **microsoft.public.webdesign.html**

➤ **macromedia.dynamic.html**

➤ **comp.text.xml**

➤ **comp.infosystems.www.authoring.html**

Magazines and Journals

There are a number of online magazines available on Web development, but very few are in print due to the nature of the paperless Internet. The following list contains a handful of the more popular publications used among Web developers. For a more thorough listing of available publications visit **http://dir.yahoo.com/ Computers_and_Internet/News_and_Media/Magazines**.

➤ *XML Developers Journal*—This is a quarterly printed magazine covering the latest issues in XML technology. This magazine includes articles and tutorials for beginning and advanced XML coders.

➤ *Web Developers Journal* (**webdevelopersjournal.com**)— This online e-zine is full of tutorials on every existing Web-based technology you can think of. You can also find the latest news on Web technology advancements on this site.

➤ *The JavaScript Weenie* (**www.javascriptweenie.com**)—Hosted by Paige Turner, The JavaScript Weenie is a lighthearted, yet very useful, e-zine that deals with all sorts of twisted things that you can do with JavaScript and advanced HTML techniques.

Web Pages

➤ *Microsoft Developers Network Web Workshop* (**http://msdn.microsoft.com/ workshop**)—This workshop is part of the Microsoft Developers Network. On this site, you can find articles and tutorials on all kinds of information relating to the Web, ranging from DHTML techniques to the Feng Shui of Web design (no kidding).

➤ *Web Developers Virtual Library* (**http://wdvl.com**)—This library is an online collaboration of articles and tutorials submitted by some of the Internet's best Web developers. Its email discussion list is one of the more active lists on Web development with an average of 150+ email postings per day.

➤ *Page Resource.com* (**www.pageresource.com**)—This online resource is a vast resource of Web design tutorials and information. There are dedicated sections for developers and Webmasters.

➤ *Intranet Design Magazine* (**http://idm.internet.com/webdev**)—This online e-zine deals specifically with intranet networks (private corporate networks). Not only are there design tips, but also security bulletins and job boards as well.

Professional Associations

The HTML Writers Guild (HWG) at **www.hwg.org** is a professional association open to all who are interested in Web development. Membership is $40 per year with benefits ranging from job boards to discounts on online classes taught by master developers. The HWG is the only association of Web developers that is a member of the W3C, and therefore has a voice in setting the standards of the WWW.

Summary

If you are a creative person who loves to learn new things everyday, the field of Web development may be a perfect match for you. With new technologies emerging everyday, even the most seasoned Web developers are compelled to experiment with the latest developments and products. This can be a double-edged sword, however. If you fall behind on your studies and training, you will soon find your skill set a bit antiquated.

Site Designer

The site designer's job role is a natural advancement from that of a Web developer. Generally, site designers design, implement, and maintain hypertext-based publishing sites using authoring and scripting languages, content creation and management tools, as well as digital media tools. Some tools that you may find useful to learn are Microsoft FrontPage, Microsoft Visual InterDev, and perhaps Macromedia Flash. Site designers are typically well versed in all areas of Web development and interface design. The primary role of a site designer is as an interface between the client, or company management, and the development team. Therefore, the site designer needs the ability to communicate the wishes of the client to the development team as well as formulate solutions that will fulfill the client's wishes. This fact typically translates into many site designers fulfilling the role of a project manager for the creation of a Web site.

Because of the fact that site designers are required to interface with people of various different knowledge levels, it is imperative that they have strong communication skills to fill this job role. In addition to being the mangers of site development, they need excellent design skills that are tailored for the Internet. They are not only responsible for the general layout of the graphics and content of the site, but also need to be able to organize the content of the site into a structure that is both easy to follow and easy to navigate.

Daily Tasks

The daily tasks of a site designer are much the same as a project manager. As a site designer, you will find yourself in meetings discussing layout concepts, business models, and organizational structure. Typically these meetings take place with the client or company management. In addition to these meetings, you will also be interfacing with content editors, artists, and Web developers. During the final phases of the development stage, you will be in charge of coordinating usability testing. With the results of those tests, you will then need to coordinate with the development team to make any necessary changes to the site that are needed. The following list contains some of the more common tasks that face a site designer:

➤ *Research/Evaluate available design technologies*—One of the more challenging aspects of being a site designer is researching and evaluating new design technologies. Although this may seem easy enough, the challenge comes when you interface with corporate management or clients that have limited knowledge of Internet technologies. A delicate balancing act must be performed in deciding when to implement new technologies that may not be compatible with older versions of Internet browsers.

➤ *Conceptualize/Plan new Web site design*—The old saying, "Familiarity breeds contempt" applies tenfold to Web design. The longer a particular Web design is staring you in the face, the more the desire to change it will grow. The challenge is to create a design that is not only visually appealing, but also functional and easy to navigate. Particular attention must be paid to creating designs that are accessible to all users, especially those with disabilities.

➤ *Interface with management/client for design needs*—The true test of good site designers is their ability to gather the necessary information from their clients or management teams as to what function(s) the site should perform. Questions like, "What do you want this site to do," and "What sort of image do you want to portray on the site," will begin a dialog that will give you an idea as to the direction the project should take.

➤ *Design site security*—It's no secret that there are those among us who would seek to break into a Web site to deface it or steal critical information. The site designer should, at a minimum, be familiar with available security technologies to provide the greatest degree of protection necessary. Ideally, a site designer would have a security specialist available to consult with to determine what steps to take to lock down the Web site from most invaders. However, there is no such thing as an unbreakable security system, so the challenge is balancing security needs with budget constraints.

➤ *Develop project plans*—As with any construction project, coordinating when all of the various parts and pieces of the project are brought to completion is an art form in itself. The nature of the Internet and its related technologies is inter-connection. Therefore, when one component is behind schedule, many others soon fall behind as well.

➤ *Develop site standards/templates*—Many Web sites that sell products or provide up-to-date information need constant updating and additions. To facilitate this process without re-creating the wheel, you should develop generic Web page standards and templates that have all of the basic elements used in your site contained in them.

➤ *Perform usability testing*—After working on a project, such as Web site, for a length of time, it becomes easy to overlook the small details that may not function properly. Ideally, you would have a team of site testers that would navigate through the entire Web site and document any challenges they found. However, in the real world, budgets don't always allow for this sort of testing. Therefore, as the site designer, this responsibility will fall on your shoulders. This type of testing requires a very detail-oriented person with good communication skills to report specific findings.

Qualifications and Requirements for Site Designers

As stated earlier, you can think of a site designer (also known as a Web site designer, Web architect, Senior Web developer, or Web site project manager) as a high-level Web developer. These two jobs share common required skills and qualifications, such as page layout and design, graphic design, and development techniques. Typically, a site designer will have been involved in Web development for a couple of years.

The primary difference between a Web developer and a site designer is that site designers interface with the client more so than the Web development team. This requires having knowledge not only of Internet technologies, but also business principles as well. Oftentimes clients will tell you what they want in terms of functionality as it applies to their business, yet not have any knowledge of how to implement it on the Internet. This is where a skilled site designer really shines. The ability to communicate the confusing and technical aspects of Internet technologies into something that can be understood by less technically savvy clients is of paramount importance. Excellent communication skills are therefore essential to this position.

On the flip side, being able to translate the business needs of a client into technical solutions that the Web development team can use is challenging as well. Again, this requires the knowledge of both sides to effectively communicate these issues back and forth.

With the increased demand for site designers, some community colleges may have Web development programs as well as many continuing education schools, technical schools, and universities. For certifications, you'll find a few options listed in the "Courses and Certifications" section later in this chapter. Of course, having the education, knowledge, and training is essential for this position, however, ultimately, it's all of these factors combined with experience in Web development that gets you a site designer position. As suggested for Web developers, for those who do not have the benefit of a job placement program, it is recommended that you create a personal Web site that showcases your abilities. Many ISPs, like America Online (AOL) and Earthlink, offer their members personal Web site space as part of their service agreement. This Web site space provides you with the ability to create an "online portfolio" of sorts that will give a potential employer a good idea of what your skills as a site designer are.

Job Demand

You can think of a site designer as a high-level Web developer. Often, they have been or are currently involved in Web development. Therefore, the availability of site designer positions is not as plentiful as those of Web developers. Even so, a visit to an Internet job site turned up over 11,000 job openings in the United States. Of course, this need will increase as more companies take their business online.

A particularly lucrative niche for site designers is in the small office/home office (SOHO) market. These are small businesses that cannot afford the time or expense of creating their own site in house and must enlist the help of a Web design consultant. These projects are typically small Web sites that provide information and some minor e-commerce functions.

Training Options and Resources

Because of the intangible qualities of a skilled site designer, the training and certifications available to potential site designers is even further limited than those for Web developers. The only way to become qualified as a site designer is by spending a lot of time and gaining experience developing Web sites. However, there are a few certification options that can be sought after.

Courses and Certifications

Even though certification options for site designers are somewhat limited today, do not expect this to be the case in the near future. Microsoft and Prosoft both offer site designer certifications that have become very well known to potential employers. Look for many other vendors of Web oriented products to release their own product specific certifications as well as other vendor neutral companies, such as iGeneration or CompTIA, to create valuable certifications for this career path.

The Internet is a valuable tool when searching for this information—try searching by using the keywords "site design" to see what you come up with. The following list contains a couple of certification options:

➤ *Microsoft Certified Professional + Site Builder (MCP+SB)*—This certification tests a candidate's abilities to engineer, deploy, and administer Web sites using various Microsoft products. Successful candidates must pass tests on FrontPage 2000, Visual InterDev, and Site Sever Commerce Edition. In addition, candidates must attain MCP+I (Internet) status before attaining MCP+SB status. The MCP+I process involves passing tests in TCP/IP, Internet Information Server (IIS) 4.0, and either Windows 98 or Windows NT. For more information, visit **www.microsoft.com/trainingandservices**.

➤ *Prosoft Master CIW Site Designer*—This vendor neutral certification requires successful candidates to pass a Site Designer exam and an E-commerce Developer exam. Additionally, candidates must have passed the Foundations exam (outlined earlier in this chapter) in order to qualify for the Master Site Designer certification. For more information, visit **www.ciwcertified.com/certifications/ciw_mcd.asp**.

Online Training

Because of the multifaceted nature of being a site designer, online study options are a bit limited compared to those available to Web developers. Many of the online schools listed in the "Web Developer" section also offer courses in site design. Some additions to that list are as follows:

➤ *Proflex CIW Training* (**208.242.10.65/go**)—This site is dedicated to Web paced training for the Master CIW Site Designer certification.

➤ *Web Monkey* (**http://hotwired.lycos.com/webmonkey**)—This site has some nice tutorials on the basics of site design, even though it is listed as a Web developer's resource.

Additional Resources

The following sections outline some of the most commonly used terminology for site designers and also provide some additional print and online resources.

Site Design Jargon Buster

The field of site design is complete with its own laundry list of terms. Fortunately, many of them are useful terms and not just acronyms.

➤ *1ˢᵗ Generation Web sites*—These Web sites are purely informational and do not incorporate many of the graphical or functionality technologies available.

➤ *2ⁿᵈ Generation Web sites*—These Web sites focus on a more commerce related approach. Often they incorporate more technology and functionality, which adds to the sales approach. Five areas that have been added to these sites are interactivity, e-commerce capability, dynamically generated Web pages, database connectivity, and Web site analysis.

➤ *3ʳᵈ Generation Web sites*—These sites take second generation Web sites and add elements that are not purely functional, but provide users with a more visually engaging experience. Often, these sites use themes and metaphors to attain a user's attention.

➤ *World Wide Web Consortium (W3C)*—This not-for-profit organization is responsible for reviewing new Internet technologies for standardization. Although many companies develop new technologies for the Internet, only those that are approved by the W3C are considered standards that should be supported by other Internet technologies. You can visit its Web site at **www.w3c.org**.

➤ *Deprecation*—Deprecation applies to technologies, especially HTML tags that are being pushed aside for better options. These technologies are not necessarily unusable, but it is recommended that you use newer standards.

➤ *Inverted Pyramid Layout*—This describes the standard layout of most Web sites. It illustrates the technique of providing an entry point to all of the information available on a Web site with very little summary or description of the various topics. As users travel down into the site, they find greater amounts of data on a particular topic. This technique can be found in most newspapers.

➤ *Usability*—This refers to the ability of users on your site to efficiently navigate your site and find the information they are looking for. Usability comes into play with navigation, design, and organization of the site. A particularly new front in this arena, established by the W3C, is extending usability to users with disabilities.

➤ *Navigation*—One of the most overlooked areas of Web design is the ability of users to traverse a site to find the information they are looking for. There are many techniques and technologies available to accomplish this task.

Books

Books that focus purely on site design are not as plentiful as they are for Web development. However, the books listed below are actually interesting to read because they focus mostly on the psychology of site design and not just the technology behind it.

Beginners Book Titles

➤ Nielson, Jakob. *Designing Web Usability: The Practice of Simplicity.* New Riders, 1999. ISBN 156205810X.

➤ Fleming, Jennifer, and Richard Koman. *Web Navigation: Designing the User Experience.* O'Reilly & Associates, 1998. ISBN 1565923510.

Advanced Books

➤ Burdman, Jessica R. *Collaborative Web Development: Strategies and Best Practices for Web Teams.* Addison-Wesley, 1999. ISBN 0201433311.

➤ Powell, Thomas, David Jones, and Dominique Cutts. *Web Site Engineering: Beyond Web Page Design.* Prentice-Hall Computer Books, 1998. ISBN 0136509207.

➤ Sano, Darrell. *Designing Large-Scale Web Sites: A Visual Design Methodology.* John Wiley & Sons, 1996. ISBN 047114276X.

Reference Books

➤ Haggard, Mary. *Survival Guide to Web Site Development.* Microsoft Press, 1998. ISBN 1572318511.

➤ Sweeny, Susan. *101 Ways to Promote Your Web Site.* Maximum PR, 2000. ISBN 188506845X.

Online Information and Resources

As with other areas of technology, the Internet serves as a great resource for a wide array of information on Web design. Listed in the following sections are some resources to get you started.

Newsgroups

The newsgroups listed in this section are discussion forums that are populated by site designers currently working in the field. A quick look into some of the postings reveals the issues and challenges that site designers face.

➤ **microsoft.public.publisher.webdesign**

➤ **microsoft.public.webdesign.html**

➤ **comp.infosystems.www.authoring.site-design**

Web Pages

➤ *Page Tutor* (**www.pagetutor.com**)—This site offers some valuable lessons in Web site design and development.

➤ *GrafX Design* (**www.grafx-design.com/tutorials.html**)—This site has been created by a Web development firm. It offers some interesting tutorials on graphics design for the Internet as well as a handsome portfolio to get ideas from.

➤ *4Web Design* (**www.4webdesign.com**)—This site is truly geared toward the site designer. It offers a number of articles and tutorials on the fundamentals of effective Web site design.

Professional Associations

The Association of Internet Professionals (**www.association.org**) is geared toward Internet professionals in all career paths. Membership is $90 U.S. and benefits include industry discounts, site hosting discounts, financial services, insurance, and representation for Internet issues at the government level.

Summary

As you have seen, the role of the site designer falls into a managerial role. The interesting twist on this career path is that not only do you need to be a very capable Web developer, but you also need a keen ability to design a Web site that represents the business model outlined by your client or management team. Having the level of perception and creativity that allows for such proficiency is obviously a great skill set to have for this job role.

Webmaster

The last career path discussed in the Internet Technology field is the role of the Webmaster (also known as Web administrator). The term Webmaster is as old as the Internet itself. It was originally given to individuals who could perform the entire gamut of tasks related to delivery of content over the Web. These tasks included

Web development, site design, e-commerce integration, and Web server administration. Because of the rapid expanse of Web technologies, it is not only difficult to find such an individual nowadays, but also is not very desirable for large corporations.

Therefore, for the purposes of this book, let's focus on the Webmaster role as being that of the person responsible for maintaining the computers on which a Web site is hosted. Like any other position, job roles may vary a bit, depending on the company for which you work, but generally, a Webmaster maintains, structures, and authors various core Web pages, implements design, monitors the presence of a business's site, and acts as a focal point for communication.

For the most part, as a Webmaster, you may be given an updated page from the Web development team to post onto the Web site. This is a very common task performed by a Webmaster. Oftentimes, however, a Webmaster is a jack-of-all-trades and a master of a couple. This can make the nature of the position a bit like a digital fireman—chasing down and solving a wide variety of challenges. For example, a problem can arise from server-based difficulties where, perhaps, a poorly authored piece of code causes the processor on the Web server to become overloaded and subsequently users are unable to connect to the Web site There may also be situations where you may find yourself performing emergency repairs on a site that is not functioning properly as a result of poorly written code. Therefore, the ability to quickly shift from one problem situation to another and still maintain a good attitude towards resolving the problem is essential.

Daily Tasks

Many of the daily tasks of a Web administrator are closely related to those of a local area network (LAN) administrator. Therefore, not only is a solid knowledge of Web design and authoring necessary, but also a strong background in Internet hardware technology. Web administrators are often called upon to put out fires related to server hardware, Web page content, and security breaches. This combination of skills makes a seasoned Web administrator very desirable in today's job market and guarantees that there will never be a dull moment. The following list contains some daily tasks that a Webmaster might expect to encounter:

➤ *Administer/Maintain Web server*—This duty includes a variety of tasks ranging from making sure the Web server is functioning properly to updating hardware and software.

➤ *Backup Web site content*—A critical task is the backing up all of the files that make up the various sites being hosted on the Web server. There are many options available to accomplish this, and it is up to you to know which options best suit your needs and how to use them.

➤ *Generate Web site statistics reports*—Many Web server packages and some third-party programs generate a slew of information that relates to how site visitors use your site. This can be of particular importance when deciding what areas of a site need frequent updating and how valuable the space is on popular areas.

➤ *Troubleshoot hardware related challenges*—The unfortunate nature of computers is that, like any other mechanical device, they break down. Fortunately, they usually don't pose a physical threat, such as a wheel falling off a car going 60 mph on the freeway. But a nonfunctioning server can cost a large corporation millions of dollars an hour in lost revenue. It is critical that you have the ability to solve these problems quickly and as seamlessly as possible.

➤ *Update security patches/software*—Like many areas of IT, there will always be the threat of outside persons attacking your site for the purposes of disrupting your business. Your most basic line of defense is to incorporate a solid security plan to protect your site. This includes firewalls, antivirus software, and logging the traffic to your site. These solutions, however, require a modicum of administration to keep them up-to-date with the latest patches and updates.

➤ *Research/Evaluate new Web hardware and software*—Perhaps one of the more enjoyable aspects of Web administration is keeping yourself up-to-date on the latest and greatest technologies available to you. The less enjoyable aspect is creating proposals and justifications for your client or management team as to why you feel that your company would benefit from these advancements.

➤ *Add/Remove user accounts*—Not all content available on a Web site or intranet site is publicly available. Controlling who has access to these areas usually involves creating user accounts for each individual and assigning permissions to these accounts to access private areas.

Qualifications and Requirements for a Webmaster

The fundamental qualifications for a Webmaster involve being skilled in the areas of Web development, network administration, and PC technician. You will need to know how Web content is generated in order to update and maintain it. In addition, you will need to know how to troubleshoot any network connectivity issues, especially if you are administering an intranet. An intranet is like a miniature WWW that is created for private use in a company. Creating an intranet is accomplished by adding a Web server to the company's network, creating a series of content pages, and adding functionality for the employees of the corporation—a large task that can invite many challenges.

You will also have to troubleshoot and replace any failed hardware in the Web server itself. For a review of the depth of these tasks, refer to Chapter 6. Problems can range from hard drive crashes to a complete system failure of the Web server.

Knowledge in Microsoft IIS 4.0 and Apache are essential in that they are the two most commonly used Web servers. Certification for both IIS and Apache are available and listed below. Because site designers are expected to be able to perform many of the similar job requirements of a Web developer, many of the training and certification option outlined earlier still apply for site designers.

Job Demand

For Webmasters, positions in the job market are again not as plentiful as they are for Web developers, however, over 8,000 job openings in the United States were found in an Internet job search. This is due to the fact that a majority of businesses host their Web sites with external hosting services, which host hundreds of different Web sites. These hosting services administer these sites using a team of Webmasters. Usually, only larger companies with large budgets host their sites internally and employ a Web administration staff.

As with most career paths in IT, job opportunities are expected to increase for Webmasters. This growth will not be as dramatic as it is for other career paths in IT, however, due in part to the fact that Web servers are becoming easier to repair and maintain. Therefore, in the near future, it will be possible for a team of Webmasters to administer scores of Web servers simultaneously. This advancement in technology will be counterbalanced with the increase in business moving to the Internet. As a result, it is expected that the demand for Webmasters will continue to increase steadily.

Training Options and Resources

Because of the multifaceted nature of Web administration, there are many various certifications available that could apply to the job of a Web administrator, but few are specifically targeted at this particular job role. Many of these certifications have been outlined in previous sections of this chapter and in other chapters.

Courses and Certifications

Given the overall depth of tasks that a Webmaster must take on, there are a number of courses and certifications available to qualify you for this position. Many of these certifications are focused on software products offered by specific vendors. For hardware certifications, a review of the CompTIA A+ PC Technicians certification is in order. Also from CompTIA comes a new certification, Server+, which focuses on administering network servers with a concentration on Internet servers.

➤ *Prosoft Master CIW Network Administrator*—This certification involves passing a number of vendor neutral exams on basic network administration, network security, and networking hardware. It does however, have a slant towards Internet-based networking concepts. Like all other Master CIW certifications, it requires that you pass the Foundations exam before attaining this certification. For more information, visit **www.ciwcertified.com/ certifications/ciw_mcasp.asp**.

➤ *Microsoft Internet Information Server 4.0*—This exam tests your ability to maintain and administer IIS 4.0, Microsoft's flavor of Web server. This exam must be passed for MCP+I and MCP+SB certification status. For more information, visit **www.microsoft.com/trainingandservices/exams/ examasearch.asp?PageID=70-087**.

➤ *Microsoft Site Server 3.0 Commerce Edition*—Site Server is an extension package to IIS, which is geared toward e-commerce sites that require frequent updating and administration. This exam is part of the MCP+SB certification. For more information, visit **www.microsoft.com/trainingandservices/exams/ examasearch.asp?PageID=70-087**.

➤ *CompTIA Server+*—Although this certification is not available until 2001, it will be very in depth in its testing of knowledge about servers and their related hardware technology. Preliminary reports are that it will have a heavy focus on Web servers and related technologies. For more information, visit **http:// comptia.org/certification/serverplus/index.htm**.

Online Training

Many courses on installing, maintaining, and administering Web servers are available online. You should look for courses on Microsoft IIS 4.0 and Apache to learn about the two most commonly used Web servers. Many of these courses are reasonably priced compared to live instructor-led courses. The challenge is creating a means of gaining some hands-on experience on the subject. You may want to consider finding an old computer and using it to practice administering a Web server. Some of the more well-known online schools are contained in the following list:

➤ *SmartPlanet* (**www.smartplanet.com**)—Students need only Web access and a credit card to sign up, pay for, and complete courses on this site. For Internet topics, students can choose from several options within tracks entitled Databases, Web Design & Graphics, Programming, Webmaster, and Networks & Servers. Within the Web Design & Graphics track, classes are offered in Photoshop, Paint Shop Pro, Illustrator, CSS, and basic design techniques. Wanna-be programmers can take courses in Perl and CGI, all things Java, and Visual Basic. SmartPlanet is a good choice for Webmasters who want to dive quickly into a new technology or become familiar with an authoring tool without going deeper than the fundamentals of usage.

➤ *Techies.com* (**www.techies.com/Develop.html**)—Purchasing a $129.95 subscription to Techies.com provides you with access to more than 200 online courses including instruction on Photoshop, Paint Shop Pro, CGI/Perl, and DHTML. The subscription is good for one year, and classes are entirely Web-based, meaning you can start a class at any time and complete it at your own pace. If you're a job seeker, one significant perk of a Techies.com registration is the automatic inclusion of your vital stats and skill set in the nationwide job bank and resume pool. Job descriptions matching your abilities and interest are emailed to the address of your choice, and employers can scan your resume online.

Self-Study Options

There are vast amounts of information on the Internet regarding Apache and IIS Web servers. Some of the better sites are kept up-to-date with the latest security holes and patches along with reviews of the latest releases of both software packages. C-Net's Web Builder site has a fantastic area devoted to Web servers for Webmasters. A quick search of "Apache & IIS & Webmaster" in your favorite search engine will turn up scores of other resource centers.

C-Net (**http://home.cnet.com/webbuilding/0-3884.html?tag=st.bl. 3880.dir.3884**) is a subsection of the infamous Web Builder section that is devoted to Webmasters. The site also has some interesting articles on Macintosh Web Servers as well as hosting your own Web site on a Commodore 64 (yes, it's possible).

Additional Resources

This following sections provide you with some additional information about Web administration including related terminology, books, and newsgroups.

Web Administration Jargon Buster

Many of the terms used by Webmasters are familiar to those in network adminis-tration. This is representative of the nature of Webmastering being a combination of Web development and network administration. Listed below are some of the more specific terms used by Webmasters:

➤ *Port*—The simplest way to understand ports and how they relate to the Internet is to think of people meeting at a specific time and place to exchange information. In order for the user and the Web server to be able to exchange information (data), they must agree to meet at a specific place (a port). In terms of the Internet, information is transmitted to a commonly known port number (in the case of HTTP, this is port 80) that all browsers and servers know to go to for information.

➤ *Apache*—This is a very popular Web server program based on the Unix/Linux kernel. It is one of the oldest programs around to host Web sites on.

➤ *IIS*—Internet Information Server is Microsoft's version of a Web server that runs on Windows NT/2000. It has many features including virtual domains (see definition), ASP support, and other functions that make it very easy to administer and integrate with other Microsoft products.

➤ *Domino*—Lotus Domino is a very popular Web integration platform that is primarily used by larger corporations and Web sites that rely on seamless database integration, messaging services, and transaction services.

➤ *ColdFusion*—A popular Web application platform from Allaire, ColdFusion relies on a number of proprietary technologies that allow for speedy database integration and other Web-based application services.

➤ *T1*—T1 refers to a dedicated digital connection typically from a Web host to an ISP. It has a transfer rate of 1.544 Mb per second.

➤ *T3*—T3 is the equivalent of 28 T1 lines with a transfer rate of over 45 Mb per second.

➤ *DSL*—A DSL is a high-speed digital connection that can reach throughputs of 1MB per second or greater. DSL throughputs are limited by the distance of the user from the central office of the local phone company.

➤ *Virtual Domains*—A relatively recent technology that allows a Web server to host multiple Web sites on a single static IP address. Virtual domains were introduced in Microsoft IIS version 4.0.

Books

Many of the books for Webmasters are valuable to both network administrators and Web developers alike. The titles listed below are a bit more focused for Webmasters.

Beginner Book Titles

➤ Tauber, Daniel, and Brenda Kienan. *Webmastering For Dummies.* IDG Books Worldwide, 1997. ISBN 0764501712.

Intermediate Books

➤ Bowen, Richard, et al. *Apache Server Unleashed.* Sams, 2000. ISBN 0672318083.

➤ Arnold, Mark Allan, and Jeff Almeida, et al. *Administering Apache.* McGraw-Hill, 2000. ISBN 0072122919.

➤ Iseminger, David. *IIS 4.0 Administrators Handbook.* IDG Books Worldwide, 1999. ISBN 0764532758.

➤ Goncalves, Marcus. *IIS 5.0 Black Book.* The Coriolis Group, 2000. ISBN 1576106748.

Advanced Books

➤ Holden, Greg, and Nick Wells, Matthew Keller. *Apache Server Commentary.* The Coriolis Group, 1999. ISBN 1576104680.

➤ Wainwright, Peter. *Professional Apache.* Wrox Press, 1999. ISBN 1861003021.

➤ McCormack, Joc. *Webmaster's Guru Pack.* MnetWeb Services, 1999. ISBN 0967227313.

Reference Books

➤ Ford, Andrew, and Gigi Estabrook. *Apache: Pocket Reference.* O'Reilly Press, 2000. ISBN 1565927060.

➤ Manhiem, Seth, et al. *Microsoft Internet Information Server 4.0 Resource Kit.* Microsoft Press, 1998. ISBN 1572316381.

➤ Spainhour, Stephen, and Robert Eckstien. *Webmaster in a Nutshell.* O'Reilly & Associates, 1999. ISBN 1565923251.

➤ Ditto, Christopher. *Webmaster Answers! Certified Tech Support* McGraw-Hill, 1998. ISBN 0078824591.

7

Newsgroups

The number of newsgroups specifically targeted for Webmasters is quite limited. The entries listed below are focused on issues surrounding Webmasters. To supplement these, it is suggested that you look into the newsgroups listed earlier in this chapter and those listed in Chapter 5.

➤ **alt.www.webmaster**

➤ **microsoft.public.inetserver.iis**

Magazines and Journals

The best magazines and journals for Webmasters are found on the Internet, although a few good ones are available in print. A few of the best titles are listed below.

➤ *Apache Week* (**www.apacheweek.com**)—Apache Week is an online magazine that is updated on a weekly basis. It contains articles ranging from upcoming releases of Apache to security alerts to Webmaster surveys.

➤ *Windows 2000 Magazine* (www.win2000mag.net/Channels/WebAdmin/)— Windows 2000 Magazine is a printed magazine issued on a monthly basis. However many of its articles are also posted online. One particular channel of interest for a Webmaster is the Web Administration channel, which focuses on issues concerning Microsoft IIS.

➤ *IIS Administrator Newsletter* (**www.iisadministrator.com**)—An online e-zine devoted to IIS administration. Issues are released on a monthly basis with about 30 percent of the featured articles available free of charge. Subscriptions to the entire e-zine cost $99 U.S. per year.

Web Pages

The Internet is a vast resource of free information for Webmasters to delve into. Many of the sites that you may find are uninformative at best. The sites listed below are some of the best in cyberspace.

➤ *Webmaster Resources* (**www.webmasterresources.com**)—This Web site is devoted to the true Webmaster with articles and tutorials on HTML authoring, Internet marketing, Web server administration, and security alerts.

➤ *Apache Software Foundation* (**www.apache.org**)—This online organization provides organizational, financial, and legal support for Apache open source software projects.

➤ *Apache Today* (**www.apachetoday.com**)—This free online resource is devoted to issues concentrating on Apache administration with a particular focus on Linux.

➤ *Microsoft Windows Web Services* (**www.microsoft.com/technet/iis/ default.asp**)—Hosted by Microsoft, this Webmaster's resource is full of useful information on IIS administration. It also serves as a portal to other Web sites with information on IIS.

Professional Associations

The International Webmasters Association (IWA) at **www.iwanet.org** is an organization "devoted to the education and professional advancement opportunities among individuals dedicated to a Web career." Full membership is $50 U.S. per year with free limited trial memberships available. Benefits include industry discounts, access to the IWA Experts-Exchange, and a host of additional monthly benefits and offers.

Summary

The career path of the Webmaster is certainly one that is and will be fast paced and challenging at best. As with all other areas of IT, the technology involved in Web server administration changes daily. As a Webmaster, you will therefore need to stay aware of changes and fluctuations in the industry by visiting the resources outlined in this section on a continual basis. If you are the type of individual who loves to tinker with many different areas of Web technology and can also endure the pressure of being called "on demand" to put out fires, then being a Webmaster is certainly for you.

A Web Developer's View

As stated earlier, the only one who can give you information about what a specific IT career path is like is someone who lives it every day. Daniel Story is a Web developer with an e-commerce company that attained over 60 million dollars in online sales last year and receives over 100,000 visitors to its site every day. Daniel's interview sheds an interesting light on what the real world of Web development looks like in a large development environment.

What is your job title, and how long have you been doing this job?

[Daniel]: Web programmer. I've been with my current employer for about four months.

What are your main duties?

[Daniel]: I work on page convergence, merging graphical mockups of Web pages with database and server-side code to produce a functional Web site. I spend time as a liaison between the design and programming teams to coordinate what the executives want done with what can be done. I'm also on the emergency response team for maintaining the Web servers. I carry a cell phone 24 hours a day as a requirement of the job and if something breaks down, I can be called in at any time from any place to fix it.

What systems are you currently working with?

[Daniel]: I'm working with a network of Windows NT/IIS 4 servers with ASP for server-side scripting attached to a SQL Server 7 database and a separate network of Solaris systems running WebLogic and Blue Martini with an Oracle backend.

What qualifications or certifications do you hold?

[Daniel]: I haven't had much formal IT training beyond college computer science classes. Most of my knowledge base comes from work experience and the fact that I've been a self-taught hobbyist ever since I was a kid, learning new technologies out of curiosity.

How long have you been working in IT, and how did you get started?

[Daniel]: I started in 1993 as a teenager teaching some simple classes on basic computer operations out of the basement of my parents' house and doing odd contract jobs repairing PCs and building Web sites and small applications.

What hours do you normally work? If you work evenings and weekends do you get paid for it?

[Daniel]: Normally, I work from about 8:30 A.M. to 5:30 P.M. with an hour for lunch. This can expand or contract based on my workload—late nights (10:00 or 11:00 P.M.) are not uncommon when trying to meet a deadline, but I've also had days when I could leave at 3:00 P.M. if I didn't have anything more to do for the day.

What do you find most interesting about your job?

[Daniel]: Balancing the functionality that the programming department can implement from a technical standpoint with what the design department can imagine. It's great to sit down with the designers and brainstorm ways to create functionality that's out of the ordinary or beyond the normal scope of a Web site.

What is the least interesting aspect of your job?

[Daniel]: Constant revisions as upper-level management gets involved in lower-level processes. It can be frustrating to redo something for the fifth time without a deadline extension because an executive VP who knows very little about the technical process decides that he wants a new feature, and it "won't take any time at all."

Do you consider your job to be stressful?

[Daniel]: Under deadline (or when my cell phone goes off at 5:00 A.M.), yes, it can be. It's not necessarily a bad thing, however; fast-track, emergency "rush" projects can be very exhilarating to work on, and the feeling of triumph, knowing you just did the impossible, is really amazing. In between crunch times, though, it's a fairly relaxed work environment—everyone here wears jeans and T-shirts to work, even the division managers don't dress up beyond a collared shirt and slacks. We have a Ping-Pong table in the corner of the cubicle block and most everyone (including the executives) gets in a match or two a day.

Do you work with other people or alone?

[Daniel]: I work with a team of programmers, graphic design artists, content writers and editors, and managers who also fill the role of architects.

If you could change one thing about your job, what would it be?

[Daniel]: I'd have the company's executive management give our division producers more trust and micromanage them less. The executives have a vision for the Web site but not the technical knowledge to know how well the vision can be fit feature for feature; the producers have both. It would make for a much smoother workflow if executive management would specify what they'd like the site to do, not how to go about doing it.

Can you see yourself staying in this area of the IT industry, or would you like to try something different?

[Daniel]: I've already moved around several times within the computer field as a programmer, a designer, an engineer, an instructor, and various other roles. One of the most important qualities in this field is flexibility—the more things you can do, the more valuable you are and the better prepared you become for the next job shift or new technology. Part of what makes this industry so exciting is its dynamic nature and unpredictability—you never quite know what you'll be doing from one day to the next.

What do you consider to be the most challenging part of your job?

[Daniel]: Getting handed a complex project out of the blue and being told, "the company president just decided to make this an expedited assignment—it needs to go live in three hours, but we know you can do it."

What advice would you give to someone who is starting out in IT?

[Daniel]: You love it or you don't; there's no middle ground. The people who are successful in this industry are those who live, sleep, eat, breathe, and dream about technology. You have to keep learning and keep adapting to stay on top of the new developments, or you'll find yourself replaced by the next generation of teenagers who have had the time and interest to pursue all the latest innovations. People who just sign up because of the money usually fizzle out quickly under the intense workloads and incredible rate of change.

A Webmaster's View

Some of the hardest working people in the Internet world are the Web administrators. They sit in the front lines and often act as a liaison between customers and their employer's administration. As you will see from this interview with Evan Kittleman, the Webmaster at Taylor University, being a Web Administrator takes a lot of skill, patience, and the ability to wear multiple hats simultaneously.

What is your job title, and how long have you been doing this job?

[Evan]: I am the Webmaster at Taylor University. I started my third year on July 1, 2000.

What are your main duties?

[Evan]: I am responsible for the overall look and feel of the university's external Web site. I also develop content for "general" areas of the site, and I oversee all of the other areas. My duties are much like those of a magazine editor. I am also responsible for the graphic content of the site. I develop templates and graphics for the site and for others to use. I create dynamic app[lication]s for the Web site including student and staff directories, message boards, database apps, and so on.

I am responsible for administration of the Web server software and hardware. I get support for the base hardware and software from our Information Services department. Anything not in the OS or "standard software" is my responsibility. This also includes user settings and permissions, security, and so on.

I am the front line for the university regarding communications with those who send questions or comments via the webmaster@tayloru.edu account, our message boards, and so on. I am a part of the university's crisis team—should a crisis occur, we need to get information to the public immediately. I provide training and support for content development on our server. Personally, I am also responsible for keeping current in the field.

What systems are you currently working with?

[Evan]: Our external Web server runs Windows NT Server 4.0 with IIS 4.0. We plan on rolling to Windows 2000 with IIS 5.0 soon. I develop in FrontPage 2000. We also plan on having a separate staging server in the next month. This is because we are looking for an e-commerce solution for the university.

What qualifications or certifications do you hold?

[Evan]: None, really. [Laughs] I did graduate from Taylor with a B.S. in Political Science and a minor in Computer Science. The Political Science degree and communications skills that come with it are actually quite useful for dealing with the politics of an educational institution.

How long have you been working in IT, and how did you get started?

[Evan]: I began working in our Information Services department as a student at Taylor, around 1995. I was a systems installer involved in setting up and trouble-shooting workstations. I did that for about three years.

What hours do you normally work? If you work evenings and weekends do you get paid for it?

[Evan]: I usually work from 8:00 A.M. to 6:00 P.M. or 6:30 P.M. I get paid for 8:00 A.M. to 5:00 P.M. I work some on the weekends—an hour here, an hour there. I'm on 24-hour call since the site is in "mission-critical". I don't get paid overtime; however, I can take some comp time.

What do you find most interesting about your job?

[Evan]: Usually the job is a constant challenge. I have lots of different projects and things to do. I also like the fact that it isn't just a technical job. It is also very much marketing and public relations. I enjoy being able to take a break from coding in order to deal with PR situations, and vice versa.

What is the least interesting aspect of your job?

[Evan]: Waiting on people for content in order to finish a project.

Do you consider your job to be stressful?

[Evan]: Yes. Between juggling multiple projects, dealing with internal politics, and relating to the public, the job can be very stressful at times. Also, this job forces me to be a bridge between IT staff and PR staff. It can be easy at times, but more often it is quite difficult.

Do you work with other people or alone?

[Evan]: The majority of my job I do by myself. Of course, I do work closely at times with other members of the University Relations department (my department) and with members of Information Services.

If you could change one thing about your job, what would it be?

[Evan]: Definitely add staff. I can only do so much myself.

Can you see yourself staying in this area of the IT industry, or would you like to try something different?

[Evan]: I like Web development and would like to stay here, although it would probably end up being in a managerial role. The field is changing so fast, and there are so many people who could probably do the technical aspect of the job a lot better than I can.

I've considered going back to systems installation or network administration. But the Web is the future, and I want to stay in it somehow.

What do you consider to be the most challenging part of your job?

[Evan]: Being the only full-time, "professional" external Web developer. And being the bridge between PR and IS. Those two roles are the most challenging part of the job.

What advice would you give to someone who is starting out in IT?

[Evan]: Be open-minded about the job. Too many times I feel that we in IT focus on our own jobs and responsibilities and do not consider how we fit into the bigger picture of the organization/institution. This leads to division between departments and people. We need to be able to relate to other departments better.

Get used to long hours.

8

Careers in Database Design and Administration

As discussed in previous IT chapters, there are many career paths in IT that have two sides or descriptions to them. This is true of the area that is collectively referred to as Database Management as well. For the purposes of this chapter, this area will be referred to as Database Design and Administration, so that you can clearly understand the two major job roles that fall under this main technical area. There is a fine line between a database designer and a database administrator, which is due in part because of the opportunities in the database world to wear many "hats" at one time. One week you can be managing a database and the next be assisting with design as well as managing the database. In this particular IT field, there are no clear lines, but there is a difference between a designer and a administrator. Additionally, the larger an organization is, the more specialized your responsibilities will be, and the more likely it is that you will need to choose whether to emphasize database design or database administration in your career. There are also different types of databases. The most commonly used database systems are Oracle, IBM's DB2, SQL Server, Access, and dBase.

In this chapter, the difference between database design and database administration is discussed and factors such as job demand, qualifications and requirements, and the daily tasks for each are addressed. You'll see that although they share similar roles and responsibilities, there is a definite difference in career paths between the two. You will see that they use the same software and programs to do each specific job, but that the day-to-day tasks each performs with the database are not precisely the same.

Before the details of those job roles are described, however, this chapter defines and discusses what a database actually is and what it's used for. A discussion regarding the job roles follows and the chapter then addresses three of the most commonly used database management systems—Oracle, DB2, and Microsoft SQL Server. Each section describes the specific management system, provides reasons for using them and what to use them for, and presents what the job demand is for a database professional working with that particular system. As in similar chapters, each major section contains various resources, such as course and certification listings, book references, and online resources. Sections entitled "Jargon Buster" present definitions for some of the terminology most commonly used in the world of databases.

The end of the chapter invites you to review two on-the-job interviews. One interview directs questions to an experienced database designer, and the other interview presents the viewpoint of a support analyst. Rather than just working toward a job or career without any background information, it's always useful to talk to those in the field so that you can learn firsthand what the job (from their perspective) really entails.

Let's start by discussing a database system.

What Is a Database?

Companies need to keep track of information. In this "information age," a lot of information (data) is accumulated, and someone or something has to manage it in a way that allows it to be useful. For example, if you had a lot of money, you would want an accountant to keep track of it and be able to tell you where it is and how much there is anytime you need this information. You would not necessarily want him to point to a pile and say, "everything's in there."

In a sense, putting data into a database does the same thing a good accountant does—it organizes a collection of data into information that is useful to those who care about it. E-commerce sites use databases to track their orders and inventory, as well as customer data. The phone company uses databases to track the physical location associated with a particular phone number along with technical information such as the wiring used. Just about every large collection of information in a company is stored in a database. As a result, there are many opportunities for those who create and maintain those databases.

The classic definition of a database states that a database consists of three elements: files, records, and fields. A file can be thought of as a grouped collection of information. The set of your city's White Pages and Yellow Pages can be considered a database, consisting of at least two primary collections of information. The White Pages would be considered a file in this analogy. An example of a record would be your name, address, and phone number entry. Each other person's telephone book entry would be considered a record in the "telephone book" file as well. So, as you can see, a file can contain many hundreds of thousands of records—far more than can be organized and sorted easily by hand. Continuing with this example, there are three individual fields where the various types of information are entered. In this case, the names of the fields are name, address, and phone number. However, a database is not limited to these three fields. In virtually any modern database, fields may be added or subtracted at will, depending on what data the organization needs (or wants) to store. In the case of older databases, a new database sometimes needs to be created, and the previous information imported to the new target database because the structure of some older databases cannot be changed once it is created.

There are two parts to a typical database system: (1) the set of actual data tables and (2) the underlying system software. The software provides the data access language, indexing system, and other utility functions needed to add and delete data from the database and retrieve specific data of interest to the organization. The software is typically bought from a vendor, such as Oracle or Microsoft, and installed by a database or network administrator. The data tables are unique to the organization using the database. Data tables are created by the database designer and are based on input from those who want to access the data. For example, if the organization wants to track phone book entries, they would create a phone book file containing names, addresses, and phone numbers. Once the data files have been defined, it is still necessary to get the actual data records into the database. Two primary means of adding data to a database exist. Adding data can be accomplished by having data entry personnel key records into predefined forms. You can also add data by using automated processes to move data between one database system and another or import it from another organization (an example of this would be the way in which money management programs import your checking account's transaction records into their files from your online banking statement). In either case, a programmer or database designer is involved in designing the automated processes or the data entry forms used to add, display, and change the data.

There are different types of databases, and each major database system software product (such as IBM's DB2) is based on a specific type. Most commonly used are "relational" types of databases. A relational database is one in which the required information is organized into tables, which are related to each other by specific rules established during the design of the database. Most databases in use today, such as SQL Server, DB2, and Oracle, are relational. So, it is important for those in the database field to be familiar with relational database terminology and concepts.

Recently, the database world has emphasized a particular type of database known as a relational database management system (RDBMS). In an RDBMS, a file is known as a *table*, and a database is considered to be a collection of these tables. A record in a table is known as a *row*. A field of a table is known as a *column*. These terms clearly describe the concept of a database to most people because in any sort of written table, such as a transit schedule, people can easily see the table's actual rows and columns. The way in which that table is implemented in a relational database is sometimes as simple as making the table's column headings into the names of fields in the table, and then adding each row of the written table to the database table as data.

Because not all databases are relational databases, the terms file, record, and field are still in common use today. Network, hierarchical, and object-oriented database structures, or organizations, also exist. These are in less frequent use than relational databases due in part to the wide industry acceptance of relational database system software, the excellent tools available for accessing relational database data, and the convenience for database designers and programmers to think about data in a relational way, which is as flat tables of data linked to each other. In particular, hierarchical database organization is becoming popular again. XML (eXtendable Markup Language) data exchanged across the Internet is structured in a manner that many call a hierarchical database format. This format consists of a master record, such as a purchase order, containing multiple subrecords for ordered items within it.

You may have seen actual databases in use in a variety of places. For example, in a small office, you have probably seen databases created with Microsoft Access. These databases usually keep track of items such as records, accounts, and even names, phone numbers, and addresses. Simply put, databases of any sort contain data. Whether or not you've seen an actual database, you've probably seen information being retrieved from databases many times. If you've visited an airport recently, you've seen the contents of the airport's Arrivals and Departures database displayed on the video monitors throughout the terminal. Your grocery sales slip contains information from a database as well. It is through a database that the barcodes on your groceries are automatically translated into the product descriptions and prices printed on the sales slip. The reality is that there are many varying uses of a database, depending on both user and end user needs.

Designer vs. Administrator

In larger organizations or in organizations that run database applications developed by third parties, different people or teams often perform designer and administrator functions and all may report to a senior database administartor (DBA). In smaller organizations, a single team or even one person may perform both functions.

The boundary between the two functions isn't absolute. For example, some organizations may determine that only a database administrator can create new database tables, even on test systems, for reasons of control and procedure. Others may give this responsibility to the database designer, figuring that a test database changes so frequently that having the designer maintain it is most efficient. Both job functions require in-depth knowledge of the organization's database software; however, each has a slightly different emphasis on the use of the software. Keep in mind that the IT industry runs at a speed sometimes referred to as "Internet Time." Up until 1998, roles of a designer and an administrator were clearly defined and distinguishable from each other. As database software has developed, roles that were once black and white have blended into a color better defined as gray. The following paragraphs attempt to describe the roles of administrator and designer, explaining the differences and similarities between the two.

The Database Administrator

A database administrator is often responsible for databases used in production, much like a system administrator is responsible for an organization's file and print servers. A database administrator's duties might include performing database updates required by the development staff on test and live systems, tuning database performance based on statistics accumulated during the use of the "live" system. In addition, the administrator coordinates with IT staff regarding server hardware and OS issues and backup and restore strategies. Additional duties include importing third-party data (such as Electronic Data Interchange [EDI] information from suppliers) into the database, and resolving errors reported by the database software (such as full log files).

The database administrator may also maintain security for the database, determining which groups of users have access to which data stored in the database and setting policies for how that data can be accessed (for instance, certain data can be viewed over the Internet; other, more sensitive data is only available on the company's intranet). The database administrator may provide input to the database designer on how frequently certain database content is used, what parts of the application might benefit from performance improvement, and other "real world" information that might impact the database design. Organizationally, the database administrator may report to the Director of Technical Support, and his or her workgroup peers may include system administrators and network administrators.

The Database Designer

A database designer is more of a business analyst/software developer than a production support technician. Although a database administrator can likely discourse knowledgeably on the fastest way to organize the indexes on a specific complex table, a database designer will know how to efficiently organize an application's required data into related tables, specifying the most appropriate characteristics for each data item being stored. A database designer is concerned with architecting a database whose structure meets the user community's current and (as much as possible) future needs for data storage and reporting. This architecture can also be effectively used by project development staff creating the programs to store data in and retrieve data from the database. In doing this, they interact with the user community and development staff, maintain the database model (usually a combination of diagrams and written documentation), and create the development database used by project staff.

The database designer sets standards for data access. For example, the designer might specify that a particular database stored procedure always be used to move an order from "data entry" to "fulfillment" status in order to maintain system efficiency and data consistency. They may also be familiar with the project's implementation language, such as Java or Visual Basic, and advise development staff on data access using that language. The database designer also serves as a resource to the database administrator in resolving production issues. Organizationally, the database designer may report to the Director of Systems Development, and his or her workgroup peers may include business systems analysts, application programmers, and application project leaders.

What's the Difference?

The database administrator can be looked at as the person whose primary responsibility tends to be the "production" version of the database. An administrator is usually more skilled at troubleshooting random problems that occur during day-to-day use (such as what to do when the database runs out of disk space), and at choosing the best way to perform administrative tasks (such as database backups).

On the other hand, the database designer can be looked at as the person whose primary responsibility tends to be the "development" version of the database. In general, the database designer is usually more skilled in programming and the precise considerations involved in database design (such as deciding whether a particular piece of data belongs in one table or another).

Because the production version of the database application tends to have more urgent "uptime" (availability) requirements, it is the database administrator who is at the mercy of a pager and can more often be found talking to Oracle support technicians late at night. Similarly, the database designer can also expect a work day to creep toward 12 hours, as a project that is behind schedule (as most real-world database projects tend to be) nears completion. For the most part, the database designer can leave work at the office for the night because trouble with the development version of the database isn't generally considered a pager-worthy issue. So, as with almost all IT jobs involving support or development of systems on which a company relies, database designers and administrators find themselves working unscheduled long hours from time to time.

Daily Tasks

As previously stated, there are many day-to-day tasks involved in the IT field of database design and administration. Not every task typically done by a database designer or administrator is performed by a specific person on a daily basis. This is partly because larger organizations usually have a team of database designers and/ or administrators. On any given day, one person may or may not be assigned a particular task because multiple people are capable of doing it. Similarly, not every important database task (such as creating a new database from scratch) is done every day—but it is still a vital task that database administrators and designers need to know how to perform.

Because there are usually specific stages in a database project, designers will find their daily job tasks evolving as the project progresses and the database itself evolves. Similarly, an administrator's daily tasks will depend on whether there are urgent system problems to resolve that day or whether the day can be dedicated to making improvements in the database or system performance. The daily tasks for this job may sound more important because the database is often the center of a business application project. A well-designed, well-maintained database can "make" a successful project, whereas a less carefully designed or not well-maintained database can "break" a project. The daily tasks listed in this section are not necessarily a complete list of all tasks you might encounter when working in this field. But they are general tasks that are common in jobs concerned with the design and upkeep of a database.

The differences between an administrator's task and a designer's tasks can be non-existent in some cases. For example, when Microsoft introduced SQL Version 7, they included a great number of automation tools called wizards. These wizards featured even more automation with the release of SQL 2000. It is now completely possible for an administrator to design a smaller project without the assistance of a designer, thanks to the wizards. This does not mean the administrator is now overworked, as some tasks that once required human intervention and monitoring are now "self-tuning."

The tasks in the following list are common for both administrator and designers, however, they do vary somewhat depending on the project, client, and company. The actual tasks may be accomplished by one person in a small firm, or may be broken up into different areas to meet specific company needs. These duties are considered a sampling of general tasks:

➤ Meet with application project team and end users to discuss the data required in the database, its characteristics, and the activities needed by end users to manipulate this data (such as summarize sales by region, exchange data with a supplier in a specific EDI format required by the supplier, etc.).

➤ Add new data entities and modify existing data entities in a conceptual database model based on end user and programmer input. (This is usually a diagramming task, which is independent of any particular vendor's database.) Update accompanying documentation with business specific and technical details of specific data items and relationships between data items.

➤ Review changes in the database model with end users and programmers to verify that the changes will meet their requirements. Receive sign-off from end users on the proposed changes.

➤ Develop and test implementation of a conceptual model using specific database software, such as Microsoft SQL Server or Oracle, on development server. Update related project documentation.

➤ Develop database specific program code to access and update database objects and ensure that proper relationships among database objects are maintained.

➤ Recommend to programmers efficient ways to access specific sets of data stored in the database.

➤ Tune database performance (analyze database statistics and add, remove, or change database indexes and tables) and recommend system upgrades to IT staff (larger disk, additional processor, etc.) to achieve system performance goals.

➤ Install database system software (and perhaps operating system software) on the database server, according to project requirements and organizational policies.

➤ Work with IT technical support staff and database system software vendor technical support to troubleshoot production and development database problems when they occur. Possibly carry a cell phone or pager and be on call during nonwork hours to address any problems that might occur.

➤ Administer database security, such as the list of users who have access to all or part of the database and the security rights they have (for example, some users are only allowed to view inventory information, and others are allowed to change it).

➤ Create quick reports as required by end users.

➤ Work with application project staff to move application upgrades from the development server to test and production servers as required.

➤ Test new version of the third-party database software being used for project implementation.

➤ Keep up-to-date on database technology and research answers to questions that come up during the day by reading relevant technical books and articles.

8

Job Outlook

In previous chapters, you may have read that the job outlook for other careers in IT is generally very good and promising. Database management is no different. There will always be databases to be created and databases to be maintained or administered. As long as there are networks and loads of information passing through them, there must be databases somewhere keeping information to run businesses day-to-day.

On-the-job demands are being set higher for database designers and database administrators as businesses are coming up with more types of data to store and more types of analysis and reports to run on existing data. Of course, existing databases constantly need to be maintained on a daily basis as well. The market for both database personnel on the administration and design sides of IT is growing along with the demand for additional database functionality. Job descriptions that may be relevant to those interested in a career in the database field range from data administrator to systems analyst. The wide variety of particular positions in which database skills can be applied is what makes the demand so high.

In order to stay on top of this particular IT field, computer companies have set out to train people in the industry through classes, online training, and even instructional handbooks on certain languages and software. Some are oriented toward individuals seeking to enter the field for the first time; others are oriented toward IT personnel who may have a background in older database technology (such as IMS, which runs on very large "mainframe" computers) and are being retrained in a new technology, such as DB2. As with most of the IT industry, to become involved with database administration or development is to make a commitment to periodic retraining as database products evolve, new tools and programming languages are introduced, and new environments, such as the Web, appear. The following sections provide a more specific focus on the job demand for database administrators and designers.

The demand for database administrators is at a very high stage and is increasing. It was projected that there were 21,200 job openings as of 1996. By 2006 there may be as many as 46,100 job openings. These statistics are just for the specific title of database administrator; there are many additional openings for other related job titles.

The idea of constantly changing job tasks involved in this area, creating a variety of new "hats" to be filled, supports this job increase, along with that of the database designer. Many narrow specializations do exist (for example, Oracle performance and tuning engineer). Additionally, individuals who work on a contract or consulting basis may be referred to by generic titles, such as computer specialists or consultants. The job titles in the field evolve rapidly with new technology (20 years ago, Web/database designer was unheard of) and thus new occupational titles are born. Of course, employer preferences and organizational structures also play a big role in demand and new specializations.

Opportunities are so wide ranging in the database field that as you are searching for a job on a Web site, you may find yourself needing to limit your search to a particular vendor's database platform, a particular programming language, or to a particular application area you're familiar with.

Qualifications and Requirements

The skills required for a database specialist vary depending on the career emphasis you choose. Some database designers may prefer to concentrate on database administration and support; others may prefer to concentrate on system design and development. In smaller organizations, a database designer may end up with responsibilities in both areas. Similarly, you may wish to align yourself with one particular database product line, such as Oracle, or you may wish to build expertise in working with multiple products. There are good career opportunities available for both database designers and administrators no matter which route you choose.

Knowledge of relational database theory and terminology is a requirement regardless of the specific RDBMS platform on which a database designer works. Similarly, for the relational database world, proficiency in SQL is generally a requirement, although new graphical tools are gradually reducing a database designer's reliance on SQL for database maintenance tasks. As mentioned earlier, SQL is an important tool for people in the database world. The ability to perform tasks with SQL is one of the hallmarks of a database expert. However, basic knowledge of the SQL language is enough to begin working with a database in a project with others who have more experience.

Basic Internet and Web knowledge is useful to both designers and administrators as well. Sooner or later someone will either ask you to make all or part of your database Web accessible or interface with the Web developers who will be doing so. Terms like Active Server Pages (ASP)—Microsoft's easy-to-use Web server programming system—and Java Server Pages (JSP)—Java's answer to ASP—are frequently encountered when discussing how to make a database accessible over the Web. Many books on various Web programming techniques are now available. In fact, the field of Web/database integration is a database area of its own.

8

Additionally, a background in computer security on your particular platform (Windows 2000 + SQL Server 7, for example) is useful.

Note: A study in 2000 found that more than a few well-known e-commerce sites had unknowingly made administrator-level access to their database available over the Web by accepting default settings during database software installation. It seems that neither the database administrators nor designers had ever checked to make sure that the database was only accessible internally.

Required Skill Set for Database Designers

Because the database designer is responsible for building a database that meets the end users' business needs, some background in general business is very useful. Additionally, more and more organizations are interested in database designers who have some knowledge of one or more of the company's specific lines of business, sometimes referred to as *vertical markets*. For example, a small hotel chain might like its database design personnel to have some familiarity with the types of data a hotel keeps on its guests (guest name, reservation number, reservation contact name, phone number, address, assigned room, length of stay, daily rates, etc.). A grocery store chain may hire multiple IT staff from its checkout and stocking staff because it knows that these individuals have a firsthand understanding of how the front line operations of the company work.

Many database designers also augment their qualifications with experience and/or certifications in one or more computer programming languages, like Java or Visual Basic, and skills in using one or more computer operating systems, like Unix or Microsoft Windows. Because a database designer often maintains the overall database diagram, expertise in a business charting program, such as Microsoft Visio, may also be useful. Although a database designer may not be called upon to use these skills on a daily basis, they are useful to possess because having them means that a database designer can pitch in and "do whatever needs to be done" to help in the development of the application programs that access the database. For example, a database designer might want to look at a particular program to determine why it takes so long for a report to run and recommend to the programmer changes to the program that would speed it up.

Required Skill Set for Database Administrators

A database administrator may wish to gain some expertise in system or network administration, or perhaps even computer or network hardware, depending on his or her interests and on the types of tasks most often done in his or her work environment. For example, a database administrator (DBA) who is part of an organization's computer technical support department might find it useful to learn about TCP/IP networking (the type of networking on which the Internet and most corporate networks is based) or the Windows NT operating system (if their databases are typically located on Windows NT servers). Knowledge of networking and a relevant computer operating system will better enable the DBA to optimize the performance of the databases for which he or she is responsible. In addition, it will enable him or her to lend assistance in performing other tasks done by those in the department, making the administrator a more valued member of the organization.

Why Different Database Management Systems?

In this section, you will find that there are at least three large Database Management System (DBMS) software products and one that is popular for smaller desktop or workgroup databases, which supports fewer users. Different DBMSs exist to fit the different needs of various companies and administrators. Each DBMS was created for its own particular purpose. You could say that they were designed to compete with one another, but that is not precisely true. They were each created to fit a particular set of database needs. Some were designed to be very fast, others were designed to be very easy to use, and still others were designed to operate almost seamlessly with the computer's operating system.

What Are Some Specific DBMS Software Products?

Some of the main products in the database world include Oracle, DB2, SQL Server, Access, and dBase. The following list contains a brief description of each of these systems. Following this list is discussion on why one system might be chosen over another:

➤ *Oracle*—Oracle is a well-known, top-tier RDBMS. It is popular throughout the industry due to its speed, efficiency, and reliability. It runs on a variety of computer hardware and operating systems and is primarily used for larger database projects. Oracle is a rather expensive, but very complete, database environment. The specifics of Oracle are discussed in the "Oracle" section later in this chapter.

➤ *DB2*—An RDBMS from IBM, DB2 is very comparable to Oracle in speed and can handle about the same workload. Like Oracle, it is expensive, high-maintenance software. Also like Oracle, it runs on a wide variety of computers under many operating systems. Because DB2 is another popular platform for "enterprise" (large-scale) databases, more information about DB2 is provided in the "DB2" section later in this chapter.

➤ *Microsoft SQL Server*—The SQL Server RDBMS is Microsoft's enterprise-class database, which runs on Windows NT and Windows 2000. It is actually a relative of the Sybase database, which runs on Unix platforms. SQL Server has handled larger and larger databases with each new version of the product, but according to most analysts, it does not yet have the workload capacity of Oracle or DB2. Still, it is considered a price performance leader in the moderate-sized database category. SQL Server is also discussed in detail in the "SQL Server" section later in this chapter.

➤ *Microsoft Access*—Access is Microsoft's smaller contribution to the database world. This program is geared more towards an office workgroup environment with fewer users (generally under a dozen, sometimes only one) than is typical of the databases listed previously, which often handle hundreds or thousands of users working with the database concurrently. Although Access does not have all of the fancy capabilities of larger databases, such as SQL Server, it also requires dramatically less administration than SQL Server does. Because many people migrate to SQL Server when their database "outgrows" Access, Microsoft has created a special tool called the "Upsizing Wizard" to assist in the conversion of Access databases to SQL Server.

➤ *dBase*—dBase is a PC database platform that is no longer popular for new development. However, if you are involved with smaller database application systems, you might encounter it, if only when asked by someone to convert a dBase application to a newer or more scalable database. The dBase series of database programs (dBase II, III, IV, etc.) was very popular in the 1980s and early 1990s to implement smaller database application systems. It was so popular, in fact, that Microsoft acquired a very similar competing product called FoxPro, so as not to be left out of the dBase market.

Unlike more modern databases, dBase is a file-based rather than relational system. Most but not all database applications that access a dBase database are written in the relatively easy to understand but proprietary dBase programming language rather than a newer language like Visual Basic. Many organizations have run MS-DOS-based dBase systems for years on the grounds that "if it ain't broke, don't fix it." But the days of dBase systems depending on MS-DOS are numbered, as Microsoft advances its Windows platform. The ability to review an existing dBase database and convert its functionality to a modern database, such as Access or even SQL Server, has earned more than one database specialist the thanks of an organization and has helped launch many consulting careers.

Choosing Database Software

Which of the previously listed databases is the best to use or become familiar with? All of them, at least to a degree. When selecting a career in this area of IT, you have to realize that different clients and different companies require different databases. As a database designer or a database administrator, you may have to use more than one of these DBMSs in your environment.

How do you choose the right one for a particular project? Generally, it's easier than you might think because the choice usually isn't up to you. Many organizations (or departments within larger organizations) standardize on one particular vendor's database software, such as DB2, and perhaps even a particular well-tested version of that vendor's software. If your project's database can be force fit into the capabilities offered by that particular software, that's the platform on which it will be implemented. That may sound severe, but there is actually a great deal of sense behind it. For example, organizations employing very highly skilled database staff often want to utilize those skilled personnel in as many situations as possible. Although a particular database project might be more easily accomplished on Oracle than SQL Server, the company may have many internal SQL Server resources but no Oracle resources other than a consultant who is not available every hour of every business day. Similarly, the company may have invested a lot in tools to administer SQL Server databases and may have no tools that would allow easy administration of Oracle databases. In some cases, the choice of database may be up to the senior database manager or the company that is your client.

Technical and Organizational Preferences

If you do have the luxury of choosing between database platforms, you might want to consider the following questions in order to include both technical and organizational considerations:

➤ Has management already decided on the computer hardware to be used for this project? If so, the database chosen must run on that hardware.

➤ Is the database likely to move to different computer hardware in the future? If so, it is better to choose a database platform that runs on multiple operating systems rather than one like SQL Server, which limits you to Windows server operating systems on Intel platforms.

➤ Can the database software in question handle the workload (number of users, number of database updates, sizes of reports) that your database will have to support? As unforeseen demands seem to creep in later, take the estimate, double it, and add another 20 percent for a really accurate forecast.

➤ Does your management or user community have a preference of database platform? The degree to which you give your "customers" what they're asking for often determines the degree to which they are satisfied with the end product. So, unless they're asking for something very unrealistic (like Oracle on a Unix machine in an organization that is Microsoft Windows NT-based), it generally pays to follow their recommendations.

➤ How much data will be stored? If the data ranges into the tens of gigabytes, you will need a true database server like Oracle rather than a desktop database like Access.

➤ In which databases do the database administration and application development staff have expertise? You will usually be better off choosing a database in which personnel are already skilled.

➤ Does the database system software you're considering have a large installed base, or does it have a smaller user base? In some cases, large organizations are hesitant to go with products developed by smaller database software companies, figuring that larger database software companies, like Oracle, are more likely to be around in 10 or 15 years, than is a smaller company.

➤ Can programmers design software to access data in this database using database-server-independent development tools, so that it is easier to move the application to a different vendor's database server if that is ever required? Along with installed base and hardware variety, this is a "safety" measure to consider when choosing a database, so that the company is not left high and dry if the database vendor goes out of business or a database capability is not supported in the current database but is supported in a similar one.

➤ If you are purchasing an application system (such as a human resources management package) from another company, does that company have a preference for the underlying database? An application may be able to run using a variety of databases, but its developers may know that it works best on one in particular.

Performance Preferences

Another criteria to keep in mind is performance. An interesting Web page for database professionals to visit from time to time is **www.tpc.org**, the home page of the Transaction Processing Performance Council (TPC). This site contains benchmark results for an assortment of database activities, listing the best-performing combinations of computer hardware, operating system software, and database system software. (A benchmark is a measurement of how fast a particular combination of hardware and software performs a very specific set of computerized tasks. Benchmarks are useful as guidelines in determining relative performance levels of several different alternative hardware/software combinations.) On the TPC site you will find the numbers to back up comments made in this chapter about the scalability of database products such as DB2 to very large amounts of data—one of the test database sizes is 300GB! You can check this site periodically to see how your preferred database software is doing compared to other popular database software without the "marketing spin" that tends to accompany vendors' press releases about their product's benchmark performance.

Ultimately, the decision of which system to use comes down to what works best given a set of organizational preferences and technical requirements. The more you know about the alternatives, the better choice you will be able to make. As a database designer or administrator, you are responsible for matching the project's needs with the available database platforms in a manner that satisfies your management.

Let's look at an example of a situation in which you might use more than one database product in your organization. Suppose Oracle is your organization's standard database. It might not be the best database platform for every database application your organization needs, but your management has decreed, "We are an Oracle shop," and for most purposes, it works well enough. So far, every major database created in your department has been created in Oracle. Your company has a sales force of 100 sales reps, each of whom carries a Windows 98-based laptop while on the road and who frequently need to call in to your organization to get price quotes and inventory information. To eliminate the need for sales reps to manually call in to the main office and ask for this data, you can extract the relevant pieces of data from the large Oracle system into a smaller database, which can be loaded onto each salesman's laptop.

Because Oracle is a server database, and one that requires a bit of maintenance, it is not a good choice for use on a small army of laptops used by nontechnical staff. Instead, you might choose to create a Microsoft Access database for each salesman that contains only information relevant to a particular salesman's territory. In these types of situations, creative thinking and knowledge of the capabilities of different types of databases allow database professionals to best serve the organization for which they work. Sometimes that means explaining to management that an "outside the box" solution, like an Access database in a primarily Oracle environment, is best. Learning at least some of the basics of the most popular platforms will be useful to you and the clients you may be serving.

Now let's take a detailed look at three of the most commonly used systems—Oracle, DB2, and SQL Server.

Oracle

Oracle is one of the most well-known RDBMS platforms. It is preferred throughout the industry due to its speed, efficiency, and reliability. It is primarily used for larger database projects and runs on a variety of computer hardware and operating systems. Over 95 percent of the Fortune 500 companies use Oracle as one of their database systems. It is a high-cost program that runs on many types of hardware, ranging from IBM's huge mainframe computers to mini-computers and even PCs, and is best maintained (kept running well) by trained personnel. Although it runs on even small Windows NT Server systems, the maintenance overhead of Oracle makes it primarily suitable for larger systems that justify the time necessary to administer the database. Oracle also sells numerous business applications, such as its Accounts Payable and Job Costing packages, as add-ons to its database. These additional applications can push the cost of an Oracle solution into very significant dollars. Many database system design and maintenance tools were developed with Oracle in mind. As a result, support for this database in the tools that make a database person's life easier tends to be as good as it gets for any database product.

Why Use Oracle?

If an organization requires a database server that has proven able to handle very large amounts of data and large numbers of simultaneous users, Oracle is definitely a contender. An organization might decide to use Oracle for a database project if it wants to use some of Oracle's prewritten business and financial applications or a third-party's application software, which works well with Oracle. In the case where an organization combines the Oracle database and Oracle applications, the IT department has the convenience of a single source (Oracle) for database server and business application support.

Oracle might also be selected if the organization has standardized on it as a database platform, which is a fairly common occurrence, or if they are required to exchange data with another entity who uses Oracle. Similarly, benchmark tests may reveal that for the anticipated work the database will be doing, Oracle is the fastest choice. (Specific situations in which this is true won't be discussed in this book because benchmark results change from month to month as different database vendors adjust their software to better their competitors' results.) Finally, as previously mentioned, Oracle has been around long enough to be trusted by management as a viable, long-term solution. Often in the IT world, business applications run for decades longer than originally anticipated. Oracle has shown that it keeps up with new computer hardware and operating system platforms, and that as a company, it is in the RDBMS business for the long run.

Job Demand

Job demand for those with Oracle expertise is among the highest for any database, and those who acquire a high level of Oracle proficiency tend to be very well compensated. Entire Web sites, such as **www.oracjobs.com**, are devoted to matching Oracle professionals with employers. Another site, **www.orasearch.com**, specializes in job seekers with one or more years of paid Oracle experience. After searching several general career listing sites, results showed more than 1000 entries at each site for each of the following searches: Oracle database administrator, Oracle database designer, and Oracle/Visual Basic programmer.

In recent years, Oracle has experienced success in the e-commerce market, where its ability to handle large transaction volumes is well known. Therefore, Oracle can be found at both large, established corporations as well as smaller startup companies for whom reliable, efficient database access is a business requirement. If you are interested in becoming involved with Oracle's financial applications, job demand is high in that area as well. For example, more than 500 organizations in New England alone run a portion of the Oracle financial suite. Consider that this is only a small subset of the large (and ever increasing) number of organizations using the Oracle database, and you can understand the demand for Oracle skills today and in the future.

Training Options and Resources

Because many Oracle database specialists work in, or in conjunction with, larger business environments that value certifications, Oracle offers a full series of certification programs. Most certification exams, and the training that leads to mastery of the material on the exams, is fairly Oracle specific. Although PL/SQL, Oracle's particular version of SQL-92 (the current standard for the SQL language) is known either as enhanced (because it contains additional functionality beyond that in most SQL implementations) or nonstandard (for the same reason) depending on one's fondness for its unique capabilities, it is still basically SQL. General experience with SQL, gained in any database environment, provides a prospective Oracle database designer or administrator with a good foundation from which to start working with the product.

Courses and Certifications

As each database product was created to meet a particular need, training and certification for a particular product naturally follows. The track for this database carries the title series Oracle Database Administrator and Application Developer. These certifications fill the demand for a popular databases for mid- and large-sized businesses. Therefore, it should not be a surprise that there is a separate certification track for each version level of the Oracle database software, in addition to separate tracks within each version, for administrator and designer specialties. As of this writing, the current version is Oracle8i. For example, to attain Oracle Certified Professional status as an Oracle8i DBA, a candidate must pass five tests: a generic introduction to SQL and PL/SQL and Oracle8i specific exams on architecture and administration, backup and recovery, and performance tuning and network administration. Because you must pass the entire series of tests before gaining an official Oracle certification title, the Oracle certification program is considered relatively demanding. A prospective database designer with some knowledge of database concepts might start by studying for Oracle's SQL and PL/SQL test because it tests SQL knowledge in a largely vendor neutral fashion. See **www.oracle.com** for more information.

Online Training

A variety of companies offer online study materials for Oracle certification exams. A sampling of available resources includes:

➤ *The Database Domain* (**www.dbdomain.com**)—For a per user subscription fee, this site offers access to its Oracle DBA exam preparation courseware as well as introductory level Oracle courses over the Web. It also offers training toward some (but not all) of the Oracle developer exams.

➤ *DbaSupport.com* (**www.dbasupport.com/cert**)—This site offers free practice guides to Oracle exams in its Oracle Certification Zone section.

Self-Study Options

As with most technology training, self-study is a viable option for those who cannot, for one reason or another, attend formal classes. First and foremost, get your hands on the product. If you do not currently have access to the Oracle RDBMS, you can download trial versions of many Oracle products from Oracle's Web site at **www.oracle.com**. Then, acquire an introductory Oracle book or two (some of these are mentioned in this chapter in the "Books" section) and perhaps a certification study guide. Review the Web sites mentioned in this chapter (and any others you might find through links at these sites) for specific information as you use the product, study, and run into questions.

Additional Resources

These following sections provide you with some additional information about database administration and design, including related terminology, books, and newsgroups.

Jargon Buster

Whether you're an Oracle database administrator or a SQL database designer, you talk the same talk to a large degree because nearly all databases follow ANSI (American National Standards Institute). Consider this list your first lesson in general database jargon, with more to follow when we get to the DB2 and SQL sections later.

➤ *Database server*—Typically used as a synonym for RDBMS or DBMS. This term may also refer to the main machine or set of machines on which the database server software and your company's data reside.

➤ *Database client*—Typically, any computers running software that accesses the database server. The software might be a generic productivity package like Crystal Reports or an application specific front end, such as an order entry system.

➤ *Table*—A set of information about a specific data object in a database. RDBMS tables are composed of rows and columns of data, similar to the tables you may have constructed in HTML or a word processor. For example, you might have a Customer table that contains information, such as Customer ID, Customer Name, Customer Billing Street Address, Customer Sales Contact, and Last Purchase Date about each of your company's customers. When doing logical database design, these tabular sets of data are often called *entities*.

➤ *View*—A logical grouping of information from a database, which may include a subset of rows and/or columns from a single table or from a combination of multiple tables. For example, a database might contain a Customer table and a New Customer view, which is defined as all the rows from Customer that were added on 1/1/2000 or later.

➤ *Column*—A type of information stored in a table. For example, Customer ID, Customer Name, Last Purchase Date, and so on would each be columns in the customer table. Each of those individual pieces of information, such as Customer ID, would be contained in one column. A column is assigned a specific data type, such as character, integer, or floating point number, and all rows' data in that column must be of the assigned type. In logical database design lingo, a column is often referred to as an *attribute*.

➤ *Row*—A specific occurrence of a set of data in a table. For example, one customer's data represents one row in the Customer table. In logical database design lingo, a specific row of a table is also known as an *instance*.

8

➤ *Relationship*—An association between two tables, which is described by connecting one or more fields (called a foreign key) in one table with one or more fields that are the primary key of another table. Relationships can be 1 to 1 (for each row in this table, there is one corresponding row in the other table), 1 to many (for each row in this table, there are one or more corresponding rows in the other table), or many to many (for each row in this table, there are zero or more corresponding rows in the other table *and* for each row in the other table, there are zero or more corresponding rows in the first table).

➤ *Key*—Identifier of a record in a table and/or a means of linking a field in one table to a field in another table. The two main types of keys are primary keys and foreign keys. A primary key is a unique identifier for one particular row of a particular table. A foreign key is a link from one row of one table to another row in another table.

➤ *Index*—A list of pointers to individual records (or records themselves) in a table, which are sorted in a specific order for quick retrieval in that order. For example, a customer table that contains customer ID, customer name, customer street address, customer city, customer state, and customer zip might have an index on customer zip, so that customer data can be retrieved quickly in zip code order.

➤ *Transaction*—A logical unit of work in a database system that generally consists of multiple modifications to the database (either multiple tables or multiple records in a table or both). Most large system databases, such as DB2 and Oracle, have excellent support for transaction processing. If a transaction is started, and fails, it rolls back to the original state.

Books

A look at the shelves in your local bookstore will convince you that Oracle must be a popular database. It is second only to Microsoft's database platforms in terms of the number of available reference and tutorial books, which range from introductory level to relatively advanced. Some available books include:

Beginner Book Titles

➤ Hernandez, Michael J. *Database Design for Mere Mortals: A Hands-On Guide to Relational Database Design*. Addison-Wesley, 1997. ISBN 0201694719.

➤ Harrington, Jan L. *Relational Database Design Clearly Explained*. Morgan-Kaufmann Publishers, 1998. ISBN 0123264251.

Advanced Books

➤ Devraj, Venkat S., and Ravi Balwada. *Oracle 24x7 Tips and Techniques.* McGraw-Hill (Oracle Press), 1999. ISBN 0072119993.

➤ Allen, Christopher, Jason S. Couchman, and Lakshmana N. Rao. *Oracle Certified Professional Application Developer Exam Guide.* Osborne/McGraw-Hill, 1999. ISBN 0072119756.

➤ Niemiec, Rich, Joe Trezzo, Richard J. Niemiec, and Bradley D. Brown. *Oracle Performance Tuning Tips and Techniques.* Osborne/McGraw-Hill, 1999. ISBN 0078824346.

➤ Snowdon, Nick. *Oracle Programming with Visual Basic.* Sybex, Inc, 1998. ISBN 0782123228.

➤ Ault, Michael R. *Oracle8 Black Book.* The Coriolis Group, 1998. ISBN 1576101878.

Reference Books

➤ Loney, Kevin, and Marlene Theriault. *Oracle8i DBA Handbook.* Osborne/McGraw-Hill, 1999. ISBN 0072121882.

➤ Loney, Kevin, and George Koch. *Oracle 8i: The Complete Reference.* Osborne/McGraw-Hill, 2000. ISBN 0072123648.

Online Information and Resources

A popular saying today refers to "Internet time." This is a reference to the fact that the world is changing faster than ever. At one point, industry pundits thought electronic media would kill the printed word. The pundits of a previous generation thought that TV would kill radio. The latter was proven wrong, and the former is being proven incorrect. Books are needed to cover a topic in depth; online information and resources assist with quick clarification and bug reports. Below you will find some excellent resources to supplement the printed word.

Newsgroups

There are many database related newsgroups available through your Internet Service Provider's (ISP) (or corporation's) standard Usenet connection. In addition to accessing the current content of these newsgroups through your ISP, you might find it very useful when researching specific questions to query the Usenet archives at the **www.deja.com/usenet** Web site. Newsgroups to check out include:

➤ **comp.databases**—This newsgroup provides generic database technology discussions or discussions referring to a database for which a specific group does not exist.

➤ **comp.databases.oracle**—This newsgroup provides Oracle discussions.

Vendor-Sponsored Discussion Areas

Oracle offers access to user-to-user discussion groups on its technologies (the Oracle database server, programming Oracle-based applications, XML, Java, etc.) and other support resources at **technet.oracle.com** with free registration to the Oracle Technology Network (OTN). Anyone can register for the OTN, and if you're interested in Oracle, it's a must.

Magazines and Journals

As with most technology oriented periodicals, database related magazines tend to maintain an online presence to augment their printed publications. Some include content not available in the actual printed versions. If your favorite magazine is not on the following list, try searching for it by title on **www.altavista.com**, and you will probably locate its Web site.

➤ *Oracle Magazine* (**www.oramag.com**)—This site includes links to the online homes of several Oracle publishing periodicals including *Oracle Magazine*. The *Oracle Magazine* site includes searchable access to current and archived articles as well as a tips and techniques section. Print subscriptions are free to qualified readers.

➤ *Oracle Professional Newsletter* (**www.oracleprofessionalnewsletter.com**)— This site is *Oracle Professional Newsletter's* online presence. It includes content from current and past issues. Some articles are freely available; others are restricted to subscribers only. Print subscriptions are $199; a free three-issue trial is also available.

➤ *Intelligent Enterprise* (**www.intelligententerprise.com**)—This site is the online presence of *Intelligent Enterprise,* a database magazine oriented more toward managers in larger organizations. Although not specific to Oracle, it contains information that is likely to be relevant to those interested in Oracle. This site also includes archives of *DBMS Magazine* and *Database Programming and Design Magazine*, which merged into *Intelligent Enterprise* over the past couple years. Print subscriptions are free to qualified readers.

Web Pages

Web sites of interest to database designers tend to fall into two categories: database vendors' technical support/marketing sites and user-to-user sites. Note that vendor maintained sites are a source of marketing spin as well as invaluable technical information, such as support knowledge base articles, product details, Web searchable documentation, and sometimes tutorials. Investigating the Oracle Web site and becoming familiar with searching it before a user calls to report an error message (and expects you to resolve the issue within three minutes) is highly recommended. As with the discussion groups, in order to access some of the site's technical content, it is necessary to sign up as a member of the OTN—don't worry, it's free. The Oracle Web site can be found at **www.oracle.com**.

Additionally, some end-user maintained sites related to Oracle include:

➤ *Dbasupport.com* (**www.dbasupport.com**)—An online community for Oracle users. This site contains discussion forums, an Oracle FAQ, sample Oracle scripts, information about Oracle certification, a mailing list sign-up, and other features of interest to potential Oracle DBAs.

➤ *The Oracle User Forum and Fan Club* (**www.orafans.com**)—Another online community for Oracle users and fans, as the name suggests. This site offers Web-based discussion groups, software that might be of interest to those using Oracle databases, and direct links to purchase Oracle related books.

➤ *Underground Oracle FAQ* (**www.orafaq.com**)—This site contains a very complete, nicely hyperlinked Oracle FAQ and discussion boards.

Why all the different third-party Oracle Web sites? Each has its own community of regulars and a unique style. If you're looking for an answer to a question, you might search all of them. If you're looking for one to visit on a regular basis just to keep up-to-date, browse each one, and choose the one that most closely fits your interests and personality. Most sites have a "Links" section that may lead you to other interesting Web sites beyond those in this list.

Professional Associations

As with most top-tier database products, Oracle has an active user community that participates in international and local users groups. In addition to groups focused on the general use of the Oracle database platform, there is another users group that concentrates on the Oracle business applications, such as General Ledger, Project Costing, and Accounts Payable.

➤ The International Oracle Users Group's Web site is located at **www.ioug.org**.

➤ *Oracle Magazine* maintains a list of regional and local Oracle users groups on its Web site. As of this writing, the list can be found at **www.oracle.com/ oramag/misc/users.html**, but because Web sites tend to be reorganized on a regular basis, you might need to search the *Oracle Magazine* Web site at **www.oramag.com** to find this information in the future.

➤ The Oracle Applications Users Group for users of Oracle business applications can be found at **www.oaug.org**.

Summary

The Oracle segment of the database industry is enjoying significant popularity, particularly in larger organizations. The Oracle platform is evolving to stay current with new technologies (such as Java) as they appear, ensuring that it will be a viable database solution for the foreseeable future. There are a variety of opportunities for those who want more business oriented database responsibilities (such as working with corporate management in the implementation of Oracle's financial applications) as well as those who want more technically oriented responsibilities (such as the ongoing maintenance of key databases for the organization). In keeping with Oracle's position as an industry leader, it maintains a challenging certification program and does an excellent job of making technical product information available on its Web site. Additionally, the third-party educational and user community support for Oracle is excellent, as shown by the number of users groups, books, magazines, and Web sites dedicated to the Oracle database and associated applications.

DB2

DB2 is IBM's "universal" database, which (like Oracle) runs on a wide variety of computer hardware and operating system software platforms. It is comparable to Oracle in performance and ability to handle huge amounts of data. Again like Oracle, it is a rather expensive, full-featured package best suited to larger environments with qualified personnel on staff to maintain the database.

Why Use DB2?

Like Oracle, the DB2 RDBMS can handle huge data warehouses (aka databases). IBM's DB2 product has a long history in the mainframe world and a growing reputation in the Unix and Windows worlds. Many organizations standardize on DB2 across the enterprise because they're familiar with using it on one platform (mainframes, for example), and the learning curve is smaller to just learn the administration and development differences on a different computer/operating system platform than to learn a completely new database. Additionally, when an organization is using IBM computer hardware and (in some cases) an IBM operating system (such as AIX, IBM's version of Unix), using a database provided by IBM means that when technical support is needed on any aspect of that system, there is only one vendor to call—IBM.

As one of the top-tier databases, DB2 is constantly battling other enterprise databases on benchmark results. In fact, DB2 may be chosen in some organizations for its excellent performance in a particular situation. (As with Oracle, specific benchmarks won't be discussed in this chapter because database software performance is continually being adjusted by vendors.) Because of DB2's years of presence in the database arena, and its IBM support, many IT organizations consider it to be another "safe" option, especially for large databases. As a company with many decades of experience in mainframe data processing, IBM has shown that it knows how to create software that can handle significant workloads, and that its staff can provide a very high level of support to mission-critical IT environments.

Job Demand

Job demand for those proficient in using DB2 is very high. Searches of several popular employment sites, such as **www.monsterboard.com**, showed that many large companies and consulting firms are interested in those with DB2 expertise. Again, more than 1000 openings appeared in the search results at each site. The DB2 Universal Database (UDB) platform is gaining in popularity as it becomes available on more platforms. As a result, job demand for DB2 professionals is expected to continue to grow in the future.

Training Options and Resources

Because DB2 is an enterprise database, many DB2 professionals work in larger business environments that value certifications. As of this writing, IBM offers DB2 certifications on two different versions of the product and includes two tracks: administration and design. The exams are fairly DB2 specific, and both the administration and design exams require SQL proficiency in addition to knowledge of the DB2 UDB product itself.

Courses and Certifications

IBM Certified Solutions Expert in DB2 UDB Database Administration for Unix, Windows, and OS/2 and IBM Certified Solutions Expert in Database Development for Unix, Windows, and OS/2 are IBM's two basic certifications. The first is for those specializing in DB2 database administration, and the second is for those specializing in DB2 database design and development. There are separate versions of each certification for different versions of the DB2 product. Currently, DB2 version 6.1 is the latest release. Each of these tracks requires passing two exams—a "fundamentals" exam, and then a second exam specific to either administration or development. IBM also offers advanced level certifications on topics such as data replication and using DB2 in a clustered system environment. For more information on DB2 certification, you can check out the DB2 section of IBM's certification site at **www.ibm.com/education/certify/certs/db_index.phtml**. You can also find information on IBM's DB2 administration and development classes including IBM's new DB2 classes for Linux users at **www-3.ibm.com/services/learning/**.

Self-Study Options

You can start learning DB2 by downloading a trial version of the product from **www.ibm.com/db2**. Then, acquire an introductory DB2 book or two (some of these are mentioned in the "Books" section later in this chapter), install the product, and work with the product. To augment your studies, check out some of the Web sites listed in this chapter, particularly the list of DB2 links, for the latest information on DB2.

Additional Resources

The following sections provide you with some additional information about database administration and design, including related terminology, books, and newsgroups.

Jargon Buster

The following terms pick up where the previous "Jargon Buster" section left off. Again, these terms are spoken and understood by database professional regardless of the database in which they specialize.

➤ *SELECT*—The SQL statement used to perform database queries, retrieving a specified set of columns in a specified set of rows from one or more database tables. For example, "SELECT CustomerName FROM Customer WHERE CustomerID='14682':" would retrieve the name of the customer whose Customer ID is 14682.

➤ *INSERT*—The SQL statement used to add rows of data to a table in the database.

➤ *UPDATE*—The SQL statement used to update one or more columns in existing rows of a table.

➤ *DELETE*—The SQL statement used to delete rows of data from a table.

➤ *Normalization*—The process of organizing a database design in a way that results in tables and relationships that adhere to the relational model, which is a set of rules of how to structure data in relational databases. The different levels of relational model compliance are known as "Normal Forms," and normalization is performed by applying rules, such as "No repeating groups of data items are allowed in a single row of a table."

➤ *Locking*—The process of restricting access to certain pieces of a database, generally because a transaction (or perhaps a program that is not formally a transaction in database terms) is updating or accessing those parts of the database and doesn't want another process to change the data until it is finished. There are many different types of locking, and not all are implemented by every database.

8

Books

DB2 may be the best-kept secret of the database world. It doesn't get nearly the attention or respect it deserves, and DB2 folks like it that way. Why? Because DB2 professionals say they make more money and get the same job done faster than the more popular database specialists. To begin your trek on this less traveled path, check out the following books available on DB2.

Beginner Book Titles

➤ Chamberlin, D. D. *A Complete Guide to DB2 Universal Database.* Morgan Kaufmann Publishers, 1998. ISBN 1558604820.

➤ Visser, Susan. *Teach Yourself DB2 Universal Database in 21 Days.* Sams, 1998. ISBN 0672312786.

➤ Whitehorn, Mark, and Mary Whitehorn. *DB2 for Windows NT—Fast.* Springer-Verlag, 1998. ISBN 3540762000.

Advanced Books

➤ Cook, Jonathan, Robert Harbus, Tetsuya Shirai, and Hershel Harris. *DB2 Universal Database V6.1 for Unix, Windows, and OS/2 Certification Guide.* Prentice-Hall, 1999. ISBN 0130867551.

➤ Lawson, Susan, and Roger A. Yevich. *DB2 High Performance Design and Tuning.* Prentice-Hall, 2000. ISBN 0132037955.

➤ Cook, Jonathan, and Robert Harbus. *DB2 Replication Certification Guide.* Prentice-Hall, 1999. ISBN 0130824240.

Reference Books

➤ Sanders, Roger E., and Janet Perna. *DB2 Universal Database SQL Developer's Guide.* McGraw-Hill, 1999. ISBN 0071353895.

➤ Mullins, Craig S. *DB2 Developer's Guide (4th Edition).* Sams, 2000. ISBN 0672318288.

Online Information and Resources

The DB2 world is a bit different from that of the Oracle or SQL databases. And this is reflected in the online information and resources supporting DB2. Professionals working on DB2 appear to have a secret, and they like to keep it that way. Drop into the quiet, yet profitable world of DB2 by looking into the resources below.

Newsgroups

The challenge with newsgroups is not every ISP carries every newsgroup. You might find it very useful when researching specific questions to query the Usenet archives at the **www.deja.com/usenet** Web site. Newsgroups to check out include:

➤ **comp.databases**—This newsgroup provides generic database technology discussions or discussions referring to a database for which a specific group does not exist.

➤ **comp.databases.ibm-db2**—This newsgroup provides DB2 discussions.

Magazines and Journals

As with most technology oriented periodicals, database related magazines tend to maintain an online presence to augment their printed publications, and some include content not available in the printed versions. Be aware that because many DB2 sites are large corporations with huge mainframe data centers, some DB2 resources are priced for that market (in other words, they are very expensive for an individuals to acquire on their own). If the company for which you work runs DB2, check your organization's technical library for copies of those periodicals. If your favorite magazine is not in the following list, try searching for it by title on **www.altavista.com** to locate its Web site.

➤ *DB2 Magazine* (**www.db2mag.com**)—This site contains a quarterly magazine about DB2 and includes content for current and past issues. Print subscriptions are free to qualified readers.

➤ *Xephon* (**www.xephon.com/db2update.html**)—This site contains a monthly journal about DB2, which includes DB2 news and issue tables of contents as well as code to accompany various articles. The list of articles in all issues is freely available. To access the code, you must subscribe to the journal. Print subscriptions are $380 per year.

➤ *DB2 Performance Journal* (**www.ylassoc.com/Journal/perfjrnl.htm**)—This site contains the *DB2 Performance Journal*, which is a technical magazine about DB2. It also includes archives of past issues, white papers, and tips and tricks. Print subscriptions are $700 per year.

Web Pages

There are two types of Web sites of interest to database administrators and designers: database vendors' technical support/marketing sites and user-to-user sites. Note that vendor maintained sites are a source of marketing spin as well as invaluable technical information, such as support knowledge base articles, product details, Web searchable documentation, and sometimes tutorials. The IBM Web site at **www.ibm.com/db2** is a valuable source of technical support information, software patches, and news related to the DB2 product.

Additionally, some end-user maintained sites related to DB2 include:

➤ *DB2 Family* (**www.dunhamsoftware.com/db2.htm**)—This site offers a substantial list of DB2 related links.

➤ *DB2 News and Resources* (**www.best.com/~arnoud/db2**)—This site is the home of a DB2 FAQ.

Professional Associations

DB2 has an international users group as well as numerous local and regional groups. You can find out more about the DB2 users groups on the Web at the following sites:

➤ The International DB2 Users Group's (IDUG) Web site is located at **www.idug.org**.

➤ IDUG also maintains a list of regional DB2 users groups at **www.idug.org/ neo_apps/url_magnet/index.cfm**.

Summary

DB2 has been popular in large IT environments running proprietary IBM hardware (mainframes and the AS/40) for many years. As the DB2 UDB product becomes more popular in Unix and Windows environments, the user base continues to grow both in number and diversity. No longer is DB2 the exclusive province of the mainframe world, although it definitely still has a strong presence in that realm. IBM's recent initiative to make DB2 available on the Linux platform shows that IBM is dedicated to supporting the most popular operating system platforms rather than simply positioning DB2 as "the database you run if you're running an IBM system."

DB2's Web database capabilities, which focus on high performance, support for complex types of data, and multiplatform interoperability, make DB2 a leading RDBMS. As with other advanced databases, there are many opportunities for those who want to work in DB2 administration or design. IBM supports those pursuing DB2 career paths by providing an excellent technical Web site for personal research as well as established training and certification options. Although third-party support for DB2 is not as great as for some other RDBMSs, this is changing as DB2 transitions from a primarily mainframe oriented product to one that enjoys significant popularity on a full spectrum of operating systems.

Microsoft SQL Server

SQL Server is Microsoft's scalable database platform. It runs exclusively on Microsoft Windows NT and Windows 2000. It is very widely used in the industry in small, medium, and large organizations and is mostly for small- to medium-sized projects. As successive versions of SQL Server have been released, its capability to handle larger amounts of data have improved. Microsoft publicly demonstrated SQL Server's enhanced large database capabilities by hosting the Terraserver aerial photography Web site at **www.terraserver.com**. It is perhaps the most popular database among those who have worked exclusively or primarily in Windows-based environments (rather than mainframe or Unix) because of its Windows user-friendly product design.

Because SQL Server is a true database server, more database administration and design knowledge is required to make use of it than is required for Microsoft's desktop database product, Access. Despite the added complexity of SQL Server, many Access-based systems eventually migrate to SQL Server because of its performance, reliability, large database support, and added functionality. As with Oracle, many database design and administration tools exist in SQL Server.

Microsoft has even included extra client/server SQL debugging capabilities in the Enterprise version of its Visual Studio product (which is Microsoft's development environment).

Why Use SQL Server?

If your organization is familiar with administering a Windows network, would like to run a true database server, and is looking for the simplest alternative to get up and running with the least amount of retraining, SQL Server is a good choice. Additionally, if your organization maintains a database in Microsoft Access, and that database has started to slow down as more users access it and more data is stored in it, moving the database to SQL Server is a logical step. Microsoft's commitment to the PC/Windows platform ensures that as long as you stay with Windows, you won't encounter the phenomenon of a vendor providing great support for most of its platforms, but only mediocre support for the one you chose several years ago. This does happen with some vendors that support many, many different operating system and hardware platforms when sales haven't justified additional product support expenditures.

Many organizations choose to standardize on Microsoft Windows as their only (or primary) operating system because they then don't have to worry about support-ing multiple operating system environments. SQL Server might also be chosen by organizations who would like to have only one vendor to call for both operating system and database issues to minimize the finger-pointing that can occur among vendors if a problem occurs. Microsoft has a tremendous presence in the technol-ogy channel, and tens of thousands of individuals are trained and certified on various versions of the SQL Server product. This fact ensures that if an organiza-tion opts for SQL Server, there are many potential sources of support in addition to those offered by Microsoft.

Job Demand

There is great job demand for those with Microsoft SQL Server expertise. As with other popular database servers, searching popular career listing sites on the Web resulted in more than 1000 opportunities for those with a background in the product. Microsoft SQL Server is also popular in the e-commerce world, with many Windows NT-based Web hosting sites also offering access to it as part of their site hosting packages. SQL Server is likely to be found in organizations of any size, from small retail organizations to large manufacturing operations. So, if you are particularly interested in working with smaller firms, SQL Server might be a good platform choice for you.

8

Additionally, many SQL Server skills are transferable to the Sybase database server environment because both were originally based on the same product. So, even though Microsoft SQL Server is limited to use on Windows platforms, the skill set you acquire while working with the product is valuable in Sybase-based projects as well. This can be seen in career listings involving Sybase database environments, which include Microsoft SQL Server as relevant experience. As with other top-tier databases in this expanding market, Microsoft SQL Server's popularity continues to grow, and there is expected to be great demand for SQL Server professionals well into the future.

Training Options and Resources

Microsoft's certification programs are among the most well known in the technology world. They have been offering certification on SQL Server since version 4 and are now up to version 7 (SQL Server 2000 is available, but training and certification opportunities for it are not yet available). Due to the popularity of the SQL Server platform and Microsoft certifications in the industry, there are an incredible number of resources available from Microsoft as well as third-party vendors to assist you in gaining SQL Server certification.

Courses and Certifications

Currently Microsoft has great popularity in the realm of certification. SQL 7 has done very well, and SQL 2000 shows great promise in extending this popularity to a scale that should make Oracle and DB2 nervous.

For SQL Server 7 certification, Microsoft offers System Administration and Database Design exams, which test relational database concepts and SQL knowledge as well as significant SQL Server specific knowledge. Passing either exam earns you the status of Microsoft Certified Professional (MCP). These exams also count as credit toward the Microsoft Certified Systems Engineer (MCSE), Microsoft Certified Solution Developer (MCSD), and Microsoft Certified DBA (MCDBA) designations, which are advanced certification programs that require passing a series of exams. The MCDBA certification requires passing Windows-related exams as well as database exams, ensuring that an MCDBA can administer both SQL Server and the Windows NT (or 2000) server system on which it runs. See **www.microsoft.com/mcp** for more information.

Online Training

Many companies offer online study materials for SQL Server certification exams. For a sampling of available resources, check out **www.microsoft.com/ seminar/1033/SQL7Overview/portal.htm**, which contains an overview of SQL Server from Microsoft.

Self-Study Options

As with most technology training, self-study is a viable option for those who cannot, for one reason or another, attend formal classes. A trial version of Microsoft SQL Server can be downloaded from Microsoft's Web site as **www.microsoft.com/sql**. There are many, many Microsoft SQL Server books available covering beginning to advanced topics. Also available are other books specifically aimed at the Administration and Design exams. Additionally, there is a tremendous amount of SQL Server information available on the Web.

Additional Resources

The following sections provide you with some additional information about database administration and design, including related terminology, books, and newsgroups.

Jargon Buster

Below is the final batch of database jargon. Becoming familiar with these terms will make your research of database technology all the more meaningful.

➤ *SQL*—SQL is the de facto standard language for accessing and updating information in relational databases. Both ANSI and ISO have issued standards for SQL, and vendors tend to closely comply with these written standards. Sometimes it is pronounced "sequel" as in a movie sequel; other times, it is spelled out letter by letter, as in "S-Q-L." SQL has roots that are found in IBM research in the mid-1970s. Since then, it has become one of the most popular database access languages.

➤ *Stored procedure*—Program code stored within the database, which operates on database contents. Typically, stored procedures provide a very efficient means of updating and querying a database, more so than programs written in other languages, such as Basic or Perl. The language used to program a stored procedure is specific to the database, such as SQL Server or Oracle.

➤ *Entity-Relationship Diagram*—A graphical representation of the entities in a database design and the relationships among them. The logical database design, which is represented by the E-R Diagram, is generally done before the database designer sits down with a specific database, such as SQL Server, and begins to implement the database.

➤ *Open Database Connectivity (ODBC)*—A database independent standard interface (called application programming interface [API]) for accessing the contents of databases, generally from Microsoft Windows-based database client computers. The idea behind ODBC is that any database client program, like Crystal

8

Reports or Microsoft Excel can, through ODBC, access any DBMS for which a piece of computer software known as an ODBC driver exists. The reality is a bit more complex than the theory, because multiple versions of ODBC drivers for most databases exist, and each version tends to have its own set of software bugs or limitations to be wary of.

➤ *Java Database Connectivity (J DBC)*—A database independent standard interface for accessing the contents of SQL-based databases from the Java language. JDBC is based on Microsoft's earlier ODBC standard, and connectors exist to allow JDBC-based client software to access ODBC databases.

Books

There are dozens of books available on topics related to SQL Server, including administration, programming, database design, performance tuning, specific certification exams, and so on. Most SQL Server books are aimed at the beginning to intermediate level user, so you should find many titles of interest when browsing your local bookstore. The following sections list some titles to get you started.

Beginner Book Titles

➤ Wynkoop, Stephen. *Special Edition Using Microsoft SQL Server 7.0.* Que Education and Training, 1999. ISBN 0789715236.

➤ Bjeletich, Sharon, Greg Mable, and David W. Solomon. *Microsoft SQL Server 7.0 Unleashed.* MacMillan, 1999. ISBN 0672312271.

➤ Robinson, William. *Teach Yourself Microsoft SQL Server 7 in 10 Minutes.* Sams, 1999. ISBN 0672316633.

Advanced Books

➤ Henderson, Kenneth W. *The Guru's Guide to Transact-SQL.* Addison-Wesley, 2000. ISBN 0201615762.

➤ Viera, Robert. *Professional SQL Server 7.0 Programming.* Wrox Press Inc, 1999. ISBN 1861002319.

➤ Siebold, Dianne. *Visual Basic Developer's Guide to SQL Server.* Sybex, 2000. ISBN 0782126790.

Reference Books

➤ Deluca, Steve Adrien, Marcilina S. Garcia, Jamie Reding, and Edward Whalen. *Microsoft SQL Server 7.0 Performance Tuning Technical Reference.* Microsoft Press, 2000. ISBN 0735609098.

➤ Soukup, Ron, and Kalen Delaney. *Inside Microsoft SQL Server 7.0*. Microsoft Press, 1999. ISBN 0735605173.

Online Information and Resources

Microsoft has a large following, which means there is no shortage of places to find the digital equivalent to the "Daily News" regarding Microsoft SQL. And today a Microsoft SQL guru may need to interconnect with an Oracle database in use at a partner's site. Therefore, the list below guides you to both generic sites as well as Microsoft specific sites.

Newsgroups

While some newsgroups are not available at all ISP's, the two listed below are popular, which means they can be found on virtually every ISP. To find others, query the Usenet archives at the **www.deja.com/usenet** Web site. Newsgroups to check out include:

➤ **comp.databases**—This newsgroup provides generic database technology discussions or discussions referring to a database for which a specific group does not exist.

➤ **comp.databases.ms-sqlserver**—This newsgroup provides Microsoft SQL Server discussions.

Vendor Sponsored Discussion Areas

Microsoft offers newsgroups at **www.microsoft.com/technet/discuss/ support.asp**, which includes forums for discussion of its SQL Server and Access database products. (Hint: SQL Server is in the BackOffice products section, and Access is under the Office section.) The archives of all **microsoft.public** newsgroups are also searchable via **www.deja.com/usenet**. These newsgroups are broken down into more specific topic areas than are the Usenet database groups. For example, there are over 20 Microsoft Access newsgroups pertaining to various aspects of the product and over 10 SQL Server newsgroups. Other newsgroups on Windows NT, Visual Basic, and other topics might be of interest to those pursuing SQL Server certification as well. The following list contains a sample of the available newsgroups:

➤ **microsoft.public.sqlserver.server**—This newsgroup provides general discussions about SQL Server functionality.

➤ **microsoft.public.sqlserver.setup**—This newsgroup discusses SQL Server installation and configuration information.

➤ **microsoft.public.sqlserver.programming**—This newsgroup discusses accessing and maintaining SQL Server databases via programming.

Magazines and Journals

Without taking anything away from the Oracle and DB2 mainframe profession-als, there are more PC users working with databases then there are mainframe professionals. SQL 7 can scale down to run on a Windows 95 laptop. This creates a great demand for Microsoft SQL publications. If your favorite magazine is not in the following list, try searching for it by title on **www.altavista.com** to locate its Web site.

➤ *SQL Server Magazine* (**www.** awitp.org)—The online companion to *SQL Server* magazine, this site includes current articles as well as archived articles from past issues, all of which are searchable. It includes a FAQ on SQL Server and a user community with end-user discussions.

➤ *SQL Server Professional* (**www.pinpub.com/sqlpro**)—The online home of *SQL Server Professional*, this site includes current and past articles and source code archives.

Web Pages

Web sites of interest to database designers and administrators tend to fall into two categories: database vendors' technical support/marketing sites and user-to-user sites. The Microsoft SQL Server product home page, which contains support links to content, such as the Microsoft Knowledge Base, Microsoft newsgroups related to SQL Server, training information, and product information, can be found at **www.microsoft.com/sql**.

Additionally, some end-user maintained sites related to Microsoft SQL Server include:

➤ *SQLWire* (**www.sqlwire.com**)—This site features news and technical infor-mation about Microsoft SQL Server.

➤ *Swynk.com* (**www.swynk.com**)—Named after its founder, Stephen Wynkoop, this site has evolved into a significant source of BackOffice information with Web-based user-to-user discussion groups, a FAQ (frequently asked questions document), sample SQL scripts, a tips and tricks library, and regular columns on Microsoft SQL Server, among other things.

➤ *SQLServer Superexpert* (**sqlserver.superexpert.com**)—This site offers a community of SQL Server experts and contains SQL Server-related news, technical information, and job postings, among other resources of interest to those working or learning about SQL Server.

Microsoft SQL Server has an active online community. As with Oracle, browse the sites available (and any links to other sites, as new SQL Server sites tend to appear frequently) and decide which ones fit your style. Each site has its own unique group of regular users and emphasis (administration, development, etc.). Then, make a point of visiting your sites of choice regularly. If you're searching for a particular piece of information, it usually pays to research your query at each available site.

Professional Associations

Many technical professionals are involved with local or national newsgroups related to Microsoft products including SQL Server. In addition to groups specific to SQL Server, user groups that cover all of Microsoft BackOffice (of which SQL Server is a part) might be of interest to those working with SQL Server. The following list contains some of these groups:

➤ The Professional Association for SQL Server (PASS) can be found at **www.sqlpass.org**

➤ The BackOffice Professionals Association's Web site is located at **www.bopa.org**.

➤ *SQL Server Magazine* maintains a list of regional and local SQL Server users groups on its Web site at **www.sqlmag.com**.

Summary

As noted earlier, Microsoft SQL Server is a very popular RDBMS, and its popularity is growing as it is adopted by more sites, including e-commerce-based organizations and Web-hosting companies. There are many resources, such as Web sites, magazines, and books, available for learning the product and maintaining your skills. Microsoft recognizes that individuals working with SQL Server may choose either a database administration or a database development career emphasis. Consequently, it includes challenging certification tracks that reflect the different career paths, each of which requires passing at least four exams to achieve certification. The demand for Microsoft SQL Server experienced professionals is strong and is expected to remain so in the future.

A Database Professional's View

The following sections contain two on-the-job interviews that may provide some insight to the world of database professionals. The first interview is with a database designer and the second interview with a database administrator.

Interview One

The following interview with Helen, a database designer, illustrates how a database professional might take on various relevant roles and responsibilities in an organization. Helen has been in this field for over 15 years. From week to week, she not only performs database work, but also performs various other job roles. Her certifications, training, and of course, experience, show that she has become a very diversified person in the IT field. Being diversified in many job skills is almost a requirement in this particular IT field. Helen brings to this interview her experience from the many database environments in which she has worked. It is helpful to be able to work with those in the field that you want to be in, learn from them, and gain experience while also working in a related field.

What is your job title, and how long have you been doing this job?

[Helen]: Right now I am a Senior Programmer Analyst. I've been in the database world professionally since late 1986, working in many DB environments.

What are your main duties?

[Helen]: My main jobs day-to-day are a cross between supporting an existing application system that is built on one database technology and assisting with the design and specifications for a new system that is similar to the old one but based on new technology.

What systems are you currently working with?

[Helen]: Unix and Windows NT. The database system software I use includes a proprietary database system on Unix. I use SQL Server and Microsoft Access on Windows NT.

What qualifications or certifications do you hold?

[Helen]: I hold an MCSE + Internet, an MCSD, and degrees in math sciences and business, which is how I got into databases.

How long have you been working in IT, and how did you get started?

[Helen]: I have been working in IT since 1983. I was hired as a computer room assistant in school and gradually proved myself, got promoted as programmer and programmer analyst, and just continued on from there.

What hours do you normally work? If you work evenings and weekends do you get paid for it?

[Helen]: I pretty much work as the job demands it. Nowadays, I would say that I spend about 60 hours a week consistently, but at his point in my career, I have a pretty flexible schedule. If I wanted to work fewer hours, I could. I am typically paid by the hour, so there is an incentive for me to work the long hours I do.

What do you find most interesting about your job?

[Helen]: I like learning about the new technology, keeping up with the new SQL Server 2000, and seeing how databases evolve all the time as technology evolves and computers get faster. People realize that new things can be done with databases, like online analytical processing, and that means more for me to learn about.

What is the least interesting aspect of your job?

[Helen]: When someone tells me, "Here go do this. We know you can find the right solution, and we're really too busy to help you figure it out." And I then have to go figure out the solution on my own without any help. At times, I find myself lacking the information I need to do the best job I possibly can because the user is too busy to provide me with more input. Sometimes, I'm just guessing at how they'd like the database to work, and I don't like to guess about things like that.

Do you consider your job to be stressful?

[Helen]: Mostly no. However, from time to time when there are deadlines to be met, it gets a little bit stressful.

Do you work with other people or alone?

[Helen]: Some of both, and I most enjoy it when I work with other people. However, the nature of the job is programming, so there will be a week or so where that is all I'm doing.

If you could change one thing about your job, what would it be?

[Helen]: I would like to spend more time on the new technologies. I am a technologist, so new technology is interesting to me.

Can you see yourself staying in this area of the IT industry, or would you like to try something different?

[Helen]: I think I'll always be involved in the database arena, simply because I really do understand it, and I have some talents in that regard. I like getting into the technology side of it as well as doing database design. So, I look for opportunities in which I get to do both sides of database work in order to maximize variety.

What do you consider to be the most challenging part of your job?

[Helen]: Balancing user requirements. Because I'm doing databases that serve accounting people, front line order taking people, and a large user community, I have to balance their needs, which is making sure people are paying for what they are supposed to pay for.

What advice would you give to someone who is starting out in IT?

[Helen]: Get into the industry any way you can in terms of just getting IT experience. This provides a good start toward doing the kinds of things I do. My first work in IT, as a school computer room assistant, was the academic equivalent of being the help desk engineer for a group of very novice users. It's the kind of environment that might not be very exciting or technically challenging all the time, but it is one in which you can practice the skills of communicating effectively with users at all levels of expertise and use all available resources to solve reported computer hardware and software problems. Being able to interact effectively with end users who often have substantial business expertise, but limited computer experience, is a key skill for many in the computer world, particularly in IT environments. And it's one that not enough IT personnel seem to have. Getting in the door of an IT organization and being able to demonstrate the ability to learn as well as the ability to work well with a variety of users often enables you to network your way into an opportunity in the particular area of IT that interests you within the organization.

Interview Two

Tina has been in the IT field for over eight months and had never seen the inside of a computer before entering this field. However, she can now build, analyze, and troubleshoot hardware and software issues. By answering emails and phone calls, Tina helps other users resolve their problems and challenges. She has learned to wear many different hats to get the job done, but is also very satisfied in the end by her success. Tina has become very confident in the knowledge she has obtained and has greatly appreciated the outcome of her experience in the field. At the time of the interview, Tina was working help desk for database challenges. Very recently, due to her success, she has been promoted to being an assistant administrator on the database product she was supporting on help desk.

What is your job title, and how long have you been doing this job?

[Tina]: I am a Support Analyst (Help Desk) and have been in the position for eight months.

What are your main duties?

[Tina] I am responsible for analyzing and troubleshooting users' technical issues received via telephone and email. I help support in-house programs that are all run off databases, so there are times when I have to go into the backend of the database to resolve issues. I also act as a focal point for communication to the associated parties on all escalated issues.

What systems are you currently working with?

[Tina]: Windows 9x and Windows NT.

What qualifications or certifications do you hold?

[Tina]: I hold MCP and Network + certifications.

How long have you been working in IT, and how did you get started?

[Tina]: I started working in the IT field eight months ago. I decided on a career change and started from scratch in this field after going back to school. I started in the Support Center and learned anything and everything I could. Currently, I am interviewing for a promotion to Assistant Network Administrator.

What hours do you normally work? If you work evenings and weekends do you get paid for it?

[Tina]: I work anywhere from 45 to 50 hours a week in the office. That translates to four 10-hour days, plus I am currently on call for two-week periods, rotating every four weeks for after hours and weekends, which I do not get paid extra for. There are times when a couple of hours at a time get taken out of my days off to work and answer calls.

What do you find most interesting about your job?

[Tina]: The thing that I find most interesting is how much I learn on a daily basis. The issues that I receive to analyze always challenge me to use my education and resources.

What is the least interesting aspect of your job?

[Tina]: The least interesting part of my job is the follow-up piece. I have to ensure that all escalated issues are being taken care of, and if they are not, I need to determine the status of the issue.

Do you consider your job to be stressful?

[Tina]: For the most part no.

Do you work with other people or alone?

[Tina]: I work on a team of seven people and basically always have another brain to tap when my knowledge isn't enough to solve a problem. I also have an office of 50 other people who specialize in all different areas of IT to use as a resource.

If you could change one thing about your job, what would it be?

[Tina]: My hours of work. I am at work from 4 A.M. until mid-afternoon, and then have an hour commute both ways. Otherwise, there isn't much I would change about my job at the moment.

Can you see yourself staying in this area of the IT industry, or would you like to try something different?

[Tina]: I would eventually like to get into the Internet part of the industry. I appreciate everything that I have learned, which is a ton, but I would like to branch out and learn different areas.

What do you consider to be the most challenging part of your job?

[Tina]: The most challenging part is supporting an application without any training or knowledge of it. Also, knowing that sometimes the company is down until you fix the problem.

What advice would you give to someone who is starting out in IT?

[Tina]: Don't be afraid of any kind of experience you are offered. At first, I was disappointed in myself for starting at the very bottom as a Support Analyst, but now I would not take any of the experience back. The position that I have is not a ticket taker or reporter but an analyst. I have to analyze and troubleshoot issues and fix them at the drop of a hat. I am ready to move up and on, but will still have to have the database background to continue in my career. You will be amazed at how much you can learn on a daily basis and how good it feels to help people resolve their issues, so that they can continue with their work.

PART III

Making It Happen

So what was your choice—programmer, network support, database developer, or did you give up on an IT career all together to pursue a passion for dance? Whatever your choice, the next section takes a specific look at how to prepare, achieve, and maintain that desired job. Part III is all about turning your career choice into a reality. For those who chose dancing, some, but not all, of the information provided in the following section may be useful!

The various chapters of Part III run in a logical and sequential order, starting first with identifying training and certification issues before moving on to the preparations for job-hunting, such as résumé writing and presentation. From there, the actual interviewing process is explored, including how to deal with technical interviews and avoid some common interview blunders. You learn how you can negotiate the best deal without underestimating your opportunities and market value, while at the same time having realistic expectations. Finally, you learn how you can keep yourself marketable so that when, or if, the time comes to move on you are still a valuable commodity.

Chapters 9 through 13 of this section are broken down as follows:

➤ *How to Prepare for a Career in IT*—In the IT field the basis of your skills must be learned and practiced before entering the workplace. The good news is that there is a broad range of educational opportunities available to assist you. We look at training in considerable detail, including the different training methods available and the benefits and potential drawbacks of each. We also examine the often mystifying world of certification.

➤ *Preparing for the Job Hunt*—After you prepare for a career and the training is complete, it's time to go out and look for a job. With your qualifications, experience, and the right attitude, you are ready for work. Don't be fooled, however, into believing that the shortage of skilled IT professionals forces employers to lower their standards for employment as this is simply not the case. Most employers would rather go without than employ a liability. Preparation is the key.

➤ *The IT Job Search*—Will your résumé go to the top of the pile or become lost in the recycle bin? There are aspects of job hunting that are specific to the IT industry. This section describes what is involved in an IT job search, including resources and information on where to look for the job, writing a résumé for a job in IT, and the interview process. Recruitment agencies add their own little twist to the process, too.

➤ *Keeping That Job*—After you have the job, you need to keep it. But how can you keep your boss happy, develop your own skills, and keep one eye on the job market all at the same time? It can be done—with a little help, of course.

➤ *Moving On*—With new opportunities and challenges around every corner, it can be tempting to look around and think about moving on. As a second-time jobber, you have more choices than you did when you were first looking for work. New opportunities such as freelance or contracted positions may be a factor that you previously had not considered.

As with the other parts of this book, Part III is designed to provide you with information you need to realize your ambitions. If things work out, by the time you have finished with Part III, this book will have served its purpose—that of helping you to secure a career in IT.

9

How to Prepare
for a Career in IT

Preparing for a career in IT can be very confusing. Upon entering the field, you are greeted with a variety of options and choices, with each choice having the potential to greatly impact your career. Even the ways of getting into IT can seem technical. What are the training options? What are the training costs? Are some training methods more appropriate than others? Do employers have a training preference? Is experience more valuable than training?

Unfortunately, there is no single universally accepted method to prepare for a career in IT. Some jobs require a bachelors degree or higher, for others technical certification is more than enough to get a foot in the employment door. Relevant work experience adds another ingredient to the mixture. How much experience do you need? How do you get it? Do you really need it? Preparation, research, and clear career direction is what you need to find these answers.

In this chapter, we address these questions. We discuss the significance of on-the-job experience, provide insight into the various types of training available, and explore certification. We help you evaluate which certification may be right for you, and discuss how certification compares to an accredited degree. In each discussion, we address both the advantages as well as the disadvantages. The intention, as in other chapters, is to assist you in making an informed and prudent decision that best suits your needs and situation. You will find that preparation, research, and a clear understanding of what career direction you choose to take will all play an integral role in your ultimate decisions.

Experience vs. Training

Two people apply for the same job. One applicant has one year of experience working in a similar environment, the other just finished a two-year training course that prepares applicants for exactly the job that is available. Who is more likely to get the job? Well, it depends on the policy of the employer, but the person with the experience is most likely to get the job. The reason is that companies can train people with relative ease. Experience can only be gained over time, which you simply can't learn in a class. In addition, the person with the experience has done the job, coped with the stresses involved, and come out the other side. The person with the qualifications may know the technical low-down, but how does this person react when the job gets stressful?

Think about this. You want to have your house repainted. Would you rather use a professional painter who has painted houses for over a year, proving time and again that he can get the job done, or would you use someone with a certificate in painting that has never actually painted a house but does know the theory? The example may seem a little flippant, but you get the point.

The Importance of Experience

No doubt about it, work experience is important. It gives you the real scoop—a look at the good, the bad, and the painfully ugly aspects of the job you are pursuing. Nothing else can accomplish this. If, for instance, you decide to become a PC technician because you enjoy fixing computers for friends and family, a little work experience will reveal that troubleshooting computers for family and friends bears very little resemblance to a career in PC repair. Your Uncle Ed for instance, is likely to be more understanding about your difficulty fixing his printer than the fifty accountants waiting to print off invoices.

Several factors make work experience an essential part of a career plan:

➤ Real work experience in your chosen career enables you to confirm, or deny, whether the choice you made was a good one. Trying the job gives you the opportunity to see first hand if it is what you imagined it to be. You can see first hand the fun and exciting aspects of the job as well as the routine and mundane. Being on the job is the only way to get a thorough understanding of what the job is like.

➤ Work experience is a résumé builder. Résumés of employee candidates are far more attractive to potential employers when they include relevant work experience. In fact, some employers do not consider résumés of those applicants without experience.

➤ Being on the job enables you to network with other professionals in your chosen field. These co-workers and contacts become a valuable resource and can often have the inside track for employment opportunities.

➤ Work experience can increase your confidence in yourself and your ability to do the job. Your first day employed as a systems administrator can be less stressful if, for instance, you already have some experience with the equipment and software used.

How Do I Get Experience?

You can get the valuable experience you need to get your IT career started in a variety of ways. Unfortunately, many of them involve self-sacrifice and some volunteer time. Rest assured, however, that your effort and self-sacrifice will pay off. Many employers actually view your volunteer efforts in a very positive light, recognizing the fact that you had the foresight to secure a position to get experience, and that you were prepared to undergo some self-sacrifice to do so. Nothing says dedication more than giving up your own time to further your experience and knowledge.

If you are interested in getting some volunteer exeprience, there are a variety of options available. Co-ops, internships, job shadowing, volunteer work, and part-time employment represent just a few of the ways to get started.

Cooperative Education and Internships

Many schools offer co-op and internship programs. These programs are formed by a partnership with the educational institution and a business. Typically, these supervised work experience programs enable students to earn a combination of academic credit and some well deserved money. Sometimes the internships are done purely for the experience. The main advantage of these programs is that they allow students to get work experience before graduation, thus better preparing students to enter the work force. Furthermore, it is not uncommon for the companies involved in such programs to offer jobs to students after graduation. The employer benefits because they get an employee who has experience working in their company, and they don't have to go through the interview process. These programs are exceptional for exposing students to a career field, giving those involved the chance to develop marketable skills.

When preparing for a career in IT, it may be a good idea to call universities, colleges, technical schools, and training centers and ask if they offer co-op or internship programs. With a little research, you may find a program that provides you not only with training but also relevant work experience, which in some cases can lead to a job.

Volunteer Work and Job Shadowing

Probably the last thing you want to hear after spending time and money obtaining a degree or technical certification is that you might have to work for free. It may not be necessary, but if you were unable to find a co-op, internship, or even a part-time job that gave you relevant technical experience, volunteer work may be a viable option.

In the right place, volunteer work provides a way of gaining marketable skills, gaining confidence in your ability to do the job, and perhaps making professional contacts that can help you find a job when your volunteer period finishes. It allows you to work in a variety of settings without making a long-term commitemnt to any one job or company.

Volunteer work, while familiarizing you with the actual work environment, cannot give you a completely true picture of the job. It is unlikely that a volunteer will be given enough responsibility to feel the pressures and rewards of a full-time position. Even so, just the opportunity to be in the environment is worth any sacrifices you have to make. Being around the technology and the people who work with it can only serve to enhance your IT knowledge and experience.

Making Experience Count

So you have figured out a way to get some experience. Now you need to make sure that you are going to use this valuable opportunity to maximum advantage. You need to make the experience count. The first thing to remember about such a situation is that you are not working per se. You have been given the opportunity to spend some time in an environment that will ultimately benefit your career, and may or may not be paid for it. The company or organization that gave you this opportunity did so out of the goodness of its heart, not because it had to. This is no time to be complaining about the coffee or the lack of sports facilities at the office.

For the period of your volunteership, especially if it is just a few weeks, you should get to the office as early as you are allowed and leave at the last possible moment. Every minute you spend at work, no matter how mundane the task you are doing, is a minute well spent. While we are on the subject of mundane tasks, let's address another issue. As a volunteer, there is a chance that you will be given routine tasks to complete, in part because they do not require a great deal of supervision, but mainly because the regular IT staff do not want to do these types of tasks. Whichever way, for you at this stage, there is no such thing as a waste of time. If you have to do mundane tasks for six hours, but then get to spend half an hour in a program project meeting or with a network technician while he upgrades a file server, your six hour investment is cheap at twice the price. Plus, if the tasks you are given are completed correctly, the more likely it is that you will be given a more interesting task next time. This advice may seem obvious, but it is easily forgotten as you start yet another morning of filing and photocopying.

While you are volunteering, take notes, ask questions, and generally soak up the atmospehere of your environment. Watch other people and how they act. Offices have a very unique working environment, as do many other situations. Again, experience is about learning the things that cannot be taught in a classroom, and not all of these things are IT related. Sometimes it is just about understanding the role that your chosen profession plays in a business. Do try to impress others. More often than not a volounteer who impresses co-workers is the first candidate to be

9

considered when a future work opportunity comes up. If you are interested in working for the company you are volunteering at, make sure that the company knows. You will not do yourself any harm by saying at an appropriate moment, "I really enjoy working here. If a position comes up, I would welcome the opportunity to be considered for it."

Sooner or later your work experience period will be over, and it will be time to go back to your studies or to your job search. You still have the opportunity to get maxium benefit from your work experience. Before you leave, get some valuable feedback on your performance. Find a quiet and convenient moment, and then ask the person you reported to for feedback on your performance. Listen carefully to what the person says. You do not necessarily have to agree or dissagree with any of the comments; just listen. After all, it was you who asked for input. After the sesson has finished, thank your supervisor for providing honest feedback, and think about what was said.

The way that last paragraph sounds, it may seem as if all the feedback will be bad, which is probably not the case at all. There may well be more good than bad, but remember that most people find it just as hard to give praise as they do criticism.

Evidence of Efforts

Last, but certainly not least, make sure that you get some evidence of your work. If the organization is unwilling to give a written reference, ask if it would be okay to include a phone number of someone who can give a verbal reference if needed. Failing that, ask if one of the more senior workers in the IT department would be willing to provide a personal reference, which is not necessarily any less effective than one from the company. Remember that although you may feel a little discouraged by a company's reluctance to give a reference, some companies or organizations have a policy of not giving them at all.

Most importantly, remember that as a volounteer, you are the one who is getting something out of the situation. It is up to you to make sure that the organization you work for gets something out of the arrangement too.

All About Training

The furtherment of knowledge is one of the most overriding features of a career in IT. Workers who elect not to learn new technologies and products will find themselves in diminishing demand. To keep up to date with technology, you must continually augment your current knowledge with new information. The process of training can take many forms. In this section, we discuss the various methods of formalized training and pros and cons of each. At some point, almost everyone will need to attend or participate in some kind of course or study.

If you are currently employed, your company will most likely choose the method of study and even the topic of study. For private individuals, however, the range of training options and the bewildering choice of training organizations can make it seem hard to pick the right situation. To help you make a decision, let's look at the various types of training and the features of each. Always remember that you need to view the relative merits of each type from a personal perspective. Self-study may be the most practical option from a price and convenience perspective. If you have self motivation issues, however, it is unlikely to be the best choice. Most of all, rememeber that training should be fun. You are not only learning an interesting subject, but also a subject that can help you build or further a lucrative and rewarding career.

Training Options

Numerous training options are available for those seeking a career in IT. The training method you choose is very important because it must prepare you with the knowledge and skills to do the job. Training options for IT range from complete self study to instructor-led classrooms and every possible combination in between. The following sections explain each category to help you understand the characteristics of each. In some cases, course curriculum may use a combination of methods. Even the most focused instructor led classroom courses require that you supplement the information learned in the classroom with that learned outside the classroom.

Self-Study

Complete self study essentially provides a student course materials and a self proclaimed deadline for assignments. Self-study training involves a process where individuals learn independently and at their own pace. Self-study is normally achieved by using a range of different mediums such as computer-based training software (CBTs), technical books and manuals, and hands on exercises and practice. Although the Internet obviously provides a veritable goldmine of resources and material, the use of the Internet does not constitute e-learning (discussed later), which is the equivalent of an Internet-based virtual classroom.

Self-study does have some clear advantages that make it a popular choice for IT training, but it also has disadvantages. Keep in mind, procrastination is the enemy of self-study. Basically, procrastination lets low priority tasks take precedent over higher priority ones. It is watching television, socializing, sleeping, or any other possible distraction that will take precedence over studying. Before embarking on a self-study program, it is a good idea to be aware of your personality and study habits. Self-paced study is not for everyone and not for the faint of heart. It requires an extraordinary level of motivation and resourcefulness. If you already have a closet full of half completed projects and courses, it may be better to try a classroom and free up some closet space.

Advantages of Self-Study

➤ Self-study is flexible. It does not require a student to attend a training institution or adhere to the time requirements of classes. People who are short on time or need to continue working a current job find training in their spare time a desirable option, perhaps their only option.

➤ Self-study is usually less expensive than other methods of training. Classroom instruction can become expensive; therefore, people on a budget may lean towards self-study.

➤ With self-study, the student typically sets the pace of the course. A student has the option of spending more time on difficult material. In addition, self-study affords the student the opportunity to delve further into areas of particular interest.

➤ Because self-study is exactly that, it is easy to fit around a part- or full-time job or other commitments such as looking after children.

Disadvantages of Self-Study

➤ If you get confused by a principle or certain piece of information, help is not at hand. You almost certainly can find an explanation that helps you understand, but this may take time and in some cases money. This disadvantage can be negated in part by joining a user group, newsgroup, or an Internet study group for your chosen subject.

➤ Some of the costs associated with self-study may not at first be apparent. Computer books, especially training materials, are surprisingly expensive. In addition, to learn many subjects you need computer hardware and software, which also may be expensive. Many companies provide evaluation or demonstration versions of software that can help a great deal, but if it becomes necessary to purchase new computer hardware for your learning, make sure that the figures add up. You may reason that you can reuse the new computer after your self-study period is completed.

➤ Some courses are simply inappropriate for self-study. Some courses require thousands of dollars of hardware to create a working environment, while others have concepts or procedures that are simply too complex to learn on your own. In these (isolated) cases, it is best to seek out a classroom or Web-based training program.

➤ You may find that you can find a study buddy who is interested in learning the same subject at the same time as you, but most likely those embarking on a program of self-study will be working alone. This isolation can lead to motivational and productivity issues. In a classroom environment, you would be amazed at how much you can learn from other students. You not only learn about the technology, but learn which companies are the big local employers, and where can you get the best deals on a new PC. Many people also find that the peer pressure, as long as it is kept in context, can be a useful motivator for studying. It is hard to put a price on either of these aspects, but they are things worth considering.

Something to Be Aware of

One challenge that those who choose self-study encounter is that of quantifying or substantiating what they have learned. Even though you spent the last six months holed up in your basement, having pizzas delivered, and sleeping at your terminal while learning the intimate details of Windows NT, how do you convey that fact to a potential employer? Most other forms of training offer some kind of course completion certificate or provide examinations that can be used as evidence of your learning experience. Self-study offers no such built-in luxuries. So, realistically, those pursuing a self-study program should do so with the aim of taking some kind of certification test that can prove their knowledge.

Classroom Instruction

Of all the training methods available, classroom-based training is the most expensive, and arguably, the most effective. Without stating the obvious, the premise of classroom-based instruction is that a group of people, led by an instructor, work their way through a course of material at an approximate preset pace. Sounds ideal doesn't it. The only fly in the ointment is that with instructor led, or classroom-based training, a significant part of the responsibility for learning is assumed by the instructor and the institution providing the course. This assumption effectively represents a loss of control by you over the learning environment and process. Although this detail does not have to be a problem, and in most cases it isn't, but it means that before you sign up for training you need to consider the following points:

9

➤ Ask for evidence of the instructor's qualifications and experience. Ask how long the instructor has been teaching, but don't necessarily back away from someone with little teaching experience. If the instructor has just come out of the workplace, you can assume that this teacher will have up-to-date and very valuable real world skills.

➤ Ask the institution if the class has a maximum number of students. Your expectations should relate to the price you are paying for the course and the type of institution that is providing the training. Private training companies offering short (two to five day) courses should generally contain no more than 12 students. Academic classes that last for months or more may have higher numbers of students, but remember that the instructor/student ratio can have a major impact on how effective the course is on an individual basis.

➤ What courseware is supplied and what do you have to provide? As mentioned previously, courseware can be very expensive. The training center most likely will provide all of the courseware you need, but may also have a list of recommendations for other materials.

➤ Before you embark on a long course, especially if you are required to pay money before the course starts, check into the background of the institution. Don't be embarrassed to ask about what happens if the institution experiences financial problems.

➤ Inquire about the equipment you will be using, and ask what additional equipment you may be exposed to during the course. Also find out what the ratio of equipment to students is. Nowadays there is no reason why the ratio should not be one to one.

➤ Some training centers offer continued support to students after they finish the course, such as email access to instructors or revision sessions. If the institution you are considering offers these facilities, and you think you may use them, check exactly what they are.

After you have your shortlist of training centers, and certainly if you are going to be embarking on a long course, ask if the training company or organization would mind if you sat in for an hour to preview a course. As long as you are prepared to be flexible with your request, many companies have no objection to this—it is a reasonable request if you are considering spending tens of thousands of dollars with them.

Advantages of Classroom Instruction

➤ Classroom attendance typically allows the students to use the equipment and software they will use on the job. For those doing self-study, the access to such equipment can often be limited by the cost.

➤ The value of an experienced instructor cannot be overstated. Experienced instructors combine relevant job experience and the course materials to provide not only the necessary education but also a glimpse into the job itself.

➤ Classroom-based training allows you to meet and work with other professionals with similar career goals. Working through the same trials and tribualtions as others can develop a sense of community that can help you through the tough times.

➤ A classroom setting provides less opprtunity for distraction, making it easier to focus on the material. If your mind does start to wander, you can try reminding yourself of the money you are paying to be in the class. That should focus you.

Disadvantages of Classroom Instruction

➤ Classroom instruction is based around a set timetable. That timetable may or may not be suited to your learning pace. The problem is that the pace cannot be altered. If you can't keep up, the money you spent on the class compared to the value you receive may be greatly impacted.

➤ Your desired training center may be in another town or city, requiring you to spend time and money traveling, which can be an inconvenience.

➤ As much as a good instructor can make a good course, a bad instructor can seriously devalue a course. This factor is beyond your control.

➤ Curriculum of instructor-led training is often very class specific. Time may not allow for you to look at at a certain aspect of the technology in more detail, although many instructors allow students to use the classroom before and after class hours.

When taking classroom based courses, keep in mind that your experience can be enhanced outisde of the classroom. Each evening you should review the material that was covered that day, and make notes about any aspect you don't understand or that you want to better understand. The next morning, catch your instructor before class, and ask if there is a convenient time when the two of you can meet to further discuss this topic. Try not to wait to ask the instructor at the end of the day, as both of you may be tired. This benefit is hard to put a price tag on when comparing training options.

9

E-learning

There is little doubt that we are in the *e-times*. Our e-vocabulary now includes such terms as e-marketing, e-commerce, e-business, and of course e-mail. Hidden within the ever-increasing collection of e-terms is one of great interest to those seeking training in IT: e-learning. E-learning, or otherwise known as *online learning* has become a viable alternative to standard classroom training and augments traditional home study method.

Essentially, e-learning, electronic learning, is the delivery of education or training with the use of computers. E-learning includes delivery over the Internet, Web-based training (WBT) as well as computer-based training (CBT) on the resident hard drive or over a network.

CBTs have become a popular method of e-learning study and are essentially an interactive training method that enables you to learn on your own computer and at your own pace. Because CBTs can be used anytime and anywhere, they offer a distinct advantage. When installed on a laptop, you can review course materials everywhere from the beach to the mall. Who can resist that?

The two types of e-learning are instructor-led or self-paced e-learning. Instructor led e-learning involves live training with real instructors training realtime over the Interent. The dates and times are arranged, and the course is taught much the same as in the classroom only over the Internet.

Self-paced learning is just that. Courses are offered online, and it is up to the student to decide how and when training is to take place. If you find that your best learning is done between 2 and 4 AM, self paced WBTs or CBTs can accommodate you. It would be much more difficult to find a willing instructor to do the same. Typically, this style of learning still requires tests and assignments to be turned in by a specified time. Flexibility has its limits.

E-learning, the Good and the Bad

On the one hand, e-learning offers huge advantages to the instructor as well as the student. On the other hand, there are potential pitfalls and shortcomings to this method of training. An understanding of both pros and cons of CBT and WBT is essential before choosing this option as a means of learning.

Advantages of E-learning

➤ E-learning is convenient because it takes learning out of the classroom. Courses can be taken from home or other locations.

➤ E-learning enables students to work at a pace that best suits them. This self-paced training can accommodate those who cannot dedicate consistent or large blocks of time to training. For those less motivated, this flexibility can be a double edged sword.

➤ E-learning can remove or at least reduce travel costs involved in training. Students who do not live near a training or education center can use this method of training to prevent the time and cost associated with traveling.

➤ While accessing courses on the Internet, students become more familiar with the Web and develop a strong knowledge of the Internet. Whether taking courses through e-learning or in the classroom, knowledge of the Internet is an invaluable resource, and the ability to navigate it effectively is a key for success.

➤ E-learning can often accommodate different learning styles; whereas, a class-room does not always have the flexibility to adapt to an individual's learning preferences. Spend 20 minutes a day or 10 hours a day training; whatever suits you better.

➤ E-learning often allows greater choice when choosing a school or training center. You can choose one that offers the specific training you may be looking for. Further, you have greater choice with regards to the availability of course delivery times and dates.

➤ E-learning is often times cheaper than classroom training. If you want to take courses, but cannot afford the standard classroom setting, you may want to investigate the costs of some of the online training. Remember that good training does not come cheaply, no matter whether you consider e-learning or a traditional classroom.

Because of these advantages e-learning is increasing in demand and popularity. Students can take control of their learning environment and conditions and customize their training experience. E-learning, however, does have its dark side. E-learning does not represent a training utopia and is an inappropriate and ineffec-tive method of training for many people.

Disadvantages of E-learning

➤ Without the encouragement and gentle nudges provided in a classroom setting, many students find it hard to maintain the interest and motivation necessary to complete a course. In the absence of a schedule, it can become all too easy in a self-paced course to put things off until tomorrow. It is important to accurately assess your level of commitment to e-learning before using this as a method for training.

9

➤ Gaps in technical knowledge may be easier to detect in an instructor-led classroom. There can often be huge chunks of technical knowledge missing that greatly hinder training progress. When working alone or with limited support, these gaps may go undetected and can lead to frustrations.

➤ Students may have to buy equipment or software to participate in the course. Classroom training includes modern equipment and all of the necessary software. Equipment, or the lack of it, should be factored into the equation when deciding on a method of study.

➤ The delivery of the course is dependent on technology, and technology is subject to technical difficulties. When equipment fails, a course on programming can quickly become an exercise in PC repair.

Before deciding on a training method, it is important to examine thoroughly all of your options. Doing a little investigative work can save you both time and money wasted on an option that is not for you. CBT and WBT are an atttractive option to classroom training both in terms of convenience and money. Remember that the reason for training, however, is not for convenience but rather to aquire the knowledge and skills necessary.

Full-Time or Part-Time?

Just when you thought you had your training organized, along comes yet another option—full-time or part-time study. Whether pursuing your training through self-study, e-learning, or instructor-led classroom, a decision needs to be made regarding your time commitment to the training.

Part-Time Study

For the most part, people want to get training as soon as possible so that they can get out there and look for work. Unfortunately, there can be numerous factors and circumstances that prevent the pursuit of training to the exclusion of everything else. Some of the more common reasons for enrolling in part-time study include:

➤ Family commitments do not allow the dedicated time needed for full-time training.

➤ Financial considerations may prevent full-time study. Paying for part-time study may be easier, especially if you have a job that you can fit your studies around.

➤ Part-time study allows you the time to enjoy other hobbies or interests. Although not a huge consideration, relaxation is an important aspect of learning, making the time you do spend studying all the more productive.

➤ For those who have to continue working, part-time programs are often aimed at balancing study time and work.

➤ Part-time education is available and practical for almost any study method. Even though self-study may seem like the obvious part-time study option, e-learning courses are often operated on a part-time basis as well as evening and weekend training courses that are provided by local colleges and training companies.

➤ Part-time studies may free up time for you to volunteer in the job you are training for. When the training is done, you leave with both the experience and the training. This situation is almost ideal, yet many people preparing for a career in IT simply don't consider it. Many people find that the best way to make this scenario work is to embark on a short full-time study period and then resort to part-time study while looking for volunteer work. Such a situation does require a high degree of motivation and dedication, especially as many people also have to hold down a part-time job as well as the studying and the volunteer work.

Part-time study is just what the doctor ordered for those with busy lives who still need to retrain or obtain qualifications. For all of the advantages of part-time study, however, there are some obvious disadvantages. Most notably, obtaining a degree or certification can take twice as long and so too will your ability to get out and get the job. Specifically in respect to degree programs, a great many of them cannot be taken part-time, which may exclude this as an option completely If, for instance, you are enrolled in a full-time degree program scheduled to take four years to complete, the same degree take when enrolled in a part-time program can take much longer to earn Time is precious commodity in the IT field.

A second, and perhaps more hidden, drawback of part-time study is the success rate for completion of programs. Because the training does take longer and there are other things in you life besides the study, you can be distracted. Many part-time programs, specifically self-study, are not completed. Procrastination becomes the enemy of the part-time student.

People in part-time study programs will tell you that they require a strategy and game plan to get you through it. Common techniques include having periods of time set aside that are dedicated to study, a dedicated space for books and other course materials, and a "To Do" list to help keep things organized and moving ahead. Part-time study is ideally suited for those with good time management skills, personal motivation, and the patience to see the training through completion.

9

Full-Time Study

If you have the money, have the means, and you have the motivation, you can train full-time. The length of training programs vary considerably. A degree in computer science may take four years, but a certification program may only take six months to a year. Having the time for full-time study means that you can complete your training in the shortest possible time. Advantages in training full-time include:

➤ Some students find it easier to stay focused on training when attending full-time because it does not give them the time to become sidetracked.

➤ Financial assistance may be easier to get for students in full-time study than part-time.

➤ Full-time students may have greater access to grants and loans.

➤ Attending training on a full-time basis shows a commitment to both the subject and to your learning goals.

Of course, full-time training does have its drawbacks. The first drawback is the fact that it is full-time, leaving a shortage of time for other activities such as travelling, working, or hobbies. Full-time training requires a commitment from students, and students not willing to make this commitment may not meet their training goals.

The Real Cost of Training

As with anything else, money is likely to play a factor in what study method you choose. At first glance, it may seem like self-study is the lowest cost option of the various methods of training, but you may be surprised at just how quickly the study guides, CBTs, and equipment costs add up. What you need to do before making a decision is calculate what exactly the costs of each training method is. Doing a mathematical calculation does not produce a definitive answer, but we'll talk about that later.

Let's start by looking at the obvious things. Course fees can be expensive and in some cases are payable in advance. If you are going to be using a bank loan or another interest charging mechanism to pay for your studies, consider what paying a lump sum up front may mean in terms of interest payments. Some organizations allow the payment of fees on a monthly or semester basis. If you are studying over a number of years, paying for your study in this way can save money on interest payments.

As well as course fees and training materials, you should figure the extra expenses that will be involved in your training. For certification programs, the cost of the exams can be surprisingly high. In addition, the costs in terms of lost wages from a part-time job or those paid out in travel expenses to travel to the testing center should be figured in (which may not necessarily be the same place that you took your training). Don't forget to budget for travel to and from your place of study if taking a course away from home. These travel costs can start to build rapidly if your training involves staying away from home overnight or paying expensive city parking rates. Basically, as far as the costs go, you really need to sit down and list all of the costs you can possibly think of, and then add them up.

Even after you have done this figuring, you should also consider the hidden cost of training. Consider this scenario. Presuming that you are going to be looking for employment as soon as you finish studying, the length of time it takes to complete your training becomes a factor. Assuming that once you complete your studies you can make a salary of $30,000 per year, if the course of study takes six months to complete, it is actually costing $15,000 in lost earnings. On the other hand, if your course of study takes the entire year to complete, then you can add $30,000 to the total cost of your training expense. In essence, working with this strategy allows you to work out which training method costs the least money, or on a more positive note, which offers the best value for money.

To work out the cost in your case, calculate what your total training costs are likely to be, and then find out what a reasonable expectation of your earnings will be. You can do this by looking at job advertisements in local newspapers, reviewing job sites on the Internet, and by speaking to employment agencies. Then do the calculation as described, and you should have an idea of the sorts of figures in question.

What You Cannot Calculate

What this formula does not help you with is choosing the most appropriate form of training for you as an individual. Forcing yourself into a $10,000 intensive training program so that you can enter the workforce quicker is not a solution. You are unlikely to learn or absorb the necessary information. You should consider the fact that in some cases, particularly that of a university education, you often can earn more when you enter the workplace as a result of your education.

College Degrees, Certification, or Both?

Way back when, if you wanted to work in IT you needed one of two things: a college degree or experience. These qualifications were valid and well recognized, but they had two major drawbacks. First, they took a long time to obtain. College courses typically ran for a minimum of one year; whereas, university degrees typically ran for at least three. Second, commercial organizations wanted people who could literally start being productive from day one. Degrees, while preparing people for the workplace in a broad sense, were too general on specific technologies, and were slow to adapt to market change. These facts meant that another method was required to validate people's knowledge. Enter the certification. Though uptake and recognition were initially slow, in time certification programs gained acceptance by both employers and IT professionals. Now, the IT certification is an industry all of its own.

Before we start to talk about the relative merits of degrees and certification, we should perhaps make something clear. University and college education does a great deal more than a certification program ever can. It provides the opportunity to develop written and verbal communcation skills, as well as providing an in-depth education on the chosen subject. It teaches organizational skills, as well as providing the chance to develop interpersonal skills. Certification is a very different animal. Certification is designed to teach you a single subject to a certain depth. In many cases, certification presumes a given level of knowledge about a subject, or at least of technology generally. It offers nothing in the way of coaching in any of ther personal skills such as communication or organization.

How Do They Match Up?

So why, if a college education offers so much, are we discussing certification as a means of getting into IT? The reality is that many people do not have the time, the money, or the background to embark on a lengthy academic program. Certification provides a way for people to enter the IT industry on their own terms and in their own time. The good thing is that employers seem willing to recognize certifications as proof of a person's knowledge, so much so that college graduates often find themselves seeking certification to add a degree of tangability to their skills. In a way, this approach is the ultimate. To have a degree and a certification makes an individual valuable indeed. Our last note on this subject is this: Certifications work, and so do degrees and diplomas. What you have to ask your yourself is which one are you most suited to. In the sections that follow, we discuss some advantages and disadvantages of both.

Advantages of Certifications

Becoming certified has a number of advantages. Here are just a few:

➤ Certifications programs offer short, focused learning. Although the longer degree program may include information on areas such as networking as part of the overall program, certification programs isolate networking as a single technology, giving you the training required to be employed as a network support technician.

➤ Certification programs are directly related to a technology and to commercial practices. Employers have a way of knowing exactly what your knowledge of a given area should be.

➤ Even though the initial cost of certification programs seems quite high, over the long run they prove their financial worth over degree programs. When in a training program, either a degree program or a certification program, you are not likely earning the money you could be. This type of focused training gets you out looking for work in the shortest possible time. The quicker you are working, the quicker you are earning.

➤ Training methods for certification programs vary greatly. From CBTs and WBT to self-study and full classroom attendance, certification training is available in every possible format. Training options are essential for students requiring flexibility in their training.

Disadvantages of Certifications

Certification programs may be the flavor of the month, but they are not without their drawbacks. Here are some of the things you should consider before embarking on a certification program:

➤ The initial costs of certification programs are high. Keep in mind that this money is going to pay for cutting edge equipment, experienced instructors, and the most recent courseware. Just remind yourself of that when it comes time to pay.

➤ Certifications require ongoing upgrading. As new products, programs, and hardware are introduced, certification programs are modified to reflect these changes. All this really means is that the training is always there; sometime soon you will need to take another exam.

➤ Degree or diploma programs often offer training in such areas as programming, but also include information on a variety of other areas as well. Certification programs generally do not. When pursuing certification training as a programmer, that is the training you will receive.

Advantages of Degrees

➤ Degrees such as computer science, offer in-depth knowledge on a broad range of materials. When on the job, degree programs can prepare for the job itself as well as other aspects of the job that certification programs simply do not have the time to cover. The broad knowledge that degree programs give can make your job easier and make you a better employee.

➤ After students earn degrees, they always have the degrees. The same cannot be said of certification programs. A student who has a computer science degree is not required to take another exam to keep those qualifications. Those with IT certifications can just look on with envy.

➤ Completion of a degree program can open doors not available to those with certifications. Some positions, and some companies, insist on a college degree from applicants. Many companies also run graduate intake programs that as the name implies, are only open to college degree holders.

Disadvantages of Degrees

➤ Perhaps the biggest disadvantage of seeking a degree is the time involved in getting it. Four years of training and out of the labor market is a long time, especially considering that certification graduates are already out there looking for work.

➤ The duration of the course, and the fact that your chosen institution may be in another city, state, or country can make things such as accommodation or travel expensive. Although the experience of studying away will almost certainly be interesting, finances may be the bottom line.

➤ Unlike certifications, the knowledge used to obtain a degree from a college may become redundant after a period of time. Graduates may find themselves looking for other ways to prove their up-to-date knowledge.

Choosing the Degree or Certification that Is Right for You

Having decided whether to pursue a degree or a certification, you now need to decide which program is right for you. In this section, we discuss important issues and factors that you should consider when selecting the appropriate educational channel. We discuss how and when to choose certain options, what those options are, and how those decisions may impact your career. What is not discussed, however, are the particulars of specific certification programs and relevant details. That information you can get from those sponsoring organizations publications that specifically focus on certification programs, or obtain from Web sites such as **ExamCram.com**.

Certifications

Choosing a certification program is relatively easy, as by now you should know in which direction you want your IT career to progress. Some areas of IT, notably networking, have a number of programs available, and it is relatively easy to match up the program with your chosen path. Others, such as programming, have less options available, though the definition of the subject means that this is not necessarily a problem. Here are some things to consider when choosing a program:

➤ Choose a program that is recognized and in demand by employers. Check job advertisements and ask other people in the industry about what is in demand. If you have a specific company in mind that you want to work for, find out if they will accept your certification.

➤ Consider whether the certification program is suited to your chosen method of study. As mentioned earlier, not all certification programs are suited to every study type.

➤ Although it may be tempting to do so, try to avoid programs that you have little interest in, even if they are in demand. Having an interest in what you do is an important part of your choice.

➤ Investigate your chosen program throughly, especially in regard to what exams you must take and when the vendor is updating the certification. Finding out during a course of study that you are going to have to immediately update your skills can be disheartening.

➤ Find out what study aids are available for your chosen certification. There is no doubt that books, sample tests, CBTs, and other resources can be invaluable no matter what study method you choose. Selecting a certification path in which there are few resources available can make it that much harder to study.

Vendor Independent Certifications

Some certification programs are vendor independent, meaning that the program itself is not run by the hardware or software manufacturer themselves. These programs have advantages over vendor operated programs because they often cover more than one technology. Note that vendor independent certification programs are often not as widely recognized as those from a major company. A good example here is the Microsoft Certified Systems Engineer certification. Because it has Microsoft's name behind it, it is immediately recognized by employers who often have an understanding of what is involved in obtaining the certification. In contrast, programs from independent organizations do not have the recognition that the MCSE has, though this is something that is changing as time goes on.

As far as your career planning goes, you may want to consider a vendor independent certification if you are unsure of exactly which products you want to learn. In addition, many vendor independent certifications offer courses and certifications that can be particularly useful for those just starting out in IT, such as those which cover the basic principles of PC technology and networking.

One Final Note on Certification

There are mixed feelings in the IT industry when it comes to certification programs. Some people believe they are the answer to the skills shortage, and the relative lack of relevance that traditional methods of education provide. Others believe that certifications prove very little about a person's relative IT skill, and more about the person's ability to remember and recollect facts and figures in exams. These latter critics have some basis, because it is very possible nowadays to become "paper" certified. In fact, the issue of people who have little knowledge of the product but who hold certification has led vendors to tighten up their certification programs.

The bottom line is that certification, as any other qualification, does not entitle the holder to anything. Certification is a material verification that the person named on the certificate has had the dedication and commitment to learn and understand principles of a certain product or technology. It is not an IOU from the IT industry or a passport to fame and riches. It is a starting point. Try to think of a certification in the same way as a driving license. When you learn to drive, you take the lessons, prove your abilities, get a licence, and take to the open road. The reality is only on that first day of solo driving do you really start to learn how to drive. Everything up to that point has been done in a controlled environment.

Degrees

Choosing an appropriate degree program is easier in some respects than choosing a certification and harder in others. The easy aspect is that you only have to decide a general direction, such as computer science or mathematics. The hard part is that you often have a choice of where to pursue your degree, and this factor can have a major influence on both your studies and your personal life.

Choosing a venue for your studies is especially important because the length of time that you spend at the institution will be huge. People studying for a certificiation only have to grin and bear a few months somewhere where they are not comfortable. In fact, these people can move to another training facility. For those enrolled in a four year university course, such flexibility is not available.

Getting the right training at the right institution makes a huge difference to the effectiveness of your studies. Here are some things you should consider when choosing a qualification and training institution:

➤ As degree programs are lengthy, consider where the market will be when your course is completed. Try to ensure that the skills you learn will be in demand when you have completed your course.

➤ As mentioned previously, those taking degree programs can often participate in intern or co-op programs. This experience can be invaluable, therefore, be sure to look into what opportunities the institution you choose offers. Consider what co-op or internships are available.

➤ Though it may not be possible to attend a high profile, world renowned university, you do need to consider the reputation of the institution you are attending. This need not be a mammoth task; it simply requires some research.

➤ The length of study means that degree programs can often include a wide variety of subjects, some of which may be elective. In addition, titles of qualification courses are not always explicit. To be sure that you are going to learn the material you need for you chosen field, investigate what exactly is included and match it up to your targets. If your chosen course does have electives, choose them wisely.

➤ If you need to study away from home, consider the effects this will have on your personal life. Although it is quite natural for recent high school graduates to attend a college away from home, those who are considering a career change later on in life may find the proposition unsavory.

Post secondary education has for many years been the key to securing good employment, and that fact remains today. What also must be considered in an IT environment is that experience is just as important as schooling. Those qualifications that can combine some element of experience with the sudy element are particulalrly benficial.

Predicting Change

Gaze into my crystal ball. I can see a programming language. Its name is...wait, it is going cloudy again...the mists of time are hiding it from me. Okay, maybe we can be a bit more scientific than the fortune teller at the carnival, but to be honest, predicting change in a market that moves as quickly as the IT industry isn't an exact art. That said, there are things you can do to make sure that you don't get left behind in the early stages.

Predicting Short Term Change

The nature of the IT industry means that nowadays there are few surprises to be had. Companies announce products months, or in some cases, years before they become available. Even once they are available, the nature of business computing dictates that not everyone is going to switch to a new technology at the drop of a hat. Whatever the size of the company, change has to be planned and implemented over a period of time, and that is the case only if the company chooses to use the product or technology in the first place.

The key to predicting short term change in the industry is simply that of keeping your eyes and ears open keeping up on what is going on. Then you need to interpret what you learn, looking at how it may or may not affect you. Let's look at an example. You decide to attend a course in computer networking at your local technical college. The course is slated to run for a full year, which means that you will be entering the workforce in July the following year. By reading the computer press and doing some investigations on the Internet, you find that a major software company is releasing a new version of its popular network operating system in June next year. The college is unlikely to be including anything to do with the new product in the curriculum, because there are no concrete details as to what the new features of the product will be, and it would also be highly unlikely that the instructor would be suitably qualified and experienced to teach the new product. You have to figure out how you are going to deal with this change by deciding a plan of action. Given that you are going to spend much of the next year doing intensive study, adding to the burden by trying to learn a new product at the same time as the current one may be a tall order. You may decide that when you finish your college course, you will take some additional training, or you may elect to do nothing formal at all, working on the principle that companies will be unlikely to upgrade in the months that first follow a new product release.

Even if you do nothing, the fact is that you are fully aware of what is occuring in the industry as a whole, which is an intergral part of working in the IT industry. Knowing what is going on can prevent those demoralizing moments when you find out three weeks into a year long course that much of the information you are going to learn will be obsolete two years from now.

Although it may seem like a continual burden, upgrading your skills offers a unique opportunity, because companies that decide to upgrade will often seek out individuals who have knowledge and experience in both areas. Although perhaps not a role a first-time job holder may be suitable for, it's worth noting for future reference.

And Long Term Change

Look at your chosen area of the IT industry as it exists today, and then look at how it affects the IT industry overall. Look forward now into the future, and see where things are headed and fit the two together. Sounds difficult? It really isn't. Here's how it works.

Let's take programming as an example. Today, the most popular languages are C++ and Java. In five years time—a long time in the IT industry—there is a good chance that even if the languages themselves are not the latest and greatest, derivatives of them will be. That means that as long as you develop a plan of ongoing education, you can ride the wave of change as it develops.

If you cannot see a market for the technology you are involved in five years from now, now is the time to think about getting out or at the very least changing direction. If you start making preparations for change now, you can continue to earn a decent living while training for your new area. You may even be able to pick up on a job that needs people with skills in both areas, allowing you to develop your skills and knowledge at someone else's expense.

9

Chapter Summary

As with the other things that we have discussed in this book, a good way of finding out which training method may be best suited to you is to ask around. Talk to people and listen to what they thought of a specific company or a type of learning. Most of all, be honest with yourself about what training method you are best suited to. Keep the following points in mind when making your decisions:

➤ When going into IT, keep your options open, and don't jump too quickly to make a decision. Consider all factors.

➤ Make sure that whatever you choose is going to get you where you want to go.

➤ Be realistic about your expectations. Don't' think you can learn everything there is to know in one quick course.

Whichever study method you eventually pick, choosing the right qualifications, study method and at the right institution can determine whether your IT training will be an enjoyable and successful endeavor.

10

Preparing for the Job Hunt

Once you have completed your degrees, certifications, and training, all you need to do is get a job so you can pay for them. Unfortunately, even with the shortage of skilled IT professionals, simply having the technical training and certifications does not provide you with a complimentary ticket into the IT industry. You still need to hit the streets and track down the job you were trained to do.

Before embarking on your quest to find that first job, it is important to do some prehunting preparation. Although you are understandably eager to begin an IT job, a little patience and planning can prevent a lot of job hunting frustration and disappointment. In some cases, prospective employers will ask you for your résumé, so having one already prepared reinforces your professionalism and organization. In other situations, particularly when dealing with employment agencies or online career sites, a résumé is a prerequisite to registration.

Job search preparation includes activities such as writing résumés and cover letters and selecting references. Effectively, it is about creating the basis of a personal marketing strategy, so that when you are ready to actually start looking for work, you will have all of the tools and information you need ready and waiting. This chapter discusses these tools—primarily your cover letter, résumé, and references. It provides both good and bad examples of these items as well as some actual examples included at the end of the chapter. Let's start by looking at developing cover letters.

Cover Letters

Most likely, you have heard the saying, "You never get a second chance to make a good first impression." A cover letter is your introduction to a potential employer, and your chance to make a good first impression. Unfortunately, it is also your chance to make a bad first impression, and therein lies the potential backlash of cover letters. A good cover letter may not actually make a great deal of difference in your job search as they are designed to be simple affairs, briefly read through as recruiters work their way toward the résumé. A bad cover letter, on the other hand, may send your cover letter and the attached résumé straight into the trash. In many cases, a recruiter will not even look past a bad cover letter to see if the résumé is any good. After all, if you didn't take the time to create a good cover letter, what are the chances that the résumé will be any better?

A good cover letter should be a brief note accompanying your résumé. Its purpose is to act as an introduction for you and your skills. The cover letter exists to pique the interest of a potential employer and nothing else. A cover letter does not stand alone. It is the bait intended to hook the reader and leave them wanting to know more. A well-written cover letter does this in the shortest and most succinct way possible. Overly wordy cover letters are rarely read, especially if they are poorly written.

Cover letters are intended to be personalized and direct. They should be addressed to the person who is doing the recruiting and refer directly to the position for which you are applying. There are some basic rules to creating a cover letter, and it is almost certainly worth generating a template letter as part of your job search preparations. For this reason, information on cover letters has been included in this section rather than the next section, which discusses conducting the actual job hunt.

An example of a good and a bad cover letter are included at the end of this chapter along with comments from a recruiting agent. You might want to refer to these examples as you read through the next section.

Writing Cover Letters

A cover letter is not an exercise in creative writing, rather it should follow a generally accepted format. Many people have a different view on the exact layout of the letter itself, but whatever the subtle nuances or differences, the content of the letter remains basically the same. The structure of the cover letter can be broken down into topical paragraphs.

10

Tip: Don't include detailed information about yourself in a cover letter. Direct people to your résumé where the information is complete. The cover letter is an introduction, not a replacement for your résumé.

The first paragraph of the cover letter is your introduction. It includes information about how you heard about the position and why the position is of interest to you.

The second paragraph is when self-promotion starts. Armed with the knowledge of what the company is looking for in terms of an employee and skills, you identify your skills and abilities to match what the company is seeking. If a position is advertising for a systems administrator, outline your skills, training, and experience specific to that area. Similarly, if a company is advertising for certain values, such as the ability to work under pressure or work in a team-oriented environment, match your values to those being sought.

Tip: Even though it is unlikely that you would do so, never make your cover letter more than one page in length. If you find that your cover letter is getting close to this limit, you are probably including too much information.

The third paragraph should continue your self-marketing. In it you should provide a little more information on your training and experience. However, try not to duplicate information given on your résumé. Instead, briefly describe your *relevant* training and experience. If the employer is advertising for a job as a programmer, you need not include the workshop you attended on PC troubleshooting. You can save that little nugget for the résumé. Remember, the cover letter is a hook meant to catch the readers' interest and make them curious to read more. This paragraph requires a balance between over promoting and under promoting.

That should be it for the self-marketing portion. Your résumé should cover the rest of your skills and experience. The final paragraph on your cover letter requires a little assertiveness on your part. This is your chance to encourage the employer to contact you. Make it easy for them by directing them to your contact information on the cover letter or résumé and offering to be available for an interview at short notice and at flexible times.

Tip: Although it appears on your résumé, always include your contact information, such as your address, phone numbers, and email address, on your cover letter. If these documents get separated, your contact information will be on both. Make it as easy as possible for the employer to contact you.

Some career experts suggest that the onus rests on you to contact the employer to arrange an interview. This is a bold move indeed. Even if you were given to such directness, you may find yourself in an awkward situation during the phone call. Not only do many companies discourage such contact, stating that they will contact individuals who are selected for an interview, a great number of other companies have a personnel department that acts as the intermediary between the hiring manager and the potential employee. In such a situation, a call to arrange an interview may in fact be damaging to your job prospect. After all, if your cover letter and résumé have done their intended job, chances are that the employer will be contacting you.

As always, there are exceptions. If the company is small enough and you get to speak to the hiring manager, then your call to set up an interview may be appropriate. However, if you want to strike some middle ground, perhaps a good way to finish your cover letter would be to add something like, "I will call you next week to discuss my suitability for the position." It sounds a little less presumptuous than, "I will call you next week to arrange a time for my interview." Keep in mind that although they may have been seasoned by years of recruiting, managers and recruiters are still people.

To round off your cover letter, include a brief paragraph thanking the employer for their time in consideration of your résumé.

Tip: Remember to be polite and courteous in your cover letters. They are a reflection of your personality, and you want to come across as a friendly and likeable person.

When you have finished your cover letter, read it through and ask yourself how you would feel if you read such a letter from someone else. Once you are happy with it, get a second opinion.

Tips for a Good Cover Letter

There are a number of ways to ensure that your cover letter says what you want it to say. The following list contains some tips to consider when writing cover letters:

➤ Use a heavy weight paper for the cover letter; it is all part of a positive first impression. Paper that matches the résumé will look sharp.

➤ Cover letters are customized for a specific job. They are intended to respond to a job posting and should be directed toward it. Unless there is literally no way of knowing who the intended reader will be, do not open your letter with Dear Sir or Madam, and never open with To Whom It May Concern. Do your homework and address it to the right person.

➤ Remember that your cover letter is an example of your written communication skills; get it right. The cover letter is actually more powerful than your résumé because a résumé offers little opportunity to demonstrate writing skills.

➤ Always sign each of your cover letters. A photocopy of your signature usually means that you are using a standard cover letter, which is undesirable, and a cover letter that is unsigned shows a lack of attention to detail.

➤ Make a copy of your template cover letter for your personal file. You will need to refer to it again to remember what you have written if you are called for an interview.

See the example of a good cover letter at the end of this chapter.

Cover Letter Tragedies

As mentioned earlier, even though cover letters are designed to work for you, they can potentially work against you. The following list contains some tips to ensure that your cover letter does not deliver the wrong message:

➤ Always check your cover letters for bad punctuation, grammar, and spelling. Most word processors have excellent spelling and grammar checking capabilities. There is no excuse not to use them.

10

➤ If writing is not your strong suit, get some help, even if you have to pay for it. Type or write out how you want the cover letter to flow, and then ask someone else to read it over.

➤ Avoid obvious exaggeration of your skills and values. A slight embellishment of certain skills may slip by, but be careful, at some point you will need to back up what you say.

➤ A poorly laid out cover letter not only looks unprofessional, it can also be very hard to read. Stay away from the temptation to impress the reader with italics, bold letters, and unusual fonts.

➤ No one likes a pushy salesman, and it is not the impression you want to give potential employers. An overly aggressive sales pitch can take you out of the running in a hurry.

➤ Conversely, a sales pitch that is not aggressive enough can be equally ineffective. Make sure the employer understands your enthusiasm for the position.

➤ Cover letters that are not directed at a specific position show a lack of preparation. Do not photocopy one cover letter for another position. Use your template, and rewrite the cover letter for each job you apply for.

See the example of a bad cover letter at the end of this chapter.

Résumés

Almost certainly, the primary tool of the job search is the résumé. Because of its importance in the job search, it is essential that you get it right. Put simply, jobs can be won and lost with a résumé. You may need to write several drafts of your résumé to get it right, or even pay to have it done properly. When it comes to the résumé, there are no shortcuts. Typically, a résumé is a summary of your training, experience, and skills. The purpose of the résumé is to catch the attention of a potential employer and get an interview.

As with other areas of this book, this section looks at résumés from the perspective of someone who is entering the IT industry for the first time. This situation brings with it special considerations, which will be covered in this section. Toward the end of this chapter, an example of both a "good" and "bad" résumé are given along with comments from a recruiter. You might want to refer to these examples as they are discussed.

Tip: Although there are no specific rules as to the length of the résumé, the shorter a résumé is the better. But don't sacrifice information just to keep the page count down. If you do go onto a second, or in extreme cases a third page, make sure you use the entire page. Lots of blank space can make it look like you ran out of things to say. If necessary, increase the font size or the spacing on your résumé to achieve this goal.

Let's start with the basics. Your résumé generally includes your name in a good-sized font at the top of the page. The font should be larger than the size used in the body of the résumé to make your name stand out. It should not, however, be so large that it looks disproportionate to the rest of the text. There is no need to include the word résumé at the top or anywhere else on the page. Everyone who reads it will know what it is. Your name should then be followed by your contact details, which should ideally list every possible way of contacting you, including email, home and cell phone numbers, and so on.

It is becoming increasingly popular for people to create Internet Web sites that act as online résumés with information about themselves. If you have done this, feel free to include the URL as part of your contact details, but only if the page is going to add something to your application. Directing employers to a poorly written Web page that expounds your passion for skydiving is unlikely to impress anyone. On the other hand, in certain situations, such as applying for a job as a Web page designer, a professional looking personal Web page is almost a prerequisite.

After your personal details, information placement gets a little trickier. As a novice in the IT industry, your résumé needs to convey the fact that you are tech savvy, knowledgeable, and keen to expand on your current skills. The fact that you may have little or no IT experience should not necessarily be seen as a negative. Everyone has to have a first job. The key to conveying this point is to structure your résumé in a certain way, so that rather than broadcasting the fact that you have limited experience, you present the many other qualities that would be of interest to the employer. These skills might include a positive attitude, excellent organizational skills, and a good-natured personality.

Tip: Whether or not they are IT related, describe past work experiences in a positive manner. Indicate other competencies like "managed a team of four" or "responsible for customer relations." These skills, although obtained in a non-IT position, are relevant to your overall ability and may be just as attractive to a prospective employer as your IT skills.

Talk about your qualifications or certifications. For formal education, list the institutions you attended along with the dates and subjects studied. Be sure to highlight any courses or modules of particular relevancy to the job position.

10

Tip: Conserve words and ensure meaning by always using active voice. Choose verbs like created, developed, managed, and executed when talking about your previous roles.

If you have attained a certification, list the certification along with the date that you achieved it. If your training and certification program included specific course components directly related to what the employer is advertising for, highlight these details. Many degree or certification programs, for example, have elective course requirements. If an elective course you have chosen matches the job requirement, make sure to reference this point.

Tip: Generally speaking, print your résumé and cover letter on good quality, bright white paper. If you really must print on colored paper, use light pastel tones not bright colors. Using colored paper may help in certain cases, but white is generally regarded as the most professional color. White also scans well.

After the education portion, your résumé should then list your IT related experience, be it details of hands-on experience or any exposure to IT in general. Conventional résumé wisdom dictates that your work experience should appear chronologically early on in your résumé. However, if you are looking for employment in a new field, it is worth focusing on your skills, certifications, and general personality characteristics first, and then listing past employment experiences. If you are lacking prior experience, you can still provide information to ensure that your résumé looks attractive to employers. The objective is to provide the employer with sufficient background information so that they understand what you have done in the past and how that can benefit them while still believing you are ready for a new job role.

If you *have* been lucky enough to obtain some experience by working on a part time or volunteer basis, discuss the tasks you performed in your roles and what you achieved. It is perfectly reasonable for you to talk about a volunteer position as if it were a permanent role. This experience is your most valuable asset. Make the most of it.

Tip: Although it may be tempting to do so, especially if your résumé is looking a little bare, do not include information such as your age, marital status, or race. Companies are legally obligated to make recruiting decisions irrespective of this kind of information, so it will have no bearing on your suitability for a position.

At the bottom of your résumé, if space permits, you can include a variety of relevant information, such as membership in associations or non-IT related achievements.

Lastly, a word of caution on those creative urges that some professional résumé writers seem to get. Looking for your first IT job can be challenging in itself. This is no time to be adventurous. Stick to the format. Do not include items such as mission statements, ideas on life, or slogans. They may work in a rare case, but they are more likely to hinder than help you. Keep in mind that you only ever hear about the rare times that these additions did make a difference and not about the many times they didn't.

And You Thought You Only Needed One Résumé!

After discussing the basics of résumé writing, let's consider other factors that will have an effect on your résumé, such as the medium by which it will be presented. Different employers, agencies, and online job sites require that résumés be sent in a specific manner. For this reason, you are likely to find yourself needing more than one version of your résumé.

Traditional Résumé

In today's high-tech world, creating a traditional résumé, meaning one that is on paper, may seem slightly outdated. Realistically though, it is very likely that even if you intend to do all of your job hunting electronically, sooner or later you will need a paper résumé. Imagine sitting in an interview and noticing that your potential employer is reading a printout of your résumé from an email attachment. Then imagine reaching inside your folder, pulling out a professional looking résumé that has been printed on quality paper, and handing it to the interviewer. Not only is the interviewer likely to be impressed that you took the trouble to bring a paper résumé with you, but he or she should also be equally impressed with the quality of the résumé you present.

Writing a Scanable Résumé

You spend lots of time and energy writing the perfect résumé and cover letter based on the assumption that someone will read it. However, experience has proven that it is never safe to assume. Technology has impacted virtually every aspect of our lives, and job hunting is no exception. To quickly and effectively shortlist numerous résumés and build a database of potential employees, some companies are now using computerized scanning.

Through a process called optical character recognition (OCR), résumés are scanned using software that converts documents into plain text. Once processed, the computer searches these documents and selects those containing keywords such as C++, Unix, Java, and other technical keywords. The computer takes the information it has collected and builds a skills inventory list, which is stored in a database. Employers then search for certain skills and attributes by querying the database, and a list of candidates who match the criteria is generated. The benefits to an employer using this method of processing are clear. It enables companies to sift through a large number of résumés in a short time and develop a huge database of potential employees.

For the job hunter, automatic résumé processing does have certain considerations. Many OCR programs make mistakes when reading words or special characters, such as underlining, italics, or bullets. Preparing résumés that are scanner friendly requires a slightly different approach to formatting than a standard résumé. The following list contains a few tips to help make your résumé ready for scanning.

➤ During the scanning process, the computer searches for a list of keywords. If the computer is unable to find those keywords on your résumé, your database entry will be incomplete. To work around this problem, try to pinpoint some of the keywords that are important to the position you are seeking. It is likely that the computer will be looking for specific words or acronyms that are related to specific computer skills. For example, on a database administrators résumé, the words Oracle, reports, and data warehousing may be selected.

➤ Fancy formatting, boxes, italics, underlining, and unusual fonts may not be clearly read by a scanner. It is best to keep your résumé simple, keeping in mind that it is just for the computer's eye.

➤ As a precaution, include both the acronym as well as full titles for technical terms. The computer may scan for either, and to miss out on an opportunity for such small details would be unfortunate.

➤ Scanners typically like a lot of white space, so try to avoid congestion and keep the layout simple.

➤ Print the résumé on a quality printer. Photocopies and poor print quality may make for a poor scan. As mentioned earlier, use white paper rather than colored stock.

➤ If at all possible, try running your résumé through a scanner to see how it looks.

Due to the convenience for employers, companies using computers to scan résumés will become even more common than they are now. When preparing for the job hunt, it is a good idea to have a résumé prepared in a normal format as well as a scanable version.

ASCII Résumés

Nowadays, résumés are often distributed to employers over the Internet. To prevent issues with formatting on various word processors, it has become common practice to use the ASCII format to publish résumés to the Web. ASCII is a very basic text format that can be used across all computing platforms. ASCII files are often referred to as "plain text" or "text only" files.

Preparing an ASCII résumé is not difficult to do. Simply save your document as a text only file, which even the most basic of word processors has the ability to do. However, be aware that when saving your résumé as a text only document, some of the formatting you have used will be removed. Therefore, when saving your résumé as an ASCII document, it is best to first remove any formatting, such as bold, italics, underlining, text alignment, unusual fonts, and word wrap. The ASCII format simply does not support these features. This file format may make the résumé seem a little plain, but as discussed earlier, fancy formatting is not needed on a résumé, and the person to whom you are sending the résumé will be expecting the ASCII document to look plain. Once the ASCII résumé is created, open it in a utility such as Windows Notepad to see how it looks prior to sending it.

The plain text ASCII format is necessary because a common method is needed for sending text over the Internet. ASCII is compatible with every word processor available as well as every version. By avoiding formatting issues, an ASCII résumé becomes the easiest way to apply for jobs online. When applying for a job by email, many employers will specify an ASCII format and will not accept résumés by attachment because attachments can carry viruses, and they may also present compatibility issues. Furthermore, if you want to put your résumé online and post it in one of the many Internet job databases, an ASCII format is usually required. Keep in mind that when your résumé is added to a database, there is a good chance it will be read by a computer, so it should be written using the keyword format for scanning.

Producing a document in a variety of formats may make it seem like designing a résumé is a complicated task, but the reality is that if you have a good idea of what your résumé should include in the first place, creating a suitable résumé in any format should not be too difficult.

Paying for Your Résumé

Of course, you may decide that instead of producing your résumé yourself, you would rather it be prepared by a professional résumé writing service. It is an approach that many people take, although whether a professionally written résumé is any more effective than generating it yourself remains questionable.

10

Many résumé writing services simply take your existing résumé and process it into a professional format. Others, particularly those that are more expensive, often take the time to meet with you in order to be able to incorporate some of your positive personality traits into the résumé. Whichever way is chosen, if you are using a reputable service, you are likely to get a professional looking résumé with very little hassle.

If you do decide to use the services of professional résumé writers, there are a few things to consider. Always be clear about exactly what it is you are getting for your money, and if you are unhappy with the work they have done, make sure that you have the option to have it redone. Also, be sure to find out what the résumé writing service will charge for any changes that may be needed to your résumé after it is completed. As with other services, if you get the chance, ask other people about their experiences with a certain résumé company, and go with their recommendations. Remember, résumés are formulaic in nature. People use résumé writing services because they believe that the résumé will be better than one they could produce themselves or because they do not want the hassle of writing one. There is no reason at all why you, with sufficient effort and research, would not be able to produce a résumé of comparable quality without the assistance of a professional résumé writer.

References—Don't Take My Word for It

The last significant piece in the job hunt preparation puzzle is references. The importance of references who can validate your experiences, training, and character cannot be overlooked. However, there is some debate concerning whether references should be included on the résumé or not. Many career counselors currently suggest excluding references and in their place providing the line, "References are available upon request." The primary reason for excluding references from your résumé is that in some cases potential employers may choose to call these references before your interview, and you may be eliminated from the running by something a reference has said. Some people contend that information about your past work experience should be obtained only after the employer has had a chance to meet you in an interview. In any case, employers will assume that you are able to provide references, so if you are in a crunch for room, omit mention of references completely.

If you do choose to include references on your résumé, be sure to choose people who will provide positive feedback on your character and performance as well as those that like you.

In the interview, however, references are mandatory. Preparation for an interview should include a list of references. For each reference, you should provide:

➤ Name

➤ Title\Position

➤ Company

➤ Company address

➤ Contact numbers

➤ Email address

➤ Relationship to yourself

Your reference sheet should be typed up neatly as a separate page, but in the same style and on the same paper as that used for your résumé. Also remember to include your contact details on the references sheet in case it gets separated from your résumé. This prevents the potentially embarrassing situation of an employer phoning a reference and inquiring about the wrong person.

How to Choose a Reference

References are not used for a popularity contest, so limit them to three or four of those people who are able to validate your technical skills as well as your personal attributes and values. Your reference choices may include past employers, coworkers, professional contacts, instructors, and even someone who has just known you for some time. Do not include family members or anyone you have a direct personal relationship with.

Just selecting people who will give you a positive reference is usually not enough. It is necessary to choose references that can provide the information the employer needs to make an informed decision regarding your potential employment. References that are only able to confirm that you are a nice person are not adequate. The following list contains some guidelines to follow when you are choosing your references:

➤ You need to choose a reference that can confirm your technical skills. This may be a coworker, a client, or a supervisor.

➤ As well as professional references, it is also worth listing personal references, but if possible, try to use people who have a recognized standing in society, such as a judge, policeman, school principal, and so on.

➤ For those just entering the IT industry, academic references from instructors are often used.

Remember to always confirm with your references *before* giving their names to employers. It can be embarrassing if your reference is called and can't remember you. If possible, discuss the job responsibilities with your references. The more information your references have about the job, the better prepared they will be to answer your potential employer's questions.

If your references are willing to provide you with written recommendations, it is always worthwhile to take them with you on interviews. However, make sure that you do not exclude the fact that these same references may be approached for other references by a potential employer.

Supporting Evidence

During your job search preparation phase, you should also make sure that you have copies of any certificates or awards you have received. Whether or not you will ever be required to produce them at an interview will depend on the potential employer, but it is a step that takes very little time and serves to reinforce a level of organization. Items that should be included are high school, college, or university graduation certificates, technical course completion certificates, and any certificates issued for the completion of a certification program.

Once you have collected all of your certificates, your résumé, your cover letters, and references, it's a good idea to buy a presentation folder in which to keep them. When attending interviews, it is often less threatening to carry a folder into the interview than a briefcase or a bag. Also, keeping your documents in a folder will protect them from becoming dirty or crumpled.

Chapter Summary

Creating a professional looking résumé and cover letter are just two of the steps necessary to prepare for your job hunt, but their importance cannot be overstated. Investing the thought and preparation they require allows you to approach opportunities with the right tools. The following points highlight the most important things to keep in mind:

➤ Cover letters should be personalized, short, and easy to read. A good cover letter will motivate a potential employer to read your résumé.

➤ Résumés provide the chance to tell a potential employer about you and your skills. Be accurate, succinct, and clear.

➤ Although references are usually provided after an interview, selecting and preparing a list of your references before you start looking for work can make things easier in the long run.

Think of your cover letter, résumé, and list of references as representations of yourself. They are the first impression you make on a potential employer, as well as the tangible reminder of who you are and what you are capable of long after the interview is over.

10

Andrew J. Wiseman
445 Coronation Street
Clarksville, VA 11111
(545) 555-4445

A.Wiseman@givemeajob.com

October 20, 2000

Ms. Judith Blais
Director of Human Resources
Translation Software Services
451 Francis Street
Hanmersville, VA 78194

Dear Ms. Blais:

I am responding to your advertisement in the Herald (dated 9/8/00) regarding the C++ programmer **①**
position. Enclosed is my resume outlining my education and experience. **②**

③ I have completed training as a C++ programmer and have practical experience working with all aspects
of the language. I find programming to be a stimulating and challenging field. Whether working as part
of a team or on my own initiative, I am able to produce work of a high standard be it coding, debugging,
testing, or writing documentation. **④**

Although my technical training has focused on C++, I have been fortunate to have worked with a range
of other programming languages. My open mindedness has meant that the transition to other languages **⑤**
has been relatively simple.

⑥ I can be available for an interview at short notice and would welcome the opportunity to discuss my
suitability for the position in more detail. I can be reached at the number provided above or via email.

⑦ Thank you for your time and consideration.

Sincerely,

Andrew J. Wiseman

Andrew J. Wiseman

Enclosures

An Example of a Good Cover Letter—Commentary and Tips

On the opposite page, you can see an example of a cover letter for a programming position. This example includes the necessary aspects of a cover letter described earlier in this chapter.

The letter is written using an Helvetica font and is well spaced and positioned on the page. There are a number of points worth noting. The numbered circles on the letter refer to the following points:

1 As discussed, the first paragraph of a cover letter should include details of how you heard about the job and reiterate the name of the position you are applying for. It is not uncommon for companies to advertise more than one position at a time, and if it is unclear as to which position you are applying for, your résumé might end up in the wrong pile.

2 This one simple sentence reinforces your interest in a position. You are directing the reader to the fact that your résumé is attached.

3 In addition to mentioning relevant training, you should also refer to practical experiences you have had. If you have little or no work experience, a phrase such as this is neutral and does not imply too much.

4 This is your chance to choose key phrases from the actual job advertisement and compare your skills with those that the employer is looking for. Positive comparison in this way will make you seem like a good candidate, and at the very least, will make the employer look at your résumé.

5 You want the employer to think that you are ready for a challenge and are keen to learn new things, both of which are characteristics an employer will be looking for in any employee, but especially if it is your first IT job.

6 This paragraph says everything it needs to. It shows a willingness and eagerness to attend an interview and directs the employer to your contact details at the top of the page. It is sufficiently positive without seeming pushy or aggressive.

7 Finally, the cover letter is rounded off with a polite thank you. This, combined with other areas of the cover letter, give the impression that you are courteous and friendly, two of the greatest assets any employee can have.

Tips from a Recruiter:

- Identify something specific about the position or company that attracted your interest. This will be more personal and show that you have done your homework.
- It is critical that you do not have any typos, misspelled words, etc. This can, and usually will, end your chances for consideration immediately, even if you are well qualified. Have it proofread by someone you trust who has a solid command of grammar.
- Project a positive, well-defined self image using as few words as possible.

10

Andrew J. Wiseman
445 Coronation Street
Clarksville, VA 11111
(545)555-4445
A.Wiseman@givemeajob.com

1 Director of Human Resources
Translation Software Services
451 Francis Street
Hanmersville, VA 78194

1 Dear Sir/Madam:

2

I am responding to your advertisement in the newspaper regarding programming vacancies. I feel I would be suitable for this position as I have just completed my training to become a programmer **3**

4 Although I have no practical experience, I have been fortunate to have worked with a range of programming languages. My skill at adapting to new languages would make me a valuable asset to any programming department. **5**

6 I can be reached most days at the number listed above, and I will be available for an interview next week, although not on Friday.

I look forward to your early response. **7**

Sincerely,
8

Andrew J. Wiseman

Enclosures

An Example of a Poor Cover Letter—Commentary and Tips

On the opposite page, you can see an example of another cover letter. Although this letter has all the same components as the cover letter discussed on the previous pages, this cover letter has some of the characteristics of a poor cover letter.

The font used, Helvetica Condensed, is difficult to read due to its small size and minimal space between letters. In addition, the text is clustered toward the top of the page, making the entire letter seem a little cluttered. If you compare this letter with the good cover letter, you will notice that the differences are relatively subtle, but the overall effect is very different.

1 Cover letters should be addressed directly to an individual. Most job advertisements will state who résumés should be addressed to. But if the advertisement does not make this clear, you should contact the company and find out who to submit your résumé to.

2 The first paragraph of the cover letter should refer directly to the position being applied for. Not only does this letter not do this, it goes on to say that you have "just" finished training. This gives the impression that you really are a newcomer to the industry.

3 The missing period at the end of this line may seem like a small error, but it indicates a lack of proofreading. Always be sure to check your cover letters for spelling, grammar, and punctuation. It is best if you can get someone else to read through a cover letter before sending it.

4 There is no need to draw people's attention to the fact that you have no experience, even if it is true. Try to focus on positive points, such as what you have done outside of the classroom to enhance your skills.

5 This phrase is very pushy and quite bold for someone with limited experience. Statements such as this are often interpreted as arrogance. Remember, your cover letter and your résumé are windows to your personality.

6 Although it is good to reinforce your availability for an interview, there is no need to outline your personal daily schedule. If you are unavailable for an interview on a certain day, you can deal with that fact when the employer contacts you.

7 This aggressive approach may work in certain situations, but it is probably better to close your cover letter with a polite thank you rather than a brash phrase such as this.

8 The fact that the letter is not signed or dated along with the lack of specific detail throughout the letter, makes the letter seem like it is just a standard cover letter being reused. This is not the impression you want to convey to a potential employer.

10

Tips from a Recruiter:
- Always make sure you take the time to put together a good cover letter. You can have all the skills and the sharpest résumé in the world, but if your cover letter does not grab the attention of the reader, you probably won't have the opportunity to compete for the potential position.

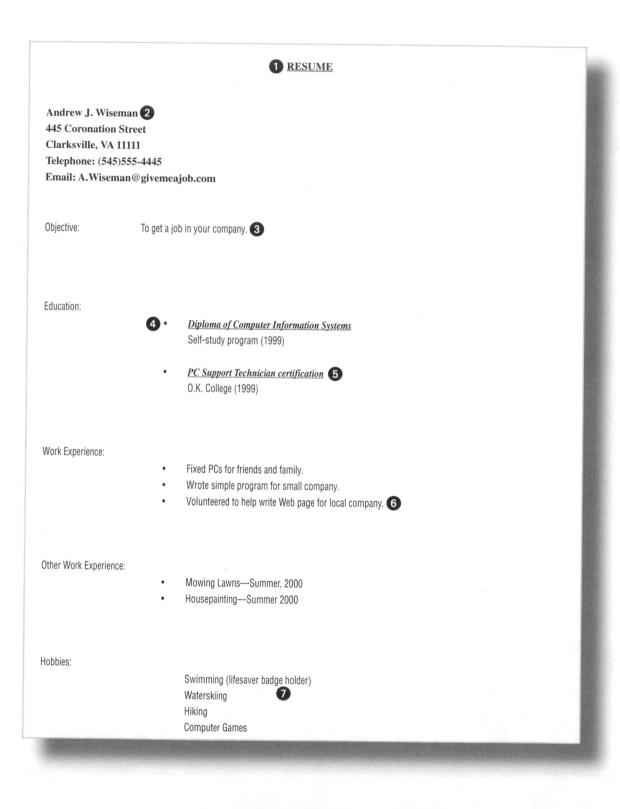

❶ <u>RESUME</u>

Andrew J. Wiseman ❷
445 Coronation Street
Clarksville, VA 11111
Telephone: (545)555-4445
Email: A.Wiseman@givemeajob.com

Objective: To get a job in your company. ❸

Education:

    ❹ •   <u>*Diploma of Computer Information Systems*</u>
          Self-study program (1999)

      •   <u>*PC Support Technician certification*</u> ❺
          O.K. College (1999)

Work Experience:

      •   Fixed PCs for friends and family.
      •   Wrote simple program for small company.
      •   Volunteered to help write Web page for local company. ❻

Other Work Experience:

      •   Mowing Lawns—Summer, 2000
      •   Housepainting—Summer 2000

Hobbies:

        Swimming (lifesaver badge holder)
        Waterskiing   ❼
        Hiking
        Computer Games

An Example of a Poor Résumé—Commentary and Tips

The résumé on the opposite page was written for Andrew Wiseman, the same candidate referred to in the cover letters. This first example has all the basic components of a résumé, but is lacking in a number of areas.

The résumé makes the page look bare, and the use of bolding is somewhat misplaced. The font used, Helvetica Condensed, looks a bit awkward and does not fill the page width, which again contributes to the scant look.

In addition to these factors, there are a number of points worthy of specific mention. As before, the numbered paragraphs correspond to the numbers on the actual résumé.

1 The word résumé appears at the top of the page, which is not necessary. It is the correct placement for your name, however.

2 The name appears in this location, but is mixed in with the other contact details. Also, the font used is different from the one used in the rest of the résumé, which is indicative of poor formatting and proof reading.

3 Although it is good to have an objective, it should be positive and ideally directed toward the desired position. This objective is too general and sounds very casual.

4 The education section is in the right place, but there is simply not enough detail. As someone entering the IT industry for the first time, you need to capitalize on your training by providing lots of detail.

5 The underline running past the end of the text, again shows a lack of attention to formatting. Combine this with the formatting error mentioned earlier as well as the lack of bullet points in the hobbies section, and it starts to look like very little time was spent on the general layout and tidiness of this résumé.

6 As with the education section, the work experience portion is too brief. Also, any experience you have needs to be discussed in positive terms. Words like "simple" and "small" will not conjure up the right image with an employer.

7 As mentioned in item 5, the bullets are missing from the list of hobbies, but hobbies really should not be on this résumé in any event. In this example, it almost looks like the hobbies section was added to fill space, whereas that space would have been better used in the preceding education and work experience sections.

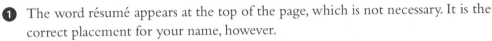

Tips from a Recruiter:
- Many times we see candidates who have very good skills, but do not have the expertise or desire to showcase those skills on their résumé. It is unfortunate because those individuals are limiting their opportunities.
- A well done résumé is one of the most critical aspects of finding the right employment opportunity.

1 **Andrew J. Wiseman**

445 Coronation Street, Clarksville, VA 11111
Telephone: (545)555-4445
Email: A.Wiseman@givemeajob.com

2 **Objective:** To obtain a position with Translation Software Services as a
C++ Programmer.

Education:

- ***Diploma of Computer Information Systems*** **3**
  Independent Learning (1999)

  Relevant Courses include:
  - Object-Oriented Programming Techniques in C++
  - C++ and OOP
  - Intermediate C++ and Object Oriented Design
  - Advanced Topics in C++: implementing graphics using inheritance
  - Object-Oriented Programming and Classes

- ***PC Support Technician Certification***
  O.K. College (1999)

  Courses include:
  - Advanced Hardware Troubleshooting Techniques
  - PC Repair and Maintenance

Work Experience:

4
- Designed and wrote an inventory tracking system in C++ for a
  local food company.
- Worked with Clarksville based Web design company to develop a corporate
  Web page for one of its clients. Authored CGI scripts for
  online customer requests.
- Extensive PC hardware maintenance and troubleshooting skills.

Personal Achievements:
- Lifeguard Certificate
- Editor of School Newspaper for 3 years. **5**

6 **References available upon request**

An Example of a Good Résumé—Commentary and Tips

This résumé follows the same basic format, but has much more chance of landing a job interview with its clean crisp look, excellent layout, and more detailed information. The résumé fills the page in both directions and the font, which is Helvetica, is easy to read. This résumé makes good use of both the education and the limited experience of the candidate, having all the right ingredients in the right quantities. There is no section on previous work experience because none of it is relevant to the position being applied for, and space is minimal.

There are a number of points worthy of specific mention.

1 The name stands out at the top of the résumé and catches the eye. Although the font size for the name could be bigger, it is nicely proportioned to the rest of the résumé.

2 The objective is clear and very specific. This type of personalized objective must be changed every time a résumé is submitted for a new position, but it is a small touch that may make a big difference.

3 Education experience is clearly laid out and details the relevant courses and subjects studied. The amount of space that the education section uses serves to draw the attention of the reader to the fact that the candidate has been well educated in these technologies.

4 The work experience is spoken of in a positive and constructive tone, and details projects that are likely to be of direct interest to an employer looking for a computer programmer. The fact that the work was performed as a volunteer is not mentioned, nor is the fact that that it was a "simple program for a small company."

5 Adding this personal achievement section gives more substance to the résumé, and the achievements themselves demonstrate a number of qualities about the candidate.

6 It may not be completely necessary, but rounding off your résumé by saying that references are available reassures the reader that the information provided can be backed up by a third party.

10

Tips from a Recruiter:

- Put yourself in a manager's position and answer the question, "Would I bring this individual in for an interview based on this résumé?" If the answer is no, then modify the résumé.

- Under work experience, show the month and year for both start and finish dates for each employer. Do your best to explain gaps. If you are still employed, then show, "to present." In listing education, include any undergraduate and graduate degrees beginning with most recent. Be sure to incorporate any meaningful distinctions, such as "cum laude."

- Always be honest; never lie on your résumé.

CHAPTER ELEVEN

The IT Job Search

It's D-day. After what may have been months or, in many cases, years of planning, studying, and preparing, it's time to translate your IT potential into a job. Finding a job in the IT industry has much in common with finding a job in any other industry, but it also has many differences. As with everything else in IT, the recruitment process is often fast. You may find that little time elapses between seeing the job advertisement, submitting your résumé, interviewing with the company, and receiving the offer. Jobs are advertised on the Internet, through computer magazines, newspapers, and through recruitment agencies. Your mission, should you wish to accept it, is to find the right job for you, and then nail the interview in such a way that the employer is left wishing there was more than one of you.

In this chapter, we discuss the following:

➤ How to market yourself to potential employers

➤ Where to look for job opportunities and the "hidden job market"

➤ How to deal with recruitment agencies

➤ How to be prepared before, during, and following an interview

➤ How to handle subsequent offers and rejections

➤ How to negotiate the best deal

Strategic Decisions

A large part of the job search preparation involves developing a strategy for self-promotion. A job search is a bit like an ad campaign, your goal is to get out there and promote your skill, training, and, if applicable, your experience to potential employers. It's all about marketing, and you and your skills are the product. Be aware, however, that the process of self-promotion is a bit of an art and runs a fine line between over promotion and under promotion. Somewhere in between these two is the best place to be.

During your job search, there are specific tools you can use to self-promote yourself. Everyone seeking employment has access to these tools, but it is the proficiency in how they are used that makes the difference. The key tools for self-promotion are the cover letter and résumé, which we covered in the last chapter. But now you must consider how the tools can best be used, and how you will convey your message to employers.

Let's Get Going

Before you start looking for a job, make sure that your résumé is complete and up-to-date, and you have all of the necessary information needed for your job hunt. In the last chapter, we discussed the necessary components of your job hunt, but it's worth doing one final check over before you start. Here is a quick checklist of what you should have:

➤ *Cover letter*—You should have a template of your cover letter ready so that you can customize it to a specific employer or position.

➤ *Résumé*—An up-to-date résumé in a paper, ASCII, and scanable format are needed.

➤ *Certificates*—Copies of your course, degree, or diploma certificates reinforce your educational background. If you have certifications, include these too.

➤ *References*—Ideally, contact all references you intend to use to prepare them for the fact that they may get a call or email from a potential employer.

It might be tempting to just launch headlong into your job search, but having things organized make it possible to take maximum advantage of opportunities as they arise.

Making Personal Decisions

Before you actually start looking for a job, you need to make some decisions about the things that are important to you. Factors to consider include the companies you would like to work for, what job roles you will consider, and where, geographically, you are prepared to work. It's important to decide these things early on because it lets you focus your job search so that you aren't wasting time on opportunities that ultimately will be unsuitable or unattractive. Be wary of narrowing your search too much though; be general in some of your decisions. The more opportunities you can consider, the more likely you are to find a suitable position quickly.

Other factors you must consider are those regarding working hours, salary, and benefits. Again, be careful not to narrow your search too much based on this criteria, but remember the bills have to be paid. Note that many employers are reluctant to include details of compensation packages in job advertisements, which makes it difficult to judge a job vacancy against this criteria.

Always remember that you are looking for your first IT position. Now is not the time to be overly fussy about certain aspects of a job, but do not put yourself into a situation where after only a few weeks you are looking to move on because the job is unsuitable. Know beforehand what sacrifices you're willing and able to make and which ones you can't make.

Making Contacts

It is likely that during your training, you have come in contact with, or have spoken to IT professionals. Perhaps an IT professional spoke in your class, maybe you met a programmer at a party or a network administrator while walking your dog. The point is that these are contacts and present a chance for networking with IT professionals. Networking with other IT professionals is very important for those looking for their first job in IT.

The function of networking and making contacts is to establish and build professional relationships. These professional relationships can give those entering the IT field two distinct advantages, relevant industry information and increased recognition.

There is no better source of information on the IT industry than from those already employed in it. They know what's hot in the field, who is hiring and who is not, which employers have a good reputation, who does not, what to expect on the job, and what the current industry trends are. Many seasoned IT professionals have the inside track to such information and usually have an established network of professional contacts from which to acquire this information. The information that can be gleaned from these professionals is a powerful part of job preparation. Assuming information is power, it may in fact be one of the most important aspects of job preparation.

The second advantage of networking with other professionals is it increases your visibility. Not literally of course, but networking and meeting other professionals gives them a chance to get to know you and your IT skills. When they, or someone they know, require such skills, you already have a foot in the door. Getting known and increasing your professional visibility can be a great asset in your job search and can really give you an edge.

Many newcomers to IT are somewhat hesitant to assertively pursue professional contacts. This hesitation and fear to establish connections is understandable, but for the most part unjustified. IT professionals are generally forthcoming and eager to tell their story. The difficulty may be determining fact from technical bravado, because like any other field, IT professionals are always keen to expound on their responsibilities and knowledge.

Remember that no matter how much experience an IT professional has, this person started off where you are now. Someday, someone may be chasing you for the inside scoop.

Looking for Opportunities

After you have been in the IT industry for some years, you may get a recruitment agent or head hunter phoning you with a new opportunity. The reality for your first position, however, is that you are likely to have to find your own opportunities. Fortunately, there are many places you can look. In the section that follows, we recommend ways to find job listings and opportunities. Keep in mind that you'll want to customize your cover letters and résumés per each job for which you apply.

Finding Vacancies

Thanks to the Internet, much of your job searching can be done from the comfort of your own PC. Even traditional paper-based media, such as newspapers and magazines, have a corresponding Web presence. The main resources for job searching are as follows:

➤ *Internet job sites*—A huge number of Internet job sites offer job listings from companies of all sizes and from every business sector. Every site provides the capability to search through the available positions on a variety of criteria including skills, location, and job role. Appendix D includes links to some of these sites, but you can find even more sites by typing *IT job sites* into any Internet search engine.

➤ *Company Internet Web sites*—Many companies now choose to advertise vacancies through their own corporate Web sites. If there is no apparent link to a careers section, use a site map or site search capability that nearly all pages offer.

➤ *Employment agencies*—In some cases, employers would rather not advertise vacancies themselves, and instead use an employment agency. Employment agencies advertise positions on behalf of the client, in most cases providing details of the position while omitting the name of the client. You can locate employment agencies by reviewing ads in the classified section of the newspaper, or, by using the Yellow Pages of your phone directory. There are also agencies that specialize in particular technical areas of IT. Appendix A lists some agencies that specialize in certain areas.

➤ *Newspapers*—Traditionally, vacancies appeared in a newspaper, and while this medium is perhaps not as popular as it once was, many companies still choose to advertise vacancies in this way. Companies may use newspapers for recruitment purposes if they feel that there is a good chance that the vacancy can be filled locally.

➤ *Personal contacts*—As previously mentioned, the importance of networking with other technology professionals cannot be overestimated. In addition to these professional contacts, make sure that everyone from Great Aunt Mabel to your dentist are aware of the fact you are looking for work.

Because there are so many different resources that are available for job searchers today, you'll probably want to try to use every resource you can to ensure that you've located the best opportunities. Aside from what's actually advertised, in whatever medium, however, how else can you find opportunities? Let's look at that next.

The Hidden Job Market

Want to know a secret? Not all jobs are advertised. Okay, so maybe you already knew this, but it is important to know that finding these unadvertised jobs may well be how you gain entry into the IT industry.

Essentially, there are two methods for a job hunt: a proactive and a reactive approach. Candidates who respond to ads placed by employers are involved in a reactive job search. Many employers choose to look for employees by using classified ads, job postings, or job banks. This approach is highly visible, and for the prospective employee, a very competitive method of job searching.

In a proactive job search, job candidates take the initiative by approaching employers before they advertise. Many employers actually choose not to advertise job openings because they receive unsolicited applications on a daily basis. When a new position opens, it is easier, and considerably cheaper, for employers to read through the résumés already on hand than to go through the process of advertising. Jobs typically are only advertised when no suitable candidate can be found within the current collection of résumés. It is estimated that advertised jobs comprise a mere 20 percent of the available job openings, meaning around 80 percent of available jobs are filled without advertising. Referred to as the "hidden job market," these unadvertised jobs offer strong opportunities to motivated job seekers. The question is, how do you find, apply for, and obtain a job that isn't advertised?

Searching for jobs using classified ads, online job agencies, and referral agencies is the standard advertised job market with which we are most familiar. Those looking for a job respond to the employer's ad along with many other candidates. It is fierce competition for the 20 percent of advertised jobs. Think about taking a proactive approach as well. Send résumés to companies with which you think your skill sets would be beneficial. The next section discuss this approach.

Where to Look

Job hunting within the hidden job market takes a bit more effort than the traditional job search. To access this market, the first thing you need to do is identify the employers, companies, and agencies that you want to work for or that may need your technical skills. The Internet is a good place to start this search. The following list provide links to sites that may help you find more about a company and, if applicable, the company's Web site address.

➤ Localeyes (**www.localeyes.com**) allows you to search for a city and industry type. The Web pages that meet the criteria are listed. This site is very useful and can help focus your job search.

➤ Infospace (**www.infospace.com/bizweb.htm**) makes it easy to search for a specific company's Web site. It enables you to access the publicly available information on the business or company.

➤ Compfind (**www.comfind.com**) allows you to search by company name, or more generally, by product or service. The site boasts access to over 700,000 business listings. Finding technology companies in this mixture is not a difficult task.

➤ Yellow pages are provided from AOL (**www.aol.com/netfind/ yellowpages.adp**) Search for businesses by category or name.

Note: Don't neglect the good old Yellow Pages when looking for businesses.

➤ GTE yellow pages (**http://yp.superpages.com**) allow you to search by many different criteria, including business name, street address, phone number, or category.

➤ Bell South Real Pages (**www.yp.bellsouth.com**) is a similar business finding tool.

11

You Don't Know Me But. . .

After you locate the companies that interest you, the real work begins. With your list of potential employers, résumé, and cover letter in hand it's time to tap into that hidden job market. Ready for a little proactive job searching?

Networking

As mentioned, networking plays an important role in finding the hidden job. It is perhaps the most effective way to find out about a job and meet potential employers. The fact is someone with a large network of professional acquaintances in the IT industry is more likely to find a job than someone responding to an ad. Every contact you make spreads your reach further. It is necessary to take the time to build your professional network.

Cold Call

Making a cold call to a company is a bold move that can at times pay off. A "cold" call refers to contacting potential employers not currently advertising positions. The intent of the cold call is to introduce yourself and offer skills to the employer. Even though no jobs are currently available, it is hoped that you are remembered when one does become available. In the best-case scenario, cold calls may land you an interview. Be forewarned, however, that many companies do not like this approach, and you may have many rejections along the way.

Informational Interviewing

Informational interviewing is a clever approach to get your name and face known with potential employers. Informational interviewing involves contacting potential employers and asking to arrange a meeting. On the surface, the intention of the meeting is to learn more about the company or the profession, but there is another intent. An informational interview gives potential employers a chance to get to know you, and this connection may assist you when the company has a vacant position. At the very least, the information you get can be beneficial in your job search. Further, just by meeting and talking, you have expanded your professional network.

Including these steps as part of your active job search campaign expands your professional network base. Persistence and perseverance are the keys to successfully break into the hidden job market. You will most certainly hit resistance along the way, but a proactive job search can pay off in the end.

Dealing with Recruitment Agencies

The complexities of technical recruitment coupled with the difficulty in finding suitable staff leads many companies to look for other ways of finding employees. When faced with the need to recruit new IT staff, many companies choose to get a little help by partnering with recruitment agencies. This technique helps them, but it can help you as well.

Recruitment agencies make money by charging the company that they are recruiting for. On permanent positions, the charge normally is a percentage based on the new employees salary, which effectively means that the service is free to the employee.

Note: Be very wary of any recruitment agency that requires candidates to pay a charge for registration or subsequent placement.

In most cases, the charge is payable after the new recruit has completed an initial employment period. On a contract position, the charge is likely to take the form of a percentage commission for each hour, day, or week that is worked.

There are two very good reasons why using a recruitment agency can be a great help during your job search. First, it can only be a good thing when someone is helping you look for work. Second, agents make their living by finding people jobs. It is in their best interest to acquire a position for you. When you contact a recruitment agency, make sure that you have a résumé to email or fax to them. To speed up the process, you may want to drop off or email your résumé in advance and then call to discuss your situation. If the agency has an opportunity that is matched to your skills, they may call you right away, but otherwise they will add you to their database so that you can be matched with future opportunities. Recruitment agents and the database systems they use are not infallible. If you see an advertisement from a recruitment agency with which you are registered that matches your skills, it is definitely worth giving the agent a call and expressing an interest. It may be that the agent feels you are not suitable, but it simply may mean that you got overlooked in the search process.

With agents, perhaps even more than employers, keeping your name in the forefront is particularly important. An employer may have five vacancies a year that it needs to fill; a recruitment agent may be working with a database of hundreds or even thousands of possible opportunities. What you need is for the agent to see a vacancy and immediately think of your name. As always don't go too far. Stalking your agent is more likely to label yourself as a nuisance rather than a great candidate.

11

It may seem to the untrained eye that an agent's job is easy, in reality it is anything but. The agent acts as an intermediary between two parties in a situation where there are many variables. Employers can change their requirements on a whim, and candidates can be equally fickle. The key to building a good relationship with an agent is simply to be honest, forthright, and upfront at all times. Do this and the agent will work hard for you.

Applying for a Job

However you find your vacancy, you need to actually apply for the job. In the great scheme of things, this is probably the easiest step of them all. Most vacancy listings detail how and by when applications for the position should be made. The simple rule of getting it right is to follow the instructions. If the listing specifies that résumés should be emailed as a Word attachment, make sure that is exactly what you do. Doing anything else is likely to guarantee that you don't get considered for the position.

When mailing résumés in a conventional manner, observe the rules that we discussed in the last chapter regarding customization, appearance, and professionalism. If you want to be doubly sure that your résumé gets to its destination before a certain date, use a registered postal service or courier. The costs are inconsequential when compared with the ultimate goal. If the potential employer is local, it is safest to drop the résumé off in person. Not only does this ensure the delivery of your résumé, but it also gives you a chance to visit the office, see what it is like, and maybe make a contact.

An important thing to do when applying for several positions at the same time is to keep a record of the places to which you have applied and the details of the position. Keep track of details such as the contact name, the job role, and the application closing date. This information enables you to keep track of your job search. If you responded to an advertisement, you may want to clip the ad or print the posting if it's a computer-based listing, for your future reference. It's always helpful, especially if you're responding to several ads at once, to quickly refresh your memory of a particular job for which you may have scheduled an interview.

Many career guides suggest making follow up calls to ensure the employer has received your résumé. Although companies may be happy to confirm receipt of your résumé, it is unlikely that placing this call will increase your chances of getting the job. In certain cases it may even be viewed as you hassling the employer. At this stage of the game, the effort you put into your résumé and cover letter are your greatest assets, and it is these that will be working for you.

Job Interviews

Hopefully, your application will be successful, and you will be offered an interview. After you schedule the interview, you need to be prepared so that you stand the best chance of landing the job. As every career guide book will tell you, finding out information about the company is an important step. With the Internet serving as a tremendous and valuable resource to us today, information gathering should not be a difficult task. A great deal of information can be gleaned from a company's Web site, as well as other publicly accessible sources. After you have read all there is to read on a company's Web site, try typing the company name into an Internet search engine to find out related news stories or product reviews, if applicable. When you do find relevant and interesting information, learn it. The reason you are going to so much effort is so you can impress the employer with your knowledge of the organization and its business during your interview.

The Day of the Interview

By the day of the interview, you should have completed all of your preparations and be ready for action. Today is the day when your IT dreams could be turned into a reality. Today you need to be more focused than ever.

If you are tackling a number of interviews in one day, pay special attention to how you intend to travel between interviews. Most importantly, make sure that you schedule more than enough time between each appointment. The worst that can happen is that you end up drinking cappuccinos or taking a stroll to fill in the time between interviews. If you don't allow enough time, you obviously will be late for your interviews and risk losing whatever potential you had to land the job. In addition, you also may stumble through the end of the interview that is going into overtime by worrying about being late for the next one! Don't make this mistake. Allow yourself plenty of time.

Although people advocate locating an office before an interview so that you do not have problems finding it, it's not always possible. If you are unable to do this, call the company's receptionist and find out which subway station, parking lot, or bus stop are nearest to your destination. Also, check your directions and ask about particular traffic problems in the area during peak commuting times so that you can plan extra time. If you do drive, try to avoid using parking meters or other time restricted parking means because sitting in an interview wondering if you car has been towed can be very distracting.

If you are going to be late for the interview, give as much notice as is absolutely possible. If you have to leave a message for someone, stress the fact that you are attending an interview and that it is imperative the message get to your interviewer. If the reason for your being late is reasonable, the employer may be sympathetic to your plight and either offer to wait for you or reschedule your interview. If you got up late and missed your train, forget it. The rule of thumb is simply don't be late.

What Goes on during a Real Interview?

If you believe the career guides or recruitment officers, you may think that interviews are highly structured meetings where a panel of seasoned pro's quiz you with probing questions designed to find out your true personality. The reality is that in many cases interviews are poorly organized and given by people who, while they may know a great deal about the job, have little formal interview training. Although not always the case, you may be surprised as to just how frequently this situation occurs, especially in smaller organizations.

In a well organized and professional company, the likelihood is that you will be faced with a highly organized interview. The panel may consist of the recruiting manager, a member of regular staff, and a representative from the company's personnel department. The person leading the interview most likely will start by going through basic information such as the layout and makeup of the organization. Even though you will know a great deal of the information from your pre-interview research, this is a time when you should just listen. From here, conversation will most likely move to the position you are being interviewed for and what's involved with that. Again, this is a time where you should be listening rather than talking. As the interviewer starts to probe into your personality and knowledge, the conversation will move to a two-way exchange. Now is your chance to impress the interviewer(s) with your positive outlook and enthusiasm.

The questions you must answer are likely to be the same as those asked in any job interview—what are your strengths, weaknesses, aspirations, and ambitions. Where the IT interview differs from the normal interview is when the discussion turns to your technical knowledge and experience. Though there may be no definite separation, you are entering the phase of technical interviewing.

Technical Interviewing

Many companies choose to give candidates a technical interview as well as a conventional one, though as discussed above they may happen at the same time. The idea of a technical interview is a simple one. In most cases, the technical interviewer, who may or may not be the original interviewer, will ask questions about your technical knowledge. Some questions will be direct, focusing on a specific product or technology. Other questions are likely to focus on trouble-shooting or configuration issues in an attempt to determine how you can apply your knowledge to a given situation.

In either case, the key to surviving a technical interview is to understand the interviewer's objective. The interviewer is trying to ascertain two things—Do you know the technical areas that you claim you do, and are you able to recall that information and apply it to a given scenario under pressure. The interviewer also may ask you questions to which you are not expected to know the answers. This strategy is not meant to trip you up, but rather to see how you react when presented with a problem to which you do not know the answer. As we have mentioned before, knowing when to ask for help is as important as the other aspects of your knowledge. When you are being technically interviewed, stay within the boundaries of your knowledge. Moving outside of them will almost certainly be visible to the employer and will ultimately erode your credibility. If you are asked a technical question that you do not know the answer to, say so, and then stress your enthusiasm and ability to learn about new products and technologies.

Telephone Interviews

Either due to geographical limitations, or simply to save time, some employers opt to do an interview over the telephone before asking you to visit their offices. This type of interview can work for you if you are good on the phone, and almost certainly guarantees a high level of interest in you by the employer if you are asked to attend an additional interview in person. For many people, however, telephone interviews can be one of the most uncomfortable interview methods and provide new challenges and rules to the interview process.

Telephone interviews tend to be relatively brief with their main use being to quickly clarify qualifications and background information. Although you may elect to dress in your pajamas and slippers, many of the rules that apply to a normal interview should still be observed. Try and ensure that while you are being interviewed, there are no distractions. The television should be turned off, and ideally you should be by yourself. Answering difficult questions from an employer can be intimidating enough without the members of your immediate family spectating from the sidelines.

What Is a "Good" Interview

A good interview is about offering both sides the chance to find out more about each other and to decide whether they can work together. Both the employer and the interviewee want things from the interview. Remember that it is a two-way street and that after you've done your share of listening and responding to the questions, you may want to ask some of your own questions. Asking questions about the company, its products, more details about the position for which you are interviewing, and the role of the position demonstrate a desire to learn with enthusiasm. It also shows that you're not afraid to ask questions when you need to.

We've listed below some things that employers want to know from an interview, as well as things that the candidate should look at learning from an interview. You may want to keep these things in mind during your interview.

Things the Employer Wants to Know

During the interview, the employer wants to get to know you better and judge whether you would be a good fit within the organization. Specifically, the employer wants to know the following types of things:

➤ *Who are you?*—The employer wants to get an idea of who you are. Are you a friendly, easy going character who will fit in with the rest of the team, or are you an intense individual who will work well in an independent role? What are your likes and dislikes? What do you do outside of work? All of these things act together to make you the person you are, and that brings us to an important point. Apart from the obvious needs such as skills and experience, an individual's personality can sometimes influence a company's decision to employ a person. Even the best database designer in the world will have problems finding work if he or she shows indications of a "difficult" personality. If you want an employer to know that you have good communication skills and can work well with coworkers, exemplify those skills well through your interview.

➤ *What do you know?*—The employer will want to get a real idea of what you actually know. Your certification or degree may say one thing, but what do you know that he needs? As mentioned in the technical interview section, this area is often tackled in a distinctively separate section of the interview, other times it will be intermingled.

➤ *What do you want?*—This question does not refer to just tangible benefits such as salary and health plans, it is more about finding out what you are looking for from a position. The employer is looking to match the job he has with your goals and aims. The closer the match, the more likely you are to be a content employee who will remain with the organization for a longer period of time.

Things the Candidate Wants to Know

The interview serves as an opportunity for you to size up the company and the work opportunity it has to offer. The interview provides the best chance you have to find out about your potential duties and how you will fit into their organization. Conventional wisdom seems to dictate that the interview is the domain of the employer, and you are almost solely there to answer their questions. This is not the case. In particular, you should focus on the following points:

➤ *What is the job?*—Get a good idea of what the job is all about. An employer is likely to give a good overview of your duties and responsibilities, but will relate this information from his or her perspective. The interviewer is unlikely to say that any of the tasks are boring or mundane. You need to factor this "rose tint" perspective into your thinking.

➤ *What is the company like?*—Any employer giving an interview is likely to give a glowing report of the company. Look at it from that perspective—no one wants to work for a bad company. Take the information given in this respect lightly, but obviously appear enthusiastic. Make your judgments based on what you have learned through your research and professional networking as much as the interviewers opinions.

➤ *What am I going to get?*—As well as the obvious things such as salary and benefits, you have the opportunity to find out what the future can hold for you. The interview is your chance to match the job with your career goals and aspirations.

It may seem that breaking the interview process down in this way simplifies it a little too much, but realistically, these are the things that each party is looking for. If you spend some time before an interview preparing yourself for answers to some possible questions, as well as creating questions of your own that might exemplify who you are and what you're looking for, then your preparedness and enthusiasm will shine.

Interview Do's and Dont's

As well as understanding what both sides are looking for from an interview, there are a number of other things you can do to make sure your interview goes smoothly. There are countless sources of advice on interview techniques and practices, and the intention of this book is not to provide a complete tutorial on interview techniques. So, as a short measure, here are our top tips on interviewing:

➤ If you do decide to be humorous, be absolutely sure of the suitability of what you are saying. Cracking the wrong joke may cost you the job.

➤ Make eye contact with your interviewer. If you are being interviewed by a number of people, make contact with each. Make it seem natural, and not as if you are staring.

11

➤ Smile. Be positive and friendly. Interviewers automatically warm to a candidate who is cheery and personable.

➤ Remember to ask questions. Questions make you appear interested and can help you understand more about the position and the company. Remember, the interview is for both of you.

➤ Appearing over confident can make you seem pushy and arrogant. Most employers are seeking someone who can fit into an existing team; these qualities are incompatible.

➤ Have a clear idea of your career goals and be ready to express them. Employers will want know where you are headed in your career and how that fits with the company.

Show Me the Money

Probably the most discussed interview question is, Should I ask what the salary is? If the employer has not brought the subject of compensation up with you, and you sense that the interview is headed toward a close, you may opt to ask the question. If the employer has mentioned a second interview, the end of the first interview is probably not the right time to be asking. If the first interview is drawing to a close and the employer has not mentioned compensation, it may signal that your talks are not going to get to that stage. Most employers today are aware that the salary and related package are a major component of a job offer and have no hesitation of mentioning it during the interview. Common wisdom, however, dictates that it is inappropriate to mention salary as it serves to cheapen the proceedings, and in reality, you may have to fly a little on faith that the salary package will be adequate.

On the other hand, the employer may not mention salary, but may ask you what you are looking for. Working on the principle that at this point you are more interested in the experience than the money, you should have a realistic figure in mind that allows you to live comfortably but does not appear to be greedy. Although there is likely to be a negotiation process, quoting too large a sum may take you out of the running.

As a first jobber, you may actually be far more interested in the experience than the money, but even so, you are going to need to make a wage. Besides, you have invested time and probably a reasonable amount of money into getting trained for a career in IT. It is not unreasonable to expect to be paid for your work, and it is not unreasonable for you to be interested in just how much that might be. Even so, the actual step of asking the question can seem daunting. Whether it should be asked depends on you and the situation you are in. If in doubt, err on the side of caution and don't ask.

The End of the Grilling

At the end of the interview, it is usual practice for the employer to ask whether you are interested in the position. If the employer does ask, you can take this as a very positive sign. However you feel at this point, even if you do not want to work for this company, enthusiastically express your interest. At least then you have the option to consider the proposition fully before making a decision. What may seem an undesirable position may become more interesting after you have had a chance to think about it, especially if there is no abundance of other offers. Also, it might be a good idea to ask what an employer's timeframe is for making their decision. This timeframe will give you some expectation of when you think you might be hearing from them, if they are interested.

The Ultimate Scenario

On rare occasions, an employer may be so enamored with you that you receive an offer on the spot. The only issue with this is that you will almost always be expected to make a decision on the spot as well. If you like what the employer is offering and believe that you can agree on mutually acceptable terms (which you will have almost certainly already discussed), then why not say YES! After all, that is the whole point of this exercise. If you feel uncomfortable making such a decision under pressure, simply tell the employer that you want some time to think about it, but beware. Not saying yes in this situation will almost certainly appear as a negative to the employer, who is looking for someone so enthusiastic about the possibility of working for them that they cannot say yes quickly enough. Before you make any decision, make sure that you had the opportunity to ask and get answers to all of your questions.

Second Interviews

For a number of reasons, employers may choose to conduct a second round of interviews. Sometimes it is because they're having trouble deciding between a number of candidates, other times it is because they want to have a more in-depth discussion or involve other members of the staff. Obviously, the offer of a second interview shows a high level of interest from the employer. Even so, there is still the opportunity to mess things up. Approach your second interview with the same level of professionalism as the first interview. Doing this will make the second time around even easier as you now have some idea of what to expect.

Do not be too casual in your approach or manner, but at the same time acknowledge you are no longer strangers. Asking how projects that were discussed during the first interview are progressing will reinforce your enthusiasm and show that you were actively listening during the first interview.

Interview Follow Up

At the end of the interview, be it the first or second, it should be established what the next step in the process is. It may be that the employer will contact you after a decision is made or it may be that you have to contact the employer. Get clarification of who is doing what and when. The information is important to you as, obviously, you are going to want to know the outcome of the interview, but it may also have a bearing on other interviews or offers you may be pursuing. There is no fixed time period between the interview and the decision, but realistically an employer should not keep you waiting for more than a few weeks. If the employer was supposed to contact you and you don't here from them, it is very reasonable for you to contact them.

Interview Thank You Letters

It is common practice to follow up an interview with a brief letter, thanking the employer for their time and once again expressing your interest in the position. As well as reinforcing your business-like approach and organizational skills, putting your name in front of the employer is an added reminder of your interview. The employer will also almost certainly appreciate the courtesy. In a tight decision between candidates, this little extra detail may just help you to edge out the competition.

Dealing with Rejection

While it would be nice to think that every interview will result in a job offer, you must deal with the fact that you may be rejected. Most companies issue rejections after they have secured the services of another individual, just in case their first choice candidate elects not to accept the offer.

If the rejection comes in the form of a letter, there is likely to be very little that you can do to ascertain the reason for the rejection. If you are fortunate enough to receive a phone call, the employer may be willing to discuss with you the reasons for the rejection. Whatever the reasoning, take note. Knowing what the employer sees as a negative can help you in your further job search.

If you are notified by email, it is probably not a great idea to reply and ask why you were rejected. Rather send a courtesy reply with a brief note thanking them for their consideration and reinforcing the fact that you are interested in any other opportunities that come up in the future.

Comparing Offers

If you are fortunate enough to find yourself in a situation where you have more than one job offer, congratulations. What you must do is to sit down and carefully consider the relative merits of each opportunity. As well as considering the obvious factors such as salary, location, and working environment, you can now add some other things into the mix. The difference that each of these factors makes in the long term is difficult to quantify, but they are worth considering:

➤ *Possibilities for advancement*—If your plan is to stay with a company for a significant period of time, considering what opportunities there are for advancement can be an important factor. The size of the company may have an influence on this, but it should not be the only condition. Small companies may grow rapidly and often promote from within. If advancement is important to you, ascertain this fact during the interview.

➤ *The technologies in use*—As discussed elsewhere in this book, the key to retaining your marketability in the IT industry is focused on your skills and how applicable they are to the market. To have the opportunity of working in an environment where you have access to the latest and greatest technologies and products will make it easy to stay ahead of the game.

➤ *Gut feeling*—Not very scientific perhaps, but in reality you are likely to have a feeling as to which of the offers represents the best opportunity. Sometimes it is better to go with your heart than your head.

Negotiating the Best Deal

To talk of negotiation when you are looking for a way to break into the IT industry may seem a little odd. Surely, you should just take what you can get? You may convince yourself in the beginning that working for poor pay and no benefits is okay as you are getting the ever valuable experience, but this will wear thin after a short time. It is far better to negotiate a package that both parties are happy with. It may mean that you will be paid low wages to begin with, but after an agreed period your wages will increase. In essence, the negotiation in this respect may not be about what you want now, but rather what you will get in the future.

That is not to say that there is no room for negotiation over things such as salary, only that the room may be a little limited. The exact amount of room depends greatly on the employer. Some employers work on a principle of paying employees the least they can while paying them enough to discourage them from leaving. Others, though not enough, work on a principle of paying them market rate, thereby giving them no monetary reason to look elsewhere. Of course, pay in this context does not just refer to salary, but extends to things such as benefits and bonuses as well.

The negotiation of a job offer is different from the other negotiations that you may undergo in life. If you have bought or sold a car, house, or if you have held a garage sale, you may have been involved in a negotiation. The difference with those negotiations was that if the purchaser didn't want to buy, someone else likely would. When looking for a job for the first time buyers may be hard to find.

What Are You Signing Up for?

Almost every company that offers employment will provide employees with a contract detailing the salary, benefits, requirements, and expectations of both the employee and employer. Things that should be covered in this contract are working hours, office, overtime, and when benefits apply. Here are some specific things that you should pay attention to on a contract of employment:

➤ *Working hours*—Your contract should specify what are regarded as normal working hours. Contracts should also define the company's policy regarding overtime on both an expected and unexpected basis.

➤ *The normal working location*—An employment contract normally states the location at which you are expected to report on a regular work day. It should also state what the company policy is regarding working away from this location, including travel, subsistence, and accommodation expenses. If the job has no foreseeable element of travel, this point is not an issue, but in field or project based roles this is particularly important.

➤ *Employee benefits*—It is likely that during the interview process the benefit element of an employment package will have been agreed. The employment contract should detail these benefits as well as the dates on which the benefits become effective. Many companies exclude new employees from benefit schemes for a number of months at the beginning of the employment period. Particularly important are those benefits relating to sickness and absence.

➤ *The duration of probation*—A great many companies place new employees on probation for a number of months. This probation period is a time when the employer has the ability to let you go at short notice, and also a period when you may not be entitled to benefits. Your contract should also make it clear about what will happen if a certain aspect of your performance falls below expected levels during this period.

Turning Down a Job

Under certain circumstances, you may find it necessary to turn down a job. There are two instances when this can happen. You may have attended two interviews close together and received offers from both companies, or you may have attended an interview and decided that you do not want the job. Either way, you need to turn one of the job offers down.

When turning down an offer, try to keep it as simple as possible. Simply inform the new suitor that you have already secured employment. Though unlikely, the employer may ask you at what stage the negotiations are, hoping that you might be tempted to also negotiate with them. This move is very unethical, but then again IT is not a particularly ethical industry. In this case it is up to you to decide the correct course of action, but realistically, sticking with your original commitment is the only practical option. It is also the right thing to do.

If possible when turning a job down, try and keep the lines of communication open. The more contacts you have in the industry, the better. You never know when you may find yourself looking for another job.

Dealing with Interview Offers after You Have a Job

If companies have been slow in coming back to you, you may find yourself in a situation where you are getting interview offers from other companies after already securing employment elsewhere. If this does happen, contact the company offering the interview, preferably by telephone or email, and thank them for their attention. Explain that you have been successful in securing employment with another employer and express regret at not being able to attend an interview with them. This courtesy may make no difference at all, but always remember that you may well be looking for another job in the future and it always pays to keep every door open.

Chapter Summary

Finding a job is the last step in your quest to become a worker in the IT industry. A carefully planned and well implemented campaign will hopefully see you attending interviews and looking at job offers in fairly short order. Although a great deal of detail was included in this chapter, here are some of the key points to keep in mind:

➤ When you start looking for work, make sure you are ready with résumé, cover letters, and so on.

➤ Don't limit your job search to classified ads and other job postings. Much of the hiring for positions is done before it has a chance to be advertised.

➤ Interviews are not just about the employer getting to find out about you, they are also an opportunity to for you to evaluate the company and the possible opportunity.

➤ Try to follow your interviews with a Thank You letter. This letter can help the interviewer remember your interview, and, if you're "high on the list" of hiring potential, it may help squeeze out some competition.

➤ Try and negotiate the best employment package possible, but remember that you are looking for a way to break into the industry. Don't be too pushy in your demands, but don't get taken for a ride.

Good luck with your job search and interviews. After you've tackled the challenges of finding a job, you're ready to start your career in IT!

CHAPTER TWELVE

Keeping That Job

So, all of your hard work, training, and financial outlay has finally paid off. You have a better understanding of yourself and your career goals. You have explored job opportunities and have impressed an employer with your slick interview style. Congratulations, you have a job!

You must now make sure that you keep your job. This not only requires hard work, but also the right attitude and approach to your new opportunity. Up to this point, you have prepared for the unknown. It would be nice to think that a degree of certainty about the challenges you will be facing would now be evident. In reality, you are not at this point yet, but you are much closer now than when you first decided to pursue a career in IT.

For many people, starting a new job is a stressful endeavor. Realistically, there is no need for this to be the case. Your employer liked you enough during the interview process to offer you a job based on your skills, training, and personality. Now the company is simply looking for you to bring those same qualities into the workplace.

Even so, the first weeks in a new job can be a testing time. It is a period when you finally find out whether or not you have what it takes to be successful in your chosen area of IT.

This chapter picks up where Chapter 11 left off, working on the basis that you have secured a job in IT and are now waiting to get started.

Prework Preparation

After the interview and subsequent offer, there is often a gap between completion of formalities and your actual start date. This gap may be as short as a few days, but rarely exceeds a month. Although it may be tempting to relax during this period and take it easy, there are a number of details you can take care of to make sure your transition to your new job goes smoothly.

The following list contains some suggestions to make the best use of this time:

➤ *Leaving a former job*—Once a new job is secured, it can be extremely difficult to maintain the energy and commitment to your current job. When moving to a new job, whether within IT or from another profession altogether, do not let your work performance and attitude in the office slip. Keep in mind that your job does not end when you have given your notice, rather it ends when you finish your last day of work. Continuing to work hard until your last day demonstrates respect for your employer and coworkers as well as yourself.

➤ *Prepare yourself technically*—Through the interview process, you will almost certainly have learned information about the technologies that your new company uses as well as what some of its working practices are. In the days or weeks before you start work, you have a valuable opportunity to find out even more about your new job. Do a little research of your own to give yourself a head start.

➤ *Increase your awareness*—Make an extra effort to keep up-to-date with the goings on of the IT industry, especially with those events that may affect you in your new role. Your new colleagues will almost certainly be aware of factors that affect their working environment, and they will expect you to understand them too. For example, if a software update is due to be released in the near future, make yourself aware of when the release will be and what issues it will address. Prepare yourself for this constant need of awareness.

➤ *Don't neglect yourself*—The days or weeks between your job offer and your start date is a good time to take care of personal needs, such as routine visits to the doctor, dentist, and/or financial planner. It is also an ideal time to attend to any special family matters as well as any particular household projects or automotive maintenance—concerns that you don't want to worry about once you start your new job.

➤ *Learn more about the company*—Obtaining a detailed knowledge of the structure and culture of your new employer can be a great asset during the initial employment period. This gives you a head start on your new job and can make the transition to the new position easier. Therefore, if you have the time, you might want to explore your company's Web site as well as any additional literature that you may have received during your interview process. In addition, learning more about the industry in which your new company operates can serve to add context to your new role. If your employer is a company outside of the IT industry, you could also direct some effort toward learning more about its industry as well. Again, the Internet can assist you with your research efforts. You might want to look up similar or competitive companies to see how they compare to yours.

➤ *Take a holiday*—At this point, you have almost certainly earned some time off. It's a great feeling to sit on the beach secure in the knowledge that you have a job and a new career awaiting you. However, if you decide to take a short holiday, make your new employer aware of this fact and, if possible, leave details of how you can be contacted should any of your start date plans change.

12

The time period between securing a job and starting that new job is an exciting one. Using this period productively can help you prepare for the new job.

Your First Day

By the time your first day on the new job arrives, you are likely to have had plenty of opportunities to think about what it will be like. Will the people be friendly? What will they expect you to know?

You may well be nervous, but you are not alone. Even seasoned IT professionals who have had many jobs ask themselves these same questions on the first day of a new job. These unknowns can make your first day seem like a daunting proposition. In any field, few things are as nerve-racking as the first day on the job. The key to survival is to keep your perspective on what the real issues are and separate those from the issues you create yourself. There are many unknowns and many pressures, some are real, but most are not. The next few sections discuss some important things to remember.

First Impressions

Some of the stress on the first day of work comes from the realization that you are making a first impression. As you all know, first impressions are lasting, which makes them very important. The way people respond to you depends greatly on how you respond to them. A smile, a firm handshake, and a generally cheery demeanor is the best way to say, "Hi, I'm new and pleased to be here." You can impress them with your razor wit and sarcasm some other time. Remember, a good first impression is easy to make, a bad one can take a while to repair.

Creating a good first impression is not difficult. The following suggestions can help you get off on the right foot:

➤ *Pleased to meet you*—Try to remember and use the names of the people you were introduced to. This sounds easy, but can sometimes be difficult, especially when you are being introduced to a large number of people in a short period of time. Remembering peoples' names makes you appear respectful and polite. Your new colleagues will notice if you have taken the time to learn and remember their names. It is an easy way to make a positive impression.

➤ *There's a time and a place*—Do not be overly eager to show your knowledge and attempt to improve on the existing way of doing things. You will have the opportunity to show your worth soon enough, but on the first day, it is best to take a back seat. Observe the way things are currently done and understand that there may be good reasons why they are done in those ways. Listen to explanations, but resist the temptation to give your opinion. As the old saying goes, "You have two eyes, two ears, and one mouth." Use them in that order.

➤ *Don't be afraid to ask*—If something is explained to you that you don't understand, ask for clarification. Rather than making you seem inept, asking for clarification on some matters, shows you are interested and want to learn. Your first day on the job is an ideal time to ask questions. It is far better to ask certain questions on the first day rather than several months down the road. A wise man once said, "The only type of stupid question is the one that doesn't get asked."

➤ *You are what you wear*—You will find that the correct company dress code is somewhere between a tuxedo and jeans and T-shirt. The way you dress on the job often has an impact on how coworkers, clients, and supervisors view you. Dress is another easy way to make a good impression. If you are unsure of what the dress code is, phone or email your new employer and ask. It is a reasonable request. If you are unable to do this and are unsure of what to wear, then play it safe and wear smart business attire.

➤ *Establish a positive attitude*—Colleagues are more likely to want to be around and work with someone positive. Be quick to talk with people and find out what they do and what role they perform in the company. Be equally slow to tell others of your accomplishments or achievements.

➤ *Remember what is expected*—Although it may not feel like it, the expectations on the first day of the job are minimal. As one seasoned IT manager proclaims, "The first day is about finding out where the washroom and the coffee machine are."

After the first day, hopefully, some if not all of your fears should be assuaged. As you leave the office for the first time, you may just want to allow yourself a little smile and a pat on the back. Now, without a doubt, you work in IT.

Your First Week

With the stress of the first day behind you, you are ready to get down to business. By the end of your first week, you should be starting to feel a little more settled and have a good idea of what is expected of you on a personal and professional level. You are likely to have had the opportunity to get to know your supervisor, coworkers, users, and clients.

The following list contains a few suggestions to remember during your first week:

➤ *Maintain a positive attitude towards the job*—It is never a good idea for the new employee to be negative about the job or the tasks given, especially in the first few weeks of a job. As a new employee, it is likely you will be given a lot of the undesirable, grunt work tasks. Do them with a smile. If all works as it should, one day you will be delegating such tasks to someone else. Be friendly and show a willingness to learn.

➤ *Gain an understanding of procedures and routines*—The first week you will be exposed to the internal procedures of the new job. Get to know how inter-office communication works, how to complete timesheets, , and how to operate the phones according to company procedures. Knowledge of the day-to-day routines can make your job easier.

➤ *Respect your coworkers' space and get to know them*—Work performance aside, as a new employee, you will have to get along and be able to work well with the existing team. It is likely that part of your evaluation during the probation period will come from the people with whom you work directly Your employer will most certainly discuss your performance with your coworkers. A recommendation and positive words from coworkers can carry a lot of weight in your current job as well as in future job references.

➤ *Evaluate and familiarize yourself with the technologies being used*—In the first week, it is likely that you will be introduced to the major technologies you will be using in the new job. If you have the time, explore this technology and become as familiar with it as you can. It can serve to boost your confidence on the job.

➤ *Observe and learn*—IT professionals have a secondary motive while working on the job, which is gaining experience. If you are working with other professionals, watch and learn from them. The more you learn, the more valuable you are both in and out of the company. A little humility and willingness to learn from others can help you become successful.

You Are on Probation!

Many companies have a probation period, which gives an employer a chance to evaluate the performance of the new employee. It also allows the employee to prove himself to the employer. There is no standard length of time for a probation period, but typically it is 60 to 90 days. Regardless of the length of the probation period, it is all the time you have to make your mark.

Completing the probation period successfully does not require a superhuman effort on your part. All you are expected to do, preferably admirably, is fulfill your job role. Many employers provide new recruits with ongoing evaluations, whereas others do not. If your employer is not providing feedback during your probation period, take the initiative and seek out an evaluation from the employer before the probation period expires. Asking for information shows you care about your job and you have a desire to meet the needs of your company. Many new employees make the mistake of waiting until the end of the probation period to find out if there is an issue with their job performance. This leaves no time to correct the problem. If, through a probation evaluation, you do learn of a shortfall in your performance, take all the necessary steps to correct the problem. If you do not, you will only have yourself to blame.

The following list contains other techniques you can use to help you get through the probation period:

➤ *Prove yourself competent at your job*—Demonstrating your value in a new position is not always easy. Perhaps the only time a network administrator wants the network to go down is during the probation period. In this situation, your value to the company is obvious. However, if you are maintaining and monitoring the network behind closed doors for the duration of your probation, your significance is not as apparent.

➤ *Work on projects with others*—One of the key factors in determining your suitability for the job is your ability to work with others and collaborate on projects or problems. Whether you work with other IT professionals, users, clients, or customers, you need to be able to work well with different people. It is essential that you are able to do this during the probation period.

➤ *Take an interest in the company*—Researching and gaining knowledge of the company can work in your favor. It allows you to discover where the company is heading and modify your skills and efforts to make yourself an asset at the present time as well as in the future. Learning about the company also shows the employer your interest and enthusiasm.

With a little hard work, your probation period will end successfully, and you will become part of the team. At this point, you should start considering your future career goals.

12

Commitment to Training

With the job in the bag, you might think that your days of exams, training, and certifications are over—think again. Remember, keeping your job in IT means that you have to make a commitment to continue your training. It may not happen overnight, but the skills you currently use as an IT professional will become dated and eventually become obsolete. Training and keeping up with current technologies is the only way to combat this outcome.

Much of the IT professionals' training is performed on the job. IT professionals need to keep on top of the tools being used in their workplace. A constantly updated knowledge of the specific systems, software, and hardware used is a key requirement of those working in the industry. This knowledge makes you a valuable employee as well as difficult to replace.

In addition to maintaining your skills and training for the products used in the workplace, IT professionals must also keep up-to-date with other technologies. To maintain marketability, IT professionals must identify and learn the newest technologies that are introduced to the IT industry almost daily. To maintain this learning pace, IT professionals can refer to a variety of resources including technical Web sites, magazines, and newspapers.

Renegotiating Your Package

When you are first looking for work, it is hard to imagine sitting down with your employer and renegotiating your employment package. Because of your experience and ongoing training, the day may come when renegotiation will take place. Like any other part of your career, renegotiation requires a strategy. Timing your renegotiation is, of course, part of the strategy. When the time comes to renegotiate, you need to know what you want, what you will be satisfied with, what your market value is in the IT industry, and what your value is to the company. You should go into negotiations with a certain frame of mind. Know what you would like from the negotiations and also know what you will settle for. Keep in mind that negotiation is a two-way process. Employees enter negotiations because they believe they have more to offer their employer than they did when the package was last negotiated and want to be compensated for their additional knowledge and skills. Employers have a certain perceived value of what the added benefit is "worth" to them, hence, the negotiation. You can only properly negotiate if you have something to offer. Also, remember that, should the negotiations be successful, you will have to continue to work with the other person, perhaps directly for the foreseeable future. With this in mind, make sure that negotiations are always kept polite and friendly.

Is There a Right Time?

Just as important as knowing what to negotiate is knowing when to negotiate. It is an inexact science, but for those looking for some guidance, the right time may be sometime between your second week on the job and your thirtieth year. Essentially, there are three occasions when it may be appropriate to approach your employer and renegotiate your package. They are:

➤ *Change in job duties*—Throughout your career, job duties, tasks, and responsibilities change. When they do, it is an ideal opportunity for you to renegotiate your employment package.

➤ *Change in qualifications*—Many IT professionals continually upgrade their knowledge and skills. As they upgrade their abilities, they increase their marketability in the IT industry. Professionals trained in the latest technologies are very valuable to companies and this expertise provides considerable leverage for negotiation.

➤ *Length of tenure*—Proving your value to an employer can often create good terms for renegotiation. In an industry where employee turnover is so high and skilled staff is difficult to find, employers are often willing to recognize the efforts of a faithful and productive employee.

What Can I Negotiate?

When renegotiating an employment package, it is important to remember that it is comprised of more than just a salary. An employment package is far more complex, making the negotiation process a little trickier. The following list contains some of the negotiable components of an employment package:

➤ *Salary*—Salary is perhaps the biggest and trickiest negotiation of them all. Salary renegotiating is that delicate balance between being greedy and underestimating your value. Finding this balance requires a detailed knowledge of your marketability outside of the company as well as your value to the company. Be aware that overestimating your value to the company and your marketability can produce very bad results. At the least, you won't get what you are after, and at the most, you will be looking for a new job.

12

➤ *Training*—After sufficient tenure within a company, some employees renegotiate their employment package to include training. In IT, having training paid for is almost equivalent to a salary increase. IT professionals need to stay competitive and training plays a large role in this objective. Training does not come cheap, so having your employer pay for some or all of your training can be a huge benefit. Some employers, however, are more likely to include a salary increase rather than training because training increases a professional's marketability within the industry. Employers do not want to pay for training and then have their employees move on to greener pastures. In many cases, employers actually require that legally binding contracts be signed by employees to ensure that they get a return on their investment from the training.

➤ *Hours*—Although not always open for discussion, some jobs in IT are flexible in the actual number of hours worked as well as when the hours are worked. For those with family commitments, this component can be a particularly important factor.

➤ *Benefits*—Many companies offer other benefits including medical, dental, retirement benefits and stock options. Many of these are not negotiable, but it is worth taking a look at them to see if improvements can be made.

➤ *Vacation Time*—After spending some time within a company, vacation time is definitely a negotiating point. Moving from a two week a year vacation package to an eight week vacation package may be overly ambitious. However, agreeing on an escalating scale of additional days on a yearly basis can present a valuable perk to you and a relatively painless one to your employer.

➤ *Telecommuting*—Many jobs in IT allow for telecommuting and working from home. It is becoming more popular to include working away from the office one or two days a week as part of the employment renegotiation. Although a great number of positions are unsuitable for telecommuting, for those that are, this presents a real incentive over other compensation options such as salary and vacation time.

When It Just Does Not Work Out

Of course, you may be unsuccessful in your negotiations and decide that it is time to move on. Chapter 13 deals with exactly that subject—moving on. Nevertheless, you can hopefully look back on the job that got you started in the IT industry with a degree of fondness. You will always be able to take with you some value from your first job.

Chapter Summary

So, it's as simple as that. You are now a full-fledged member of the IT community. From here, it is onward and upward. A great deal of very useful information was covered in this chapter. Let's review some major points and try to keep them in mind when you start a new job:

➤ Make good use of the time between getting your job and starting work. Taking care of personal and other business beforehand can help you stay focused on the job and lessen the stress that always comes with starting new job.

➤ Develop a strategy for your first day as well as the first week on the job. This strategy should include making a good first impression by learning the names and job roles of your coworkers, learning more about your company, and learning about the internal operations and procedures. Assess where you and your role in the company "fit in" and how you can best benefit the company as well as your career.

➤ Use your employment probation period to your advantage. This time period allows your employer the chance to evaluate your skills and allows you the chance to prove and demonstrate your value to the company.

➤ Decide very carefully how, when, and why to renegotiate your employment package. As your knowledge and your experience grows, so too does your marketability in the IT industry. Renegotiation is part of the game plan for the IT professional, but it must be approached carefully.

Starting a new job, and potentially a new career, can be an exciting time. Although it may seem like there is a lot to remember, have fun. It may be work, but there is no reason why you cant enjoy it.

12

CHAPTER THIRTEEN

Moving On

With the IT industry moving at an ever faster pace, it should come as no surprise that the turnover of staff has a tendency to follow the same regimen. In today's environment of skills shortage and high staff demand, job changing has become commonplace. The days of leaving a company after 40 years of faithful service with a gold watch and a great retirement package are long gone. Today, changing careers and job roles in the IT industry has become an integral part of maintaining and enhancing a professional's career portfolio. It is not uncommon for a professional to change careers and job roles numerous times over a lifetime. That is not to say that you can't work for the same company for many years and be very content and successful. That scenario, however, is the exception rather than the norm.

Changing jobs may not be uncommon, but that is not to suggest that it is an easy process. On a personal level, it can be difficult to leave co-workers and the security and familiarity of a job. People who work in IT tend to create strong bonds between themselves and their co-workers. These relationships often enable them to discuss issues that non-IT workers may not necessarily understand. These bonds can be hard to break.

On a professional level, job transition requires a direction and a strategy to ensure that you have the right reason for leaving, and that you make the right choice for your next position. Before leaving a job you need to consider carefully why you are leaving, have a strategy for doing so, and have some idea of where you are headed and what you need to get you there.

In this chapter, we discuss some important issues that you should consider when thinking about changing jobs. We've addressed some of the more common issues that you face when considering a change and make some suggestions on how to approach each one. Before that, however, you need to seriously consider why you're looking to move on.

Why Do People Change Jobs?

Generally speaking, within a profession there are three general factors that may force a job move. These factors include personal, professional, or external situations. Personal factors include such things as difficulty relating to co-workers, incompatible values with the company, or an overall dissatisfaction with the job. Some areas of IT require intense teamwork and collaboration with co-workers. Personality conflicts can disrupt this process making it very difficult to work in that environment.

Professional factors are a major concern to the IT professional. IT staff need to be technically challenged on an almost continual basis. If they are not, they run the risk of losing the skills they need to be competitive in the future, almost certainly damaging potential career prospects. As discussed earlier in this book, with the exclusion of money, continuous education and experience are almost certainly the most prevalent factors governing people's career wanderlust. Keep in mind that the erosion of an individual's skills may not be readily apparent when the person stays in the same working environment, but will be harshly exposed if the individual elects to look for other work. Consider these factors carefully before making a decision to "move on."

Other significant professional factors to consider include such things as a company's attitude towards employee training, on-the-job diversity, and exposure to other professionals and accessibility to current technology. IT professionals need to be aware of what a company has to offer their career and the direction towards which a company intends to grow.

Much of the skills and knowledge of IT professionals is gained through practical experience. A quick look through any online employment agency reveals that hands-on experience using the latest technologies is a hot commodity in the IT field. Effectively, the more jobs, responsibilities, and products an IT professional is exposed to, the more marketable the person becomes. Within IT, experience is money. Knowing this, job diversity becomes very important.

Finally, external factors are those circumstances not directly related to the job but which can have an impact on the direction of a career. These factors can include such things as needing or wanting to relocate to another area based on various personal and family-related reasons.

Of course it is reasonable to say that these factors can influence people in any industry, but few other industries experience the staff turnover that IT does. The skills shortage can play a major factor in this respect. Whereas in other industries an individual might work through a difficulty with a co-worker, or attempt a salary renegotiation with a manager, a worker in IT might just as easily decide to leave, working on the assumption that the skills shortage will make it easy to find another job. Another way that the skills shortage can have an influence in this respect is that alternative employment opportunities appear at seemingly every turn. Every IT and many non-IT related Web sites have a link to employment opportunities, and online job sites offer electronic résumé services and a list of tempting employment opportunities. For those who are dissatisfied in their current job, this is a bit like looking through the menu of an exclusive restaurant knowing that they can order without leaving their desk. In other words, people may be

13

willing to change jobs because it is just too easy. The question that career movers need to ask is whether this degree of ease leads people to change jobs on a whim—something that does not necessarily help themselves, their employers, or the IT industry as a whole.

The first thing to do when you get the feeling of itchy feet, therefore, is to ask yourself what is wrong with your current situation. Depending on the situation, changing jobs may seem like the cure all for whatever issues are at hand, but beware! Before you jump to any conclusions or make any decisions, you need to ask yourself, Why do I want to leave? You need to carefully examine not only what your particular issues are, but whether moving from one job to another will actually resolve them. The next section will assist you with this decision by discussing some common issues that you might face in evaluating whether to change jobs.

Reasons for Moving On

An IT professional may have many reasons to consider changing jobs. In fact, to stay competitive in the profession, an IT professional often *must* consider job changes. This section addresses some of the more common reasons to switch jobs, along with some suggestions of alternative ways to deal with these issues without switching jobs or companies.

Boredom

Working for a long time in the same job can make the routine functions, duties, and responsibilities mundane. Network administrators, for instance, may become bored with monitoring networks and the responsibilities involved in keeping them running. Similarly, PC repair technicians may become bored with troubleshooting the same errors over and over. When boredom hits, job performance often falls and daily tasks and responsibilities can suffer. Rather than looking for a job elsewhere, consider asking for more or varied responsibilities for your current role. Chances are if you're the type of person who bores easily, you may just as quickly become bored with one job as another. Consider taking a proactive approach to create additional or diverse responsibilities to your role.

Lack of Upward Mobility

If, after working for a company for some time, it becomes apparent that the job lacks any possibility for advancement, it may be necessary to change jobs to meet your career goals and keep your skills current. The possibility for advancement is more of a concern for some IT professionals and not for others. You may not want to work towards being the senior database programmer responsible for the entire programming department in a large company. Knowing your career goals is the answer to the advancement issue. Look carefully at your current company and see whether there are other departments in which advancement is possible. Alternatively, consider a path toward a managerial position that may be available. Many large companies offer managerial training programs, and encourage current employees to take part in these programs.

Money

Let's face it, the possibility of earning more money can provide strong motivation for a job change. No doubt about it, jobs in IT can be financially rewarding. If your company doesn't offer a competitive salary and benefits package, an experienced IT professional should not have a problem finding a higher-paying job elsewhere. IT professionals should keep in touch with the value of their skills and experience. Ways to do this include monitoring online employment agencies and reviewing what other IT professionals are earning for similar job responsibilities. If you can prove that you are being underpaid, broach the subject with your manager. Be prepared, however, for the fact that your manager may not see things in the same light that you do. You also may want to factor in some things that you might perceive as an added value to your straight salary—things such as benefits, work environment, opportunities, growth prospects, the size and type of company, and how this all sizes up in light of your needs.

Dislike of the Job

Some people spend considerable time and money training and becoming certified for a particular occupation only to discover they really don't like it. Unfortunately, you may make this discovery only after you are actually doing the job. If you continue to work at something you don't like, even though it offers good pay and an opportunity for advancement, you are wasting your time and are working below your capacity. Although this can seem like a no-win situation, there are often changes that can be made to allow you to continue in your current technical field, while at the same time changing the way you work. For example, if you have a few years experience in a given field, you can consider becoming a trainer or try and get a technical sales role. You may be surprised at the demand for technically capable individuals in these fields, too.

Self-Employment

Many IT professionals choose to take the skills, knowledge, and experiences gained from working and use this to start their own businesses. In fact, some businesses and

13

companies prefer to hire freelance IT contractors rather than permanent IT professionals on regular payroll. However, self-employment in the IT industry is not necessarily your ticket to easy street. Permanent positions often come with a string of benefits which, as a self-employed professional, you must obtain and purchase for yourself. It is also worth mentioning that often people find themselves uncomfortable with the fact they are no longer guaranteed a paycheck each month.

Businesses today require a constant stream of self-employed individuals to contract new IT business. Therefore, as you're working on one project, you need to be thinking about what other contacts you need to make to secure yourself with future projects. Many IT professionals fail as freelance contractors not due to technical skill, but to a lack of business savvy. If you are considering self employment, consider all the things you don't get by being self employed, such as pensions, health and dental plans, and other corporate benefits. If it is possible to do so, assign a dollar value to each of these things and add up the total. You might just be surprised at how much extra money you need to make as a freelancer to pay for all of these benefits.

If you do decide to become an IT freelancer, you should approach the situation with caution. Find out what other professionals with skills and experience similar to your own are earning, and try to ascertain how easily they are finding work. Also consider that the fluid nature of an IT contractor means that it is often necessary to relocate, sometimes frequently, to find suitable positions. Relocating may not be as much of a problem if you live and work in a large city. If you live in a smaller city, however, it may be an issue.

What many people forget when they decide to become an IT freelancer is that the work does not end when you finish at the office. Tasks such as accounting and bookkeeping must be done after the normal work day. Although you can offload much of the related paperwork on agents and accountants, all of these tasks cost money. You may find yourself paying out more than you expected, eroding any financial advantage that you gained from going freelance in the first place. In addition, keeping your skills up to date can prove to be problematic. No one can do that for you, and you need to consider that every day spent away from work on a training course is lost income, not to mention the fact that you now have to pay for the training course rather than an employer.

Having said that, if you can gain a financial advantage, don't mind the extra work, and can cope with the fluid work situation that freelancing brings, it may be right for you. Many experienced IT personnel have made successful careers as freelancers. If you want to know what it is really like, it is worth talking to a freelancer to gain a deeper perspective.

Keeping Up with Industry Trends

IT professionals who are not keeping their skills current may find themselves in an awkward situation if the demand for what they do decreases. How many employers do you know looking for a DOS programmer? Jobs in the IT industry change and even dissolve over time. You must stay current with new trends and technologies in the industry. You need to constantly match yourself to current industry needs to ensure that you're marketable. This situation can take the decision whether or not to change jobs right out of your hands. It may be a long shot, but there is no reason why you could not suggest new products or technologies that could be implemented to improve the business. However, if there is no real business case (or no money) to implement these ideas, you may be fighting an uphill battle, and may need to seriously consider your issues. Then consider whether, regardless of what more you can do, your current company offers you the opportunities and experience necessary to keep yourself competitive as an IT professional.

Skill Development

Have you stopped learning? Skill development is paramount for the IT professional. If the job has become technically stagnant, training opportunities are nonexistent, and you are unable to broaden your technical skills and experiences, a move may be in your future. If you enjoy the other aspects of your work, you should discuss with your manager the possibility of attending training courses. If management understand your frustration, they may be willing to accommodate your need for additional training. It is far more expensive to recruit new members of staff than it is to place an otherwise happy member of staff in a training course. Recruiting new staff is not only difficult, but is surprisingly expensive. If employment agencies are used, there are commissions to be paid. If the company advertises for positions, the costs of placing ads and processing applicants can pay for a training course of an existing employee many times over.

Stress\Environment

Long hours, long commutes, and impossible deadlines can make for a stressful environment. Working in such an environment can be more than enough motivation to consider a job change. Money and experience can offer little consolation when working in a highly stressful environment. Stress can affect not only work performance, but your health. Is it worth it? If you believe it is, try and identify which components of your work are the biggest factors and then try dealing with them on a one-by-one basis. If appropriate, discuss the matter with your manager, and see about adding another member to the staff or try to reduce your workload.

13

If, after serious consideration, you decide that it is time for you to make a move, you need to prepare a plan and then follow it. A little time planning may save a great deal of hassle later on.

How to Move On

You can prepare for a career change in several ways. The common denominator for all successful job changers is the preparation behind the move. Understanding what is required for the job change and the reasons behind the move are essential. From there you can formulate a plan of action. Changing jobs can be tricky. Some moves, such as promotions, may require very little skill upgrading but come with an increase in responsibility that may cause a certain level of stress. Other career changes may require extensive technical training or certifications to upgrade skills. When a career change requires additional skills, you need to factor in the time and money needed to acquire the skills. Learning additional skills normally requires training. Most likely you will have to pay for the training, and unless you can find training in the evening hours, you will lose income from not working during your training period. In exceptional circumstances, your new company may pay for your training, but companies that do this are few and far between. All this means that changing jobs can be a complicated procedure.

Making a Plan for Change

Successfully completing a job change requires a strategy. You need to know everything from the type of company you want to work for, the area of IT to work in, whether to try self-employment, and even the predicted future of the job. Here are a few things to consider when planning your job change:

➤ Make a list of companies you may want to work for. Get to know a little about these companies—what is the nature of the company, in what direction is it going, its commitment to training, and its competitiveness. A little legwork can prevent you interviewing for a company that doesn't suit your needs.

➤ Check the predicted job demand. The Occupational Handbook published by the U.S. Bureau of Labor Statistics (**http://stats.bls.gov**) is a valuable resource for seeking information on careers and the occupational outlook for the future. To check current demand for a job, you can also refer to online employment agencies.

➤ Determine educational requirements. Can you switch jobs with minimal upgrading or will it require a larger educational commitment? Fortunately, many skills in IT overlap.

➤ Brush up on current industry trends. Get to know what is out there and what is in demand. Talk to people already employed in the area, and get first hand information on the job.

While you are doing all of this, you must not lose sight of the fact that no matter how disillusioned you are in your current role, you are still being paid to do it. Your professionalism needs to be at the highest level, and you need to be working hard. Pretty soon, it is likely that someone is going to be asking for a reference on you. If you spent your last few weeks in a job with an "I'm outta here" attitude, that is what is likely to be remembered rather than the years of faultless service. Be careful who you mention your plans to. Someone leaving a company is good gossip—too good for certain people to keep to themselves.

Resignation

After many sleepless nights, careful consideration, and discussions with anyone who will listen, you decide to quit your job. Believe it or not, even quitting a job requires a strategy. Although your first instinct may be to march into your boss's office and offer your decision to quit in a, shall we say, animated fashion, you may want to refrain. Resigning should be handled professionally. It is always best in IT, as in other professions, never to burn a virtual bridge. Some day you may be looking for work again in the same company or need technical assistance from past co-workers. In addition, IT managers have a tendency to move around just as much as the workers. Nothing is worse than going to an interview and unexpectedly finding out that the interviewer is your old boss!

What should you expect when you resign? Well, assuming you have done a good job, your employer will be sorry to lose your services. Depending on how much, you may get a counter offer from the employer, making your decision that much more difficult.

13

Counter Offers

Considering the shortage of skilled IT professionals, companies can scarcely afford to lose their IT staff. When faced with a resignation, some employers may choose to sweeten the pot to retain its staff. Some IT professionals tender a resignation in an attempt to motivate the employer to add a little incentive. Best be careful with that strategy; it has been known to go entirely the other way.

Counter offers can serve to muddy the waters. It can be very flattering to get an incentive from an employer to stay at the job, making the decision to leave that much more difficult. In a counter offer situation, take the time to consider the option, and keep in mind your original reason for leaving.

Whether a counter offer is involved, resigning a position can be difficult made worse when you have established relationships and become part of a team. These are the people you have spent long hours with on the job and often off the job as well. You have depended on them as they have on you. Fortunately, in today's world of email, there is no reason not to keep in touch with them if you want to.

How to Resign

Resignations are best if kept short and positive. Lengthy discussions about new opportunities or past grievances can serve to make the process more difficult. It is a good idea to let the employer know about your decision first. Employers do not want to hear about your decision by overhearing a conversation at the water cooler.

Many employers prefer to hear of your resignation face to face, through a verbal resignation. They want to know why you are moving on and perhaps what your future plans are. Resigning orally can be difficult if you are asked questions you are unprepared for. Choose your words carefully, it is not a good time to ramble. Keep the message short and positive. Be thankful for being able to work in the company and maybe take the time to mention your co-workers. If possible, refrain from trying to explain your decision on the spot. An explanation of your decision can sometimes give the opportunity for the employer to reason away each factor, which can be particularly awkward.

Other employers prefer, and in some cases insist, on a written resignation, which does have a few advantages over an oral resignation. Writing gives you the chance to choose your words carefully, allowing you to say what you want to say, nothing more and nothing less. After receiving your resignation letter, your employer will almost certainly want to meet with you to discuss your decision. For one thing, there seems to be more finality to a written letter, making it seem more like a considered career decision than a salary renegotiation strategy. Just remember, there is usually no turning back when the letter reaches the boss's hands.

Upon hearing of your resignation, employers and co-workers may take the news of you leaving personally, especially if you're going to another company that may be perceived as a competitor. How you deal with this will be personal to you, but the reality is that most people leave a job sooner or later. Whatever you do, and whatever your reason for leaving, do not encourage other members of staff to leave for the same reasons you do. Not only is it completely unethical, but other people's circumstances may be different in ways you do not understand. It is unlikely that another member of staff would leave on your advice alone, but it can serve to sow the seeds of thought.

When it is your last day, take the time to say good-bye to your co-workers, support staff, and anyone else you worked with. It is a courteous thing, but in IT there is a secondary motivation. Many successful IT professionals have a wide network of other professionals to call on when they need a hand or information. Leaving a job on a positive note allows you to maintain past co-workers as an information resource.

Remember, leaving on the right note means that you can keep a door open. The nature of the IT industry means that it is not uncommon for people to return to the same company at a later date, either in a permanent or a contracted role.

Second Time Around

So far, this book has given an overview of the IT industry, outlined some specific IT areas, and offered information on choosing and preparing for a career in IT from the perspective of someone starting out. Although this information is important, your approach to getting your second job requires additional thought. This time you have gained the relevant experience, and you have more to offer a potential employer. You also have more to ask for. When it comes time to start looking for your second job, you need to be aware of what will be different from your first time around.

A Little Experience Goes a Long Way

With a little experience under your belt, you can employ a different strategy for job searching than the first time you looked for a job. The most important thing to do is update your résumé to reflect the experience gained. Your new and improved résumé should outline your role, including the relevant experience, the technology used, how it was used, and your responsibilities using this technology. In addition, it is almost certainly worth putting your experiences into context, explaining how they fit into the overall strategy of the business. This approach may seem difficult, but needs to be included. No matter what role you had, you can always find some connection between the work you did and the success of the business.

Your new and improved résumé should also show that your work experience and exposure to the IT industry has allowed you to further develop your personal and professional attributes, in conjunction with the technical skills that employers are looking for. Included are such aspects as proven ability to work in a team, time

13

management, ability to work under pressure, proven technical skills, self-confidence, ability to adapt to situations, industry awareness, and a displayed ability to put learned theory into practice.

With experience, you can now afford to be a little more selective in choosing your next job. In many ways you need to be. The next job should utilize your current skills and at the same time enable you to expand on those skills. Choosing the wrong position can land you in a situation where you are neither utilizing your old skills or learning new ones. When you first looked for a job, these kind of things were of less relevance; you just wanted the workplace experience. Now you need to consider them fully because even six months of working with old technology can leave you lagging far behind.

Of all the tangible skills gained through experience, there are the intangible ones such as confidence and communication skills. You may be surprised just how much of a difference these skills can make when you are going for a new position. Not only do they enhance your overall worth, but they can make you suitable for positions as a team leader or project manager, where personality and organizational ability is as important as technical skill.

Interviewing the Second Time Around

For your second job, and for every subsequent one, the interview process will almost surely be different. Technical interviews are likely to be more aggressive with the intention of exposing weaknesses in your technical ability rather than exploring the strengths. For this reason, résumés should be blatantly truthful about your level of technical knowledge. Chances are that the person interviewing you knows how to find out what you don't know just as easily as what you do. Be honest, and if you are asked a question to which you don't know the answer, say so. Never lie, or even be tempted to talk your way around the answer. Both are likely to end badly for you.

At the same time, be confident about what you do know. You are an IT professional with practical field experience. You have the right attitude and you want to contribute. You also want to leave them with little doubt as to why they want to employ you. Talk comfortably about the technology you have been working with, but avoid making judgments about what products or technologies are good and bad. You may say the wrong thing, and there really is no need to be making those sorts of statements. People in IT often have allegiances to certain products and technologies and want their new employees to feel the same way about them.

And If All Goes to Plan

If things work out the way you want, you will get the job you were after. Now the work starts again, but hopefully without whatever made you look for a new position in the first place. You have completed a full cycle of a job in IT, and our work here is almost done. But just before we go, here are a couple of things to think about before your first day in a new job. After this, you are on your own.

Hitting the Ground Running

When you started your first job, your employer almost certainly expected there to be a period of time when your productivity was not at its peak. It was your first time in an IT job, and you were still getting your bearings both technically and professionally. The second time around, you are less likely to be extended the same courtesy. As a professional with some experience, your new employer will have a certain level of expectation. You will be expected to know the technology that you said you did, which is likely to have been verified during the interview process. You also will be expected to know how to react in certain situations. Your employer also will have expectations of your professionalism, and your ability to interact with other staff. In effect, starting your second job can be somewhat more daunting than starting your first, when not a great deal was expected, and a certain degree of tolerance was exhibited.

A Little Respect

As if there were not enough to think about already, starting a new job brings with it the consideration of the other members of the staff. In your first job, as a new recruit, the other technical individuals in the company did not see you as a threat and were happy to help you along. As mentioned in other areas of this book, technical people tend to be very jealous of their knowledge and their position within an organization. In the new company, to begin with at least, you can expect a degree of probing from them while they sound out your expertise. The key to getting along is to be confident without being arrogant. If your skill is at a higher level than that of your co-workers, it will become apparent soon enough through day-to-day operation. There is no need, and it would be very unwise, to tell them of it at the outset. Try to remember that it is reasonable for them to be curious about your skills and knowledge, and that a small piece of them is thinking about self preservation. As the adage goes, respect has to be earned. In the early days of a new job, you are trying to earn the respect of your co-workers and your new boss. It is a time when you should be listening, watching, and cooperating. Respect the fact that your new co-workers know the environment and work ethic better than you, and have things that you can learn from. Treat them with respect, and over time they will come to respect you.

Chapter Summary

Moving on in your IT career is often as big a step as starting out. It is a time when you must tread carefully, ensuring that you leave open doors behind you and that you approach your new challenge with a measured confidence. Your ability to deal with the process of changing jobs and your attitude in a new role will both serve to reinforce your professionalism, and ultimately your marketability. Below are a few of the key points that we discussed in this chapter:

➤ Only move on if you are certain that you are going to improve your situation in some respect.

➤ Resign carefully. Not only will it make the process easier, but always remember that you are likely to need a reference from your current employer.

➤ Choose your next position with the same degree of care as you chose your first. Consider all of the factors regarding the position, not just the ones that you perceive will be better than the last.

➤ When you start your new job, treat your new colleagues with a degree of respect. People who work in IT can be very proud and protective.

And one last thing: Never, ever, resign from a job before you have found another. It is much easier to find work when you are working—please remember this!

Good Luck!

Specialized Placement Services

This appendix was developed with the intention of assisting you with identifying recruiters or placement services that specialize in very specific areas of IT. You should not consider this list to be a complete accounting of recruiters and employment agencies because such a list could comprise an entire book! To locate some general IT recruiters in your area, we advise you to look in the employment section of your area newspaper or phone book. To locate additional recruiters of any type, you also may want to try your local library or bookstore for additional resources, as well as the Internet.

This listing includes a brief description of the organization named, along with its Internet address and other contact information. What's important for you to note is that you don't necessarily have to limit yourself to recruiters in your local area. Most IT recruiters, particularly those specializing in placement for particular areas of industry, will recruit for a position in a location of your choice. If there are not many opportunities in an area that you might be interested in, then they will advise you of that.

We hope you find this list helpful—Good Luck!

ArtSource, Inc.

Specializing in placing top artistic and design professionals in touch with companies carrying out cutting edge high-tech projects, ArtSource, Inc. provides placements for digital graphic artists, user interface and Web designers and animators.

www.artsource.com

Bellevue, Washington
188 106th Ave NE, Suite 400
Bellevue, WA 98004
USA

Telephone: 425-688-0094
Fax: 425-688-0095
Email: info@artsource.com

The BionicSearch Corporation

Believing in the need to provide a human perspective in the job placement process, the BionicSearch Corporation serves employers and job seekers in the shrink-wrapped and Web-deployed software development community.

www.bionicsearch.com

711 Daily Drive, Suite 106
Camarillo, CA 93010
USA

Telephone: 805-383-3338
Fax: 805-383-3337
Email: info@bionicsearch.com

Compuvac Personnel Services Limited

With over thirty years in the business, this company is one of the most successful and popular IT recruitment agencies in the United Kingdom, specializing in the UK and European marketplace.

www.compuvac.com

66 Great Eastern Street
London
EC2A 3PP
England

Telephone: 0-207-613-7000
Fax: 0-207-613-7001
Email: cv@compuvac.com

Consultis Information Technology

A pioneer in IT job placement, Consultis Information Technology has an IT-specific model that is valuable in its successful operation. Consultis provides staffing for PC technical support, help support, network administration, data center operations, Internet and E commerce solutions, project management, analysis and design, programming, and database management.

www.consultis.com

1615 S. Federal Highway, Suite 300
Boca Raton, FL 33432
USA

Telephone: 561 362 9104
Fax: 561-367-9802
Email: garyl@consultis.com

Haas & Associates

Specializing in E-commerce and software development, Haas and Associates provides placements for software engineers, project managers, programmer analysts, Web developers, systems engineers, network administrators, database analysts, software testers, technical writers, and technical trainers.

www.haasrecruiting.com

1606 Willow View Rd, Suite 2D
Urbana, IL 61802
USA

Telephone: 217-384-7424
Fax: 217-384-7454
Email: dhaas@haasrecruiting.com

Jobs International USA

This recruitment and relocation agency offers to support you in all aspects of international job placement, including resume writing, interviews, legal issues, driver's licenses, and so on.

www.jobsintl.com

406 Pacific Street South
Oceanside, California 92054
USA

Telephone: 760-967-5810
Fax: 760-967-0103
Email: jobsintl@jobsintl.com

Kelly IT Resources

A division of the second largest staffing company in the US, Kelly IT Resources offers opportunities in a variety of areas, including platforms and operating systems such as Unix, Windows NT, and IBM mainframe; programming languages including C/C++, Visual Basic and COBOL; database developers featuring Microsoft Access, Oracle, and Sybase proficiencies; applications such as client server, GUI, and Telephony, Web site developers, desktop technicians, AS/400 specialists, and software engineers.

www.kellyit.com

3815 River Crossing Parkway, Suite 180
Indianapolis, IN 46240
USA

Telephone: 317-573-9510
Fax: 317-573-8859
Email: deckesl@kellyservices.com

Manpower Professional

A division of the second largest staffing company in the world, Manpower Professional handles employment needs in all aspects of the IT profession from E-commerce to network administration.

www.manpowerprofessional.com

5301 N. Ironwood Road
P.O. Box 2053
Milwaukee, WI 53201-2053
USA

Telephone: 414-961-1000

QED National

Providing per-diem and full-time placements of IT professionals, this agency strives to provide both clients and candidates with consulting which will lead to successful placements.

www.qednational.com

172 Madison Avenue
Suite 403
New York, New York 10016
USA

Telephone: 212-481-6868
Fax: 212-951-7027
Email: info@qednational.com

Strategic Search and Staffing

This national staffing agency specializes in the highest quality IT professionals, arranging placements for IT executives, hardware engineers, software engineers, Web developers, E-commerce specialists, system programmers, network administrators, database analysts, HTML/CGI programmers, technical writers, PC technicians and technical support staff and more.

www.teams3.com

7720B El Camino Real Ste #106
La Costa, CA 92009
USA

Telephone: 760-634-1991
Fax: 760-634-1998
Email: S3@S3inc.com

Tech Specialists

A division of Randstand, the fourth largest staffing company in the world with 1700 branches in 12 countries, Tech Specialists does placements in the areas of C/C++/Unix programmers, Visual C++ programmers, Oracle DBA programmers, VB/Access developers, SAS programmers, technical writers, Web developers, NT developers, and software quality assurance.

www.techspec.com

486 Totten Pond Road
Waltham, MA 02154
USA

Telephone: 781-890-2727
Fax: 781- 890-1672

Volt Information Sciences, Inc.

One of the leading staffing agencies in the US, they have over 400 offices in the US, Canada, and UK. Volt has a division specializing in computers and offers services to developers, software test engineers, technical support professionals, PC technicians, programmers, software design engineers, database administrators, and more. Visit their Web site to find details of the office nearest you.

www.volt.com

Major Information Technology Employers

This appendix provides links to Web sites and contact information for some of the major US. technology companies. All of these companies have job listings on their sites, along with information regarding corporate culture and locations. For those embarking on a career in IT, these large organizations offer a wealth of career opportunities and avenues. Most companies list career opportunities along with the qualification and experience requirements. As leaders in their respective fields of technology, they offer a valuable insight into what the general requirements are for certain types of positions.

This list is by no means complete, but provides some useful links to get you started.

ADC Telecommunications

ADC Telecommunications deals with network equipment, software, and services that deliver data, video, and voice communications over a variety of media including telephone, cable television, Internet, broadcast, wireless, and enterprise networks.

www.adc.com

P.O. Box 1101
Minneapolis, MN
55440-1101

Telephone: 1–800–366–3891
(North America Only)
952-938-8080

America Online

America Online provides a great variety of Internet services including email, computing support, interactive magazines, newspapers, Internet access, online and Internet services, Web properties and client software, as well as providing software and services to businesses to assist them in providing services to customers in E-commerce markets.

corp.aol.com/careers/

22000 Aol Way
Dulles, VA
20166-9323

Telephone: 703-265-1000

Automatic Data Processing

This company offers technology solutions for payroll and benefits administration, securities processing and investor communications services, computing solutions for auto/truck dealers and manufacturers, and auto repair estimating and claims processing solutions.

www.adp.com/home/careers.html

One Adp Boulevard
Roseland, NJ
07068   Telephone: 973-974-5000

BMC Software

BMC Software creates software that provides systems management solutions for both mainframe and distributed information systems extending to operating systems, databases, middleware, Web application servers, transaction servers, and applications. Recently BMC introduced e-business management solutions, which manage the IT enterprise in the Internet environment.

www.bmc.com\careers

2101 Citywest Boulevard
Houston, TX
77042-2827   Telephone: 713-918-8800

Cabletron Systems

Cabletron provides business solutions to global customers for enterprise connectivity, service provider infrastructures, software and professional services supporting a range of networking standards.

www.cabletron.com/corporate

35 Industrial Way
Rochester, NH
03867   Telephone: 603-332-9400

Cisco Systems

A worldwide leader in networking solutions for the Internet, Cisco offers end-to-end solutions.

www.cisco.com/pcgi-bin/jobs.pl

170 West Tasman Dr.
San Jose, CA
95134   Telephone: 408-526-7208

Comdisco

Comdisco is a technology service company assisting organizations in reducing technology costs and risks, offering equipment leasing, continuity services, managed network services, and desktop management solutions.

www.comdisco.com/career

6111 North River Road
Rosemont, IL
60018   Telephone: 847-698-3000

Computer Associates International

A leading business software company, Computer Associates International provides comprehensive solutions to empower all aspects of e-business through applications, services, and education.

www.cai.com

One Computer Associates Plaza
Islandia, NY
11749   Telephone: 631-342-5224

Computer Sciences

Active in outsourcing, systems integration, information technology and management consulting, and e-business, Computer Sciences can operate all or portion of a customer's technology infrastructure, advise clients on the acquisition and utilization of information technology services, and create internet based business-to-business solutions.

www.careers.csc.com

2100 East Grand Avenue
El Segundo, CA
90245   Telephone: 310-615-0311

Compuware

A developer of an integrated set of systems applications, Compuware provides both software and professional services to information systems departments of a wide variety of large commercial and government organizations.

www.compuware.com/careers

31440 Northwestern Highway
Farmington Hills, MI
48334-2564   Telephone: 248-737-7300

Dun & Bradstreet

Dun & Bradstreet is a firm which services clients by delivering information
relating to credit, marketing, purchasing, and receivables management containing
databases of more than 57 million public and private businesses.

www.dnbcorp.com/careers

One Diamond Hill Road
Murray Hill, NJ
07974   Telephone: 908-665-5000

Electronic Arts

Electronic Arts is the creator of interactive entertainment software for 38 different
hardware platforms including the most popular systems in today's video and
computer game industry.

www.jobs.ea.com

209 Redwood Shores Parkway
Redwood City, CA
94065   Telephone: 650-628-1500

Electronic Data Systems

A professional services company, Electronic Data Systems provides business
solutions through the innovative application of information technology in the
areas of Management Consulting, e-solutions, Business Process Management, and
Information Solutions.

www.eds.com/careers

5400 Legacy Drive
Plano, Texas
75024-3199   Telephone: 972-604-6000

Equifax

Equifax provides credit reports, check authorization, credit card processing services, database marketing advice, credit risk consulting, and software products to banks and retail stores in the US, Canada, Latin America, and the UK.

www.equifax.com/about/jobs/jobs.html

1550 Peachtree St. NW
Atlanta, GA
30309   Telephone: 404-885-8000

First Data

Specialists in electronic money transfers, First Data has divisions working in payment instruments, card issuer services, merchant services, Internet commerce, and beyond.

www.firstdata.com/Pages/Work/3000.jsp

5660 New Northside Drive, Suite 1400
Atlanta, GA
30328   Telephone: 770-857-0001

Lucent Technologies

Lucent Technologies is a leader in network communications solutions, including wireless, wireline, optical, voice, data, software, services and silicon.

www.lucent.com/work

600 Mountain Ave.
Murray Hill, NJ
07974   Telephone: 908-582-8500

Microsoft

Microsoft is a leader in software development for the home, office, and school.

www.microsoft.com/jobs

One Microsoft Way
Redmond, WA
98052-6399   Telephone: 425-882-8080

Novell

Novell is a provider of network and Internet directory software and services that include directory-enabled server platforms, directory-enabled applications, education and consulting, and pre-directory products.

www.novell.com/company/careers

1800 South Novell Place
Provo, UT
84606   Telephone: 801-861-7000

Oracle

Oracle is a leading developer of information management software providing databases, applications, and tools along with support, consulting and education.

www.oracle.com/corporate/employment

500 Oracle Parkway
Redwood Shores, CA
94065   Telephone: 650-506-7000

PeopleSoft

A developer of enterprise application software, the company provides e-business applications and other products to meet the needs of large and medium sized corporations, higher education institutions, federal, state, and provincial government agencies. In addition, PeopleSoft also supplies services including maintenance, training, installation, and consulting.

www.peoplesoft.com/en/us/careers

4460 Hacienda Drive
Pleasanton, CA
94588   Telephone: 925-694-3000

Science Applications International

A specialist in technical and research and development services for government and commercial customers, SAIC has been branching out into such commercial industries as health care, the environment, telecommunications, and information technology.

www.saic.com/career

10260 Campus Point Dr.
San Diego, CA
92121   Telephone: 858-546-6000

Tellabs

An innovator in the communications industry, Tellabs specializes in the design,
manufacture, and service of optical networking solutions and next generation
switching and broadband access solutions for communication service providers
around the world.

www.tellabs.com/careers

4951 Indiana Avenue
Lisle, IL
60532-1698   Telephone: 630-378-8800

Unisys

Leading financial services institutions, communications providers, commercial
market leaders, and government agencies turn to Unisys for business solutions,
software, hardware, and support.

www.unisys.com/careers

Unisys Way
Blue Bell, PA
19424   Telephone: 215-986-4011

3COM

3COM is a provider of networking solutions and products for consumers, small to
mid-size commercial locations and IP-based carriers and service providers.

www.3com.com/inside

Santa Clara Site
5400 Bayfront Plaza
Santa Clara, CA
95052   Telephone: 408-326-5000

Internet
Career Resources

This appendix provides links to sites on the Internet that can help you prepare for a career in the IT industry. Sites include a variety of information—from getting a free email address to getting tips on posting an electronic résumé—it's all here.

Useful Web Tools

The Internet is an incredibly valuable job search resource. The links provided in the following sections can help you get a free email address and learn how to use newsgroups. Both are essential for those using the Internet to look for work.

Email Addresses

It is often convenient to have a free Internet-based email account in order to send and receive key career, job, and training information. This site offers a listing of free email services and their features including user comments and discussion groups:

www.emailaddresses.com/email_web.htm

Charles Stuart University Newsgroup Tutorials

Usenet newsgroups are a powerful tool to obtain information on a variety of topics or to network with others who share a common interest. This is a great tutorial that explains the basic concepts of newsgroups and all aspects of using newsgroups:

hsc.csu.edu.au/help/software/news/tut

Deja News

Deja News is one of the most popular search engines for finding a newsgroup. This site offers a great place to contact people in your chosen or prospective profession:

www.deja.com/usenet

Tips for Using the Web in a Job Search

With so much information available on the Internet, finding relevant material can be a challenge in itself. The following site is one of the best places to start for anyone using the Internet as a job search tool.

Career Journal from the Wall Street Journal

This site is a valuable source for job search tips and also contains a wealth of other information about careers:

www.careers.wsj.com

Career Planning Sites

A successful career does not happen by accident. Careful planning can help you maximize your opportunities. The sites listed in the following sections can help you with your career plan.

Career Planning

Not only does this site aid you in deciding on a specific career or a college major, it also takes you through the decision making model, which allows you to plan for a particular career, put the plan into action, and evaluate the results periodically:

www.csulb.edu/~tstevens/c15-carp.htm

University of Waterloo Career Services

The Career Development Manual found at this site is an excellent resource for planning and making decisions regarding your career:

www.adm.uwaterloo.ca/infocecs/CRC/manual-home.html

Occupational Outlook Handbook

Revised every two years (currently the 2000-01 edition), the Occupational Outlook Handbook provides a valuable perspective on what it is like to work in a given occupation as well as what can be expected in the way of earnings and employment potential:

stats.bls.gov/ocohome.htm

Résumé Writing

A first class résumé is a major asset in your job search. Visit the following Web sites for help with résumé writing and other job search resources.

Career Lab

The Career Lab offers great advice on how to identify and document your accomplishments for the purposes of résumé writing:

www.careerlab.com/art_homeruns.htm

Job Hunter's Bible

The Job Hunter's Bible site is fantastic. It includes advice for building your résumé, posting it (if you wish), and even reviews other résumé sites. It's a great resource:

www.jobhuntersbible.com/resumes/resumes.shtml

Résumé Tutor

The Résumé Tutor is an interactive workbook that is very helpful in preparing you to write an effective résumé. The site also contains some good examples of résumés:

www1.umn.edu/ohr/ecep/resume

Top Ten Technical Résumé Writing Tips

Writing a technical résumé presents an extra challenge. This site includes ten solid tips to help you with the task:

www.taos.com/working/tips.html

Electronically Posting a Résumé

Posting a résumé on the Internet is becoming increasingly common and brings with it challenges not found in a paper version. The following sites can help you maximize your online résumé opportunities.

Job Choices Online

Job Choices Online provides a clear, understandable description of how an electronic résumé is processed:

www.jobweb.org/jconline/resumes/resumes/Resmatch.shtml

ProvenResumes.com

ProvenRésumés.com provides a collection of résumé writing and job search workshops including suggestions for writing an electronic résumé:

www.provenresumes.com/reswkshps/electronic/electrespg1.html

eResumes

eResumes provides an excellent tutorial on using keywords to increase the effectiveness of your electronic résumé:

www.eresumes.com/tut_keyresume.html

My Job Search

My Job Search provides an extensive list of sites where résumés can be posted electronically:

www.myjobsearch.com/cgi-bin/mjs.cgi/resumes/posting.html

Riley Guide

Riley Guide offers résumé writing advice and information about sites where you can post a résumé:

www.dbm.com/jobguide/letters.html

Letter Writing

Letter writing is an art in itself. The following Web resources can help you add flair and imagination to your résumé cover letters.

MSN Careers

A cover letter can be the determining factor in whether your résumé will be noticed or passed over. This how-to-guide helps you create an effective cover letter to strengthen your résumé. The following link will take you to the MSN career page, from there you can link directly to cover letters:

http://careers.msn.com

Career Lab

The Career Lab offers a great collection of sample letters for any stage of the job search process:

www.careerlab.com/letters/default.htm

Interview Techniques

There is no shortage of information sources when it comes to interview techniques. The following sections contain just a few resources to get you started.

Capital University Career Services Interview Page

This interview site covers all the bases in preparing you for a successful interview:

www.capital.edu/services/career/csinterview.htm

Western Illinois University Career Center

This career center site helps you to prepare for the different types of interviews that prospective employers might use. There are also links to other interview pages:

wiuadm1.wiu.edu/mioip/interview/i_type.asp

KnockEmDead.com

KnockEmDead.com contains some sample interview questions that cover three common types of questions that you might be asked:

www.knockemdead.com/interview

Job Interview Net

Job Interview Net is one of the best sites on interviewing. It includes tips, sample questions, and mock interviews:

www.job-interview.net

Human Resources Development Canada

The Human Resources Development site contains some good guidelines to help you prepare for interview questions, evaluate your interview performance, and follow-up your interview:

www.hrdc-drhc.gc.ca/hrdc/hrib/hrif/leis/career/lm288_e.html

Searching Company Information

Whether you are looking for prospective employers or are preparing for an interview, obtaining information about an organization can be an invaluable asset. The following sites can provide you with a range of indispensable information.

Dotcomdirectory

The Dotcomdirectory is a handy site that allows you to look up a company's contact information by searching on the company's domain name or Web site URL:

www.dotcom.com

Hoovers Online

Hoovers Online is a source of business information relating to companies that you may be seeking employment with:

www.hooversonline.com

MSU CIBER

Information on companies from all over the world can be accessed from the MSU CIBER meta site maintained by the Michigan State University Center for International Business Education and Research:

ciber.bus.msu.edu/busres/company.htm

My Job Search

My Job Search contains a listing of directories that you can use to research prospective employers prior to your interviews:

myjobsearch.com/cgi-bin/mjs.cgi/employers/research.html

Salary Guides

Online salary guides can provide you with a regularly updated account of current market rates. The following sites are worth a visit when you are either looking for work or considering a job move. The information that they supply may be helpful in negotiating a salary.

Economic Research Institute

A variety of software applications are available at the Economic Research Institute site to help you compare salaries within the United States as well as internationally:

www.erieri.com

Job Star

Job Star provides links to 300 salary surveys on the Internet:

jobstar.org/tools/salary/index.htm

Professional Associations

Professional associations are valuable resources for information and a good way to network with others in your field. Although many professional associations are national, a number of them have localized chapters or user groups.

Information Technology Career World

Information Technology Career World provides contact information, Web addresses, and email addresses for major Information Technology Professional Associations:

itcw.com/associations.html

Associations and Societies

The Associations and Societies site provides a very thorough listing of professional associations for a variety of disciplines including North American and International listings:

www.ntu.edu.sg/home/ctng/assoc.htm

Appendix C

Internet-Based
Job Search Resources

Once your training is over, you will need to start searching for a job. The Internet hosts many valuable sites to assist you in your search. Whether you are looking to apply for a certain job or research your chosen career, the links provided in this appendix will give you the information you need. The following sites offer listings of technical job vacancies within the United States as well as international listings. Many of these sites offer much more than job listings: They also include articles, examples of résumés and cover letters, job search tips, industry information, and other job searching tools. Even if your training is not yet finished and you are not actively looking for employment, these sites can be a great information resource.

AskJobs.com

AskJobs.com is a meta search engine that allows you to search many of the largest job boards simultaneously. The user can specify keywords, job title, and location (state or city).

Web site: **askjobs.com**
Email: **support@askjobs.com**

Best International

Best International is an international recruiting firm that offers a global job search.

Web site: **www.best-people.com**
Email: **corpinfo@best-people.net**

BrassRing.com

BrassRing.com is one of the largest online high-tech job directories with almost 60,000 jobs in its database. The site also offers extensive resources for the high-tech professional.

Web site: **www.brassring.com**
Email: **webinfo@brassring.com**

Canada Job Search

Canada Job Search enables you to search job postings placed from companies across Canada using both keywords and location. By subscribing to the mailing list, you can be notified of both job opportunities and other resources that become available through Canada Job Search.

Web site: **www.canadajobsearch.com/jobs.htm**
Email: **info@canadajobsearch.com**

CareerMarketplace Network

CareerMarketplace Network provides listings of contract and permanent job opportunities for a variety of information technology careers. The site contains links to Software Developer.com, ProgrammerAnalyst.com, WebsiteBuilder.com, and several other technology specific sites.

Web site: **www.careermarketplace.com**
Email: **rp@careermarketplace.com**

CareerNet

CareerNet is an extensive database of high-tech jobs that can be searched by keyword, job title, company, or 25 most recently posted positions.

Web site: **www.careernet.com**
Email: **careersupport@careernet.com**

CareerShop IT

CareerShop IT provides the information technology professional with an easy to use job search that allows the user to specify skill areas through a user-friendly drop-down menu. Searches can also be restricted based on keywords and location.

Web site: **it.careershop.com**
Email: **cshopinfo@careershop.com**

Computer JobBank

Using the Computer JobBank, it is possible to search over 123,000 jobs in 45 different technical areas.

Web site: **www.computerjobbank.com**
Email: **sales@computerjobbank.com**

ComputerJobs.com

ComputerJobs.com is an excellent site that is organized into regional, state, and skill sites. Combining this helpful interface with the capability of searching by keywords provides a very appealing site.

Web site: **www.computerjobs.com**

Computer Related & IT Jobs Digest

Computer Related & IT Jobs Digest provides access to information on computer and information technology related work at home opportunities.

Web site: **www.intlhomeworkers.com/cp**
Email: **help2@intlhomeworkers.com**

ComputerWork.com

ComputerWork.com provides a national job search for temporary, contract, and permanent placements. This site has over 50 regional and skill sites, which can be searched by keyword.

Web site: **www.computerwork.com**
Email: **agossett@computerwork.com**

Datum Online

The Datum Online site contains links to Datum USA, Datum Europe, and Datum Asia-Pacific. Specialized Datum IT sections allow you to search for available high-tech positions around the globe.

Web site: **www.datumeurope.com**

Developers.Net

Developers.Net is a site for software developers and IT professionals boasting 80,000 job listings from a diverse range of IT disciplines including Windows, Web, IT, Java, Linux, DBMS, Unix, firmware, freeware, wireless, and bilingual jobs.

Web site: **www.developers.net**

Dice.com—High Tech Jobs Online

Dice.com offers over 156,000 permanent, contract, and consulting placements from across America. It allows you to search by keyword, state, or metro area. Advanced search features even allow you to restrict your search based on the tax term you want your position to have.

Web site: **www.dice.com**
Email: **www.dice.com/help/contactus/supportmail.html**

Games Jobs

Games Jobs is a site for the programmer who works in or wants to enter the exciting field of game development. This site allows you to register for entry-level positions as well as positions listed for an experienced programmer.

Web site: **home.earthlink.net/~joynisha/game_job.htm**
Email: **joynisha@earthlink.net**

InfoWorks USA

InfoWorks USA is an extensive database for IT/IS and high-tech professionals. This site also contains links to The Works Canada and The Works United Kingdom for those interested in international employment.

Web site: **www.infoworksusa.com/index3b.cfm?appid=1**
Email: **info@Infoworksusa.com**

ITI People.com

ITI People.com allows you to search for jobs using all the conventional search restrictions or search by position including SAP, Web developer, COBOL programmer, DB2 DBA, Oracle DBA, HTML, CICS programmer, networking, technical and software developer, and so on.

Web site: **www.itipeople.com**
Email: **www.itipeople.com/contact/contact.htm**

JobEngine.com

Computer industry professionals can search JobEngine.com for jobs based on location, job title, job description, and company name.

Web site: **www.jobengine.com**
Email: **support@jobEngine.com**

Jobnet Australia

Jobnet Australia is the largest IT job search Web site in Australia listing over 20,000 jobs from nearly 400 agencies.

Web site: **www.jobnet.com.au**
Email: **administrator@jobnet.com.au**

The Job-Search-Engine

The Job-Search-Engine site offers a job search engine and a list of other job search resources including résumé distribution services, job boards, and so on. The job search engine allows you to search up to ten job boards at a time using keywords and location. It's a great time saver.

Web site: **www.job-search-engine.com/searchjob/engine.html**
Email: **support@job-search-engine.com**

JobServe.com

JobServe.com offers the largest IT job listings in the UK. Nearly 60,000 IT jobs from the UK and Europe are listed at this site.

Web site: **www.jobserve.com**
Email: **support@jobserve.com**

Jobs for Programmers

In addition to allowing you to search by keyword and location, the Jobs for Programmers site also has a unique feature that allows you to specify many special characteristics about the position you desire including benefits, work hours, and vacation time. This site also provides links to the Jobs for Networkers and Jobs for Database Programmers sites.

Web site: **www.prgjobs.com**
Email: **prgjobs@jfpresources.com**

Jobs Now for Computer Professionals

IT Recruitment firms from across Britain advertise their contract and permanent vacancies on the Jobs Now for Computer Professionals site. Job listings can be searched by job type, location, and keywords.

Web site: **www.jncp.com**
Email: **Use feedback link on site**

JustMyJobs.com

On the JustMyJobs.com site, the user initially selects from an extensive list of technology and skill areas, thereafter, the intelligent search allows the user to specify location, entry level, job skill, keyword, and company.

Web site: **www.justmyjobs.com**
Email: Skill specific, please see site contact information.

Linux.com

Linux.com is one of the premier sites for Linux resources and job placements.

Web site: **linux.com/jobs**
Email: **rednix@linux.com**

Mainframe Developers Network

Mainframe Developers Network provides several resources for mainframe professionals including job searches, job postings, recruiting, message boards, mainframe challenges, and articles.

Web site: **www.mainframer.net**

Search Tech Jobs Network

The Search Tech Jobs Network is a job search site for information technology professionals and engineers. This site offers job searches, message boards, featured sites, hardware/software resources, and more.

Web site: **searchtechjobs.com**
Email: **Customersupport@searchtechjobs.com**

Softwarejobs.com

Softwarejobs.com is a job search service specializing in all aspects of software development and information technology. This site also offers technology specific publications, which contain weekly technology specific job listings.

Web site: **www.softwarejobs.com**
Email: **inbox@softwarejobs.com**

TechJobBank

Applicants can search TechJobBank for jobs in a variety of disciplines. Searches can be defined by state, region, country, category, company, and keyword.

Web site: **www.techjobbank.com**
Email: **info@techjobbank.com**

Techopps.com

Techopps.com provides high-tech positions that can be searched by job description, job title, location, company, and whether or not the employer offers nationwide employment opportunities.

Web site: **www.techopps.com**
Email: **www.techopps.com/techopps/tech10.html**

USTechJobs

USTechJobs is a state-of-the-art search engine that allows you to search for jobs by skills, location, benefits, and more.

Web site: **www.ustechjobs.com**
Email: **contact@ustechjobs.com**

WebJobsUSA.com

The WebJobsUSA.com site has links to job searches for 17 different areas of specialization including database programmer, software developer, programmer/analyst, technical writer, and a variety of Web-based disciplines.

Web site: **www.webjobsusa.com**
Email: **jobs@webjobsusa.com**

The WorkSite.com

The WorkSite.com is a job search site exclusively dedicated to programmers.

Web site: **www.theworksite.com**
E-mail: **webmaster@theworksite.com**

Recommended Reading

You would think, with all the books that have been written on the subjects of computers and technology, that finding one that is both useful and interesting would be a simple task. Unfortunately, that is not the case. Typing "computer" or "technology" into a search engine yields thousands of titles on almost every topic imaginable, but most are training books. That's good news if you want to learn the intricacies of a certain program or system, but not so good if you are just looking for some general information.

To make things easier, we have compiled a list of titles on a variety of subjects that would be of interest to someone starting out in the IT industry or those simply wanting to find out more information. We've categorized these by subject area and have included topics such as certification and education, history, culture, general reading, and reference. Although this list is by no means inclusive, the publications that are listed might also lead you to other works on similar or relevant subject areas.

Information Technology History

Ceruzzi, Paul E. *A History of Modern Computing (History of Computing Series)*. MIT Press, 2000. ISBN 0262531690.

Greenia, Mark W. *History of Computing: An Encyclopedia of the People and Machines that Made Computer History* (CD-ROM). Lexikon Services, 2000. ISBN 0944601782.

Naughton, John. *A Brief History of the Future: Origins of the Internet*. Overlook Press, 2000. ISBN 1585670324.

Segaller, Stephen. *Nerds 2.0.1. A Brief History of the Internet*. TV Books Inc, 1999. ISBN 1575000881.

Technology Today

Curtin, Dennis P. (Editor), Kim Foley, Kunal Sen, and Cathleen Morin. *Information Technology: The Breaking Wave*. Richard D. Irwin, 1998. ISBN 0075613212.

The Future of Information Technology

Pearson, Ian, and Chris Winter. *Where's It Going? (Prospects for Tomorrow)*. Thames & Hudson, 2000. ISBN 0500281378.

Certification and Education

Tittel, Ed. *IT Certification Success Exam Cram, 3d ed.* The Coriolis Group, 2000. ISBN 1576107922.

Martinez, Anne. *Get Certified & Get Ahead, 3d ed.* McGraw–Hill, 2000. ISBN 0072123958.

Job Searching

Criscito, Pat. *Designing the Perfect Résumé.* Barrons Educational Series, 2000. ISBN 0764112686.

Kendall, Pat. *Jump Start Your Online Job Search in a Weekend.* Prima Publishing, 2000. ISBN 0761524525.

Technology Culture

Jonscher, Charles. *The Evolution of Wired Life: From the Alphabet to the Soul-Catcher Chip-How Information Technologies Change Our World.* John Wiley & Sons, 1999. ISBN 0471357596.

General Information and Reference

Petska, Karen. *Computer Industry Almanac, 9th ed.* Computer Industry Almanac, 2000. ISBN 094210711X.

Juliussen, E. Karen Petska. *Internet Industry Almanac, 2d ed.* Computer Industry Almanac, 2000. ISBN 0942107152.

Pfaffenberger, Bryan. *Webster's New World Dictionary of Computer Terms, 8th ed. (Dictionary).* IDG Books Worldwide, 2000. ISBN 0028637771.

Wolfinger, Anne (Preface). *The Quick Internet Guide to Career and Education Information.* Jist Works, 2000. ISBN 1563706229.

General Reading

Kaplan, David A. *The Silicon Boys and Their Valley of Dreams.* Harper Perennial Library, 2000. ISBN 0688179061.

Simson, Garfinkel. *Database Nation: The Death of Privacy in the Twenty-First Century.* O'Reilly & Associates, 2000. ISBN 1565926536.

Appendix E

IT Lingo

The Information Technology industry uses a great deal of terminology and acronyms in everyday speech that can sometimes seem like alphabet soup to someone not familiar with the jargon. This section is not meant to be a complete glossary of all terms used in IT, but rather an introduction to some of the more common and frequently used terms. If you are looking for terms beyond the scope of what's included here, check out **www.webopedia.com** or **www.techweb.com/encyclopedia.**

A+

The name given to the exam created by the Computing Technology Industry Association (CompTIA) that is designed to certify individuals who are competent PC technicians and whose knowledge covers hardware and software products, principles, and technologies from many vendors.

AATP (Authorized Academic Training Program)

A Microsoft term referring to an institution of higher learning (usually a community college, four-year college, or university) that offers the official Microsoft training curriculum under a special license to academic institutions. This program has been discontinued, but you may still see occasional mention of this acronym.

Abend

Derived from the programming term Abnormal End. Occurs when a program causes the system to halt unexpectedly from an error. Also referred to as a crash.

Active Server Page

An HTML page containing VBScript or JScript that displays dynamic Web page content; Microsoft's alternative to JavaServer Pages.

ActiveX

A Microsoft Windows-only technology, based on OLE (Object Linking and Embedding) technology, that competes with Java as the language of choice for Web content.

adaptive tests

Tests that recognize when a test taker misses a question and pose simpler questions on the same topic, then ask gradually more difficult questions on that topic until the test taker's expertise (or lack thereof) in the category is established.

AFSMI (Association for Services Managers International)

A worldwide professional organization devoted to the areas of technical support and IT services management that cooperated with the Computing Technology Industry Association (CompTIA) to help develop its certification tests (that arrangement has since been dissolved). For more information, visit the AFSMI Web site at **www.afsmi.org** or contact the company at 1-941-275-7887. Also known as AFSM International.

AOL (America Online)

The world's largest Internet Service Provider.

AppleTalk

Apple Computer's local area network architecture for Macintosh computer systems.

ATM (Asynchronous Transfer Mode)

A networking architecture based on B-ISDN (Broadband Integrated Services Digital Network) in which data is transferred in small, fixed-size packets at rates up to 622Mbps.

ATS (Associate Technology Specialist)

The Chauncey Group's credential for entry- to intermediate-level IT professionals. ATS covers a range of skills and requires candidates to pass one core exam along with two exams in one of eight career clusters.

Authentication

The process of verifying that someone or something is who or what they say they are. The most common authentication method is that of a username and password.

awk

An input-processing and pattern-matching language that scans one or more input files for lines that match any of a set of patterns specified in a set of directives. All input files are read in whatever order is stipulated; if no input filenames are provided, awk reads data from the standard input as defined for the local runtime environment.

Backwards compatible

Software or hardware that will run or work with older versions of software or hardware.

Bandwidth

The amount of data that can be transmitted over a given medium. The one rule of bandwidth is the more the better, though more also costs more money.

Beta version

Software is developed in stages. The beta version is the version after Alpha and before full commercial release. Companies issue beta products to allow others to evaluate their new technologies.

BGP (Border Gateway Protocol)

A modern exterior routing protocol for TCP/IP networks that provides a way for routers at the edges of their respective routing domains to exchange messages and information. BGP is widely used on the Internet and is described in RFCs 1266 and 1269, among others.

Boot disk

The disk with which a computer systems is booted or started. Most commonly used to refer to a floppy disk, but can be any disk that starts the system.

BorderManager

A software application that provides a secure connection to the Internet from Novell NetWare networks.

C++

A widely used object-oriented programming language created by Bjarne Stroustrup, based on C.

cable modem

A device that uses cable television lines to send and receive Internet data.

Cache

Term used to refer to temporary storage that can be either software or hardware based, used to speed up the retrieval of commonly used data. For example, a Web server cache contains images and text from frequently accessed sites.

capacity planning

In the IT/business arena, a process in which a company's computer resources are evaluated against the company's goals, from which a plan is developed to meet IT and business requirements against budgets and timing constraints.

Glossary

CCDA (Cisco Certified Design Associate)

Cisco's entry-level design credential, which requires individuals to be able to design and deploy simple routed and switched networks as well as configure, operate, and maintain them. To obtain this certification, applicants must pass a single exam.

CCDP (Cisco Certified Design Professional)

Cisco's middle-tier design credential, which requires individuals to be able to design and deploy complex routed LANs and WANs, plus switched LANs and LANE environments. Likewise, individuals must be able to configure, operate, and maintain such networks and connections. To obtain this certification, applicants must first obtain Cisco Certified Network Associate (CCNA) certification for all tracks, a Cisco Certified Design Associate (CCDA) certification for the Routing and Switching track, and a Cisco Certified Network Professional (CCNP) certification for the WAN Switching track, and then pass either two or four exams, depending on which exam track they elect.

CCIE (Cisco Certified Internetwork Expert)

The top-tier operational Cisco certification, aimed at individuals who have advanced technical skills and knowledge and who know how to configure networks for optimum performance. They must also understand how to maintain complex, far-flung, multivendor networks. Applicants must pass two exams for this certification: a written exam and a laboratory evaluation.

CCNA (Cisco Certified Network Associate)

Cisco's entry-level operational certification, aimed at individuals who must manage simple routed LANs or WANs, small ISPs, or smaller switched LAN or LANE environments. Applicants must pass one exam to obtain this certification.

CCNP (Cisco Certified Network Professional)

Cisco's middle-tier operational certification, aimed at individuals who must install, configure, operate, and troubleshoot complex routed LANs, routed WANs, switched LAN networks, or Dial Access Services. Applicants must first obtain Cisco Certified Network Associate (CCNA) certification and then take either two or four additional exams, depending on which test option they elect.

CDE (Certified Directory Engineer)

A Novell certification that identifies exceptionally qualified professionals with directory knowledge for the IT sector. Applicants must hold a primary IT certification—for example, CNE, CCNP, CCIE, Compaq ASE, or MCSE—and be able to use Novell Directory Services (NDS) and associate directory technologies in the management of operating systems, applications, enterprise-level installations, and directory solutions used in business environments. This certification requires passing two written core exams and a laboratory exam.

CDIA (Certified Document Imaging Architech)

CompTIA certification. Applicants must demonstrate skill in planning, defining, and specifying every feature of document imaging systems.

certification ladder

The progression from entry-level to senior-level certifications.

Certified Java Architect

Sun's elite Java Designer credential for individuals who demonstrate their expertise in planning, designing, deploying, and maintaining complex distributed Java applications. Applicants must demonstrate an understanding of systems design in both business and technical environments. There is a multiple-choice and an essay exam for this certification, along with a programming assignment.

Certified Java Developer

A Java certification in which individuals must pass an essay exam in addition to creating a full-blown Java application based on specifications from Sun.

Certified Java Programmer

A Java certification in which individuals must take a written test aimed at a specific Java Development Kit (JDK).

Chauncey

The testing and certification organization, a subsidiary of the Educational Testing Service (ETS), that offers occupational and educational certification programs, including CTT (Certified Technical Trainer) and ATS (Associate Technology Specialist).

Cisco

The market leader in routing and switching hardware. Cisco certification is among the most difficult of all vendor-based certifications.

CIW (Certified Internet Webmaster)

The credential offered by Prosofttraining.com that includes an entry-level CIW Professional certification in addition to three different certifications.

CMOS

Acronym for complimentary metal oxide semiconductor. It is a chip used to store configuration information about a device and holds the data even when the device is powered down.

CNA (Certified Novell Administrator)

Novell's entry-level certification. Obtaining a CNA requires passing any one of five tests: basic administration for three versions of NetWare (5, 4.11/intraNetWare, or 3.12) or for two versions of GroupWise (5 or 4).

CNE (Certified Novell Engineer)

The most sought-after Novell certification. CNEs specialize in a particular version of NetWare (presently 3.x, 4.x, or 5) and must pass five or six required tests (depending on the track) and one elective test to qualify.

CNI (Certified Novell Instructor)

Novell's instructor certification. CNIs must meet both an instructional requirement and training and examination requirements for whatever Novell courses they may wish to teach.

Cold Boot

The process of starting or restarting the computer by turning on the power.

CompTIA (Computing Technology Industry Association)

An organization that includes most major PC hardware and software manufacturers. This organization offers several certifications: A+, Network+, i-Net+, and CDIA.

CPU (central processing unit)

The basic printed circuit board or chip that supplies fundamental computer functions; the "brain" of the computer.

CTEC (Certified Technical Education Center)

A location where you can take a Microsoft Official Curriculum course taught by Microsoft Certified Trainers.

CTT (Certified Technical Trainer)

Chauncey Group's trainer credential for which applicants must demonstrate strong

Glossary

teaching skills. The certification requires both a multiple-choice exam and a 20-minute videotape substantiating the candidate's teaching ability.

DBA (database administrator)

A generic term for the job description of those individuals who must create and maintain databases. Also makes up part of the name for Oracle's Certified Database Administrator (DBA) track.

DBO (database operator)

Oracle's entry-level Oracle8 certification, for which students must pass only a single exam.

DHCP

An acronym for Dynamic Host Configuration Protocol. System that automatically issues IP addresses and associated configuration information. In most cases, the addresses are leased to the device for a predetermined amount of time.

DMA (direct memory access)

A method of transferring data between the memory components of devices (for example, hard drive to controller to RAM) while bypassing the CPU.

DNS

Acronym for Domain Name Service. The system by which Internet names are translated into IP addresses. DNS servers process requests from a specific client, and if necessary, ask other DNS servers for assistance in resolving the query.

Download/upload

The process of copying files from or in the case of uploading to another computer. It is most commonly used to refer to the retrieval and transmission of files over the Internet.

Driver

Term used to refer to a small piece of software that enables a computer's operating system to talk to a device such as a network card, graphics card, or other peripherals. Sometimes also called a device driver.

DSL

An acronym for Digital Subscriber Line. A technology that allows the high-speed transmission of data on a conventional copper phone line. Has two variations, Asymmetric (ADSL) and Symmetric (SDSL).

E1/E3

The European cousins of T1/T3 lines; EX lines were devised by the ITU-T (Telecommunication Standardization Sector of the International Telecommunications Union). An E1 line supports signals at 2.048Mbps (32 channels at 64Kbps). An E3 line is the equivalent of 16 CEPT (Conference of European Postal and Telecommunications Administrations) E1 data channels, with a maximum bandwidth of 34.368Mbps.

EDI

An acronym for Electronic Data Interchange. The term used to refer to electronic communication between businesses of information.

EGP (Exterior Gateway Protocol)

An exterior routing protocol for TCP/IP networks that provides a way for routers at the edges of their respective routing domains to exchange messages and information. EGP is now outmoded and has been replaced by the Border Gateway Protocol (BGP). EGP is described in RFC 1093.

Emoticons

The smiley faces and associated expressions used to enhance email or chat room conversations. For example, a happy face :-) or a wink ;-).

Encryption

The process of scrambling data into an unreadable format. The data can only be decrypted by using a key number, which must be supplied by the person or program attempting the decryption.

Enterprise Resource Planning (ERP)

A special-purpose software environment, such as those available from SAP, Baan, JD Edwards, and other similar companies, that permits organizations to use financial, human resources, and other data resources to analyze current organization trends and behavior and to plan future business or strategic activities.

FAQ

An acronym for frequently asked questions. A list of the answers to the questions most commonly asked about a product or technology.

Firewall

A system, which can be hardware- or software-based, which acts as an intermediary between two networks to manage the flow of data. Most commonly used to protect an organization's network from attack from outside sources.

Firmware

Chips commonly found in devices that store small computer programs that enable the device to perform basic functions.

Flame

The sending of abusive email directed at another individual or organization. The term *flame war* is used to refer to a string of communications of this type.

FoxPro

Also called Microsoft Visual FoxPro, an Xbase development system for building Windows database applications; one of the three programming languages accepted as part of the Microsoft MCSD developer certification.

FRU

An acronym for field replaceable unit. Term used to refer to any component or piece of hardware that can be replaced on a customer's site, as opposed to being returned to the manufacturer.

frame relay

A digital network packet-switching protocol that most commonly is used over T1 and T3 lines.

FTP

An acronym for File Transfer Protocol, a commonly used protocol for the uploading and downloading of files over a TCP/IP connection. Although security can be provided by usernames and passwords, many download sites use anonymous FTP, which does not require the user to input any authentication information.

Ghosting

The process of copying an image of a computer's hard disk to a single file so that it can be restored onto the hard drive of another computer of the same configuration.

GNU

GNU stands for "GNU is Not Unix." Broadly speaking, GNU represents an important body of "copyleft" (programmers can freely use and modify the code as long as they make it available to the public under the same licensing condition) code and utilities that many versions of Unix, including Linux, treat as part of the overall operating environment.

Help file
Text file that contains information about a product that may not have been included in the printed documentation.

HTTP (Hypertext Transfer Protocol)
The protocol or set of rules used for Web-based communications (that is, to connect to Web servers and transfer HTML pages).

IBM (International Business Machines Corporation)
The largest computer company in the world, IBM offers a broad range of certification programs, including those from its subsidiaries, such as Lotus Development Corporation and Tivoli Systems, Inc.

IEAK (Internet Explorer Administration Kit)
A set of software tools for customizing and distributing Internet Explorer in a networked environment.

ILT (Instructor-Led Training)
Oracle Education's comprehensive set of classroom courses for exam preparation and general training. Ultimately, the Oracle exams are derived from classroom experience with students, and Oracle indicates that ILT classes will always cover all the material necessary to take and pass the related test.

i-Net+
A vendor-neutral credential for Internet and Web professionals offered by CompTIA.

internetwork
A network made up of multiple physical networks (local and wide area networks).

Intranet
A Web site located within a company that is used for communication with and between employees in an organization.

IPX/SPX (Internet Packet Exchange/Sequenced Packet Exchange)
An important Novell NetWare network protocol. IPX is in layer 3 of the OSI (Open System Interconnection) Model; SPX is in layer 4.

IRQ (interrupt request)
One of 16 specific signal lines in a PC that exist between a computer's CPU and bus slots. An IRQ signals the CPU when a peripheral event process has started or stopped.

ISDN (Integrated Services Digital Network)
A digital communication standard for sending data, voice, and video at a maximum bandwidth of 128Kbps. PRI ISDN has voice and data transfer rates of up to 1.544Mbps.

ISP (Internet Service Provider)
A business that gives you access to the Internet, usually for a monthly fee.

Java
A compact, powerful, platform-independent, object-oriented programming language developed at Sun Microsystems, widely used for Web-based and distributed applications.

JavaServer Pages
An HTML page containing Java code that works with Java servlets to display dynamic Web page content.

JDK (Java Development Kit)
Sun's software tool set for creating Java applications. Current versions are 1.1 and 2.

Kerberos v5

A networked user authentication system developed at the Massachusetts Institute of Technology as part of Project Athena; now used as the authentication mechanism on many Unix and Windows 2000 networks, among others.

laboratory evaluation

The second test for the Cisco Certified Internetwork Expert (CCIE) certification. Applicants are subjected to a variety of simulated situations to test their hands-on abilities and diagnostic skills. They must implement a network or a communications environment from scratch, reconfigure existing environments, and troubleshoot multiple environments that have been deliberately misconnected, misconfigured, or otherwise messed with.

LCA (Linux Certified Administrator)

Officially, the Sair Linux and GNU Certified Administrator. An entry-level certification that identifies individuals who are Linux power users and can provide assistance as help desk staff members for Linux topics or as entry-level Linux administrators.

LCE (Linux Certified Engineer)

Officially, the Sair Linux and GNU Certified Engineer. An intermediate-level certification that identifies individuals who can perform everyday Linux administrator duties and can design, install, configure, maintain, and troubleshoot Linux sytems.

LCP (Linux Certified Professional)

Any person who passes the Sair Linux Install and Configuration test or the System Administration test at any of the three certification levels attains LCP status. It's the basic entry-level Sair Linux and GNU certification, much like the MCP is for Microsoft.

Linux

A free, open-source operating system created by computer science student Linux Torvalds in 1993. Linux is quickly becoming the operating system of choice by ISPs.

long-haul communications provider

A communications company whose business involves transporting digital voice and data traffic over long distances. Such communications can involve land lines or terrestrial communications or may require broadcast to satellites for relay around the world.

LPIC (Linux Professional Institute Certification) Level 1

The Linux Professional Institute's entry level Linux operator certification. Certificants must have knowledge of the installation, configuration, networking, maintenance, and troubleshooting of workstations or servers running Linux. Two exams are required.

LPIC (Linux Professional Institute Certification) Level 2

The Linux Professional Institute's intermediate-level Linux certification. Individuals must demonstrate a level of knowledge and competency that's roughly equivalent to the RHCE. Two exams are required.

LPIC (Linux Professional Institute Certification) Level 3

The Linux Professional Institute's advanced-level Linux certification. Individuals must demonstrate a deep and thorough knowledge of the Linux kernel and one or more subsystems and meet IT management requirements. This certification is still under development.

MacOS

Originally referring to Apple's System 7 operating system, MacOS now commonly refers to all versions of Apple's operating systems.

MBT (Media-Based Training)

Oracle's term for self-paced, computer-based training materials. There's a substantial overlap between MBTs available from Oracle and the various certification exams, but sometimes it's necessary to complete two MBTs to adequately prepare for an examination.

MCDBA (Microsoft Certified Database Administrator)

An intermediate-level Microsoft certification that works for individuals pursuing either the MCSE or the MCSD tracks, this certification requires passing four or five tests, depending on the track. It aims to certify database professionals who work on Windows networks with SQL Server and database applications or services.

MCNE (Master CNE)

Novell's most elite certification, which designates recipients as certified specialists in one of seven areas of expertise. The requirements vary from specialty to specialty but involve anywhere from four to six tests beyond CNE certification.

MCP (Microsoft Certified Professional)

A Microsoft certification that certifies anyone who's qualified for any Microsoft certification credential. It encompasses more than 60 exams at present. Passing almost any exam (except Exam 70-058: Networking Essentials or any of the Office-related exams) qualifies an individual as an MCP. This is a stepping-stone to the much-vaunted Microsoft Certified Systems Engineer (MCSE) credential, which requires passing six or seven tests.

MCP+I (MCP + Internet)

A Microsoft certification that certifies Microsoft Certified Professionals (MCPs) who prove their Internet expertise and who qualify to plan security, installation, and configuration of server products; implement server extensions; and manage server resources. Three core exams are required to pass.

MCP+SB (MCP + Site Building)

A Microsoft certification that certifies individuals who can design, build, and maintain corporate Web sites. It requires that individuals first become Microsoft Certified Professionals (MCPs), then pass any two from a pool of three tests.

MCSD (Microsoft Certified Solution Developer)

A Microsoft certification aimed at developers rather than systems or network managers. Candidates for this certification prove their abilities to build Web-based, distributed, or e-commerce applications. Knowledge of solution architectures, application development strategies and techniques, and development tools is required of all candidates, who must pass three core exams and one elective exam to qualify.

MCSE (Microsoft Certified Systems Engineer)

A Microsoft certification that certifies individuals who prove their expertise with desktop and server operating systems, networking components, and Microsoft BackOffice products. To qualify, candidates must pass six or seven exams—four or five core exams and two electives.

MCSE+I (MCSE + Internet)

A Microsoft certification that certifies individuals who prove their expertise in using Microsoft products and technologies in Internet or intranet environments.

Candidates must first become Microsoft Certified Systems Engineers (MCSEs), then pass three Internet core exams and two Internet-specific electives.

MCT (Microsoft Certified Trainer)

A Microsoft certification that identifies individuals who are qualified to teach elements of the Microsoft Official Curriculum (MOC). Individuals obtain MCT credentials on a topic-by-topic basis by passing the related MCP exam and meeting classroom teaching skills requirements. MCTs must also maintain current certification as an MCSE to qualify to teach Microsoft courses.

Microsoft

Currently the market leader in operating system technology and productivity applications. Microsoft offers the most varied selection of all vendor-based certifications.

Microsoft exam IDs

The numbers assigned to specific Microsoft certification tests. For example, the exam ID for the TCP/IP test is 70-059.

MLCE (Master LCE)

Officially, the Master Sair Linux and GNU Certified Engineer. This is the highest level of certification in this program. Certificants can function as senior Linux administrators and specialists and can handle complex design, installation, automation, configurations, maintenance, and troubleshooting of Linux.

MOC (Microsoft Official Curriculum)

Elements of the collection of official courseware developed by Microsoft for use in-house and at Microsoft-authorized training facilities, such as CTECs and AATPs.

MOUS (Microsoft Office User Specialist)

The certification is at the bottom of the Microsoft certification hierarchy. This program recognizes three levels of certification: a Proficient (or Core) Specialist for Word and Excel, Expert Specialist, and Master for those who are experts in all Office components.

Multitasking

Defines the fact that a computer can be performing more than one task at a time. Also refers to what practically everyone working in the IT industry has to do on a daily basis.

needs analysis

In the IT arena, a review of a company's computing and networking needs from which budgets, procurement, deployment schedules, and long-range IT goals are determined. *See also* **capacity planning**, a key element of needs analysis.

NetBEUI (NetBIOS Extended User Interface)

A network protocols suite developed to transport NetBIOS (Network Basic Input/Output System) information over a network.

NetBIOS (Network Basic Input/Output System)

A DOS and Windows network interface that is required for communications over a NetWare network running NetBEUI, TCP/IP, or IPX/SPX systems.

Netscape

A company acquired by America Online in 1998 that provides the popular Web browser Netscape Navigator.

NetWare

A popular network operating system developed by Novell. The versions available are 3.x, 4.x, and 5.

network administrator
The individual responsible for the maintenance of a company's network.

Network+
An exam from the CompTIA that aims to provide vendor-neutral credentials for network technicians (who seldom work in single-vendor environments, in any case).

NIC
Network Interface Card. An adapter card that allows devices, most commonly computers, to connect to a network. Also referred to as network adapter, LAN card, or network card.

Novell
The networking software giant that offers some of the most respected technical certifications available.

object-oriented design
The process of creating an application or system based on objects (program modules) from a model.

OCP (Oracle Certified Professional)
A catch-all term that identifies anyone who obtains an Oracle certification, either as a database administrator (DBA) or as an Oracle application developer.

Office User Specialist
See **MOUS (Microsoft Office User Specialist)**.

Offline
Used to refer to a device or other computing component that is not currently connected to a network, be it the Internet, company network, or other. Sometimes used to refer to the fact that a server is unavailable for some reason.

OLA (Oracle Learning Architecture)
Oracle's term for its Web-based training materials. Although these are largely self-paced and entirely computer based, OLA training also includes the opportunity to interact with an instructor via email or online chat facilities. Thus, it strikes a balance between the ILT (Instructor-Led Training) and MBT (Media-Based Training) approaches.

Oracle
The leading relational database vendor in today's marketplace. Oracle's database products are used in many corporations and organizations around the world.

Oracle Certified Application Developer track
An Oracle certification that focuses on preparing database professionals to use Oracle's Developer/2000 Releases 1 and 2 tools and technologies to build state-of-the-art, database-driven applications. It requires you to pass five tests.

Oracle Certified Database Administrator track
One of the tracks for Oracle Certified Professionals (OCPs). Obtaining this credential requires passing four or five tests. *See also* **DBA**.

Oracle Certified Financial Applications Consultant
An IT professional credential for applicants who demonstrate ability in installing, maintaining, and configuring financial applications in an Oracle environment. Applicants must pass three exams: two core exams and one elective exam that covers either Order Procurement or Fulfillment.

Oracle Certified Java Developer
An Oracle certification that recognizes those Web developers who master using

Oracle8i to create e-commerce, information delivery, and other Internet-related applications. There are three levels of certification that require up to five exams, including performance-based and essay exams, depending on which level you decide to pursue.

Oracle8 Certified Database Operator track

One of the tracks for Oracle Certified Professionals (OCPs). Obtaining this credential requires passing a single test. *See also* **DBO**.

OSPF (Open Shortest Path First)

An interior routing protocol based on a spanning tree routing algorithm for TCP/IP protocols developed by Dr. Radia Perlman and described in RFCs 1246 and 2329, among others.

Patch

Refers to a software update that cures specific issues with or adds features to a program.

Patch cable

Common term used to refer to a short length of network cable that connects devices to the network.

Patch panel

A device commonly found in modern computing environments that allows cables from various areas of a building to be managed from a single point. Patch panels are often grouped together in a cabinet called a wiring closet.

PCI

Acronym for peripheral component interconnect. Modern PC architecture that facilitates the high-speed communication between the computer's processor and the PCI interface cards.

PCMCIA

Acronym for Personal Computer Memory Card International Association. Standard to which credit card sized interface cards designed for portable computers are made.

PDF

Acronym for portable document format. Created by Adobe, PDF is a format in which documents can be written and read. PDF has become an extremely popular format. PDF files can be read by using Adobe Acrobat Reader, which is distributed free of charge.

Perl (Practical Extraction and Reporting Language)

A programming language developed by Larry Wall. Perl may either be interpreted at runtime or compiled into binary executables and is highly regarded for its powerful string-handling and pattern-matching facilities. Perl is widely used for CGI programming and other Web-related applications.

PING

Utility that verifies the network connectivity state of remote devices. Although the utility is called PING, it actually works by issuing Internet Control Message Protocol Echo packets and then waiting for a reply.

PKI (Public Key Infrastructure)

A set of protocols for exchanging information about digital certificates. PKI defines a mechanism whereby two parties can turn to a trusted third party, called a certificate authority, to obtain proof of each other's identities. PKI is described in RFC 2510, among others.

Glossary

Platform

Phrase used to describe a specific hardware or software architecture. For example, Microsoft Windows is a software platform.

Plug-in

A program that works with and inside another program to add specific functionality.

PostScript

Printer control language invented by Adobe that has become the standard for high resolution graphics applications.

POTS (plain old telephone service)

The ordinary analog telephone system that most homes use.

program tests

Tests that use traditional multiple-choice questions, graphical exhibits, and simulations. They follow a regular, predictable sequence of questions drawn at random by category from a database of potential questions. Everyone sees the same number of questions and gets an equal amount of time to finish.

Prosoft

A moniker for Prosofttraining.com, a company that offers the CIW (Certified Internet WebMaster) certification, among other vendor-neutral certifications and IT training opportunities.

Prosoft Certified Linux Administrator

The credential conferred on an individual who completes the requirements for basic Linux knowledge and Linux system and network administration. This is a vendor-neutral Linux certification.

Python

An interpreted, interactive, object-oriented programming language that combines an understandable and readable syntax with powerful built-in commands and operators.

RAID

Acronym for redundant array of independent, or inexpensive, disks. A fault-tolerant disk system that allows a computer system to write data to multiple physical disks.

RAM (random access memory)

A group of memory chips that comprise a computer's main workspace. Each byte of memory may be accessed "randomly" by its address rather than sequentially.

RFC

Acronym for Request for Comments. Documents used by the Internet Engineering Task Force (IETF) to define technologies associated with networking and the Internet.

RHCE (Red Hat Certified Engineer)

Linux credential for experienced systems administrators who demonstrate their abilities in installing, configuring, and maintaining Red Hat Linux and related services.

RHCX (Red Hat Certified Examiner)

Red Hat's train-the-trainer credential; required for individuals who wish to teach RHCE courses and administer the laboratory exam.

RIP (Routing Information Protocol)

A simple distance vector-based interior routing protocol used on TCP/IP networks. The current version of RIP in use on the Internet is RIPv2, which is described in RFC 1923.

Router

Device used to connect networks together. Routers make decisions about whether data should be passed onto another network based on their protocol addresses.

Sair

A wholly owned subsidiary of the international training company Wave Technologies. Before it was acquired in early 2000, Sair was recognized as a leading source of Unix training, exams, and consulting.

SCSI

Acronym for Small Computer Systems Interface. High-speed interface for the connection of peripherals such as hard disks and tape backup devices. SCSI is available in a variety of versions.

sed (stream editor)

Originally implemented as a built in Unix facility, sed is a powerful stream editor that includes various pattern-matching and substitution facilities, which explains why it's so often used to automate processing of text and command files.

Service Pack

An update issued by a software manufacturer that includes fixes, patches, and updates for a specific product.

Shareware

Software that can be freely distributed for no charge. Most shareware developers leave it up to the user to register the software if they want to. In many commercial environments, shareware must be registered.

Shrink wrapped

Term used to refer to software that is written and manufactured for the mass market.

SQL (Structured Query Language)

A specialized language for obtaining information from databases that allows multiple users on a network to access the same data.

Sun

A Sun Microsystems subsidiary that produces the JDKs (Java Development Kits) along with other resources for programming developers and IT professionals.

system administrator

Generally, anyone who is responsible for managing and maintaining a computer system, usually a network server of some type. *See also* **network administrator**.

T1/T3

Dedicated phone connections that support data transfer rates of 1.544Mbps and 45Mbps, respectively. The lines consist of multiple 64Kbps channels: a T1 delivers 24 64Kbps channels; a T3 line consists of 672 voice channels.

TCP/IP (Transmission Control Protocol/Internet Protocol)

An adaptable protocol developed by ARPA (Advanced Research Projects Agency) that connects dissimilar computers into complex collections of networks, such as the Internet.

TechNet

A monthly CD subscription available from Microsoft that includes all the Windows NT BackOffice Resource Kits and their product documentation, the Microsoft Knowledge Base, white papers, training materials, service packs, interim release patches, supplemental driver software released since the last major version for most Microsoft programs and all Microsoft operating systems, and more. Available online at **www.microsoft.com/technet/**.

Unix

One of the earliest multitasking, multiuser operating systems that is still one of the most popular in use today. Most Web servers run on Unix.

USB

Acronym for Universal Serial Bus. A technology that allows devices such as keyboards, mice, digital cameras, and other peripherals to be connected to a PC. USB devices can be plugged in or out while the PC is running. This capability is referred to as "hot-swappable."

Visual Basic

Microsoft's alternative to the Basic programming language, used mainly to create client front-ends for Windows applications.

VoIP

Acronym for voice over IP. A technology that allows the transmission of audio data, such as a telephone conversation, over a network designed primarily to carry data.

VPN

Acronym for virtual private network. A secure network link that is made using a public network such as the Internet. VPNs allow data to be transmitted between two points securely.

Warm boot

The process of restarting a computer without actually turning off the power. The most common implementation of this is the Ctrl+Alt+Delete key sequence on a PC.

WINS (Windows Internet Name Service)

A Microsoft Windows network service that resolves NetBIOS names to IP addresses.

WSH (Windows Scripting Host)

A built-in script interpreter found in Windows 98, Windows NT, and Windows 2000. It provides a moderately powerful and useful script processing facility for multiple Windows operating systems.

X Windows

A Unix and Linux GUI (graphical user interface) developed at the Massachusetts Institute of Technology.

X.25

The international CCITT (Consultative Committee for International Telegraphy and Telephony) standard for wide area packet-switched communications.

Zip file

A file that has been compressed using a compression utility. Originally coined by the makers of the utility PKZIP, *zip file* is now used by many IT professionals to refer to a compressed file of any format.

Index

Related Certification Insider Press Titles

IT Certification Success Exam Cram, Third Edition

By Ed Tittel • ISBN: 1-57610-792-2
$19.99 US • $29.99 CAN
Media: None • Available Now

Certification is a vital element of the successful career in Information Technology. This comprehensive book features insider details on the most popular certification programs such as Microsoft, Novell, Oracle, CompTIA, Cisco, Sun/JAVA, Linux, Chauncy, Prosoft, and more. The reader will get valuable information on the unique characteristics of each vendor's certification programs, including changes that could affect candidates.

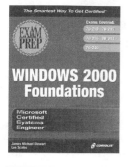

MCSE Windows 2000 Foundations Exam Prep

By James Michael Stewart, and Lee Scales • ISBN: 1-57610-679-9
$49.99 US • $74.99 CAN
Media: None • Available Now

Windows 2000 is the basis for the next generation of Microsoft certifications. Our Foundations book provides the reader with key concepts necessary to pass the new exams, including a thorough comparison of Windows 2000 and NT architectures and detailed explanations of Windows 2000 installation, troubleshooting, and service pack deployment. Also features an exclusive Self-Assessment section to help the reader evaluate their readiness for Windows 2000 certification.

MCSE Windows 2000 Core Four Exam Prep Pack

By CIP Author Team • ISBN: 1-57610-771-X
$159.99 US • $239.99 CAN
Media: CD-ROM • Available Now

This economic bundle is the ultimate test preparation system for the Windows 2000 Core Four exams. Includes four Exam Prep books covering the MCSE Windows 2000 Professional, Server, Network, and Directory Services exams. Each book includes two complete practice exams with questions designed to assess the reader's readiness to sit for the exam and answers and explanations that reinforce the reasoning behind the correct answers.

A+ Exam Prep, Third Edition

By Scott Reeves, Kalinda Reeves, Stephen Weese, and Chris Geyer • ISBN: 1-57610-699-3
$69.99 US • $89.99 CAN
Media: CD-ROM • Available: January 2001

Our popular A+ Exam Prep is now in its third edition. The book contains a comprehensive study guide for a solid understanding of the fundamentals that are standard across the entire computer vendor base for hardware and software, including update information on new technologies of AGP graphics, Linux, and Windows 2000. The reader is also provided with hands-on lab practice that is necessary both to pass the exam and to work in the real world.

THE CORIOLIS GROUP, LLC   Telephone: 800.410.0192 • www.coriolis.com
Coriolis books are also available at bookstores and computer stores nationwide.

Related Coriolis Technology Press Titles

Open Source Development with CVS

By Karl Fogel
ISBN: 1-57610-490-7
$39.99 US • $58.99 CAN
Media: None • Available Now

Learn the best practices of open source software development with CVS—a tool that allows several individuals to work simultaneously on the same document. CVS is covered in detail, as is the GNU license, software design and development, coding styles, documentation procedures, testing, release of software, and troubleshooting.

HTML Black Book

By Steven Holzner
ISBN: 1-57610-617-9
Price: $59.99 US • $89.99 CAN
Media: CD-ROM • Available Now

Explores HTML programming thoroughly, from the essentials up through issues of security, providing step-by-step solutions to everyday challenges. This comprehensive guide discusses HTML in-depth, as well as covering XML, dynamic XML, JavaScript, Java, Perl, and CGI programming, to create a full Web site programming package.

Java Black Book

By Steven Holzner
ISBN: 1-57610-531-8
Price: $49.99 US • $74.99 CAN
Media: CD-ROM • Available Now

A comprehensive reference filled with examples, tips, and problem-solving solutions. Discusses the Java language, Abstract Windowing Toolkit, Swing, Java 2D, advanced java beans, the Java Database Connectivity Package, servlets, internalization and security, streams and sockets, and more.

The Mac OS 9 Book

By Mark R. Bell
ISBN: 1-57610-776-0
Price: $39.99 US • $59.99 CAN
Media: MacAddict CD-ROM • Available Now

In-depth coverage of powerful new technologies—including improvements and bug fixes in 9.0.4—and over 50 new features available in Mac OS 9. Includes trouble-shooting tips to help beginners and intermediate users utilize important new features and leverage the Internet using this newer, more robust OS.

Game Architecture and Design

By Andrew Rollings and Dave Morris
ISBN: 1-57610-425-7
Price: $49.99 US • $74.99 CAN
Media: CD-ROM • Available Now

Teaches design principles, architecture, and project management, and provides real-life case studies of what works and what doesn't. Covers object-oriented design, core design, gameplay, and game balance. Written for PC, Mac, and Unix platforms.

Windows® 2000 Professional Upgrade Little Black Book

By Nathan Wallace
ISBN: 1-57610-748-5
Price: $29.99 US • $44.99 CAN
Media: None • Available Now

This book includes complete guidance on newly introduced technologies to help administrators upgrade or migrate users of Windows 9x, NT 4, Unix and Macintosh. Covers advanced features of Windows 2000 Professional using a concise task-oriented approach for quickly accessing solutions.

THE CORIOLIS GROUP, LLC   Telephone: 800.410.0192 • www.coriolis.com
Coriolis books are also available at bookstores and computer stores nationwide.